Intercultural Business Negotiations

Negotiations occupy a prominent place in the world of business, especially when it comes to international deals. In an increasingly global business environment, understanding and managing cultural differences is key to successful negotiations.

This book highlights two basic components of negotiations: the Deal and the Relationship. Countries and cultures place different value and priority on these components both in the negotiation process and in the outcome. *Intercultural Business Negotiations* provides a guiding framework that is both refined and contextualized and provides managers with the key skills necessary to navigate difficult negotiations where partners may differ in terms of culture, communication style, time orientation, as well as personal and professional backgrounds. The book systematically examines both dispositional and situational aspects of negotiations in interaction with cultural factors.

Intercultural Business Negotiations is an accessible resource for managers, leaders, and those interested in or studying business negotiations globally. It is accompanied by an author run companion website containing negotiation simulations, instructions for players, and teaching notes for instructors.

Jean-Claude Usunier is Emeritus Professor in the Faculty of Business and Economics at the University of Lausanne, Switzerland. He has more than 30 years' experience in cultural and linguistic aspects of international marketing, intercultural business negotiations, and comparative management and has published 15 books and many research articles in international journals.

"In this impressive book, Jean-Claude Usunier helps businesses to avoid pitfalls in negotiation with parties from other national backgrounds, applying insights from intercultural management to international deals."

Geert Hofstede,
Professor Emeritus,
School of Business and Economics,
Maastricht University, the Netherlands

"Professor Usunier's new book builds on established theories of international negotiations and offers a novel approach of linking culture and communication patterns of negotiation behaviour with the equally important legal and political contexts of international negotiations, namely ethical standards, bribery and buying of influence."

Raymond Saner,
Director,
Diplomacy Dialogue,
Geneva, Switzerland

Intercultural Business Negotiations

Deal-Making or Relationship Building?

Jean-Claude Usunier

Routledge
Taylor & Francis Group

LONDON AND NEW YORK

First published 2019
by Routledge
2 Park Square, Milton Park, Abingdon, Oxon OX14 4RN

and by Routledge
711 Third Avenue, New York, NY 10017

Routledge is an imprint of the Taylor & Francis Group, an informa business

British Library Cataloguing-in-Publication Data
A catalogue record for this book is available from the British Library

Library of Congress Cataloging-in-Publication Data
Names: Usunier, Jean-Claude, 1951– author.
Title: Intercultural business negotiations : deal-making or
relationship building? / Jean-Claude Usunier.
Description: 1 Edition. | New York : Routledge, 2019. |
Includes bibliographical references and index.
Identifiers: LCCN 2018022750 (print) | LCCN 2018025327 (ebook) |
ISBN 9781351268165 (eBook) | ISBN 9781138577022 (hardback : alk. paper) |
ISBN 9781138577015 (pbk. : alk. paper) | ISBN 9781351268165 (ebk)
Subjects: LCSH: Negotiation in business. | Intercultural communication. |
Business communication. | Conflict management. | International trade.
Classification: LCC HD58.6 (ebook) | LCC HD58.6 .U78 2019 (print) |
DDC 658.4/052–dc23
LC record available at https://lccn.loc.gov/2018022750

ISBN: 978-1-138-57702-2 (hbk)
ISBN: 978-1-138-57701-5 (pbk)
ISBN: 978-1-351-26816-5 (ebk)

Typeset in Sabon
by Out of House Publishing

Contents

List of figures and tables

Preface

The essence of this book is to provide managers with key knowledge and skills for negotiating international business with partners who differ in terms of culture, communication style, time orientation, as well as personal and professional backgrounds. The acronym ICBN (InterCultural Business Negotiations) does not imply that culture has a static, direct, and univocal influence on negotiation behaviour. On the contrary, the effect of cultural differences on ICBN is dynamic and complex, shaped by cultural borrowing, pretence, and adaptation. Culture is fuzzy, however meaningful, and dynamically combines/interacts with other antecedents of negotiation behaviour to shape the process and outcomes of ICBN. The market background is always considered in this book, along with culture-based influences. Both dispositional (e.g., profession, gender, personality) and situational aspects (e.g., repeated interactions over time, relational history, market-based price references, and partnering alternatives) of ICBN are also systematically examined in interaction with cultural factors.

The conceptual approach to ICBNs is based on the two basic components of negotiation: the *Deal* (i.e., the concrete attributes in a discrete transaction) and the *Relationship* (i.e., connections based on feelings, joint experience, and social/emotional bonds). This serves as a guiding framework, essentially because countries/cultures do not value and do not order these two key aspects of negotiation in the same way, both in the negotiation process and as negotiation outcomes.

The distinction between the IT1 and IT2 paradigms of ICBN is used throughout this book. The IT1 paradigm starts from a "deal first" assumption in which relationships are a non-necessary by-product of negotiation. Conversely, the IT2 paradigm of ICBN places priority on Relationship-Building, profitable Deal-Making coming only second. However, this is an ideal-typical framework, which needs to be constantly refined and contextualized. That is why most chapters explain how a number of dispositional (e.g., organizational culture) and situational negotiation cues (e.g., long-term association between business partners in B2B markets) encourage the adoption of a deal-first or a relationship-first perspective and combine with the IT1 and IT2 cultural paradigms to shape ICBN.

The choice of the adjective "intercultural" rather than "cross-cultural" is important. While the text partly builds on now classical comparative accounts of cultural differences as they impact business, individuals, and organizations (i.e., "cross-cultural"), it focuses on ICBN interactions in their full complexity. Each intercultural business negotiation is singular.

Part one

Calculative vs. relational rationality in intercultural business negotiations

1 Deal and/or relationship

> *As we have no immediate experience of what other men feel, we can form no idea of the manner in which they are affected, but by conceiving what we ourselves should feel in the like situation."*
>
> (Adam Smith, 1790, p. 4)

The entire book uses a conceptual approach to InterCultural Business Negotiations (ICBN) based on the Deal and/or Relationship model which serves as a guiding framework, essentially because nations and cultures do not make the same use of these two key aspects of negotiation, do not value them similarly, and do not order them in the same manner. Priority and assumed causality are the central issues in explaining Deal-Making versus, or, and/or Relationship-Building framework.[1]

The introductory chapter explains and illustrates the main dimensions of the Deal and/or Relationship model of ICBN. It does so by starting from definitions of business negotiation, highlighting the origin of knowledge about negotiation, and showing that there is a strong Western bias (e.g., the deal is of paramount importance and the relationship is a non-necessary by-product, in fact a non-pivotal issue). Because Deal and Relationship tend to intermingle and interact in complex manners, I highlight how they are likely to combine in ICBN settings. Deal-Making corresponds to an ideal-type (IT) of calculative rationality (IT1) while Relationship-Building corresponds to relational rationality (IT2).[2] In IT1, deals come first and relationship may (or may not) follow. IT1 is interest-centred and to a certain extent rights-centred. In IT2, the relationship comes first and deals are the (supposedly) natural consequence of good relationships.[3] This chapter first defines negotiation and discusses the predominantly U.S. (IT1) origin of knowledge about negotiation. It further presents the Deal and/or Relationship paradigm and examines key negotiation concepts in the light of this paradigm. The last section explains how this book is organized.

Negotiation defined

Let us start with an example, that of negotiations between airlines and aircraft manufacturers (the same holds true if you add aircraft engine manufacturers, a triangle of relationships). They have regular deals (e.g., buying or leasing aeroplanes) over long periods of time. Each time they negotiate a particular contract, they maintain or develop relationships since the airline will keep the planes for many years and will often tend to be loyal to a particular aircraft manufacturer (e.g., Boeing and British Airways). Whether deals are more important than relationships, whether deals can be closed without a relationship (in an either/or perspective), whether the deal or the relationship should be prioritized, and how deal and relationship combine in ICBN (in an either/and perspective) are the topics of this book.

The scope of business negotiation is quite large, virtually infinite: including sales contracts, business deals, agency contracts, company takeovers, mergers and acquisitions (M&As), joint ventures, and individual as well as collective agreements between employers and employees (i.e., industrial relations). In many countries, there is some leeway for large taxpayers in negotiating with taxation authorities. Similarly, lobbying implies negotiating business regulations with public authorities. Beyond signing contracts, when conflicts arise from implementation, litigation and out-of-court settlements appear as extended negotiation activities.

A general definition of negotiation

Negotiation generally is a **face-to-face** activity with two or more players who, facing interest divergence and feeling that they are **interdependent**, choose to actually look for an arrangement (**deal**) to put an end to this divergence and thus create, maintain, or develop a **relationship**. Let us go through the individual elements of this definition one by one.[4] Negotiation is first and foremost an activity with start and end dates involving joint **task**(s) and a **doing orientation**. Not all human activities involve negotiation. **Communication** *per se* is not negotiation. Individuals and organizations do not constantly negotiate. Negotiation, being bilateral or multilateral by nature, takes place between two or more players. The parties share a sense of being interdependent, which involves objective (e.g., shared interests and mutual dependence) as well as subjective (i.e., perceived) dependencies on both sides. These dependencies are neither necessarily symmetrical nor balanced. Conflict, which involves the ways in which parties "play" their interest divergence, can be increased, but also mitigated by interdependence. The parties choose to provisionally put aside the interest divergence they face, that is, downplay conflict, so as to actually (**effectively**) look for an arrangement. The adverb "effectively" implies that, in some negotiations, a party may not really look for an agreement, but rather try to obtain proprietary information through data gathered during the negotiation process without being willing to close a deal, which would force it to pay for the other party's knowledge.[5]

The next point ("and thus...") misleadingly seems a consequence of the previous **deal**-related sequence. "Creating, maintaining or developing a

relationship between the negotiating parties", although frequent, are not necessary sequels of the deal. Rather than an unmanaged and somewhat unintended consequence of Deal-Making, Relationship-Building may be a condition, a necessary antecedent of Deal-Making. This is a major divide in terms of cross-cultural/intercultural business negotiation. Certain cultures are deal-prone and find it normal to search for a one-shot contract, a discrete transaction with no future. In other cultures, the relational emphasis is much stronger: negotiation has a lot to do with developing a long-term partnership, which is assumed to be an asset if difficulties arise when implementing deals negotiated within the relational frame (e.g., in the oil business, between drilling operators and oil companies).

Alternative functional definitions of negotiation

Negotiation can first be seen as a resource allocation activity. This leads to emphasis on its deal-oriented bargaining side, in a mere calculative and single issue setting (i.e., exchanging cash against an item), evident in trade and economic exchange (a lot of single-issue, one-shot bargaining takes place in a relational vacuum). Examples are buying second-hand cars, *souk* bargaining, or haggling. Second, negotiation is often related to the search for solutions (e.g., creating a common venture, dividing joint outcomes, designing joint rules that will solve a number of recurrent conflicts). This **problem-solving orientation**, which is still deal-oriented albeit much more relational, is fundamentally related to the objective of increasing **joint utility**: there are many alternatives available and, among these, one or possibly two options are the best. However, a party that is sincerely engaged in problem-solving may at times reveal information that will be used by the other party to increase its share of the pie. The third functional definition of negotiation, more relational and also quite meaningful, emphasizes its nature as a **collective decision-making method** in situations in which there are no rules and/or hierarchy. The scope of negotiation increases as and when rules and hierarchy play a diminishing role. In a traditional society in which hierarchical relationships dominate there is less room for negotiation, which is a basically horizontal type of interaction between peers. If a society were organized along detailed, imperative, and impersonal rules, there would be no place for negotiation. However, since most rules require regular updates, exceptions, and adjustments, drafting joint rules (institutionalization) is a frequent negotiation activity. Common rules in an intercultural setting are understandably more difficult to design and to mutually comply with than intraculturally.[6]

The negotiation system

The negotiation system is a combination of relational dynamics, information exchange, persuasion, and bargaining processes which result in drafting agreements with joint as well as individual outcomes (for each party). In an international setting, relational dynamics are very likely to be culturally and linguistically coded because they are based on communication, **communication styles**, conflict resolution, information exchange, persuasion, and consensus building, and therefore differ both cross-nationally and cross-culturally. That is why several chapters are dedicated to these issues (especially Chapters 3, 4, and 5). Similarly, negotiation processes and strategies tend to display inter-national/-cultural variance (Chapter 7 and 8).

Bargaining versus negotiation

Bargaining is sometimes used as a synonym of negotiating and is also considered a subset of negotiation situations centring on price vs. object. However, in the toughest case a definition of bargaining would border on haggling, a single issue negotiation, one shot, with relational rituals rather than true relationships. Khuri (1968, p. 701) describes the rituals involved in bargaining in the Middle East. Bargaining always begins with standard signs of respect, affection, common interest, and trust. The seller's speech evokes affection and creates an impression of friendliness and fraternity. As soon as the potential buyer shows interest in an item and asks for information, the seller replies:

> Between us there is no difference; we share the same interest, price is not what pleases me, what pleases me is to find out what pleases you; pay as much as you want; brothers do not disagree on price; for you it is free; it is a gift.

Nothing in this (IT2) speech should be taken literally. The opening incantation is a way of expressing a social bond of mutual interest and trust through allusions to a probable family tie in a metaphorical sense. Relationships in fact, may be fake, simulated, and forged rather than real. Westerners sometimes feel guilty when walking away after bargaining with a *souk* vendor for half an hour without making any deal, with the impression that they are responsible for the seller's wasted time and efforts. The *souk* vendor may simulate anger and possibly shout at naive buyers in the hope that increased feelings of guilt will make them come back. In general, it is the exact opposite that occurs. The buyer never comes back. This example suggests how culturally coded and sensitive relational processes are.

Bargaining deserves a special note. In many "developed/industrial" countries, there has been a strong decline in traditional bargaining activities. This largely relates to the compulsory display of price tags imposed by regulation and to the generalized practice of self-service in retail stores. Even though bargaining exists for equipment goods and for some large ticket items in consumer durables, a significant part of the world population (including many readers of this book) are not exposed to the daily rituals of exchange price exploration. Bargaining in *souks* or *bazaars* is good hands-on training for

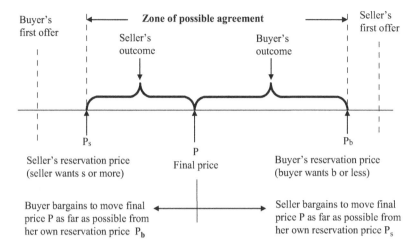

Figure 1.1 Bargaining and the Zone of Possible Agreement (ZOPA)
Source: adapted from Raiffa et al. (2003)

business negotiation. People from countries where bargaining is legally for-bidden may be at a disadvantage because of their lack of practical experience.

Bargaining and reservation price

In Figure 1.1, we imagine a situation where a buyer and a seller face each other with the hope of agreeing on a price. They both have a **reservation price** (assuming that they have prepared before entering into negotiation), that is, the price below/above which they are not willing to sell/buy. Naturally, neither of them, if rational, is willing to reveal their reservation price, which remains purely private information. Thus their first offer will be under (buyer) or above (seller) their reservation price. In the Figure 1.1 the range between buyer and seller reservation prices defines a zone of possible agreement (often clipped into ZOPA). If the ZOPA is negative (the buyer's reservation price is superior to that of the seller), they should walk away and not reach an agreement. Within the agreement zone, negotiation talent (among other factors) will decide how surplus is shared between both bargainers.

The negotiation setting

Conditions, objects, and context

There are three main conditions for entering a negotiation. First, the percep-tion by both parties of their actual interdependence (see Chapter 3) must be strong enough for them to decide to formally start a negotiation. Second, the expected utility increase derived from the process must be greater than the expected negotiation expenses (a condition rarely explored in practice). This seems a near tautology. However, many individuals and companies do not assess the costs of negotiating (e.g., travelling, time spent in the process, paying lawyers, experts, and other third parties) and may end up in small ticket deals (e.g., a licensing agreement in a small-size market), in which cumulative returns do not match actual negotiation costs, which are a significant part of transaction costs. Third, there should be a "reasonable" power differential between the parties so that the agreement is really bilateral, not unilaterally imposed and dictated by hierarchy and/or dominance. There often is some sort of power differential: non-unionized workers, for instance, may suffer a disadvantage in relation to their employers. However, power asymmetries are not a final hindrance to negotiation, provided that they remain tractable for the weaker party, especially if and when the stronger party does not overexploit its power advantage.

The **object(s) of a negotiation** sometimes seems at first so obvious that it (they) are not explicitly addressed by the parties. However, it is always advisable to first discuss what is actually negotiable and to be negotiated. There can be different issues/objects, some of which are implicit. For example, instead of buying a controlling share in a company it could be possible to buy or lease its key assets to establish cooperation without merging the companies. The initial discussion on negotiation objects can be creative because it enlarges the realm of alternative solutions and facilitates problem-solving. It also remedies a possible dissymmetry in perceived negotiation objects (e.g., employees think they are coming to negotiate a salary increase when management is willing to discuss training and working conditions). The degree of formalization in defining the object(s) of a negotiation is always to be considered before entering the process itself.

Multiple objects (synonyms: "issues", "goods"), such as social negotiation of salaries, holidays, working conditions, and work schedules (four objects), increase the potential for **creating value.** Value creation in such multi-issue negotiation is all the more increased 1) by the number of objects under negotiation and 2) by divergence between the parties in preferences and utilities for these objects. For example, an industrial subcontractor may swap shorter delivery delays and smaller order sizes with its powerful buyer which has an interest in changing to a *just-in-time* relationship and is therefore ready to concede on price, payment delay, and offer a long-term agreement. At the end, joint utility is increased through negotiation, one party exchanging lower utility objects (but higher utility for the other party) and vice versa.

Any negotiation, even the simplest, has a **context** and circumstances that are relevant to the process. Context plays a role in shaping final outcomes. For example, a pleasant place, personal affinities between the parties, and shared educational background may help negotiators in reaching a high level of joint outcomes. If properly taken advantage of, context is an asset. If not, context may become a liability. For example, a global pharma company wanted to downsize its research and manufacturing operations in a small town near Lake Geneva (Novartis in Prangins), which was bad news for the local community with many jobs potentially lost. A negotiated solution was found after a number of negotiation rounds and the active involvement of the macro-environment (local public authorities). The multinational company locally maintained most of its operations against the award of a large piece of constructible land at almost no cost. The local authorities simply changed the legal status of this large piece of land, from farming to constructible land, at no cost for them; however, at a considerable advantage for Novartis.

The **history of the relationship** between the parties is the most significant contextual feature. History should be taken *lato sensu* (i.e., in a broad sense), that is, not only past but also possible future interactions which are discounted in the present and combined with previous interactions. A first-time interaction between partners unknown to each other cannot be compared with an interaction between companies which have repeatedly negotiated over the last 30 or 40 years and will continue to do so in the long run (e.g., an airline with an aircraft manufacturer). A particular context is that of "first-time/last-time" interaction (e.g., buying real estate, selling a second-hand car) where negotiation is largely **deal-centred**, non-relational, and quite susceptible to **opportunistic behaviour** and concealed exploitative attitudes.

At first glance, it seems that a negotiation is limited to the **parties** that decide to enter it. However, other **stakeholders** sometimes pop up in the negotiation process and signal their willingness to participate in some way. They generally come from what is called the "macro-environment" of a negotiation, including private organizations (e.g., banks, confederation of industries or employers) and public organizations (e.g., local governments/ authorities) as well as trades unions and advocacy NGOs (e.g., Greenpeace, WWF).[7] They are not necessarily invited to the main negotiation table; however, they may be involved in ad hoc sessions, especially if they bring resources and solutions that help in solving problems, or when their nuisance capacity, especially in public debate, is significant enough to involve them in some way.

The third group of relevant contextual circumstances that build a negotiation context is place, date, and "climate". Where the negotiation takes place can be divided into three simple categories: "at our place", "at their place", and in a neutral site. In the case of international negotiations, place is of utmost importance as I will show in some chapters of this book. It is especially important for those who cannot master their agenda far away from home and in a foreign location as they may fear that they are being manipulated, have to decide under time pressure, and make unnecessary concessions. "Date" is a general category for many time-related issues in negotiation. These issues are analysed in detail in Chapter 4.

Nature and origin of knowledge about negotiation

The history of how negotiation knowledge developed over centuries includes famous names such as Von Clausewitz (German), De Callières (French), and Sun-Tsu (Chinese), all concerned with diplomacy and war, not business. A large body of business negotiation knowledge has been accumulated over the last 70 years, mostly based on North American contributions, representing a variety of academic disciplines from game theorists and microeconomists to social psychologists and political scientists. Where does negotiation knowledge come from in terms of language and culture background? The answer is simple: from English speaking academics and the culture associated with it (i.e., task-oriented, low-context/precise communication style, utilitarian, pragmatic, liberal, and open-minded culture). Negotiation knowledge is predominantly North American, conceived, written, and published in English.[8] This typically leads to prioritizing deal-related, utilitarian aspects, and to considering people and relational issues as secondary (e.g., "separate people from interests" (IT1) can be understood as "ignore people because they can distract you from seriously considering your interests").[9]

What kinds of educational background do these negotiation researchers have? The answer is not straightforward: there is no unified disciplinary origin for negotiation knowledge. On the contrary the educational backgrounds of well-known negotiation researchers are extremely diverse (see Table 1.1). As a consequence, research in negotiation is a sort of template for interdisciplinary knowledge.

To what extent can negotiation knowledge be considered universal or relative? The answer to this question is not at all simple. Negotiation knowledge can be considered universal because it is widely adopted worldwide, without even minor criticism of its lack of appropriateness for many local contexts. This is in fact the main objective of this book; to show what in negotiation knowledge should be considered universal (and much is) and what remains culturally relative.

The interdisciplinary nature of negotiation research and knowledge

As noted above, research in negotiation has developed out of the collaborative work of many disciplines (e.g., mathematics, microeconomics, game theory, social and experimental psychology, political science, law, experimental economics, business studies). Negotiation is an applied research topic which is present in many individual and organizational situations, from bargaining a second-hand car to joint venture negotiation. Major contributors include, for instance, John Nash (the Nash equilibrium), Raymond Cohen (diplomacy, international relations), Jeffrey Rubin, Harold Kelley (social psychology of negotiation), and John L. Graham (buyer-seller negotiations). The negotiation knowledge corpus is very open in terms of its contributing disciplines because of the capacity of academics in this field to cooperate within

Table 1.1 Disciplinary background of some well-known negotiation researchers

Negotiation researcher	Educational background (disciplines)
Max H. Bazerman	Economics, organizational psychology, accounting, business administration
Jeanne M. Brett	History, labour and industrial relations, organizational psychology
Herb Cohen	Law school
Roger Fisher	Law school
Michele J. Gelfand	Psychology, social, organizational, and cross-cultural psychology
John L. Graham	Cultural anthropology, management, marketing
David A. Lax	Statistics
Roy Lewicki	Psychology and social psychology
John Forbes Nash	Mathematics
Margaret A. Neale	Pharmacy, psychology, business administration
Dean G. Pruitt	Psychology and social psychology
Lucian Pye	Political science
Howard Raiffa	Mathematics, statistics
Jeswald W. Salacuse	Etudes Françaises, law school
James K. Sebenius	Mathematics, English, engineering, business economics
Richard G. Shell	English, law school
Leigh Thompson	Speech, education, psychology
Catherine H. Tinsley	Anthropology, organizational behaviour
William Ury	Social anthropology
Stephen Weiss	French, international affairs, conflict analysis and peace research
William Zartman	International relations

joint academic conferences and journals, and being non-territorial and not narrowly confined within the boundaries of academic disciplines, contrary to academia in general. This is evidenced by Table 1.1.

Why is negotiation research interdisciplinary in nature? Negotiation is about collective decision-making with undefined, uncertain, non-deterministic outcomes. Joint as well as individual outcomes are conditional not only on the other party's behaviour and on one's own behaviour but also on the interaction between parties (process). Negotiation is in a sense (very) applied game theory, hence the meaningful use of mathematics to formalize negotiation. However there are limits since the human, cultural, and subjective side of negotiation does not lend itself easily to formalization (Sebenius, 1992). Since negotiation is related to preferences and utilities (both individual and joint), bargaining appears as a starting base taken from microeconomics. Negotiation is also about social interactions involving interests, rights, and power, as well as disputes and conflict resolution (Tinsley, 2004). This explains why social and organizational psychology, political science, and international relations are major contributors. The negotiation process is mostly based on communication in its various forms (i.e., oral and written, face-to-face, verbal and non-verbal, through letters, emails, etc.); hence the importance of language and the relevance of interpersonal/intercultural communication research. Last, negotiation is related to formal agreements, contracts, and (possible) litigation, explaining the relevance to negotiation knowledge of law and legal studies, including business law and comparative law.

Negotiation research, being based on experiments and observation, and negotiation education, being based on experiential learning, are strongly related. They are both largely grounded on simulated negotiations with a scenario, common and private information corresponding to roles, and a context the complexity of which is kept under control. Similar instruments (negotiation games, exercises, and simulations) are used in both classroom settings and experimental research in negotiation.[10] Examples of such negotiation simulation are Kelley's game or Sharks. No individual negotiation being fully comparable to any other one (see checklist of the basic characteristics of a negotiation in Chapter 8), there is a need for experimental research based on simulated negotiation. Such experiments (in research) are in some way deeply related to experiential learning (when teaching negotiation). A large variety of research paradigms and data collection techniques are used (experiments, case studies, participant observation, content analysis, etc.), making negotiation research a template of both interdisciplinary knowledge and proper linkage between education and research.

A favourable picture nuanced

The organizational structure of universities, the constraints of academic careers, and publication systems should be taken into account as possible obstacles. For instance, a "negotiation researcher" would have some difficulty finding an academic job because she may not be properly "labelled" in disciplinary terms. A key issue for interdisciplinary research and education is the territorial nature of academia (i.e., disciplines are abstract territories and academics are members of ingroups). As a consequence, researchers have focused mindsets and may become entrenched in "paradigmatic isolation". Moreover, recruitment and careers are based on typical achievement paths that are closely codified within disciplinary ingroups. Academics need to belong to a particular discipline (i.e., they still need to be defined in disciplinary terms, different fields having their own negotiation literature). Negotiation courses in top schools and large faculties[11] most often reflect a particular paradigmatic orientation (more so in the U.S. than in Europe). Negotiation courses are most often offered as uncoordinated elective courses (unless they are embedded in a specialized educational programme). Consequently, students might acquire a biased view of negotiation, based too much on game theory, law and litigation, communication, and so on.

Another limitation is related to the programmed arch-dominance of the IT1 paradigm, through the English language as well as the associated mindset: doing oriented, facts-based, and utilitarian culture. The IT1 with its strong normative and prescriptive stance, necessarily reflects a hidden ideological background, very much related to non-positional, calculative, rational "principled negotiation", but also weakly relational, and afraid of the risk that "wine and dine" will obscure the ability to be lucid and balanced in negotiation.[12] The consequences of a particular cultural and language origin are paramount for ICBN as concerns the time frame of negotiation and issues of socialization (e.g., recommending mere friendliness rather than friendship).

Even if the academic system in general is fundamentally territorial, negotiation research and education fortunately remain non-territorial. Typically, negotiation academics are non-territorial because they have a strong leaning for the exploration of multiple territories. They do not feel threatened by multiple paradigms. As a consequence, they have not created a new territory for which they can raise barriers to entry and defend positions. There are journals, conferences, and programmes, but they are all quite open to interdisciplinary talks. Despite its limitations, the IT1 paradigm probably is the "least bad" candidate for seemingly universal knowledge about negotiation.

Deal or, and/or Relationship

Definitions of deal and relationship

Let us start with definitions of deal and relationship. It is always better to start from clear meaning.

Definition of deal: A deal is composed of the concrete, sometimes physical, most often measurable, in any case objective attributes of a discrete transaction (e.g., type of good or service, order size, delivery date and conditions, payment terms). It is based on material, financial, and precisely defined numbers for quantity, price, and time-related issues. A standard deal is a one-shot transaction, isolated in the fabric of time. As such, it has no automatic, foreseen, and/or intended future. A deal can, however, be repeated over time, unchanged or updated between the same business partners. A pure-deal negotiation can take place when it is a first time negotiation (i.e., business partners who have never had an exchange), with a relatively strong market background (e.g., clear price references). There is little subjectivity in the face-to-face encounter, and business partners usually look for a merely calculable arrangement with minimal or even no socialization at all. Deals as such are cold and dry, even if lip-service rapport may be feigned. Rationality is based on calculation, measurement, numbers, and hard facts. However, what at first may appear to be a deal (during the negotiation) may in fact be based on the relationship at the post-agreement, implementation stage. Over time, successive deals between the same partners inevitably generate some form of – largely unintended – relationship.

Definition of relationship: A relationship is based on human connections and/or feelings/emotional bonds, and generates a sense of being in some way attached to the other person/party. It progresses on the ground of joint experiences, sympathy, or antipathy. Relationships are sometimes but not necessarily based on common kinship, shared ingroup, and any form of social bondage. They may develop because of pure personal affinities. A relationship has an implied element of continuity. However, relationships can be broken, discontinued, or on the contrary resist the test of time and the negative occurrences of misunderstandings and quarrels. Relationships are people-related, personal, with all the vicissitudes of human bondage; that is, they have ups and downs, and misunderstandings may at times occur.[13] In the IT2, relational paradigm, rationality is people-based with the view that nice partners generate good deals. Many negotiators, consciously or unconsciously, strive for warm relationships with their partners. However, they do not always attain such wholeheartedness. Relationships may be exploited by one partner. Relationships are in no way an absolute guarantee against relational opportunism (i.e., unduly extracting value because of a "good" connection).

Deals and relationships may be split-up or mixed. The split-up results from the IT1 assumption, in its extreme form, that people (e.g., their identity-related bonds and connivance, *inter alia*: age, gender, shared ingroup, common educational background, shared language) can be divorced from interests. Being sensible is not being sensitive as the title of Jane Austen's novel *Sense and Sensibility* suggests. A look at the definitions of Sense, Sensitivity, and Sensibility, as well as common sense advocates in favour of mixing Deal and Relationship and therefore acknowledging that there is a complex interplay between them, especially in ICBN. What is cultural sensitivity in intercultural negotiation? First, cultural sensitivity in ICBN assumes awareness that interests and people cannot, in most cases, be completely separate. Cultural (or, better, intercultural) sensitivity implies being rationally interpretive within a constantly updated evaluation of the other party.

Should deal and relationship be separated, divorced from each other?

If the answer to the above question is, yes, why? If no, why? The assumption that deals and relationships should be separated as much as possible is based on the solid ground of *Business is Business*. The subjective side of interpersonal relationships is resented as it is likely to bias decisions, to alter judgements, and possibly to lead to suboptimal transactions. There is a latent view that too much pathos may obscure the negotiation, restricting the consideration of alternative partners and solutions, possibly leading to collusion, etc. In the pure deal version of negotiation, complicity and connivance are avoided, with very minimal socialization at the (short) beginning of a face-to-face encounter; that is, a minute icebreaker with a joke and an invitation/command to use first names from the very start.

The contrary assumption, which exists in many cultures, is that deal and relationship just cannot be divorced from each other. Human beings are negotiators, not economic robots. Inexorably, a relationship will emerge between them. Inevitably, feelings and emotions will intermingle and coalesce with the material side of the deal. It is often assumed that relationships have by and large a positive influence on the quality of Deal-Making for both sides. It is not that clear in practice. While relationships may help foster cooperative behaviour, promote trust, and help overcome obstacles in the negotiation process, they may also be unilaterally exploited by one party to extract concessions and advantages beyond a fair division of joint outcomes. Relationships are not a panacea.[14]

What comes first? What should come first?

IT1 and IT2 differ in their answer to the following (fundamental) questions: What comes first? What should come first? A strong argument in favour of starting with a Deal-Making oriented negotiation (IT1) is that relationships are the non-necessary by-product of negotiation. They are an outcome variable (building, maintaining, or developing a relationship), which evolves over time through successive negotiation rounds between the same partners. Relationships are neither necessary nor sufficient for successful negotiation.

A strong argument in favour of starting negotiation from a Deal-Making perspective is that relationships are only the by-product of negotiation. They are an outcome variable ("building, maintaining, or developing a relationship" as in the definition above), which evolves over time through successive negotiation rounds between the same partners. The IT1 paradigm is meaningful and it is often prevalent in negotiation practice.

However, a contrary – and quite defendable – assumption is that the relationship should come first. How could people negotiate without being acquainted? How can they fruitfully interact without shared knowledge of who the other negotiator is? In this view (IT2), people come first; deals follow relationships. If the tough confrontation of Deal-Making comes first, it could definitively damage relationship development. Therefore, negotiation should not focus on the down-to-earth details, before partners (and possibly the companies they represent) have developed a relationship.

As a consequence we have two polar ideal-types, which will be found in all chapters of this book. Power can intervene in both IT1 and IT2 types of negotiations. However, power is played in a different manner according to cultural background and negotiation style (Chapter 11).

Combination of deals and relationship patterns over time

Time and time frames in negotiation and contractual arrangements are extremely important. A typical deal time frame is that of a real estate agent who meets buyers of houses and flats only once, in a pure one-shot interaction with no past and no future. Conversely, a relationship time frame develops, with a past, a present, and a future in Business-to-Business (B2B) transactions which are repeated over years between the same business partners. Similarly, as soon as implementation and post-agreement negotiation, including possible renegotiation, are likely to take place, a relationship time frame must be accepted. Time issues are both cultural and business-related. This is examined in Chapter 4 and Chapter 10 (different time frames of ICBN contracts).

Deal patterns

In Deal-Making, **exiting** is the preferred solution when it seems that the parties will not reach an agreement. Exiting as such is facilitated by the absence of a relationship and would be made more difficult by subjective bonding. Alternatives to a Negotiated Agreement (ATNAs) and among these the best (BATNA)[15] are constantly reviewed against the present state of negotiation and its probable outcome. If the proposed deal is inferior to the BATNA, the walk-away option is quickly activated. Time lost in abortive negotiation is resented as mere *sunk costs*. Litigation appears as the most likely solution when interdependence is too high for exiting and conflict resolution methods seem impossible without the intervention of a third party (e.g., arbiter, judge). This is called an "Arm's length contractual relationship" (ACR in Table 1.2).

Relationship patterns

In relationship-oriented negotiations, *exit* is considered as a failure (however, not unlikely). This is not only a matter of time and money; human

Table 1.2 ACR and OCR models

ACR (arm's-length contractual relation) Deal-first negotiation	OCR (obligational contractual relation) Relationship-driven negotiation
Specific and discrete economic transactions (discontinuity between transactions)	Involves an economic contract covering manufacturing and commercial exchange
Explicit legal contract	Interactions are embedded in personalized social relationships
Unforeseen events are dealt with on the basis of normative legal or contractual rules (law of the parties)	Between exchange partners who have a sense of mutual trust
Arm's length: a distant relationship in which partners must avoid any undue familiarity	Transactions may take place without prior formal screening on all terms and conditions of the exchange
The exit option (A.O. Hirschman, 1970) is easy when the contract comes to an end	Parties expect that acts of goodwill will be reciprocated by the other side

Source: adapted from Sako (1992, pp. 11–12)

expectations are not met. Litigation is even worse than exit. It should be avoided at any cost. Reciprocity and voice appear as standards for conflict resolution. Even loyalty can be considered a standard relational pattern. This corresponds to the obligational contractual relation (OCR) model in Table 1.2.

As will be seen in the coming chapters, in ICBN, deals and relationships intermingle with inevitable ambiguities in combining them. What seems at first a pure deal (during negotiation) may appear as dominated by the relationship at the post-agreement stage, because partners have to jointly solve problematic implementation issues.

Wrong assumptions about relationships

Some final caveats help to avoid an exceedingly positive view of the relational orientation.

- A relationship is generally an asset, with a positive influence on the negotiation process and outcomes. However, a relationship may also be a liability, difficult to manage, and have a somewhat negative influence on the negotiation process and outcomes. Too high expectations may result from overestimated relational assets.
- Even if a deal is always cold and rational, there is no reason why a constructive relationship could not be built on successive successful deals, with progressive warming up. Often a relationship emerges from successive pure deals, with satisfactory outcomes on both sides, which lead the parties to develop a relationship through multiple encounters over time.
- The interaction between deals and relationships is complex. Successful deals may be exploited to simulate fake relationships. Conversely, apparently successful, bilateral, and stable relationships may be misused to generate exploitative, non-balanced deals, especially when the relationship is coming to an end and only one party is aware of this imminent termination.

Key negotiation concepts in the light of the deal versus relationship paradigm

Walk-away options: The Best Alternative To a Negotiated Agreement

Putting emphasis on walk-away options makes sense. A no-deal exit may appear as the best alternative. Paradoxically, not closing a deal is typical of short-term deal-oriented negotiation, in line with the seemingly rational ACR model in a one-shot perspective. However, a no-deal exit might later appear as a lost opportunity for creating value over a longer period of time.

A central issue in negotiation is conflict and **conflict resolution** (hence, Chapter 2 is dedicated to negotiation as conflict resolution). Conflicts in business and commercial/industrial matters cannot be compared with conflicts between nation-states, which are solved by confrontation, belligerence, war and/or diplomacy. Metaphorically, a price war or litigation between companies can to a certain extent be compared to a sort of armed fight. However, companies have many more exit solutions and alternatives than nations. They can decide to search for other markets, other products, and other solutions, as well as other partners. Alternatives (As) reside both in the negotiation process itself and beyond the negotiation table. The overall set of out-of-negotiation alternatives can be called ATNAs. For any negotiator or negotiating company it makes sense (especially in the IT1 paradigm) to constantly compare what that party can get out of the present negotiation with what can be gained by breaking off the process. Within this set of ATNAs, there is one that is presumably the best: the BATNA.[16] In many cases, negotiators tend to forget about the possibility to break off negotiation and choose a solution outside the negotiation process. The simplest ATNA is the *status quo ante*. Finding another business partner or further operating an activity that was due to be sold may be other ATNAs. If, after careful assessment of each ATNA, the continuation of the business that was due to be sold is the best, it becomes the BATNA. If further negotiation does not allow a more favourable outcome than this BATNA, the negotiator will logically and justifiably withdraw.

Comparing the BATNA with the potential agreement, there are four possibilities in terms of exit versus deal closure as shown in Table 1.3. If the BATNA is superior to the Agreement, it is not rational to close a deal (cell 1). If the BATNA is inferior to the proposed Agreement, it is rational to close a deal (cell 2). If the BATNA is superior to the Agreement, it is rational to walk-away (*exit*) without closing a deal (cell 3). If the BATNA is inferior to the Agreement, it is not rational to walk-away (*exit*) without having closed a favourable deal (cell 4).

The two "faulty" cells are likely to occur because 1) of the difficulty to make precise calculations, especially for the BATNA, so that alternatives would be perfectly comparable (i.e., with figures); 2) when engaged in negotiation and having spent time and effort in the process, negotiators often

Table 1.3 Four possibilities of exit vs. deal in terms of BATNA vs. negotiated agreement

	BATNA > Agreement	*BATNA < Agreement*
Deal closed	Unfounded agreement	Justified agreement
Negotiation failure	Justified failure	Unjustified failure Walking
(Exit)	Walking away made sense	away was a mistake

hesitate to leave the table empty-handed; and 3) the walk-away option especially in the IT2 paradigm is resented as a relationship fiasco, and begrudged
as a relational failure. In the IT2 paradigm, there is much reluctance to
admit that the relationship may be broken.

The BATNA, in a negotiation context, is akin to the reservation price in
a pure bargaining context, that is, a threshold commanding withdrawal.
However the BATNA is more about strategic stakes in a multi-issue and
more complex exchange context than mere bargaining.

Integrative orientation versus distributive orientation

Integrative (cooperative) versus distributive (competitive) orientation is
arguably more universal than the BATNA and exit options described in the
previous section. The integrative orientation can be found both in the IT1
and IT2 paradigms because maximizing joint gains requires a combination
of the IT1 calculative rationality with the IT2 other-regarding perspective.
In business negotiations, the purchaser (or team of purchasers) and the
vendor (or group of vendors) are mutually interdependent, and their individual interests clash. The ability to choose an effective negotiation path
largely explains individual outcomes on the one hand, and the joint outcome on the other. In pitting themselves against each other, the parties may
develop opposing points of view towards the negotiation strategy which
they intend to adopt: **distributive** (i.e., territorial, **zero-sum game**, **win-lose**
frame) or **integrative** (i.e., less territorial, **win-win** type, cooperative) where
achieving a higher **joint outcome** is, provisionally, privileged by one or preferably both players over **individual outcome(s)**. In the distributive strategy
(or orientation), the negotiation process is seen as leading to the division
of a specific "cake" which the parties feel they cannot enlarge even if they
were willing to do so.[17] The distributive orientation is also termed "**competitive negotiation**". It leads to a perception of negotiation as a war of
positions – territorial in essence. Distributive negotiations are of the "win-
lose" type: "anything that isn't yours is mine" and vice versa. The negotiators
hold attitudes and objectives that are quasi-conflictive. Interdependence is
minimized beyond common sense whereas opposition is emphasized, sometimes beyond reason. The (unfortunate) climax of the distributive orientation
takes place when both sides, playing **negative reciprocity** in a competitive
and escalating manner, choose a **lose-lose** avenue whereby the final objective
is to invest in costly punishment so that the other party loses the most. This
not so infrequent option in relations between nation-states is quite rare in
business negotiations.

At the opposite end of the spectrum is the integrative orientation.[18] The
central assumption is that the size of the "cake", the joint outcome of the
negotiations, can be increased if the parties adopt a cooperative attitude.
This idea is directly linked to the problem-solving orientation.[19] Negotiators
may not be concerned purely with their own objectives, but may also be

concerned by the other party's aspirations and results, seeing them as almost equally important. The **integrative orientation** has been termed "coopera-tive" or "collaborative". It results in negotiation being seen as an attempt to maximize the joint outcome. The division of this outcome is to a certain extent secondary or is at least perceived as important but coming later. Here negotiation is a "**positive sum game**" where the joint outcome is greater than zero when compared with the initial endowment.

Concern for the other party's outcomes

Concern for the other party's outcomes is not altruism.[20] Rather, it is a rational other-regarding orientation, based on enlightened, broadened rather than narrow, selfish, and calculative self-interest. It is self-interest moderated by sympathy in the Smithian sense (see epigraph at the start of the chapter), with the expectation that this sympathy will positively backfire on one's own outcomes. The importance of concern for the other party's outcomes is normatively mentioned by most, if not all, negotiation authors (often with the aphorism "Put yourself in their shoes"). However, it is not that easy for ICBN (i.e., "their shoes are not yours").

In practice, effective negotiation *combines* the distributive and integrative orientations at different stages in the negotiation process. The "dual concern model"[21] (see Table 1.4) explains negotiation strategies according to two basic variables: concern for one's own outcome (horizontal axis) and con-cern for the other party's outcome (vertical axis). This leads to four possible strategies.[22] According to Pruitt's model, the ability to envisage the other party's outcome is a prerequisite for the adoption of an integrative strategy.

The problem-solving orientation can be defined as an overall negoti-ating behaviour that is cooperative, integrative, and oriented towards the exchange of information. Fair communication and the exchange of infor-mation between negotiators are important. "Problem solvers" try as much as possible to exchange representative information; that is, true, honest, and objective data. There is self-restraint in manipulating the other party, contrary to **instrumental communication**,[23] in which the key objective is to influence. Exchanging **representative information** is considered a basic

Table 1.4 The dual concern model

Concern for the other party's outcomes	Concern for one's own outcomes	
	Low	*High*
High	Yielding (accommodative)	Integrative strategy (problem-solving)
Low	Inaction (avoidance)	Contending (competitive)

constituent of the problem-solving orientation. Empirical studies (experimental negotiation simulation) have shown that this orientation positively influences joint negotiation outcomes.[24] Normatively, the general superiority of cooperative negotiation can be demonstrated by developing a model whereby a new, more cooperative contract provides both the buyer and the seller with cost reduction, compared with a previous adversarial contract.[25]

There are, however, some conditions to developing an integrative approach; the first is the availability of cost-related data, the second is the release of this data to the other party during negotiation. Willingness and capacity to share information is obviously conditioned by culture, language, and communication-related issues. The adoption of an integrative strategy is facilitated by the following:

1) A high level of aspirations on both sides.[26]
2) The ability to envisage the future (therefore it is related to time orientations and national cultures (see Chapter 4).
3) The existence of a sufficient "*perceived* common ground"; that is, enough overlap between the interests of the two parties (not only their objective interests, but also their subjective perception of what these interests are).

The concept of the problem solving approach (PSA) is based on culturally relative assumptions. First, the *doing* orientation is strong in PSA – to solve a problem is to *do* something – and quite often PSA is posited as the *task*-related part of negotiation. Second, the PSA assumes that both partners are *fair*, an English word untranslatable in many languages, which use *fair play* as a borrowed phrase. *Fair* means "'open and honest in communication and interaction", a value which is not shared by many cultures. Third, PSA assumes reciprocal behaviour, based on quick response to the other party's openings, on a give-and-take basis where concessions on each side are precisely measured and balanced. PSA appears to make sense for IT1 negotiators; however PSA may work differently when applied to non-U.S. negotiators.[27] Some countries' cultures (CCs) are more PSA-prone and achieve higher joint gains in cross-cultural, comparative studies.[28] A reason for this is cross-national differences in the perceived compatibility of self-interested goals (i.e., claiming value) and the maximization of joint outcomes (i.e., creating value).[29] In ICBN, PSA has been shown to have a contagious effect: when a negotiator uses PSA, the partner's satisfaction may increase especially if he reciprocates in using PSA leading to an increase in individual and joint profits.[30]

Two meaningful metaphors about negotiation: Card game and theatre play

In the card game metaphor, negotiation can be symbolized as a game with players and stakes. Equality between opposing negotiators is only formal.

The stakes are most often different in both camps. The proper sense of "stake" is the money or valuables that a player must jeopardize in order to buy into a gambling game. This draws us to a fundamental characteristic of negotiation: it is a **game** to be played between two or more **players**. It involves some form of calculated gambling, of rational betting, in which any move (e.g., disclosing private information, making a concession, lying by omission) is conditional on the expected reaction of the other side. Game theory and experimental economics have been significant contributors to negotiation theory (see Chapter 1). Like in a card game, players have an **initial endowment** (cards they have in their hands with indistinguishable backs shown to other players) and, according to their talent, they can reach certain **payoffs**, especially when monetary bets have been made. Players keep the cards in their hands carefully, with card faces hidden from other players. Part of the information, essentially the rules of the game, is common knowledge. However, players keep **proprietary information** for themselves. If revealed, this information would put the other party at a significant advantage. This is exactly the same in real life negotiation: negotiators tend not to disclose key **private information**. Like in a card game, players hide their cards, especially trump cards, in order to be able to act strategically and to keep their "hand" invisible to other players.

In the theatrical metaphor of negotiation, negotiators are like actors performing scenes of a sort of drama (in the original Greek sense; that is, about action rather than tragedy). In negotiation, actors (players in game theory) commonly have a role (e.g., buyer vs. seller; purchaser vs. subcontractor; teacher vs. pupil) and a status (e.g., mandatory negotiator, CEO, vice-president, prime minister). While **role** and **status** are not involved in the whole of the negotiation process, they influence communication patterns and power dominance in negotiation for a particular script that is akin to the text of a play (e.g., buyer-seller, employee-employer, principal-agent). A role corresponds to a set of behaviours that others legitimately expect from a person being assigned this role. Individual negotiators are supposed to talk and listen within the confines of their role. Particular behaviours will be expected from a negotiator in a given role (e.g., buyer) under specific contexts and circumstances. For instance, a buyer's role may be to search for the lowest possible price. However, if he or she is primarily concerned with quality and delivery date, he or she may decide to downplay the price issue. In the U.S. management and organization literature, concepts such as **role ambiguity** (i.e., a role is ambiguously defined and rather vague) and **role conflict** (i.e., the same person experiences conflicts between two aspects of a role and/or has to combine two conflicting roles) are frequently used. In the IT1 paradigm, roles are paramount.

Status on the other hand is a set of behaviours towards oneself that an individual holding this status legitimately expects from others, a definition that seems at first symmetrical to that of role. Due to status, there are words and statements that can be voiced and others that cannot. A status-conscious person expects certain behaviours from others and tries to send signals that he or she deserves to be treated and addressed in a respectful manner. Status has therefore a strong impact on communication behaviour. It is also strongly dependent on national culture, as it reflects hierarchies, positions in the society, power distance, etc. While role is more IT1 related, egalitarian, horizontal, task-driven, and doing oriented, status is more IT2 related, non-egalitarian, vertical, rank-driven, and being oriented (concepts explained in Chapter 3).

Information, power, and asymmetries

Information is power, especially when it is not common knowledge. It is clearly not the only source of power, but information plays a key role in **power relationships**. Taking an intercultural and comparative perspective, as is the standpoint in this book, it is clear that ways of dealing with information (e.g., asking questions versus answering, equivocating, being precise versus vague, lying versus telling the truth) vary cross-nationally and cross-culturally. Some sources of power are universal: a large organization facing a much smaller one, an order taker facing a subcontractor, a well-off company facing a near-to-bankrupt partner, a negotiator with full power to close the deal facing another who has a **negotiation mandate**, etc. However, power asymmetries may not be played in the same way; that is, the extent to which they will be used to create a balance of power. Power relationships differ cross-nationally. Certain **negotiation roles** (e.g., buyer or seller) may be favoured in particular countries/cultures (e.g., the buyer role in Japan or the seller role in Germany). During the negotiation process, three types of asymmetries, **information asymmetry** (i.e., one side has more information and is not ready to reveal it), **cognitive asymmetry** (i.e., each side treats information in its own way), and **power asymmetry** (i.e., misbalance in power), should be considered. In "domestic" negotiation (people on both sides share culture and language), these asymmetries play a significant role in shaping negotiation outcomes. In intercultural negotiation, information asymmetry is played according to different cultural codes, while cognitive asymmetry, that is, how people differently select, interpret, treat, deliver or retain, and finally use information, is significantly increased (see Chapter 5).

The market background of ICBN

In Von Stackelberg's typology of market situations (Table 1.5), the standard situation for negotiation is assumed to be a bilateral monopoly, two players and no alternative partners. In this case, only negotiation strategies and tactics explain the final outcome and the IT1/IT2 contrast is fully relevant. However, alternative partnering opportunities with other buyers or sellers (some and many) encourage walking away from negotiation and going back to the market, for buyers in an oligopoly and for sellers in an oligopsony. In

Table 1.5 Typology of market situations

Sellers Buyers	*One*	*Some*	*Many*
One	Bilateral Monopoly	Contraried Monopsony	Monopsony
Some	Contraried Monopoly	Bilateral Oligopoly	Oligpsony
Many	Monopoly	Oligopoly	Pure and Perfect Competition

Source: Von Stackelberg (2010)

pure and perfect competition (e.g., most financial markets), the price is fixed by the market; price level is common knowledge especially if the item is homogeneous; transaction costs are low and there is no dominant player. In this case negotiation is reduced to the extreme, even in an ICBN setting: reservation prices being known by each party, the negotiation tends to be a pure deal. In global B2B markets, bilateral oligopolies are frequent, with few players on both sides, long-term relationships, however with alternative partnering opportunities; deal and relationship tend to combine in subtle ways. A few aircraft manufacturers facing airline alliances such as OneWorld and Star Alliance are a typical bilateral oligopoly. Finally, the rare situation – in practice – of monopsony and monopoly, especially in global markets, tends to favour the powerful and dominant party, which will impose its ICBN model. Last, an interesting situation is the symmetrical market background of contraried monopsony and contraried monopoly, where a few players, facing a single monopolistic/monopsonistic player, make a coalition to negotiate with more buying/selling power. In these market types, aggressive deal-orientation and IT1 negotiation may combine with a hate–love relationship orientation and IT2 type of negotiation.

Do negotiation concepts apply cross-culturally and interculturally?

Many negotiation concepts reviewed above seem at first sight perfectly valid (equivalent) across nations and cultures.[31] However, as noted previously, most of them are largely permeated by the IT1 paradigm; for example: BATNA, walk-away options, creating value, and claiming value.[32] Microeconomic concepts apply relatively well cross-culturally and interculturally (e.g., preferences, utility, reservation prices, ZOPA), provided that negotiators think in numbers, prepare and come to the negotiation table with a reservation price, that the negotiation is not too complex and multi-issue, etc. Some general concepts, especially in game theory, seem to apply cross-culturally and interculturally, such as cooperate/defect or problem-solving. However when entering into the details of cooperate/defect moves, it becomes much less clear: Is lying by omission clear defection? Is equivocating in communication an uncooperative move? Is indirect communication a sign of duplicity, falseness, or hypocrisy? There is no clear answer to these questions, suggesting that as soon as negotiation deals with communication, personal interactions, ethically acceptable behaviour, and the like, concepts are no longer cross-culturally equivalent, posing a potentially serious obstacle to ICBN. A last example to reveal the lack of cross-cultural invariance of supposedly universal concepts is the concept of "interests", which is omnipresent in negotiation theory. However, the literature understands "interests" mostly as being utilitarian and deal-related, while many ICB negotiators see it in a relational (IT2) perspective as relating to "interest" in people, in relationships, and in social capital.

How this book is organized

Chapter 2 explains the role of culture in negotiation, by means of the IT1-IT2 distinction which is used throughout this text as the basic ICBN paradigm. IT1 is related to the doing orientation (tasks are central), utilitarianism, and out-groupism. IT1 negotiators are interest-centred, individualistic, and tend to use low-context, precise communication, as well as to adopt linear, mechanical time attitudes. IT2 is related to the being orientation (people are central), identitarian (i.e., emphasizing identity rather than mere utility, placing identity needs[33] over utilitarian concerns), collectivistic, and ingroupist (emphasizing membership in the ingroup). Identity cannot be traded (culture especially is non-negotiable) and may prevail over interest. Status is important as well as personal (being) characteristics of negotiators. While IT1 tends to use a legal, impersonal, positive approach to common rules (i.e., contract as *law of the parties*), IT2 privileges relationships, natural rather than legal rights, and power. At the beginning and at the end of Chapter 2 and in Chapter 6, a number of caveats explain how cultural influences are subtly mediated by and interact with a number of dispositional characteristics of the negotiator (e.g., age, gender, profession). The influence of culture on ICBN is also complex because of cultural borrowing, pretence, and cultural adaptation.

Chapter 3 deals with conflict and sources of conflict (e.g., dependence, interdependence, divergence of interests and positions, rival value claims, opportunism, and opportunistic behaviour). Following the IT1/IT2 paradigms, this chapter explains how deal conflicts differ from relational conflicts, but also how they combine as well as the role of relationship and deal orientation in both conflict escalation and de-escalation. It sets out to explain deal opportunism, based on the opportunistic instrumentalization of contracts, for instance by precisely drafted clauses that can however be misleading and abusive, generating *lock-in* situations (i.e., a buyer is unable to shift to another seller without substantial switching costs), abusive delay penalties, future litigation planned from the outset, or negotiating with no real intention to close a deal, etc. Basic relational models and how they contribute to avoid and/or solve conflicts in ICBN is explained in Chapter 2.

Chapter 4 is dedicated to the pervasive influence of time-related representations and behaviours at different stages of ICBN, from pre-liminaries and socialization to agreement and beyond. Deal (IT1) time is linear-separable with a clear timeline when signing the contract, while relationship (IT2) time is fuzzy, holistic, cyclical, and extends over the whole period from pre-negotiation to post-agreement, implementation, and possibly renegotiation.

Chapter 5 covers verbal – oral and written – and non-verbal communication. It shows how IT1 negotiators use low context communication, precise and digital, relatively context-free, with a conversational style by segment, and privilege written communication formats (memos, emails, drafts, contracts, etc.), not necessarily face-to-face communication. The IT1 communication style tends to prefer representative, objective communication. It is therefore stronger on truthful and non-manipulative information exchange than IT2. IT2 relates to high context communication, with implicit messages that need context-bound interpretation to be fully understood. Conversational overlap style is frequent and a positive sign as concerns the quality of the communicative interaction. The chapter further shows how IT2 people display a preference for speech (over writing) and for non-verbal communication as well a preference for instrumental communication, which means that IT2 negotiators are on average stronger on persuasion and manipulation attempts.

Chapter 6 serves as a counterpoint to the ideal-types of deal and relationship, showing how individual characteristics including personality and gender, professional, and organizational culture substantively and subtly mitigate the IT1/IT2 paradigms. Negotiators may behave rather differently from what the ideal-types related to their cultural belonging and nationality would lead us to expect. This is because their own personality may be far from the modal personality in their culture/nationality. Their professional culture may dominate over other behavioural cues and lead to typical attitudes in negotiation (e.g., lawyers being rather distributive in general; aerospace negotiators being long term and relationship-oriented). Organizational culture may translate into a stronger Deal-Making or Relational orientation in ICBN.

Chapter 7 covers how the process of Intercultural Business Negotiations is influenced by the IT1/IT2 distinction, at each stage of the negotiation process, especially in the final stage (i.e., before signing, when transforming an oral agreement into contractual text and written joint rules) and during post-agreement negotiation (e.g., renegotiation). While for IT1 renegotiation is taboo, for IT2 negotiators it appears as standard because the relationship is supposed to prevail over the deal and to allow renegotiation. Misunderstandings about renegotiation can be related to the nature of commitment, whether impersonal in IT1 (to rules and text; "Get it in writing") or personal in IT2 (to people; "My word is my bond").

Chapter 8, ICBN strategies and tactics, discusses how to develop *interest-based* strategies (a rather universal concept, however discernibly marked by IT1) and implement them through negotiation tactics that enable us to reach goals without damaging either the relationship or a mutually profitable deal. It sets the strengths and the limitations of a Western style (IT1) typical strategic framework for negotiations such as the IRP model (Interests, Rights, and Power) or "Principled" negotiation in an intercultural perspective. The design and the preparation of a negotiation strategy are based on 1) a strategic analysis checklist, and 2) a cultural analysis checklist. A number of tactical issues in negotiation (first offer, opening, persuasion tactics, especially when they are *hardball* tactics) are examined in the light of their impact on both deals and relationships.

Chapter 9 – Negotiating different types of ICBN contracts – also serves as a counterpoint to the ideal-types of Deal (IT1) and Relationship (IT2), like in Chapter 6. It builds on the checklists presented in the preceding chapter to determine what should be treated in each major type of ICBN contract, on the basis of deal, relationship, and a combination of both. The basic characteristics of each type of international contract are discussed in detail. Time issues presented in Chapter 4 are one of the guiding frameworks: one-shot (sales/procurement contracts) vs. repeated deals, time span of the agreement, strong future orientation of the deal (e.g., joint ventures), implementation issues beyond signing the contract (e.g., licensing/franchising contracts), etc. Expectations of both parties as to the durability of the agreement as well as possible discrepancies between these expectations are examined in detail with illustrations. A number of legal issues related to particular agreements are discussed in detail such as the termination of contracts (e.g., licensing and franchising contracts), the distribution of equity and managerial power (e.g., joint ventures, M&As), the winner's curse (e.g., international corporate acquisitions), and non-disclosure agreements when key proprietary information is disclosed before finalizing the deal (e.g., know-how licences).

Chapter 10 is about ICBN ethics and starts from the view that deals can be bought or at least made easier and can be artificially closed by buying information or influence. Ethical issues in ICBN are largely related to the negative side of relationships (e.g., collusion, complicity, keeping outsiders at bay). In large project deals, collusive manoeuvres can be kept at bay (hindered) by the World Trade Organization (WTO) Code of Public Procurement. IT1 ICBN ethics are rule- and compliance-based, individualistic, impersonal, and legally enforced. Frankness and honesty are valued as universal values, even if they are not always practised in actual negotiations. Universalism is assumed: the "right" ethics should apply everywhere; universal rules cannot be challenged by local ethical standards. Personal connections and their possible abuse (e.g., nepotism, favouritism, anticompetitive alliances, and the like) are frowned upon. Conversely IT2 ethics value collectivistic assumptions: the group in all its forms, from the national group and the ethnic group (ingroup), to the clan and the extended family, is paramount. Loyalty to people is more important than "blind" compliance with anonymous rules.

Chapter 11 describes some elements of the national style of business negotiations for Americans (US-IT1), Black Africans (IT2), Brazilians (IT2), British (IT1), Chinese (IT2), French (IT1), German (IT1), Indian (IT2), Japanese (IT2), Mexican (IT2), Middle Eastern (IT2), and Russian (IT2) negotiation styles. One way to enhance negotiating power in ICBN is to identify a set of cultural traits in negotiation that can be used by negotiators to better understand their counterparts and therefore ease the ICBN process and improve joint outcomes.

A conclusive section highlights key recommendations for successful ICBN.

Notes

1 Tinsley et al. (2011) similarly oppose relational to economic goals. Hernández Requejo and Graham (2008, p. 66) oppose information-oriented to relationship-oriented cultures.

2 Foster (1995, pp. 272–274) and Maude (2014, p. 65) support the IT1 vs. IT2 distinction in terms of relationship vs. deal priority as well as Cohen (2007), Colson et al. (2013), and Graham et al.'s Chapter 4 on building personal relationships (2014, pp. 43–56).

3 Hernández Requejo and Graham (2008, pp. 65–67) make a distinction similar to the IT1/IT2 paradigm when they oppose relationship-oriented (IT2) versus information-oriented cultures (IT1).

4 Colson et al. (2013).

5 My definition is derived from Dupont (1994, pp. 11–17).

6 On average, *intercultural* negotiators are less cooperative and achieve lower profits compared with *intracultural* negotiators (Gelfand et al., 2011), especially when cultural differences are exacerbated by high ambiguity and tense situations (Morris et al., 2004).

7 For examples and reflections on negotiation between international organizations, see Faure and Rubin (1993), Cellich and Jain (2004), Cohen (2007), and Saner (2008).

8 The origin of knowledge on negotiation is evidenced by the first chapter ("Going forward to the past: A brief history of negotiation") in Graham et al. (2014, pp. 9–18), as well as by Bazerman and Neale (1992), in their section on "history of negotiation knowledge" (1992, pp. 280–295) and by Fisher (1980, pp. 11–16).

9 The U.S. origin of negotiation knowledge entails a potential bias when applied to ICBN. See for instance Hernández Requejo and Graham's (2008, pp. 17–31) first chapter on the American negotiation style which cites typical IT1 statements such as "A deal is a deal" and "I am what I am" (p. 30). A similar view is expressed by Foster's (1995, pp. 145–193) chapter on Americans at the (ICBN) negotiation table. See also Chapter 11 in this book.

10 ICBN instructors can find teaching materials and instructions (negotiation and dispute resolution simulations, cases, and exercises) from Northwestern-Kellogg's

DRRC (Dispute Resolution Research Center) (www.kellogg.northwestern. edu/research/drrc/teaching-materials.aspx) or from the Teaching Negotiation Resource Center at Harvard Law School – Program on Negotiation (PON) (www.pon.harvard.edu/store/). My own teaching materials can be found at www.hec.unil.ch/jusunier?set_language=en&cl=en. Private instructions, the Instructor's Manual and Teaching notes are available only to course instructors (for access, contact npjcu@hotmail.com).

11 For example at Harvard, INSEAD, Kellogg's, Stanford, and Wharton.

12 See Schweitzer and Kerr (2000) about bargaining under the influence of alcohol.

13 Support for the key importance of relationships in ICBN comes from many sources, for instance Fisher (1980), Cohen (1993, 2007), Kopelman and Olekalns (1999), Li and Labig (2001), Graham and Lam (2003), Shell (2006, Chapter 4, however only as the fourth foundation of negotiation out of six), Tinsley et al. (2011), Ramirez and Brett (2011), Khakhar and Rammal (2013).

14 Ramirez-Marin and Brett (2011), comparing Latin American (IT2) and Anglo cultures (IT1), give such an overly positive view of IT2, relationship-oriented cultures. They propose that negotiators from relational (IT2) cultures, compared with IT1 negotiators, would be 1) less extreme in their goals and opening offers; 2) less distributive; 3) use integrative strategies to generate [relational] compromise rather than [calculative] trade-offs; 4) display positive emotions across the whole process and not only when achieving high value outcomes (as IT1 negotiators); and 5) target relational rather than economic outcomes. While I do agree with most points, these propositions may not be true in all ICBN, since each negotiation is unique and situational variables (e.g., interdependence, power asymmetries, market background, relationship history) as well as dispositional variables (e.g., personality, organizational, cultural) may change the picture.

15 See Fisher et al. (2011). Baber and Fletcher-Chen (2015, pp. 13–15 and 45–46) offer practical guidance for defining one's own and the other party's BATNA.

16 See Fisher, Ury, and Patton (2011). See also PON (2012) document on BATNA basics from the Program on Negotiation (PON) at Harvard Law School.

17 Bazerman and Neale (1992) call the illusion that the cake cannot be increased the "Mythical Fixed Pie" (pp. 16–22).

18 Walton and McKersie (1965). See chapter 11 in Bazerman and Neale (1992, pp. 89–101), which describes rational strategies for creating integrative agreements using differences at different levels.

19 For a definition of the problem-solving orientation, see Pruitt (1983).

20 See Brülhart and Usunier (2012).

21 Pruitt (1981) and Pruitt (1983).

22 Some models of conflict handling (Thomas-Kilman) envisage a fifth, intermediate position; that is, "compromising" (Thomas, 1992; Pinkley and Northcraft, 1994).

23 In instrumental communication (Angelmar and Stern, 1978), information is not true or false as such, but packed in such a way that it intends to influence and persuade the other party. Conversely, representative information is factually true with no manipulative intention.

24 Pruitt (1983).

25 Rubin and Carter (1990).

26 See Pruitt and Lewis (1975).

27 Graham et al. (1994), through an empirical comparison across ten countries/ cultures, show that the PSA model works differently across some countries' cultures (CCs), and that a claim for PSA's universality cannot be made.

28 See Graham (1993) for 15 countries, Brett et al. (1998, p. 71) where Japan and the U.S. intracultural negotiators have the highest joint gains, followed by France and Brazil, with Russia and Hong Kong lowest. See also Graham (2003, p. 85) for 18 CCs plotting joint gains against the percentage for the buyer's role. Graham and Meissner (1986) have shown in a study comparing five countries that the most integrative strategies are adopted by the Brazilians, followed by the Japanese. On the other hand the Americans, the Germans and the Koreans choose intermediate strategies that are more distributive.

29 See Tinsley et al. (2011) and Lax and Sebenius (1992).

30 The mirroring effect of PSA in ICBN is shown in Graham et al. (1992) and Mintu-Wimsatt and Graham (2004); however it is only partially supported in Graham et al. (1994). Movius et al. (2006) propose a prescriptive model of "Mutual Gains Approach" (MGA = PSA) for ICBN and explain how to adapt and implement MGA with Japanese, Chinese, and Korean negotiators.

31 On conceptual equivalence across cultures, see Usunier (2011) and Usunier et al. (2017).

32 See Brett (2000).

33 On needs, see Saner (2008).

2 A cultural perspective on deal-making versus relationship-building

Society may subsist among different men, as among different merchants, from a sense of its utility, <u>without any mutual love or affection</u>; and though no man in it should owe any obligation, or be bound in gratitude to any other, it may still be upheld by <u>a mercenary exchange of good offices according to an agreed valuation.</u>

(Adam Smith, 1790, p. 77, my emphasis)

What I want to explain in this chapter is how culture relates to the two polar ideal types, IT1 (i.e., Deal-Making) and IT2 (i.e., Relationship-Building); that is, how cultural differences shape the deal vs. relationship model as well as the influence of culture on important aspects of ICBN, especially the negotiation process and the outcome orientation. These explanations offer linkages to each chapter, dedicated to a particular topic (e.g., communication, time, and ethics) in greater detail.

Some areas of the world dominate the global arena, essentially with an English language base and utilitarian, individualist, and task-oriented values, and a market and explicit contract-based negotiation philosophy. As opposed to a quite heterogeneous non-Western group of cultures/countries, often formerly colonized, corresponding to sometimes very old civilizations (i.e., China, India) that have been, to various extents, dominated by the Western mindset and power.

I start by addressing the issue of whether cultures matter for negotiation, and to what extent. The answer is, yes, but not without limits. Culture directly influences the negotiation process and only indirectly negotiation outcomes through its impact on the negotiation process. The two ideal types (Deal-Making/IT1 and Relationship-Building/IT2) are opposed in this chapter and the cultural assumptions on which each ideal type rests are explained in detail and illustrated with examples from ICBN. The Deal-Making/IT1 orientation is related to a *doing* mentality, predominantly utilitarian (mostly centred on interests; however not exclusively on self-interest), a preference for an objective/hard facts assessment of reality, a discrete and economic view of time, direct and explicit/context-free communication, proactive behaviours reflecting deliberate decision-making, and a strong concern to sign favourable (for oneself) written contracts. Relationship-Building/IT2 orientation is related to a *being* mentality, people rather than objects being at the centre of the negotiation interaction, a preference for a subjective assessment of reality (even though facts also matter, but may be (mis)interpreted), a holistic, non-economic, and relaxed view of time, indirect and implicit/context-bound communication, decision-making and implementation being difficult to disentangle, and a strong concern to develop relationships mainly based on personal and oral agreement rather than detailed written contracts. Caveats are necessary because the perspective on Deal-Making versus Relationship-Building is far from being exclusively driven by culture and communication style. Caveats are provided in the first section ("Does culture matter for international negotiations?"). Culture is defined, and the next sections discuss "Task-orientation vs. people-orientation", individualism/collectivism and their influence on ICBN, as well as power play in horizontal and vertical negotiation interactions There is nothing like simple and direct, mechanistic causality, especially directional causality, between cultural orientations and negotiation styles. The IT1 vs. IT2 opposition rather than dichotomous, is based on fuzzy linkages, resulting from two different bundles of associations between cultural orientations and negotiation styles, broadly privileging tasks over people (IT1) or vice versa (IT2). The last section deals with interaction and mirror games in ICBN: stereotyping, pretending, adapting, and adjusting.

Does culture matter for international negotiations?

Introductory caveats

I start here with a brief definition of culture, followed by 13 caveats for the influence of culture on intercultural business negotiation. Culture is useful to the group (i.e., a society) and to the individual because tasks are made easier through a set of unwritten, implicit rules that are shared since early childhood. Culture may be defined as a set of beliefs or standards, shared by a group of people, which help the individual decide what is, what can be, how to feel, what to do, and how to go about doing it.[1] Negotiators may share different cultures learned when interacting with distinct groups. Ideally, such culturally proficient negotiators might "switch into" the culture that is operational within a given group. The adjective "operational" describes a culture shared by people who cooperate on tasks, a definition that is *per se* culturally relative, however quite applicable to ICBN.

The concept of operational culture assumes that negotiators can choose the culture in which to interact at any time and in any negotiation situation, subject to the overriding condition that cultural rules have been appropriately internalized by individuals through past experiences. These cultural rules have been *so well learned that they can be forgotten*. The concept of operational culture is debatable, especially because it is excessively task-oriented. However, it advantageously highlights the multicultural nature of our global society, which includes bi-nationals, multilinguals, and negotiators who share an international professional or corporate culture. The concept of operational culture draws our attention to the complex sources of a negotiator's acculturation. Therefore, I start this chapter with a series of caveats aimed at avoiding simplification due to over-attribution to national culture, what Sebenius (2002, pp. 126–128) calls "The Rosetta Stone Fallacy".

1) There are *multiple sources of culture*. The national element is not always the main source of culture when regarded from an "operational culture" perspective. Social class may be a distinctive source of culture, to a greater or lesser degree, depending on the country. For instance in France and England, where there are traditions of accepted birth inequalities and a strong historical orientation, social class is a distinctive source of culture; the way one speaks reveals one's social class. However, in many other countries (e.g., the United States, Japan, and Scandinavian countries), social classes are not so marked. The sense of belonging to an important ethnic group may override the feeling of belonging to a particular nation-state.

2) The second caveat deals with the *risk of equating country-nation with culture*. In general, there are no clear-cut borders between nation-states and cultures, even though a particular cultural group (and often linguistic and cultural group) may be locally dominant, such as the Kikuyu in Kenya. Country or nation therefore cannot be equated with culture. Many countries, especially large ones, comprise many different cultural groups (e.g., India). Even smaller countries often comprise different cultural and linguistic groups (e.g., four groups in Switzerland), showing diversity despite their limited size. Finally, some cultures may exist without a corresponding nation-state, because they have been historically denied a nation-state status, and because they live in several neighbouring countries, such as the Kurds spreading over Iran, Iraq, Syria, and Turkey.

3) A third caveat is related to the *universality of many negotiation behaviours*, as I have described them in the first chapter.[2] Because many negotiation concepts have an economic base (e.g., ZOPA, reservation prices), they tend to be universally meaningful. However, even if it is a universal activity, bargaining, for instance, is carried out in a significantly different manner according to the cultural background of bargainers.

4) *Individual personality matters as well as the multicultural background of some international negotiators*.[3] Many societies include bi-nationals, multilinguals, and even people who have a particular national identity as well as an international professional or corporate culture, which are shared with negotiators from other national/cultural origins. How

negotiators can build on their own personality and background is presented in Chapter 6. Cultural similarities as well as differences must be contextualized. There are no absolutely general rules: culture mixes with age, gender, organization, profession, education. It may be relevant in certain contexts, not in other contexts.

5) A fifth caveat deals with *cultural diversity* not only across negotiation camps but *within negotiation teams*. A party's team of negotiators often comes from diverse backgrounds, blurring the influence of their company's particular cultural and national origin. Diversity in negotiation teams is examined in Chapter 6.

6) *Organizational culture* also plays its role as a moderator of culture. Companies have their own history and often have developed a corporate culture, which includes significant characteristics (e.g., long-term oriented, partnership-prone, stable employer, customer-oriented) influencing both negotiation behaviour and the negotiation process itself (e.g., coming well prepared to meetings) as well as negotiation outcomes (e.g., looking for a stable business relationship). How organizational culture combines with cross-cultural aspects of business negotiations is presented in Chapter 6.

7) A *shared professional-educational background* matters because it largely reduces the impact of basic cultural differences. For instance, medical researchers or computer hardware specialists, whatever their nationality or culture, share a common education, mutual interests, and the same professional culture. This is developed through similar education, working for companies in the same industry, reading the same worldwide academic and professional publications, and sharing global practices in their field. How ICB negotiators can play on shared professional-educational backgrounds is presented in Chapter 6.

8) Another caveat relates to the B2B-B2C divide, because it largely influences the nature and the length of the business relationship. ICBN will be more relationship-oriented in a Business-to-Business compared with a Business-to-Consumer setting, due to the average duration of such B2B bonds, and therefore to successive negotiations, which often extend beyond a period of ten years.

9) Chapter 9 describes how *the type of ICBN contract*, whether export sales, agency and dealership agreements, licensing contracts, joint ventures, project and package deals, and cross-border M&As, moderates the divide between Deal-Making (IT1) and Relationship-Building (IT2). Each of these deals has a particular time frame and relational setting which combines with cultural aspects of ICBN, making them more or less relevant.

10) Chapter 1 has outlined the crucial importance of *market situations and competitive scenes* behind the negotiation process. Even though ICBN is supposed to correspond to a bilateral monopoly setting, many negotiations have a more open market background, which offers alternatives

and exit options to both partners, makes the consideration of a possible BATNA more likely, and finally tends to favour a deal-orientation (IT1), rather than Relationship-Building (IT2). Broadly speaking, relationships become less important than mere deals when the numbers of potential suppliers and/or potential buyers increase.

11) Another caveat is that *culture does not impact all of negotiation behaviour*, negotiation process, and desired outcomes. In any negotiation, there are some strong universals, related to economic rationality, self-interest, dependence, and interdependence as they have been explained in the first two chapters. Hard facts may sometimes override cultural differences.

12) According to hard globalizers, the "supposed" difference between "traditional" and "modern" cultures could progressively vanish and cultural differences disappear. "Traditional", often past-oriented and collectivistic, countries and cultures evolve because of shared technologies, immigration, global exchange, and the dominance of English as the language of international trade and international business. In such a view, "traditional" cultures could progressively adopt a "modern" stance, being increasingly individualistic, utilitarian, and market based. Negotiators in "traditional" cultures could progressively dismiss people-based agreements and accept contract-based, formal and legal, agreements as negotiation outcomes. If this is true, IT2 negotiators could progressively convert to the IT1, modern, Deal-Making paradigm of negotiation. This is, however, far from being self-evident because these countries/cultures had made a formidable identity comeback since political independence. A good example is Vietnam where French colonial influence has left virtually no trace.

13) Last (caveat), the depiction of cultures is based on ideal-types that may give a misleading sense that cultures entirely and exclusively adopt a particular cultural trait (e.g., individualism versus collectivism). This is not the case. For instance, the individualist/collectivist divide is not always clear cut. In individualist societies, people still belong to groups, live in communities and think of themselves as integrated into a larger whole. In collectivist societies, people still feel a need to express their personal identity, and often strive for individual success and self-actualization. Cooperation takes place in all societies, but people cooperate in culturally appropriate ways. Negotiators from individualist societies are more likely to rely on individuality and rationality as motivations for cooperation, while negotiators from collectivist societies are more likely to be driven by collective rationality and social forces.[4] As I will argue in this book, the *either/or* approach (dichotomous, binary) can be misleading and a paradoxical *either/and* approach (in which seemingly incompatible cultural orientations can coexist) should be preferred.[5] Negotiators in ICBN interactions always adapt, they sometimes implicitly pretend to be like the other party, and they borrow behaviour and manners

with the intention to adjust. Consequently, the influence of culture is often dynamically blurred by the *make-believe* use of the other party's cultural norms.

However, culture matters ...

The importance of culture in negotiation is debated, with some arguing that cultural differences only impact on rather superficial negotiation behaviour and others insisting that they impact not only the negotiation process but, through the relative importance given to Relationship-Building, the desired negotiation outcomes as well. Some negotiation researchers have questioned the very fact that cultural differences have an impact on international business negotiations, arguing that negotiation is negotiation irrespective of where and with whom it takes place. William Zartman (1993, p. 19) has phrased it in strong terms:

> Culture is to negotiation what birds flying into engines are to flying airplanes or, at most, what weather is to aerodynamics – practical impediments that need to be taken into account (and avoided) once the basic process is fully understood and implemented.

To this "sceptic's view", Raymond Cohen in the same volume (*Culture and Negotiation*) opposes an advocate's view, highlighting the powerful effect of culture on international negotiation.

> I argue not only that culture affects the negotiating behaviour of inter-national actors – clearly it is simply one among many influences – but also that cross-cultural antinomies between the parties may affect the course and outcome of negotiations. ... When incompatible philosophies of life and behaviour come into conflict, serious misunderstandings may arise and the parties fail to synchronize their actions.
>
> (Cohen, 1993, pp. 22–23)

Nonetheless, there is now much empirical support for the view that culture has an impact on business negotiations.[6] When negotiating internation-ally, one needs cultural knowledge and skills in intercultural communica-tion. Many agreements have to be negotiated, drafted, signed, and finally implemented: sales contracts, licensing agreements, joint ventures and various kinds of partnerships, agency and distribution agreements, turnkey contracts, etc. Negotiation is not only based on legal and business matters, hard facts which are often emphasized as being the sole important facts. It is also based on the quality of human and social relations, "soft facts", which become of the utmost importance in an intercultural encounter. Various types of "distances" between the potential partners – geographical distance certainly, but also economic, educational, and cultural distance – tend to inflate the cost of negotiating interculturally. Difficulties in interacting, negotiating, planning common ventures, working them out, and achieving them together are deeply rooted in the cultural, human and social, background of business people. ICBN complications are not related to superficial variance of business customs. Therefore, simple empathy or sympathy is not enough for avoiding misunderstandings. As the following sections show, people with different cultural backgrounds often do not share the same basic assumptions. This has an influence on several levels of intercultural business negotiations including behavioural dispositions and the concept of what is negotiation and what an appropriate negotiation strategy is. Cultural misunderstandings may undermine trust between the parties. This chapter is an introduction to the cultural aspects of ICBN; it indicates which particular dimensions of cultural differences affect intercultural business negotiations as well as where in other chapters they are examined at greater length.

It should be stressed that cultural differences are not only impediments and obstacles to a smooth negotiation process. They can also work as an asset, a set of opportunities for reaching a better joint outcome between widely different partners. The ambiguous status of culture being both a liability and an asset in ICBN is beautifully expressed in a metaphoric sentence by Jeswald Salacuse (1993, p. 199):[7]

> Conventional wisdom holds that differences in culture among negotiators are almost always an obstacle to agreement. But culture in a negotiation can be much more than an obstacle: It can be a weapon, a fortress, or a bridge.

Culture defined

Culture as learned and forgotten norms and behavioural patterns

Sometimes culture has a reputation for being rather vague, for being a somewhat "blurred" concept. The Swedish writer Selma Lagerlöf defines culture as "what remains when that which has been learned is entirely forgotten". Thus depicted, culture may appear to be a "rubbish-bin" concept. Its main use would be to serve when more precise explanations have proved unsuccessful. It would also serve as an explanatory variable for residuals, when other more operative explanations seem inadequate. Nevertheless, Selma Lagerlöf"s definition does have the important merit of identifying two basic elements of cultural dynamics (at the individual level):

- It is learned.
- It is forgotten, in the sense that we cease to be conscious (if we ever have been) of its existence as learned behaviour.

For example, if a negotiator has been told during childhood that modest and self-effacing behaviour is suitable when addressing other people, especially at first contact – which is the case in most Asian cultures – he or she may be unaware of this programming and be shocked by the assertive, apparently boastful, behaviour in some other cultures. Although largely forgotten, culture permeates daily life and collective actions. Individuals find, in their cultural group, preset and agreed-upon solutions which indicate to them how to properly articulate their behaviour and actions with members of the same cultural group. Culture is entirely oriented towards adaptation to reality (both as constraints and opportunities). Since culture is "forgotten", it is mostly unconsciously embedded in individual and collective behaviour,[8] which remains unquestioned as long as negotiators do not meet "alien partners".

Definitions of culture

Culture has been defined extensively, precisely because it is somewhat all-encompassing. After having assessed its nature as learned and forgotten, we need to provide some additional definitions of culture. Ralph Linton (1945, p. 21), for instance, stresses that it is *shared* and *transmitted*: "A culture is the configuration of learned behavior and results of behavior whose component elements are shared and transmitted by the members of a particular society". However, we should not go too far in considering the individual as simply *programmed* by culture, and this applies particularly well to negotiators in ICBN. At a previous point in his landmark book, *The Cultural Background of Personality*, Linton clearly indicates the limits of the cultural programming which a society can impose on an individual:

> No matter how carefully the individual has been trained or how successful his conditioning has been, he remains a distinct organism with his own needs and with capacities for independent thought, feeling and action. Moreover he retains a considerable degree of individuality.
>
> (Linton, 1945, pp. 14–15)

In this respect, intercultural negotiation between different organizations may result in creating a new operating culture, a common set of shared beliefs and solutions, which is especially true in the case of joint ventures.[9] The following sections present some significant elements of culture that have an impact on intercultural business negotiations: basic cultural orientations (doing versus being; ingroup vs. outgroup), interaction patterns (individualism vs. collectivism, power distance), language (as it influences worldviews and mindsets), religion, values, institutional and legal systems.

Should culture be quantitatively measured or thickly (qualitatively) described?

It is surely useful for negotiators to look at simplified dimensions and indicators of culture that allow cross-national/cross-cultural comparisons because they are quantified in the form of indexes. Hofstede's dimensions are probably the most popular cultural dimensions enabling simple cross-national comparisons. Two of these fundamental dimensions, individualism vs. collectivism and power distance, are relevant for ICBN. They influence interaction between negotiators, not only between two parties, but also between mandatory negotiators and their counterparts and between members of culturally diverse negotiation teams.[10]

However, not all measured dimensions of culture are relevant to negotiation: for instance Hofstede's Uncertainty Avoidance and Masculinity-Femininity have little empirically demonstrated influence on intercultural negotiation.[11] The same holds true for the Schwartz value system, which is mostly an individual value framework usable if one believes in modal personality.[12] These dimensions are irrelevant or very weakly relevant for ICBN. Tinsley and Brett (1997) have argued that Hofstede's cultural dimensions lack predictive power and cannot be used to predict negotiation behaviour in isolation of negotiation variables related to process (e.g., conflict-handling styles) and behaviour (e.g., seeking help from a boss). As outlined in Bazerman et al. (2000), cultural as well as personality traits influence negotiation in conjunction with key elements of the negotiation game itself.

To compare is to put side by side two objects or phenomena to study their similarities and differences. In intercultural negotiation we often implicitly compare cross-nationally or cross-culturally. The question seems to be "Is the phenomenon similar **or** different?" implicitly assuming that the object or phenomenon cannot be similar **and** different at the same time. However, what looks similar in the eyes of marketers (researchers) may actually be perceived as different by consumers (respondents, informants). This may result in marketing blunders, often treated as mere anecdotes that cannot be generalized, and are assumed inevitable. From a pragmatic perspective, the issue is whether overlooked difference will result in marketing policy failures. However, too quickly similarities between negotiators can be self-fulfilling prophecies, the global solution being imposed on the other party. Geertz (1983: 41) writes about differences and similarities (his emphasis on *do* and *are*) as follows:

> The differences *do* go far deeper than an easy men-are-men humanism permits itself to see, and the similarities *are* far too substantial for an easy other-beasts, other-mores relativism to dissolve.

Qualitative approaches to cultural differences between negotiators, based on studying the other party's history, culture, reading novels, considering it(s) language(s), etc. support the discovery of differences in an *emic* perspective because they emphasize local meaning and interpretation. On the other hand, quantitative or *etic* approaches[13] *favour* similarities because they assume shared concepts, and use directive questioning that channels informants' insights into the observers' pre-established frames. We have to take into account not only actual versus perceived similarities/differences but also differences in *nature* (incommensurable) versus differences in *degree* (commensurable). The best solution for negotiators willing to prepare for ICBN is to combine both perspectives in an *etic-emic* country profile, taking into account measured cultural dimensions as single, isolated cues, and combining country scores on particular cultural dimensions with qualitative information. Chapter 11 on elements of the national style of business negotiation uses this combined approach.

Task-orientation versus people-orientation

I review below the consequences of two types of basic cultural assumptions (value orientations[14]) on ICBN: the *doing-being* and the *ingroup-outgroup* contrasts. The *doing-being* divide relates to what a culture prioritizes, either what people *do* or what people *are*. Consequences for ICBN are obvious: doing-oriented cultures centre on *tasks* to be performed, agenda (in Latin, what has to be done), and tend – at the extreme – to negotiate almost without caring about who their opponents are, not only in terms of culture, but also in terms of race, gender, age, status, etc. (*being* characteristics). Conversely, *being*-oriented cultures need to know who it is they are negotiating with, take time to *build rapport* and understand the human context of the negotiation. However, such cultures are less preoccupied with tasks, planning, and scheduling the process, as they are convinced that success in negotiation is mostly a matter of personal, human alchemy.

Doing orientation

It is remarkable that the *doing-being* divide is not mentioned in the international business negotiation literature. People with a *doing* orientation, as opposed to *being*, conceive themselves as defined by what they *do* (also by what they *have done* in the past and what they *will do* in the future) rather than by what they *are* (also by what they *were* in the past and what they *will be* in the future). Achievements, diplomas, experiences subsumed in the curriculum vitae are essential. In evaluation procedures, necessary for recruitment and job negotiation, elements unrelated to the capacity to perform tasks, which could blur the evaluation, should be removed. Thus the practice of the anonymous curriculum vitae is related to the doing mentality. A typical *doing* orientation is present, for instance, in Anglo-American and Scandinavian cultures.

A *doing* orientation comes therefore with a significant degree of *depersonalization* implying that, when negotiating, it is not absolutely necessary to know who a person *is* to decide what that person can *do*. Therefore, it is not necessary to spend time discovering who the person *is*, especially if time is short and strongly economic. Depersonalization means that belonging to particular groups (e.g., extended family, social class, ethnic background, religion, gender, and age) is less important than the negotiators' individual *doing* characteristics (e.g., abilities, talents, achievements, and education).

A strong *doing* orientation assumes that what people are *does not* naturally, nor legitimately, influence the roles, power, and capabilities they have in society. What is important is what people can achieve, given their individual talents and abilities. In the purest version of the *doing* orientation, even character and personality are considered unimportant in what individuals can achieve. At the extreme, tasks are viewed as standard and people as fully interchangeable, provided that they have the necessary skills. Deeds are separated from emotions and *doing* belongs to a world of its own, rather radically separated from *being*. In negotiation, the *doing* orientation is strongly associated with task orientation, planning tasks, monitoring tasks, financially measurable outcomes, clear scheduling of tasks, which imply being intensely time-conscious. It goes with a *"can-do"*[15] mindset, where being the master of one's own destiny means having a strong sense of individual responsibility. Doers are driven by their cultural orientation to feel individually accountable for their tasks and outcomes. In negotiation, they will value professionalism, objectivity, preciseness, and compliance with preset task-formats, to-do lists, and negotiation follows a relatively well-structured process, ending with written contractual formalism. *Doing* negotiators are task-oriented in negotiation, favouring agenda and schedule vs. non-planning, respecting different phases in the negotiation process, preferring linearity over (what they consider as) chaos, as a preferred route to Deal-Making and/or Relationship-Building. For pre-negotiation, they always recommend coming well prepared rather than unprepared or half-prepared. Doer negotiators value problem-solving as an exploration task and think that it is possible, and even recommendable, to separate people from interests (see Chapter 8). For *doing*-oriented negotiators, negotiation roles are important. Using the metaphor of theatrical plays, negotiating is like acting, following a script, and performing according to scenario and role (including being sometimes tough); the frequent use of the word "players" for "negotiators" draws attention to the predominance of the *doing* orientation in game-theoretic approaches to negotiation.

Being orientation and ICBN

The influence of the *being* orientation is not mentioned in international business negotiation books. *Being* relates to attitude to life as a whole.

People are defined by what they *are* rather than by what they *do*.[16] Achievements, diplomas, and experiences subsumed in the curriculum vitae surely are important elements. However, they are assumed to be rather unrelated to capacity to perform tasks if not associated with *being* characteristics (e.g., age, gender, race, name, status, family relationships). Consequently, *being* characteristics are important for assessing the fit of applicants with positions. For instance, non-anonymous CVs (related to the *being* mentality) are considered necessary for applicant evaluation in job interviews. The being orientation favours an "identitarian" approach to negotiation (i.e., you should know the person you negotiate with) and therefore Relationship-Building is needed. This people orientation implies that no exchange can really be anonymous and completely depersonalized.

The contrast between a *being* and *doing* orientation is based on the concepts of personalization and depersonalization. Personalization means that assumptions about what a person can *do* depend on who the person *is*. Since not all is *prima facie* visible, it will be necessary to spend time to understand who the person is. This is evident in cultures with a *being* orientation.

A *being* orientation emphasizes belonging, based on shared characteristics, including categories: 1) those you are born into, such as gender, family, social class, ethnic background, religion, or nationality; and 2) those you currently belong to, such as age (young versus older people) and marital status. A strong *being* orientation therefore assumes that who the negotiator *is*, naturally, legitimately, and forcefully, influences the roles, power, and capacities he or she has. A strong *being* emphasis is evidenced by what people call themselves and others. In many traditional societies, language designates people by a term meaning "human being". "'Bantu'' for instance, means human being. This, more or less, emphasizes that others may not be *real* human beings. Without going so far, the Japanese language also divides "we" and "they". Japanese people call themselves *Nihon-jin* and foreigners *Gai-jin* (those from the outside). Similarly, Pakistanis in the UK call themselves *Apney* (our own people) and white British *Gorey*.[17]

I, we, and they in ICBN: Interacting with foreigners

Ingroup and *outgroup* orientations influence the individual (**I**) or collective (**We**) negotiation interactions with outsiders, that is, with the other camp (**They**), which may be considered as opponents, adversaries, rivals, antagonists (i.e., words associated with negative/hostile value judgements) or conversely, partners, associates, contacts, with neutral or positive value judgements. Every person, whether ingroup or outgroup oriented, belongs to several ingroups – most often embedded into one another – family, clan, tribe, religious and/or ethnic group, nation, and the like. However, ingroup-oriented cultures tend to highly value shared belonging and consider members of outgroups, including foreign negotiation partners, as outsiders, with whom it may be difficult to build a trustful rapport. Conversely, outgroup oriented negotiators tend to assume that anyone anywhere is a possible negotiation partner, with a universalistic view of human beings.

Outgroup orientation: We (including They) are – fundamentally – the same

In contrast to the ingroup orientation, the outgroup orientation is based on the assumption of the fundamental unity of mankind, beyond the borders of ingroup spaces (e.g., families, nations, and cultures). A direct consequence is that outgroupists will feel relatively open and comfortable in ICBN when interacting with non-kin, foreign, different people, especially at an individual level. If the two cultural orientations are roughly opposed, it is not a complete opposition. In certain cultures they coexist. For instance, Nordic European cultures combine a strong sense of national identity (ingroup) with a universal focus on mankind, manifested in their strong commitment to peace, development of poorer countries, and international organizations (i.e., typically outgroupist values).The outgroup orientation values universal rules, applied to everybody. Human rights ethics are a typical feature of outgroup orientation. Objectivity and reciprocity are preferred over loyalty. Loyalty is neither to the group, nor to people, but to the rules and values that govern the society as a whole and activities in particular, including negotiation. This relates to personalization (*people orientation*) versus depersonalization (*rule orientation*), as discussed previously. The depersonalized approach in outgroup-oriented cultures should not be misunderstood. Paradoxically, it leads to greater sensitivity to the problems of human beings far away from their own motherland. The tendency to behave in a more universal way, in no way means that outgroupists are less other-oriented.

All societies combine some elements of ingroup and outgroup orientation. For example, "affirmative action, equal opportunity" is a strong outgroupist motto, typical of Western cultures. Despite this, people cannot freely choose their nationality. If they could, it would illustrate the strongest form of outgroup orientation. Extreme positions in either ingroup or outgroup orientation present drawbacks. The pitfalls of excessive outgroup orientation in negotiation include: 1) unrealistic universalism; and 2) global village ethnocentrism.

Ingroup orientation: We and They are fundamentally different

Belonging to the ingroup (or reference group: family, tribe, clan, club, professional society, nation, etc.) may be considered a *necessary condition* for being considered a reliable, *bona fide* partner in negotiation. When partners (opponents) belong to the outgroup, something is missing in terms of a minimal joint identity, even provisional and somewhat fake. A shared acquaintance is the necessary condition for entering into negotiation. Ingroup membership, based on *territoriality*, requires individual characteristics that cannot be acquired or learned by outgroup adults. Here, ingroup criteria are most likely to be related to birth, socialization, and education. In cases where it is impossible to gain membership, one must behave as a friendly, but realistic outsider. Often outsiders too quickly view cultures with an ingroup/being orientation as being narrow-minded, provincial, and hostile towards foreigners. Ingroup orientation in ICBN is quite complex and often unapparent. It involves patterns of kin-based loyalty and obligation. The pitfalls of excessive ingroup orientation include: 1) tribalism – only kin ingroup are considered worth interacting with and caring for; 2) localism – only people belonging to a small geographical unit are considered interesting; and 3) provincialism – only values and behaviour that are in use in the community are considered appropriate.

What does ingroup membership involve in terms of rights and obligations in ICBN? Ingroup bonds involve loyalty relationships that may not extend beyond the borders of the ingroup space; that is, to outgroup negotiators. Loyalty can be based on kinship or patronage, which is often an extended form of kinship based on symbolic adoption. Loyalty is based on allegiance, even in the face of conflicts with other members of the ingroup or when experiencing unfair treatment from the most powerful members. Loyalty is fundamentally non-reciprocal: people do not expect other ingroup members' loyalty because they are loyal themselves. There are little time constraints on loyalty: one may wait for 50 years to be rewarded for loyalty or one may never be rewarded.

Strong ingroup orientation increases an insider's loyalty (to one's own negotiation camp), but simultaneously decreases the feeling of obligation towards those perceived as outsiders (i.e., the opposing negotiation camp). Ingroup morality is space (in/out) related. It might, for instance, be considered acceptable to lie to or steal from outgroup people to whom no loyalty is owed. The Mafia is a good illustration of an ingroup-oriented society.[18] Morality is based on a set of values favouring strict loyalty, treason being punished in the worst cases by the death sentence. The Mafia godfather who has ordered the elimination of a traitor from his own family may, however, attend the burial ceremony because the godfather still "loves" the betrayer. The ingroup/outgroup divide has a deep influence on the system of ethics and morality in a society. Ingroup orientation partly explains behavioural relativity. Some national groups have a reputation for their compliant behaviour at home (where rules are strictly enforced) and for looser conduct abroad. When they are away, ingroup-oriented negotiators sometimes no longer feel the need to observe the rules that apply at home.

Interaction patterns: Individualism vs. collectivism

Interaction patterns concern how the individual relates to the group, either behaving rather independently (*Individualism*) or in a more interdependent and subordinated manner (*Collectivism*). These patterns affect intercultural business negotiations through the style of interaction between people, the decision-making process, and the way in which they mix human relationships and business matters.[19] Individualism vs. collectivism describes the degree to which the individuals are integrated into groups. In individualist societies the ties between individuals are rather loose: everyone is expected to look after him or herself and his or her family. Conversely, people in collectivist societies are integrated into strong, cohesive ingroups; often their extended families continue protecting them in exchange for unquestioned loyalty.[20]

Individualism[21]

Individualism is associated with egalitarianism (thus low Power Distance, see below), horizontal interactions between peers, "informality" in addressing other negotiators, and a seemingly relaxed and informal way of communicating with others.[22] Individualists tend to stick to universalistic morals, and may be felt, probably wrongly, as being at the limit of depersonalization (individualistic, however paradoxically impersonal). Individualists have loose ties and value independence.[23] Virtually all ICBN books are written from an individualistic and outgroup-oriented perspective, so that discriminating individual characteristics such as race cannot be mentioned, because they could appear as politically incorrect. For individualists the Western style of human rights remains unquestioned, because it is the legitimately global solution. Negotiators' age or their belonging to a particular ethnic, cultural, or linguistic group are not important issues in ICBN because they are supposed to have no impact on the deal.

Since the Middle Ages, the awareness of self has become less shared and more individualistic, which is evidenced by the growing popularity over centuries of self-oriented objects such as mirrors, self-portraits, and chairs (rather than benches). Modern individualism has its roots in 16th and 17th-century England, English tradition since the *Habeas Corpus* (1679) and the *Bill of Rights* (1689),[24] reflecting the ideas of philosopher John Locke, largely before the French issued their own declaration of human rights (1789). It is based on the ideas of English and Scottish philosophers (More, Bacon, Hume, and Locke) and was generated in large part by the Act of *Habeas Corpus*, the first legal edict forbidding the Sovereign from jailing somebody without lawful reason. The United Nations Universal Declaration of Human Rights is in the same vein: it favours an individual-based view of what is a "good" society. The individualist view of human rights is also typical of Amnesty International, Human Rights Watch, and similar NGOs which have heated debates with some governments holding a different view of what human rights are.

Graham et al. (1994)[25] expect negotiators from individualistic cultures to behave in a more self-interested way, being competitive and confrontational rather than problem-solving-oriented, and achieving higher profits. However, in individualist societies, people still belong to groups, live in communities and think of themselves as integrated into a larger whole. In collectivist societies, people still feel a need to express their personal identity, and strive often for individual success and self-actualization. As noted above, negotiators from individualist societies are more likely to rely on individuality and calculative rationality as motivations for cooperation in negotiation, with a preference for rational problem-solving and for the separation of people from problems.[26]

Collectivism

Because of interdependence between people, the interaction process in negotiation is arguably more complex for collectivistic than for individualistic cultures, as suggested by the following collectivistic assumptions:

1) Initiative, effort, and achievements can best be developed at the group level, because people function in groups (the organic view) rather than as independent entities. Therefore there is a strong association between ingroup orientation and collectivism.
2) Collective achievements are fundamentally different in nature from individual achievements, and the combination of parts (if such a computation is even possible) is much greater than the parts themselves (the multiplicative model). This is important for negotiation teams which behave differently in individualistic vs. collectivistic cultures.
3) Group coherence and social harmony have to be protected, even at the expense of individual opinions and moves in the negotiation process, and if need be, minimizing individual achievements (the concord orientation) will result in lower outcomes.

Collectivism is often associated with "traditional cultures", whereas individualism is a strong component of "modern cultures", especially in the area of consumption, which is an excellent domain for the expression of individual freedom and difference from others. On the contrary, individuals from collectivistic societies are likely to be driven by collective rationality and social forces.[27] Similarly, conflicts need to be handled in all societies. People from collectivist societies are more likely to rely on formal rules and procedures to handle disagreements, which preserves ingroup harmony, while those from individualist societies rely more on their own experience and training to handle disagreements.[28] The individualist/collectivist divide is, however, not always clear cut (see Chapter 11).

Collectivism will lead to a need for stable relationships, so that negotiations can be carried out among persons who have become familiar with each other over a long time (often several years). Every replacement of one negotiator by another may be a serious disturbance of the relationship and consequently perceived as a hurdle in the negotiation process, which has to be almost re-established from scratch. In collectivist cultures, mediators or go-betweens have a more important role in negotiations than in individual cultures. Formal harmony is very important in a collectivist setting; overt conflict is taboo. Mediators are able to raise sensitive issues with either party within an atmosphere of confidence in order to avoid confrontation.

This is in line with the opposite preference of collectivist cultures (compared with individualists: competitive and confrontational; that is, with low conflict avoidance) for the maintenance of formal harmony and the avoidance of overt conflict, often a direct consequence of individualistic and competitive values which promote self-enhancement and an independent self rather than self-transcendence and an interdependent self (Markus and Kitayama, 1991). Leung (1997) shows that in a number of studies comparing Chinese and Americans, Chinese score high on yielding and avoidance consistent with the harmony-seeking orientation of collectivist cultures;[29] but also high on contending, what seems inconsistent with Graham et al.'s (1994) findings. Leung argues that animosity reduction is a major goal in dispute resolution in collectivist cultures while previous research shows that collectivists have a weaker preference for compromising and a stronger preference for avoidance than people in individualist cultures. To overcome this contradiction, Leung proposes that collectivists are concerned with "disintegration avoidance"; that is, the major issue for them is whether the conflict has the potential to disintegrate an ongoing relationship. Contending will be acceptable as long as it does not threaten the relationship itself. Leung phrases it in the following terms (1997, p. 645):

> The general prediction is that compared to individualists, collectivists will avoid behaviour that may lead to the disintegration of the ongoing relationship. That is, collectivists should prefer yielding and avoiding more strongly, and problem solving and contending [in terms of Pruitt's *Dual Concern Model*] less strongly than individualists.

We will see in Chapter 10, about ethical issues in ICBN, that collectivism associated with ingroup orientation has a strong influence on the likelihood and legitimacy of nepotism and corruption. However, collusive connections and bribery can be renamed, in the more politically correct terms, *networking* and *lubrication payments*. This is the – slightly hypocritical – tribute paid by IT1 Deal-making, individualistic negotiators to the reality that contacts, acquaintances, and some degree of connivance, if not collusion, matter for negotiating business.

Culture, concern for the other party's outcome, and the "mythical fixed pie"

Balanced concern for one's own outcomes and for the other party's outcome, as described in the *dual concern model* in Chapter 3, is not necessarily found across all cultures. Cultures place a weaker or stronger emphasis on group membership (e.g., a) the group is important, collectivistic assumption, and b) the other party is/is not a member of the ingroup) as a prerequisite for being considered a trustworthy partner. In cultures where there is a clear-cut distinction between the ingroup and the outgroup (according to age, sex, race, or kinship criteria), people tend to perceive the interests of both groups as diametrically opposed. This is related to what has been called the concept of "limited good", in which all social games, including negotiation, are assumed to be zero-sum games, when not negative (*win-lose* or even *lose-lose*, however I lose less than you lose).

According to the concept of "limited good", if something positive happens in favour of the outgroup, the wealth and well-being of the ingroup will be threatened (Foster, 1965). Such reactions are largely based on culture-based collective subjectivity: they stem from the conservative idea that goods and riches are by their very nature restricted (i.e., the "fixed pie assumption" in negotiation). If one yields to the other party even the tiniest concession, this is perceived as directly reducing what is left for ingroup members. The concept of "limited good" induces negotiators to adopt territorial and distributive strategies. It favours the view of negotiation as a zero sum game, where "I will lose whatever you may win" and vice versa.[30] The concept of "limited good" may often be found in Mediterranean and Middle Eastern societies where the ingroup is highly valued (clan, tribe, extended family); it slows the adoption of a problem-solving orientation, since cooperative opportunities are simply more difficult to envisage.

It has been argued that members of collectivist cultures make a sharp distinction between ingroups and outgroups, because harmony enhancement is only viewed as possible with ingroup members. However, there is always some free room for negotiating insider/outsider status not only within but also across cultures. Case studies show how people can gain status as partial insiders by leveraging on common features that transcend the borders of cultures, such as gender or professional cultures. A shared professional culture tends to blur the ingroup/outgroup borders in an increasingly globalized world. In the context of the fisheries industries, for instance, research findings show that there is no significant impact of cultural differences on the international buyer-seller relationship whether trading partners of Norwegian exporters are European or American (individualistic and outgroup-oriented) or Japanese (ingroup-oriented and collectivistic). As Haugland (1998, p. 27) points out:

> It is not unlikely that industries or trades which are very international will develop a specific industry culture, serving the role of unifying persons and companies from different nations and ethnic groups.

Cultural orientations favouring an integrative strategy

Do negotiators from certain CCs display an integrative orientation? It seems that American negotiators show trust more willingly and more spontaneously than other cultural groups and have a stronger tendency towards a problem-solving and integrative orientation.[31] The level of their profits as sellers depends on the buyer's responding positively by also adopting a problem-solving approach.

American negotiators are reported to have a stronger tendency to exchange representative communication, making clear and explicit messages a priority, and to exhibit less suspicion towards the other party, than most other cultures.[32] This is in line with the American appreciation of frankness and directness and their low-context communication style which Graham and Herberger (1983) call the "John Wayne Style", even though it has been called "the John Wayne versus Charlie Chan fallacy" because it borders on stereotyping (Sebenius, 2002, p. 12). They often encounter certain difficulties in cultures where people take more time in the preliminaries: getting to know each other, that is, talking generally and only actually getting down to business later. As a result, Americans may not foster feelings of trust in negotiators from other cultural groups who feel it necessary to get to know the person they are dealing with.

The literature on joint gains in ICBN based on cross-cultural comparisons (based on intracultural negotiations) is very mixed and largely inconclusive (see notes 27 and 28 in Chapter 1, and accounts of 11 national styles of business negotiations in Chapter 11). No empirical study has shown, for example, that Middle Eastern Arabs are more distributive than Americans.[33] Americans tend to see the world as problems to be solved whereas Arabs see it more as a creation of God. The concept of integrative strategy, like the problem-solving approach discussed above, is strongly culturally influenced by the American tradition of experimental research in social psychology applied to commercial negotiation. As explained by Leung (1997, p. 648): "In individualist societies, negotiation is seen more as a task than as a social process. The primary role of negotiators is to work out a solution that is acceptable to both sides". It is also based on a "master of destiny" orientation which feeds attitudes of problem resolution.

ICBN versus intracultural negotiation

There is general agreement that the results of negotiation are less favourable when the negotiation is intercultural as opposed to intracultural, all other things being equal.[34] Van Zandt (1970) suggests that negotiations between Americans and Japanese are six times as long and three times as difficult as those purely between Americans, due to intercultural communication hurdles. Brett and Okumura (1998) have shown that intercultural U.S.–Japanese negotiations result in significantly lower joint gains than both intracultural U.S. and Japanese negotiations, in which both Japanese and Americans achieve similar joint gains. It seems that intercultural negotiators lack sufficient skills to adapt successfully and need a lot more clarifying statements than do intracultural negotiators (Adair et al., 2001). Another possible explanation is that American negotiators tend to use harder tactics, engaging in threats, demands, and sanctions, when there is more cultural distance with their partners' culture (Rao and Schmidt, 1998). The subjective satisfaction of the negotiators (measured by a questionnaire) in their result tends to be lower for intercultural than for intracultural negotiation.[35]

However, empirical findings have partly disconfirmed this. In Brett and Okumura (1998) intercultural negotiators were more happy and satisfied with the negotiation than were intracultural negotiators. This can be explained either by the subjective reward effect of achieving an obviously more difficult negotiation task (i.e., inter- as compared with intracultural negotiation) or by people being satisfied in both cultural groups by different – and not competing – outcomes (i.e., joint gains for Americans versus outcome parity for the Chinese).[36] Consistent with the IT1/IT2 distinction, a focus on social relationships vs. tasks facilitates ICBN skills (Gunia et al., 2016). And finally, cultural differences offer an opportunity for integrative potential in ICBN, especially when negotiators adapt to the other side's information sharing strategies.[37]

Problem-solving depends on a collaborative attitude which is easier with same culture partners. Similarity, in general, leads to more trust and an enhanced level of interpersonal attraction.[38] People need to evaluate others before entering into interaction: similarity facilitates accurate appraisal in social interactions. It facilitates awareness and exploration between parties and leads to more cooperative behaviour in negotiation. Perceived as well as actual similarity may influence the parties. For instance, many business people in the Middle East have a good command of either English or French. Middle Eastern negotiators are often perceived by their American or European counterparts as being similar to themselves, whereas Middle Eastern negotiators know that their Western counterparts are different. In ICBN encounters, misunderstandings may arise from misinformed perceptions of similarity. For instance, a European negotiator may perceive a Westernized Arab buyer as being similar, while the reverse is not true. The Arab buyer is aware that the American seller knows little about Arabic culture and language. The European seller may adopt a problem-solving approach because of perceived similarity, whereas the buyer may exploit the seller by adopting a covert distributive strategy.

Power play: Horizontal and vertical negotiation interactions

Status and power are important

It is important to note that negotiation is first and foremost based on a horizontal and egalitarian setting. In principle, negotiators form one camp are not in a power position to give orders to negotiators on the other side in a hierarchical manner as if they were the "boss". In practice, it is more complex because 1) mandatory negotiators have a vertical negotiation interaction with their principal, a frequent situation in ICBN; and 2) commanding the other party and treating them with a suggested hierarchical stance is sometimes used as a negotiation tactic.

Power plays are important in ICBN for at least two other reasons:

- It is often needed, and not completely obvious, to have a sense of who holds power in the other camp. Actual power may not be associated with power display and status exhibition, but on the contrary to power concealment and cover-up, clout suppression, and even authority camouflage. Powerful negotiators are sometimes those who listen, remain silent, and act as seemingly unimportant participants.
- Power is deeply related to status and to face. There is a formal side to power (e.g., showing respect) that costs little in negotiation and can be a facilitating move.

Status (i.e., having definite expectations as to how others treat you) has an ambiguous role in negotiation (as noted above, negotiation is an activity based on horizontal interactions between peers). Being status minded may generate a number of expectations.

- Facing negotiators of the same hierarchical level in the opponent team.
- Being treated and respected according to one's own high status by the negotiators in the opponent team (which may not share the same status codes).
- High-status "full-fledged" negotiators, negotiating as principals, may frown upon facing lower status mandatory negotiators, negotiating as agents.

Power distance measures how far a society and its members tolerate an unequal distribution of power in organizations and in society as a whole. It is shown as much by superiors' behaviour, who show their power and exercise it, as by the behaviour of subordinates who expect their superiors to openly display their status and power, and feel uncomfortable if superiors do not do it. In high power distance societies, superiors and subordinates feel separated from each other. It is not easy to meet and talk with higher ranking people, and the real power tends to be very much concentrated at the top. In low power distance societies, members of the organization tend to feel equal, and close to each other in their daily work relationships. They cope with situations of higher hierarchical distance by delegating power.

The prevailing values in a particular society, and the extent to which they are respected in the everyday behaviour of individuals, are important because they affect the willingness to take risks, the leadership style, and the superior-subordinate relationships. This is true for the relationships between negotiators within a particular team, antagonistic negotiation teams, and the negotiators on both sides and those from whom they have received the mandate for negotiating.

Influence of low/high power distance on ICBN

Power distance is strongly correlated with individualism /collectivism.[39] In a review of negotiation research involving power distance, Leung (1997, pp. 650–653) shows that power distance is systematically related to conflict behaviour. In low power distance societies, subordinates (e.g., negotiators who have to report to a constituency) will have a stronger tendency to resolve disputes on their own or to rely on their peers for conflict handling, than in high power distance societies.

Hofstede (1989) and Hofstede and Usunier (2003) hypothesize that large power distance will lead to a more centralized control and decision-making structure because key negotiations have to be concluded by the top authority. In fact, Fisher notes in the case of Mexico, a typically high power distance country (score of 81 on Hofstede's scale), that decision-making is rather centralized, based on individuals who have extended responsibility at the top of the organization. They become frustrated when confronted by the Americans who tend to have several negotiators in charge of compartmentalized issues:

> In another mismatch of the systems, the Americans find it hard to deter-mine how much Mexican decision-making authority goes with which designated authority. There, as in many of the more traditional systems, authority tends to reside somewhat more in the person than in the pos-ition, and an organization chart does little to tell the outsider just what leverage (*palanca*) the incumbent has.[40]
>
> (Fisher, 1980, p. 29)

Moreover, high power distance results in greater tolerance for unjust events, unfair treatment, and promotes the acceptance of higher differentials in negotiators' roles, to the extent of even tolerating insulting remarks if it comes from a high status person belonging to the same ingroup.[41]

Formal vs. actual power orientation in ICBN

One must make a distinction between the formal power orientation on the one hand and real decision-making power on the other hand. The first has to do with the display of status and how it may enhance credibility, especially in high perceived-potency societies. This involves the kind of meetings, societies, clubs, alumni organizations which assemble potentially powerful people. Belonging to such circles gives an opportunity for social-izing and getting to know each other. The simple fact of *being* there and *being* a member of a certain club is a credibility message. The formal signs of power and status differ across cultures; they may range from education

---

Box 2.1 Door-keepers

The story takes place in the corridor to the office of the Minister of Industry in the Republic of Guinea. Whether you have an appointment or you come to request a meeting, you have to be let in by the door-keeper. Besides, the door is locked and he has the key. He is a little man, looking tired and wearing worn-out clothes; his appearance leads foreign visitors to treat him as negligible and to pay little attention to him. When visitors have a lengthy wait while seeing other people being given quick access to the minister, they often speak unreservedly to the old man who seems to have only limited language proficiency. In fact, the door-keeper speaks perfect French and is the uncle of the minister, which gives him power over his nephew according to the African trad-ition. It is well-known that the Minister places high confidence in his uncle's recommendations. Thus, some foreign contractors never under-stand why they do not clinch the deal although they think they have developed winning arguments with the minister himself.

Source: reported by Professor Gérard Verna, Université Laval.

---

and titles (English public schools, French *Grandes Ecoles, Herr Doktor*, etc.) to belonging to a particular social class or caste.

Real power orientation is a somewhat different issue. As illustrated in Box 2.1, there may be wide differences between formal and actual influence on the decision-making process. When making contacts, in a cross-cultural perspective, people should be aware of the following: 1) status is not shown in the same way according to culture; 2) influential persons are not the same and individual influence is not exerted in the same way; and 3) the decision-making process differs.

Synchronizing tasks or prioritizing personal bonds

If negotiation is primarily about tasks, it makes sense to maximize the utility of these tasks (e.g., information exchange, problem-solving, exchanging concessions), to try to communicate as clearly and explicitly as possible on issues at stake, and to coordinate the parties in what is supposed to be joint tasks (e.g., by setting a formal agenda and linearly scheduling the negoti-ation process). Conversely, if negotiation is primarily about building a rela-tionship between the negotiating parties, it makes sense to spend much time exploring and bridging the differences between the parties and developing some sort of provisional joint identity. Communication will be less precise, at times even implicit, and a more holistic and relaxed approach to clock time will be in order.

(Joint) utility vs. (shared) identity

Utilitarian, privileging utility

In the IT1 paradigm, interests come first. The cultural characteristics outlined above (task-oriented, outgroupist, individualist, low power distance) are typically associated with a priority to Deal-Making over Relationship-Building. Reciprocity is preferred over loyalty and it comes as no surprise that the goal is the maximization of joint utility while preserving a fair share of the pie; the appropriate approach for such a process is problem-solving. In an ideal-typical rather than stereotypical perspective, priority given to deal-related utility (see Chapter 8) can be traced back to English philosophers Adam Smith and Jeremy Bentham.[42] The search for maximizing utility is outgroup- as well as doing-oriented, because the extended quest for the best possible partner (not necessarily the most loyal) is related to the capacity to search beyond borders and to find the best possible associate to increase utility. Competitive, anonymous exchange, depersonalized and fake lip-service socialization, is the direct consequence of utility maximization in the IT1 paradigm. Because of the dangers linked to anonymous exchange (low trust, high potential opportunism), the deal must be embedded within a formal, detailed, and precise contract. A reliable institutionalized litigation system must be maintained to bar or at least curb opportunistic behaviour. Since utility maximization has top priority, the deal need not be actually personalized. It is implicitly understood that deals could be blurred by undue socialization, compromised by relational illusions and spoiled by mixing real business interests (utility) with a misguided sense of solidarity. Tabulated reciprocity based on a finely defined system of *give and take*, where each favour must be compensated in corresponding size and appropriate time, is the preferred relational model. At best, it should even be a zero-relationship type of deal, for instance purely based on online commerce in which negotiation is completely automatized (such as on B2B marketplaces). Utility is interest based (objective), not people based (subjective). The utilitarian framework is that of global negotiation, mostly Deal-Making with relationship development mentioned only as a possible consequence.

Identitarian, privileging identity

The IT1 recommendation to "separate people from interests" violates most cultural assumptions in the IT2 paradigm: people and ingroup orientations, collectivism, etc. Literally identity is the quality of being unique, distinctive, particular, and singular. Privileging identity in negotiation implies that potential business partners are not *ad libitum* interchangeable. Beyond this, we often use "identity" as a shortened substitute for "shared identity" either because people belong to the same ingroup or because they share some common characteristics (profession, education, age, gender, etc.);

or – and this is very important – because, despite huge differences, negotiation partners have been able to develop shared principles, to cultivate a common understanding of issues at stake, and a mutual sense of how to resolve conflicts in practice. There is social capital built into negotiated relationships. The sense of partnership, marked by reciprocity, trust, and cooperation produces a "pawl effect", preventing partners from quickly exiting, probing for BATNA, and finally walking away too easily and possibly to the detriment of their actual business interests. Shared identities in a negotiation interaction are multifaceted with self-directed questions such as "What *do* I share with this person in front of me? What *could* I share?" That is where Relationship-Building is really necessary in the IT2 paradigm. It should be stressed, however, that the identitarian need for a relationship is not easy to cultivate when potential partners are outgroup people. Precisely because of this, the relationship is logically given priority over the deal. People-based contexts must be taken into account. Finally, utility counts also in the IT2 paradigm; however, following the *post hoc ergo propter hoc* principle (i.e., *after this, therefore because of this*), joint utility increase is a consequence of appropriate relationship development, not vice versa.

In cultures where people have a strong sense of identity, negotiators may display a concern with preserving a sense of honour,[43] avoiding shame and saving face. Extreme face concerns may at times override purely utilitarian interests (a redundancy), for instance by walking away from a negotiation renouncing a profitable deal for one's side, which may also be a loss in opportunity for the other party (also not closing a profitable deal), because they have proved culturally insensitive. Important to relationship builders are identity, status, power, and (sometimes unfortunately) instrumentality. This is the utilitarian side of IT2: it is by manipulating, persuading, gaining the complicity of others, that negotiators get access to utilitarian consequences (linked to objects and material outcomes) not by rushing directly to deal negotiation. Chinese Stratagem 7 (*"Make a sound in the East, then strike in the West"*); that is, create an expectation in the enemy's mind through the use of a feint, is an example of such an indirect and manipulative search for utilitarian outcomes.[44]

Language and communication styles

Communication is essential to ICBN for establishing rapport, information exchange, being persuasive, and possibly making concessions, as well for finalizing an agreement. The way in which people communicate in negotiation (that is both emit and receive messages) and the extent to which their native language frames their world-views and attitudes directly affects intercultural business negotiations.[45] They require a dialogue, although partners may have different native languages, writing contracts in a foreign language (at least foreign to one side), using interpreters, trying to express ideas, concepts which may be unique in a particular language, etc. Efficient information exchange in ICBN with outgroup negotiators requires an understanding of how they communicate. Briefly in this chapter, and in much greater detail in Chapter 5, two polar communication styles are opposed: HC (high-context, implicit messages) and LC (low-context, explicit messages) communication.

Low-context communication style

In LC communication most information is vested in the explicit code, which ideally could be transformed into digits (e.g., Yes/No corresponds to 1/0). LC communication cultures use explicit, precise messages, so that understanding does not require context-bound interpretation of messages. Thought patterns in LC cultures are linear and emphasize rationality and logic. This LC communication is practical (doing-oriented) in essence, the best possible applicant for efficient information exchange on a global scale (outgroupist). Messages are cogently decontextualized because they are intended to reach a very wide range of possible partners, differing in culture, language, and communication style. Because LC communicators may be obsessed with preciseness, completeness, and clarity of information, this style may border – especially in written communication – on formalism, idealism (possibly), even though a pragmatic doer attitude is constantly claimed at a value level. LC negotiators tend to prefer direct communication, expressing their views straightforwardly and unswervingly, at the risk of displeasing or even vexing the other party.[46]

High-context communication style

Conversely, and briefly summarized, in HC communication, generally related to IT2 cultures, little is in the coded, explicit part of the message while most of the information lies in the physical and social context. HC cultures communicate in a non-linear way with less emphasis on calculative rationality, favouring implicit, context-bound messages. In the HC communication style, interpretation (decoding) of messages is context-bound. The context of HC communication style is composed of many elements surrounding the communication process, which a priori do not matter in a low context communication, for example: Who speaks to whom? Where? When? Why? What brings the locutors together in this communication attempt?. Such interpretive features surrounding the communication process do not matter at the outset in low context communication. The HC–LC divide is the source of communication misunderstandings which may result in confused information exchange, complications in establishing credibility and fostering trust between the negotiating parties.

HC negotiators tend to use an indirect communication style (understating, going around issues, swerving, substituting this for that in the hope that the receiver will properly decode). Being direct and frank may be resented by HC negotiators as rough and rude, not only because the message is felt as somewhat intrusive, but also because there may be a risk the receiver will lose face. Moreover, HC communicators are often not native English-speakers and are in a difficult position to respond rapidly to quick and direct messages. They need time to understand the message and prepare an answer. This is especially true for HC negotiators, negotiating in English as non-native speakers and trying their best, even though they do not react as quickly as expected by LC negotiators.

Mindsets

Whether called "mindsets",[47] "intellectual styles",[48] or "mental models",[49] another major difference in ICBN concerns the way people reflect on issues and articulate thinking and believing with action and decision. To form opinions and positions, do negotiators prefer to rely on data, ideas, and/or speech, and which combination of these? How does this influence the way they relate their words (e.g., what they claim they will do, when, and how) and their actions (i.e., what they actually do afterwards)? Mindsets influence the ways of addressing negotiation issues, of collecting information, of choosing relevant pieces of information and assessing their "truthfulness", so that finally they influence the negotiation process and the resulting decisions. They are also directly reflected in communication since mindsets have a deep and often concealed relation to the native language.

Synchronizing with others: Time orientations

Attitudes towards time and how it shapes the way people structure their actions have a pervasive yet mostly invisible influence. Differences in punctuality, reflected in everyday negotiation behaviour, may probably appear as the most visible consequence, but differences in time orientations, especially toward the future, are more important as they affect long-range issues such as the strategic framework of decisions made when negotiating, the expected outcome, and the timeline of the negotiation process (see Chapter 4). Broadly stated, two time patterns, the Linear-Economic (LE) vs. the Holistic-Cyclical (HO) time pattern, corresponding to deep religious and cultural differences, are respectively associated with the IT1-deal-oriented paradigm and the IT2-relationship-oriented paradigm. They are presented in detail in Chapter 4 along with their influence and consequences on the ICBN process. In the LE pattern, time is linear, abstract, economic, divisible, and task-oriented; the timeline for negotiation is clear and the schedule is clear. In the HO pattern, time is holistic, not really separable from people, tasks are subordinated to people, and time is not akin to an economic resource. In negotiation, time pressure is not felt by HO negotiators. On the contrary, for them time should be abundantly allocated for getting to know each other between the negotiation partners before the negotiation process starts. For HO negotiators, the key to joint achievements is not agenda and schedules but socialization.

Outcome orientation: Comprehensive contractual arrangement versus broad relational agreement

Contract versus relationship

In line with their sense of preciseness, the outcome orientation of IT1 Deal-Makers is to complete negotiation with a detailed, written contractual document. For them, to close a deal, you have to *get-it-in-writing*, with a strong inclination for legally drafted contracts. Bazerman et al. (2000) emphasize that previous research has shown that negotiators from individualist societies are more concerned with preserving individual rights and attributes whereas the collectivist negotiator is more concerned with preserving relationships. Rather than relying on written contracts (which in fact they draft and sign), the outcome orientation of relationship-builders is not to end the negotiation with a detailed, written contractual document, which is for them not an end to the negotiation process. Rather than on written contracts, they rely on people-based agreements, following the traditional motto, *my word is my bond*. Person-based agreement and personal trust is preferred over written agreement; this almost always exists in global business, however it does not have the same level of importance as in the IT1 Deal-Making model.

Different attitudes to litigation and (the threat of) legal disputes

In the IT1 paradigm, legal disputes are a natural (even if unpleasant) complement of formal contracts. After the contract has been signed, contractual clauses have to be complied with by each party as the *law of the parties*. Penalties for not respecting particular obligations (e.g., delivery dates, quality) can be settled by contract clauses. Not complying with a contractual clause or asking for renegotiation may be a legitimate reason for formal litigation.

For the IT2 paradigm, litigation (or even simply the risk of it) is a major threat to the relationship. This does not mean that there are no conflicts, which exist in every negotiation. However, they should be managed within the confines of the parties and not necessarily by introducing third parties and/or a formal court procedure. As litigation is threatening, it will be avoided as much as possible. This difference in attitudes toward litigation is reflected in institutional and legal systems, which differ greatly worldwide. Differences in legal systems, contractual formalism and recourse to litigation, express contrasts in how societies are organized in terms of rules, third-party intervention in conflict resolution, and decision-making systems. The level of formality in addressing public and private issues has to be considered in any kind of negotiated partnership, including the discussion of joint-venture contracts, the registration of subsidiaries and the addressing of sensitive issues with the public authorities of the host country. There are contrasts in drafting contracts, using the threat of litigation, etc. between the two ICBN paradigms. They are examined in detail in Chapter 7.

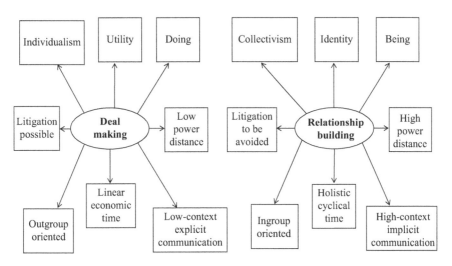

Figure 2.1 Cultural differences underlying the deal versus relationship model

A summary of cultural orientations associated with a Deal-Making versus a Relationship-Building style

Figure 2.1 presents a summary of cultural differences underlying the deal vs. relationship model, in relation to various aspects of negotiation behaviour, process, and expected outcomes.

The association of cultural orientations with either a Deal-Making style or a Relationship-Building style should not be considered as due to causality; it is more a bundle of linkages, with the caveats on other sources of culture introduced earlier in this chapter. The negotiation style of Relationship builders is broadly associated with certain areas of the world: Latin America, Africa, the Middle East, Russia, and Asia are all more or less in the IT2 paradigm of negotiation while most of Western Europe, North America (excluding Mexico), and countries such as Australia, Canada, New Zealand, and the Nordic countries, tend to adopt the IT1 Deal Makers' negotiation style.

Mirror games in ICBN: Comparing, stereotyping, pretending, adapting, and adjusting

Comparison is not interaction

A large part of the academic literature on the influence of culture on international business negotiations uses a comparative, cross-national, and/or cross-cultural setting.[50] For instance, a laboratory experiment (e.g., a negotiation simulation involving the sale of rights to a television channel) helps in comparing negotiations between businesspeople from different nationalities. Nationality is often used as a proxy and summary variable for culture, providing a basic description of cultural traits of different camps in ICBN, which are a basis for research hypotheses on either negotiation process or outcomes. This has led to significant advances in understanding cultural diversity in negotiation behaviour. However, *comparative* (*intra-cultural*) findings on negotiation behaviour and/or strategies when subjects negotiate with their fellow citizens cannot be directly transposed to *inter-cultural* negotiation. Some traits may not recur when people are negotiating with partners of different cultures: if Italian businesspeople negotiate with American counterparts (*inter*-culturally), they may adopt different behaviours and strategies as they do when negotiating *intra*-culturally with other Italians. It has been shown that negotiators tend to adapt their behaviour in ICBN. Negotiators in intercultural encounters do not strictly behave as predicted by observations derived from intracultural negotiations. For instance, French-speaking Canadians are more problem-solving oriented when negotiating with English-speaking Canadians than they normally are when negotiating among themselves.[51] Therefore behaviour and strategies as observed in intracultural negotiation can only serve as a partial basis for the prediction of negotiation style and strategies with negotiators from other cultures. Hence, the word "intercultural" in this text directly relates to the study of interaction between people with different cultural backgrounds. The word "cross-cultural" relates to a research design that is generally comparative but may also be centred on the encounter/interaction.

Pretending

Cultural borrowing is very frequent in a global world dominated by Western-style ideologies, markets, and management knowledge.[52] It is all the more likely that negotiation is considered a universal business activity with a global body of knowledge and practices.

Cultural similarity is often presumed for convenience.[53] Misinterpretation quickly arises as well as misunderstandings out of pretence behaviour. A classical situation is that of an English-speaking party making an initial "icebreaking" joke, quickly said in American slang. Non-native negotiators fear losing face if they ask for explanations, revealing that they are not completely proficient in colloquial English and run the risk of being considered as humourless. As a result, confronted by such jokes, some negotiators may pretend to understand by laughing like (and with) the others (all of whom may or may not have understood the joke) or simply expressing fake comprehension by a smile, even a faint (and phony) smile. This make-believe solution is misleading both about real language abilities, especially if it takes the form of a *fuite en avant* (*relentless pursuit* of masking real language competencies) and may later cause problems.

The deep cultural difference is revealed by visualizing that this "icebreaking joke" is merely the iceberg's tip. "Icebreaking jokes" are used for quickly creating a friendly atmosphere (i.e., letting the icy ambience swiftly melt down into a friendly one) shortening the non-task sounding stage, avoiding wasting time as an economic resource. This relates to deep cultural orientations such as the doing mentality or the linear-economic patterning of mechanical Newtonian time (see Chapter 3).

Adapting and adjusting in ICBN

A simple AKA (i.e., Awareness, Knowledge, Adjustment) model for the intercultural learning process in ICBN would linearly involve three successive stages: 1) *Awareness*, that is, becoming aware that there are cultural differences and that they matter; 2) *Knowledge*, that is, picking up and understanding what kind of cultural differences have an impact on which negotiation behaviour, on communication style, and under which circumstances; and 3) being able to *Adjust* to the other negotiating party in a way that will increase the joint outcomes, and maximize one's share of the total pie while by and large respecting a rule of fair division of outcomes.

The process of intercultural encounter in negotiation has been described as akin to a performance in which one dancer dances a waltz while the other dances a tango.[54] There is, however, much adaptation in intercultural negotiation; negotiators tend to adjust to the other party's behaviour in ways that sometimes derive significantly from what would be the stereotypical attitude in their native culture.[55] It is naturally difficult to step out from one's own culture. However, negotiators exchange masses of information during negotiation and process it in complex ways that do not aim at an intellectual understanding of the beliefs and attitudes of the other party, but rather target mutual adjustment in view of maximizing outcomes. Negotiators therefore tend to adapt their behaviour to the other party, at least to the extent they perceive as useful for smoothing the process and improving the outcomes. On average cultural adaptation done properly – without naive imitation – is positively experienced by the other side. Neither the Japanese nor the Thais feel that their social identity is threatened by high adaptation coming from American sellers in sales negotiations. The Japanese buyers positively experience cultural adaptation by American sellers despite the marked tendency in Japan to make a clear-cut distinction between ingroup members (*nihon-jin*) and outgroup members (*gai-jin*).[56]

Adaptation and adjustment in ICBN is simultaneously based, constrained, and biased by expectations and stereotyping. There may be a number of typical expectations, for instance, that negotiators are fluent in English, or that they are prepared for negotiation. In the IT2 paradigm, preparation is not done in isolation before negotiation but can be understood as starting with preliminaries in face to face negotiation. Contrary to a negative stereotype, not preparing is not necessarily a sign of a lack of professionalism. Rather, it could be that preparing without prior personal knowledge of the other side's negotiators is resented as problematic and that it is somewhat meaningless to prepare unilaterally, *in abstracto*. There are arguments in favour of open-minded and flexible unpreparedness while there are also arguments in favour of coming well-prepared (see Chapter 7). Adaptation to the other party's culture is not a panacea: adaptation increases, however without guaranteeing the chances of favourable outcomes.[57]

Culture clash in negotiation may be strong, especially at the start, when negotiators expect behaviour from the other side which normatively corresponds to what they are used to as well as to what they consider the most appropriate for effective negotiation (see Sebenius, 2001). Inadequate expectations based on one's own and not the other party's behavioural standards are the general rule in ICBN. Misled expectations often give rise to self-explanation based on negative stereotypes of the party which did not match what was expected of them. Moreover, cultural adaptation is not necessarily symmetrical. For instance, Japanese negotiators tend to adjust to Americans by using more direct information sharing and less indirect communication than in negotiations with their compatriots, whereas Americans adapt less to their Japanese counterparts.[58] A common professional culture may also help overcome the barriers related to cross-cultural understanding.[59] That is why culture often appears as an incomplete predictor of the negotiation process and outcomes and should not be directly used to predict negotiation behaviour[60] but rather in combination with other variables (see Chapter 6).

Emotions in ICBN

Emotions are subjective and transitory states.[61] They may later be reinterpreted. Emotions are often related to issues of cultural misunderstandings, opportunistic behaviour, fairness, distributive or procedural justice, and whether a party's goals have been met or not.[62] The persistence of emotions relates to the timing of norm violation: they can be disconfirmed and forgotten, for instance, when the partner moves towards more fairness in outcome distribution, or when it appears that a fair division of the outcome has emerged at the implementation stage. Emotions can also further increase and escalate, when the fairness issue remains unaddressed by a dominant negotiation partner. Communication misunderstandings in ICBN quite often result in an increased level of emotions, that is, negotiators tend to depart from the rational and objective evaluation of issues at stake and to mix subjectivity and feelings with business matters. Morris et al. (1998, p. 730) outline two types of misunderstandings that frequently arise between Asian and American negotiators:

> In one type of misunderstanding, U.S. managers make the error of reading silence of their Asian counterpart as an indication of consent...

A different type of misunderstanding occurs when Asian managers make the error of reading a U.S. colleague's direct adversarial arguments as indicating unreasonableness and lack of respect.

Emotions such as anger result in negotiators being less accurate in judging the interests at stake, more self-centred on their own interests; it also has a general effect of reducing joint gains. Kumar (1997) makes a sharp distinction between positive and negative emotions in negotiation. Emotions contain both an element of affect and an accompanying physiological arousal. For him, positive emotions result in being more flexible in negotiations, as well as helping negotiators be more persistent, especially since a positive affective state increases the confidence level of negotiators. However, a positive affective state may also heighten expectations and result in negotiators' disappointment with actual outcomes. Conversely, the expression of a negative emotion may have a positive effect on the negotiation process by drawing the attention of the other party to an unfair situation or an opportunistic move that needs to be corrected.

Negative emotions, on the other hand, may result in conflict escalation, that is, actors take matters personally when they should see them with a more distanced attitude. Likely consequences are attributing to the other side the responsibility for conflict, and possibly discontinuing the relation. While negative emotions may serve to inform the parties that an existing situation is untenable, they may also snowball and result in a negative conflict spiral. Negative spirals are partly based on selectively choosing those information cues which will confirm the negative feelings of a negotiator leading her or him to an escalation of negative feelings toward the other party which are no longer based on hard facts. They also result from systematic reciprocation of contentious communication. Negative spirals are particularly likely to occur in cross-cultural negotiations due to differences at three levels: differences in internalized values and norms, differences in emotional expression, and differences in linguistic styles. A conflict spiral appears as circular as it is based on repeated contentious communication whereby each side "responds" to the other side's contentious communication by negative reciprocation.

Negative emotions may arise from cultural misunderstandings between IT1 and IT2 negotiators. Kumar (1999) shows how IT1 task-oriented Americans and IT2 relationship-oriented Japanese negotiators experience a goal conflict, which generates negative emotions increasing behavioural incompatibility and therefore damaging the relationship. A further consequence of negative emotions is to reduce information processing and the quality of information exchange. Negative emotions generate frustration in both American and Japanese negotiators, who react by being aggressive (U.S.) or by escaping (Japanese negotiators). Conflict escalation occurs because aggression amplifies the Japanese desire to escape while Japanese withdrawal increases American frustration.

The way to solve negative spirals in negotiation has to do with both models of conflict resolution and with strategic communication styles in negotiation which may help to manage discrepancies in the process and outcomes of negotiation. Monitoring emotions in negotiation has to do with the avoidance of negative spirals but also with the avoidance of being too systematically conflict avoidant. A number of communication strategies have been recommended for breaking negative spirals in cross-cultural negotiations. George et al. (1998) recommend that negotiators engage in what they call "motivated information processing", that is, a process whereby information is selectively processed in ways that are supportive of motivational goals; motivation for certain outcomes, rather than affect, guides interpretation.[63] A mix of reciprocation combined with non-contentious communication is likely to help break negative spirals in negotiations.

To conclude this section, it is useful to stress that emotions are informative and convey messages. Adam Smith (1790, p. 188), after a long plea in favour of expressing emotions (called below "passions"), explains:

> In civilized nations, the passions of men ... are often clamorous and noisy, but are seldom very hurtful; and seem frequently to aim at no other satisfaction, but that of convincing the spectator, that they are in the right to be so much moved, and of procuring his sympathy and approbation.

Adjusting rationally by combining different rationalities

The key issue in rationally (or at least as rationally as possible) adjusting in negotiation is that there are different types of rationality in ICBN, the first being based on a calculative and utilitarian logic, the second on a subjective and relational reasoning. Models linking emotions to rationality question whether emotions are a threat to being rational in negotiation or an element of being rational; if and when it is assumed that emotions can be controlled, consciously created, and directed to influence the other side. Is it possible to be both rational and emotional simultaneously? The key issue is then interpretation, preferably objective rather than subjective; however, interpretation is language- and culture-based and misunderstandings are likely to arise. Objectivity implies not being caught in the trap of prejudices, negative stereotypes, ethnocentric views, biased evaluations, and the like. Negotiators in ICBN should make a clear difference between *normative* statements (i.e., relating to, or deriving from a standard or norm, especially as concerns suggested behaviour) and *positive* judgements (i.e., based on verified facts, evidence, proof, and shared experience). An example of successive (however, somewhat contradicting) *normative* statements addressed to negotiators are: "Be nice, understand your partner, put yourself in their shoes, and however separate interests from people. Be relationship oriented but do not lower your aspirations, don't be soft, yielding, and so on". Conversely, an example of a *positive* recommendation is: "look at people and relationships as they are, that is, search for empirical cues, facts, and evidence".

What is interactive and cooperative rationality in an ICBN perspective? The original meaning of rationality bases decision-making on an individual calculative, precise, and explicit logic. It is therefore more economic, Deal-Making, and utilitarian, all of the value orientations mentioned above around the IT1 paradigm.

In an individualist society people are seen as more mature if they act in a manner that is consistent with their attitudes, whereas people in a collectivist society are seen as more mature if they can put aside their own personal feelings and act in a socially appropriate manner.[64]

Is there such a concept as "relational rationality", based on more fuzzy calculation, which is indirect and imprecise, and which however leads to a cognitively and intellectually articulated judgement? A challenge of this book is to show that the pure economic rationality (IT1 paradigm) can be at times opposed to a "relational rationality" (IT2 paradigm), and in most cases both rationalities can be astutely combined in ICBN, following the *either/and*, *or/and* disjunctive/conjunctive approach.

Notes

1 Goodenough (1971).
2 As emphasized by Foster (1995, p. 68): "It is not always cultural. Cultural differences alone do not, of course, explain why communications and negotiations fail, why your counterparts *act as they do*, or *why you can't get things done*" (my emphasis on the last, very IT1, phrase).
3 See Sebenius (2002), Kalé (2003), and Elfenbein et al. (2008).
4 Chen et al. (1998).
5 See Karsaklian (2017).
6 See for instance, Faure and Rubin (1993); Faure and Sjöstedt (1993); Kremenyuk (1993); Graham et al. (1994); Leung (1997); Brett and Okumura (1998); Bazerman et al. (2000); Adair et al. (2001); Adler (2002); Wade-Benzoni et al. (2002); the various contributions in Gelfand and Brett (2004), as well as Bülow and Kumar (2011); Lee et al. (2013); and Ribbink and Grimm (2014). Support is coming as well from authors actually involved in international negotiations (Foster, 1995; Cohen, 2007; Schuster and Copeland, 1999; Saner, 2008).
7 See also Salacuse (2004) on the top ten ways that culture affects negotiation.
8 This is why it is not possible to really simulate cultural differences in intercultural negotiation training. Role instructions in negotiation simulations may at best give a small sense of what is a natural culture. The cultured mind is wired, organized, categorized, programmed in a largely unconscious way, following Hofstede's (1991, 2001) metaphor of culture as *software of the mind*.
9 See Madhok (1995), Brannen and Salk (2000), and Kumar and Patriotta (2011).
10 See Hofstede and Usunier (2003), Inglehart (2004), Cellich and Jain (2004, pp. 34–36), as well as Trompenaars (1993), Trompenaars and Hampden-Turner (2011).
11 See Hofstede and Usunier (2003).

12 See Schwartz (2009) and Perrinjaquet et al. (2007).

13 A classic distinction, *emic* versus *etic* cross-cultural research, was originated by Sapir (1929) and further developed by Pike (1966). The *emic* approach holds that attitudinal or behavioural phenomena are expressed in a unique way in each culture. Taken to its extreme, this approach states that no comparisons are possible. The *etic* approach, on the other hand, is primarily concerned with identifying universals. The difference arises from linguistics where phon*etic* is universal and depicts universal sounds which are common to several languages, and phon*emic* stresses unique sound patterns in languages. See Usunier et al. (2017).

14 The *doing-being* divide is due to Kluckhohn and Strodtbeck (1961).

15 See Foster (1995, pp. 178–184) on the American "*can-do*" mindset.

16 In the negotiation literature, *being* characteristics are called "dispositional" variables because they predispose negotiators to *doing* (i.e., behaving in a certain way).

17 Chapman and Jamal (1997).

18 See Gambetta (1988) and Bigoni et al. (2016).

19 See Leung (1997).

20 Hofstede (2003) in Hofstede and Usunier (2003).

21 Individualism is measured as a cultural dimension by Hoftede's (2001) scores.

22 See Foster (1995, pp. 73–87). A seemingly relaxed and informal way of communicating with others may, however, be considered another kind of formalism.

23 See Bazerman et al. (2000, p. 297) and Markus and Kitayama's (1991) contrast between the independent mindset of individualist cultures and the interdependent mindset of collectivistic cultures.

24 https://en.wikipedia.org/wiki/Bill_of_Rights_1689.

25 Graham et al. (1994) compare negotiation behaviour across 11 cultures (United States, Canada (Francophone), Canada (Anglophone), Mexico, United Kingdom, France, Germany, Former USSR, Taiwan, China, and Korea). Correlation coefficient of individualism with profits is 0.67; correlation of individualism with problem solving orientation is 0.83; correlation of individualism with the relationship linking problem solving orientation to profits: 0.64 (all $p < 0.05$).

26 Fisher, Ury, and Patton (2011).

27 Chen et al. (1998).

28 Smith et al. (1998).

29 See also the empirical findings of Morris et al. (1998).

30 Evans (1963).

31 Druckman et al., 1976; Harnett and Cummings, 1980; Campbell et al., 1988; Tinsley and Pillutla, 1998.

32 Harnett and Cummings (1980), and in fact in most ICBN empirical studies in which Americans are part of the empirical design.

33 Or it may be that Middle-Eastern negotiators hold a fixed-pie assumption as concerns economic and relational goals (Tinsley et al., 2011).

34 Sawyer and Guetzkow (1965); Ghauri and Usunier (2003); Brett and Okumura (1998); Bazerman et al. (2000); Adair et al. (2001).

35 Weitz (1979); Graham (1985).

36 Tinsley and Pillutla (1998).

37 Brett (2000).

38 Evans, 1963; Graham, 1985; Pornpitakpan, 1999.

39 See Bazerman et al. (2000), Hofstede and Usunier (2003), Cellich and Jain (2004), Gelfand et al. (2011), Gunia, Brett and Gelfand (2016).
40 See also Foster (1995, pp. 264–272) and Bazerman et al. (2000).
41 Gudykunst and Ting-Toomey (1988).
42 Adam Smith gives a perfect account of pure deal-related utility in this chapter's introductory epigraph. Utility was later formally defined by Jeremy Bentham as "that property in any object, whereby it tends to produce benefit, advantage, pleasure, good, or happiness…or…to prevent the happening of mischief, pain, evil, or unhappiness" (Jeremy Bentham's *Introduction to the Principles of Morals and Legislation* (1789, 1996).
43 See D'Iribarne (2003). On the need to protect one's identity as core of the Self, see also Dupont (1994, p. 333) and Tinsley et al. (2011) about Quatari negotiators' concerns with defending honour and saving face.
44 The 36 Chinese stratagems are famous in the negotiation literature (see Ghauri and Fang, 2003; Fang, 2006). Although frequently attributed to Sun Tzu, they have an earlier and complex origin. The keywords denote their origin in military strategy and tactics: battlefield, enemy, knife, sword, destroy, surrender, fight, move in for the kill, etc.
45 See for instance, Adachi (1998).
46 See Fisher (1980), Foster (1995, pp. 212–215), Bazerman et al. (2000, p. 298).
47 Fisher (1988).
48 Galtung (1981).
49 Bazerman et al. (2000), Thompson, Neale, and Sinaceur (2004).
50 See Usunier et al. (2017).
51 Adler and Graham (1989) consider comparisons based on intracultural negotiations as somewhat misleading because of cultural adaptation in ICBN. Other empirical ICBN studies disconfirm cultural adaptation in ICBN. For instance, in a study on conflict resolution strategies of Canadian and Chinese executives, Tse, Francis, and Walls (1994) showed that neither group adapted its negotiation strategy when negotiating interculturally. Interestingly, both Canadian and Chinese preferred to negotiate with Canadians.
52 See Holden (2002).
53 Saner (2008, p. 259) considers similarity presumed for convenience a source of "cross-cultural noise".
54 Tinsley et al. (1999), Adair and Brett (2005), Barkai (2008).
55 Adler and Graham (1989); Bazerman et al. (2000).
56 See Pornpitakpan (1999) about cultural adaptation of Americans selling to Japanese and Thais.
57 Adler (2002) and Weiss (1994a, b) suggest that the party who has greater knowledge and familiarity with the opponent's culture should do the most adaptation. However, this view is far from being shared by other ICBN authors.
58 Adair et al. (2001).
59 Haugland (1998).
60 Tinsley and Brett (1997).
61 There is no reason to suppose that words such as "emotions", "affect", or "mood" are cross-culturally equivalent, especially due to different expressivity and emotional restraint norms across cultures, this combining in fine-grained behavioural norms with gender roles, public and private circumstances, taboos

(about crying, shouting, being verbally aggressive, insulting), etc. However, I use the word "emotion" as short-duration affective states responding to stimuli related to people and situations, because there is clearly a universal side to the inner affective state that underlies an emotion, irrespective of the manner in which it is manifested. For an overview of the role of emotions in negotiations and in ICBN, see Mesquita (2001), Barry et al. (2004), Thompson et al. (2004), and Kumar (1997, 1999, 2004).

62 See Bazerman and Neale's (1992) Chapter 13.
63 See George, Jones, and Gonzalez (1998); Brett, Shapiro, and Lytle (1998).
64 Triandis (1995).

3 Quandaries in negotiation
Dilemmas, conflicts, and disputes in ICBN

Caveat venditor, Caveat emptor
(Symmetric Latin proverbs, meaning "seller beware", "buyer beware")

Negotiation has often been defined as conflict or dispute resolution. Many terms are used almost interchangeably (e.g., dilemmas, conflicts, and disputes). The first objective of this chapter is to clarify terms and definitions, starting from the antecedents of conflicts and disputes; that is, a combination of dependence (each party's dependence on the other), interdependence, and divergence of interests. This allows us to successively introduce dilemmas based on game theory, conditional decision-making, and opportunistic behaviour as well as how they can be applied in an ICBN perspective (e.g., "telling the truth" versus "lying"). Universal dimensions of economic and social behaviour, such as reciprocity, trust, and loyalty, which have been the object of much recent literature in experimental economics, are introduced to set a firm foundation for clarifying basic behaviour at the Deal and Relationship interface. Further chapters will explain how reciprocity and trust may vary across cultures and the kinds of misunderstanding that arise from hidden differences on how reciprocal and trusting behaviours are culturally coded in ICBN.

Quandaries (i.e., delicate and difficult situations, involving embarrassment and perplexity, and possibly leading to an impasse) result from the combined and somewhat contradictory blend of interdependence and interests' divergence (ID). If there is no interdependence, there is no reason not to walk away in case of unresolved ID. An industrial purchaser who has the choice between myriad potential suppliers does not hesitate to switch to another seller. If there is interdependence, but no or little perceived and/or actual ID, agreement will be rather easy and quickly reached. The blend of interdependence and divergence creates three forms of quandaries that are successively described in this chapter. Subsequently, the chapter will explain how they develop in ICBN. It is first necessary to give a detailed view of what interdependence and ID actually mean and what they imply for ICBN. Building/construction contracts for the Olympics are a nice example of high interdependence levels.[1] ICBN offer a fertile context for conflict escalation: linguistic and cultural dissimilarities may cause misunderstandings due to poor understanding or miscomprehension, especially because of discordant communication styles (see Chapter 5). Conflict escalation in ICBN may result in feelings of being cheated, trapped, exploited, mistreated, abused, etc., causing a decrease in trust or even the collapse of any trusting relationship.

Interdependence and divergence of interests, concerns, and goals

The basic ingredients of conflicts

There are two basic ingredients for a conflict to arise between business partners: 1) there must be a divergence in concerns and goals between them; 2) the parties must be interdependent. In the absence of any divergence, they quickly reach an agreement. If not interdependent, it is easy for one or both partners to walk away, dodge the conflict, and search for alternative partners. A "concern" is built around issues that affect persons or businesses and contributes to the formation of their expectations and negotiation goals, for example the nomination of a CEO for an international joint venture (IJV). Each partner has a vested *interest* in having somebody from their own side as CEO of the IJV. One partner may think that they have a *right* to nominate the CEO because they bring the most resources to the IJV. *Power* is also at stake since the CEO as the IJV's top manager will therefore exercise control, authority, and influence over its operations. According to the negotiation literature, concern divergence exists in three areas: interests, rights, and power, often clipped into the IRP acronym.[2]

- Divergence of "interests", that is, *economic interests*, described in Chapter 1 as deal-related concerns; interest divergence is basically utilitarian and exists in both the IT1 and IT2 paradigms; however, it occupies a central role in the IT1 paradigm.
- Divergent "rights" are a frequent ingredient of conflicts, especially if interdependence is high and consequently, when an *exit* is not possible as a straightforward solution to the conflict. A right is any claim, pretension, request, title (or entitlement) that accords with the principles of legal texts, customary rules, and/or moral justice; and is allowable or due to a person or an organization. Rights are highly subject to cultural differences and culture-based interpretation. An example could be non-written "nepotism rights" (e.g., "as a local partner, it is my right to appoint family and friends in our Joint Venture") versus an open, competitive, and non-discriminatory hiring procedure. Rights, codes, and entitlements form a complex set of formal and informal rules and customs that are often not shared in an ICBN setting. In licensing and franchising agreements, claims, entitlements, and concerns around

industrial property rights are a key element in the negotiation process (see Chapter 9).

- Power corresponds to people-related concerns; *lato sensu* power deals with how to have people and/or organizations act as one intends them to act. Power is a broad concept with at least four facets (ability, might, authority, and prerogative). Power means 1) the ability to make, the capability or capacity to produce a desired outcome, related to competence, expert knowledge, and a faculty to create; 2) a might, energy, and force facet, which may be related to (large) size and resources, a forceful and potent sense of purpose, combined with strength, vigour, and determination (willpower); 3) one facet relates to authority and command, which gives ascendency, control, influence, and even dominance over the less powerful party; 4) the last facet is related to the power granted to a particular individual or organization through licence, prerogative authorization, or warrant. All of these facets are fully meaningful for negotiation.[3]

Interest divergence is rather deal-related. However, ID contains a subjective element related to the objective (actual) versus subjective (perceived) divergence of *concerns* as in Pruitt's definition of PCG (perceived common ground) which is better applicable to the IT2 paradigm of negotiation. Divergence of interests (*concerns*) is bound to dynamically generate quandaries unless parties have a very low level of interdependence, such as being both on an open market near to pure and perfect market competition with large opportunities for finding alternative partners.

High ID does not imply that a Deal is not profitable. ID does not reduce the possibility of a win-win solution. It may complicate the negotiation process and increase the likelihood that both parties will walk away, relinquishing a deal that was nevertheless better than their respective BATNAs (defined in Chapter 1). There are two sides in ID like heads or tails for tossing a coin. The first issue deals with the degree (magnitude) of PCG. ID is inversely related to the ZOPA or PCG. The larger the common ground, the smaller the interest divergence. The second issue relates to how demanding in terms of joint exploration it is to find the optimal solution, that is, the degree of complexity and uncertainty in the problem-solving task, especially when it is a multi-issue negotiation. If the parties must accept significant losses on some items against high gains on others, they are likely to subjectively experience a much larger ID than if they traded larger against smaller gains per item.

Dependence

As for previous keywords in this chapter, I make a systematic use of definitions (semantics), the origin of words (etymology), and language comparisons to highlight the facets of the concept at hand.[4] To define dependence, we must first look at the original verb *to depend* in different languages (Latin, English, German, French). The Latin verb *Dependere* (*de* – down and *pendere* – to hang), is the origin of the French verb *dépendre*, translated into English as *to depend*. The image is the same in German with *abhängen*. The English verb *to hang on* illustrates that a cord links an object to some steady piece above it. Dependence is first and foremost deal-related, objective, actual dependencies being the most important. *Technological dependence (TD)* relates to plans, procedures, patents, licence agreements, know-how, shared equipment, single-source supply, etc. which bind one partner to the other, a frequent situation in industrial/B2B markets. *Economic dependence* results from one partner needing the other to survive (e.g., when a negotiating company has a disproportionately high percentage of its total sales with the other party as a buyer), to be supplied with key (strategic) inputs that have no substitutes, or when customers are shared, distribution channels are vertically integrated, in case of cross-advertising, and/or when there is a joint salesforce. *Financial dependence* takes many forms, the simplest being that one of the negotiating parties owns part of the other party's equity capital (e.g., parent company and subsidiary) as is the case of negotiations within multinational companies between headquarters and large national subsidiaries. Other forms of dependence are payment dates (and possible payment delays), loans that are to be repaid by one party to the other at some point in time, etc.

Dependence asymmetry and interdependence: A multiplicative casting

Dependencies (from one side vis-à-vis the other side) and interdependence should be carefully assessed beforehand, starting from a review of elements of dependence on both sides. Dependencies are in no way symmetric and of similar magnitude: a business B can be very dependent on company C (dependency 1) with which it negotiates whereas firm C does not depend much on B (dependency 2). Therefore, interdependence is a combination of both dependencies. Let us imagine two formulas for interdependence: a multiplicative versus an additive model for both levels of dependence.

Interdependence = Dependency 1 x Dependency 2
(multiplicative model)

Versus

Interdependence = Dependence 1 + Dependence 2 (additive model)

For example: if D_1 is small or even zero, even if D_2 is quite large, the multiplicative model results in a very low level of interdependence. Partner C can easily exit, possibly leaving partner B in a tough situation. Very asymmetric dependencies result in low levels of interdependence.

An order giver, for instance, may be a large company, but a particular subcontractor represents a small percentage of its supplies for an item. Moreover, the item can be easily supplied from other suppliers with low transaction costs, little exit cost, etc. Conversely, the subcontractor may be a small company and the order giver may represent a high percentage of its total sales figure. Additionally the subcontractor has a lot of competitive pressure and little or no proprietary assets to enhance product differentiation. The resulting situation is completely *asymmetric dependence*. The order giver may impose an *open book* policy, whereby the subcontractor must give access to all of its accounting records, corporate and managerial, generating a huge information asymmetry in favour of the order giver. If in addition the subcontractor must bid on an industrial B2B marketplace,[5] we reach the climax of *asymmetric dependence*. The additive model above often features unrealistic dependence compensation, which is not the case in the real world. Levels of dependence and interdependence (LDI) change over time, as in the case of two companies in the early stage of negotiating a manufacturing joint venture (low LDI) or cooperating after the IJV has been agreed upon (high LDI).

Interdependence

Balanced interdependence occurs when dependencies are rather similar in degree (if not in nature), which results in relatively high levels of interdependence. Strongly symmetric dependencies, in which each party depends on the other party, result in a high level of interdependence; that is, shared and reciprocal dependence that leads companies and their negotiators to be in some way *locked into* the obligation to reach an agreement. High levels of interdependence can be observed between aircraft manufacturers such as Boeing and Airbus and the aircraft engine manufacturers (e.g., General Electric, Rolls-Royce, and Pratt & Whitney) or between aircraft engine manufacturers when they have a long standing cooperation for R&D and manufacturing (as in the case of General Electric and Safran for manufacturing aircraft engines).[6]

Interdependence mitigates the conflict because it constrains opponents to cooperation. In case of high interdependence and large "distances" between the negotiating partners (e.g., geographic, cultural, linguistic distance), relationships become important to manage interactions and negotiate. Fortunately, it has been shown that the Zone of Possible Agreement in case of high geographic and cultural distances is often pretty large compared with intracultural negotiation; that is, $ZOPA_{ICBN} > ZOPA_{domestic}$. Large distance between negotiation parties paradoxically provides for increased efforts and costs as well as great potential joint outcomes.[7]

Assumed deal dependencies progressively develop into relational interdependence

In the IT1 business perspective, relational interdependence seems a priori less important than deal-related, objective interdependence. However, if high deal dependencies are assumed in a long term relation (acknowledged and accepted), they progressively develop into relational interdependence.[8] For example, when Singapore Airlines experienced major problems with its A380 Rolls-Royce engines, both companies were able to find mutually satisfactory solutions because of their long-standing relationships and the shared history between Singapore and the UK.[9] Similarly, when large ICBN contracts (e.g., turnkey plants, building contracts) extend over many years, dependencies and interdependence dramatically change before and after signing the contract. The background market situation evolves over time from a monopsony to a bilateral monopoly or even a more complex out-of-market situation (e.g., through a takeover or by signing an exclusive cooperation agreement). In the case of a stadium for the Olympic Games, if construction is late, conflict escalation seems inevitable. Rights can be invoked (e.g., a clause foreseeing jumbo delay penalties in favour of the buyer); however if power is exercised for the worst, the stadium will not be ready for the Olympic Games; the final outcome will be extreme lose-lose. Cooperation seems inescapable even though it may set teeth on edge for both sides. The level of conflict may be quite high; however deal interdependence is likewise at its highest point. Rationally understood interests must dominate over rights and power. Conflict resolution becomes more or less compulsory and relational interdependence is progressively acknowledged by the negotiation partners. Deal dependence is reversed and the two parties are in dire need of a relationship that will help them to reasonably cope with their disagreement, overcome the conflict of interest, and achieve a satisfactory joint outcome. In this case, a relationship built beforehand appears as a tremendously useful asset.

A key function of relationships as well as the genuine acknowledgment of both relational dependencies and interdependence is to help repair damaged deals and compromised joint projects. It is especially important during implementation, in the post-signature phase when confronted with unforeseen negative events. And therefore a function of the relationship is to secure future collaboration and profitable deals for both parties. This is where IT2 (defined in the previous chapter) is really strong as a background negotiation model.

Interdependence should be analysed in full detail on three levels: Deal, Relationship, and the interface between Deal and Relationship. Interdependence should be assessed concurrently with the divergence of basic concerns (interests, rights, and power) as well as with the divergence in identity and relational needs, especially when IT1 face IT2 negotiators. This requires learning both about the deal and about people and organization(s) in the adverse camp in order to a) assess possible opportunistic behaviour and control it; and b) possibly develop the relationship. It should be recalled that relationship development is hardly possible within an anonymous setting.

Dilemmas, conflicts, and disputes

The three concepts in the heading above are sometimes used as if they were almost synonyms (at least for conflicts and disputes). However, dilemmas are the real starting point because of the conditionality (on the other party's behaviour) of any move in a negotiation and the risk of facing opportunistic behaviour as an unexpected reply to one's own cooperative move.

Dependence asymmetry, interdependence, and opportunism

Oliver Williamson defines opportunism as "self-interest seeking with guile".[10] Opportunism is the deliberate practice of taking advantage of circumstances, with little regard for the consequences for others. Opportunist actions are almost exclusively driven by self-interested motives. Opportunism is likely to be greater and easier in case of high geographic and cultural distances, especially deal opportunism, because it is difficult to observe the partner from far away. For example, a Danish exporter shipping goods to Lagos, Nigeria may be opportunistically exploited by the local Nigerian customer who falsely claims that half of the goods arrived damaged in Nigeria and asks for a very significant rebate.

The conditional cooperation/defection framework in game theory finds its origin in the following (tricky) issue: How to make a decision the outcome of which depends on the (yet) unknown decision (attitude, action) of the other party? Conditionality is related to expectations of reciprocal behaviour that may not always be met (understatement). Figure 3.1 plots the degree of opportunism (U-shaped curve) against both dependence asymmetry and interdependence. Interdependence (horizontal axis) and opportunistic behaviour are strongly related to the degree of dependence asymmetry (vertical left axis). The higher the dependence asymmetry, the more the independent partner, because of its powerful position, tends to exploit the dependent partner in a situation of actual subordination.

Opportunism decreases when interdependence (horizontal axis) combines with low dependence asymmetry in the U-shaped curve: Both negotiation partners would go against their own interests. The lowest level of opportunism is reached in the case of medium interdependence with balanced dependencies (little or no asymmetry). On the ascending part of the curve on the right, opportunism is likely to generate ill-feelings, frustration, and a need to take revenge on the part of the party who has a sense (true or not) of having been opportunistically exploited. Even low levels of paranoia may play a role in fuelling conflict escalation.

However, what looks like opportunism may not be real opportunism, due to differences not only in the appreciation of "facts", but also in cultural codes. Cultural misunderstandings may arise from delayed reciprocation by one side interpreted as non-reciprocation by the partner, expectations

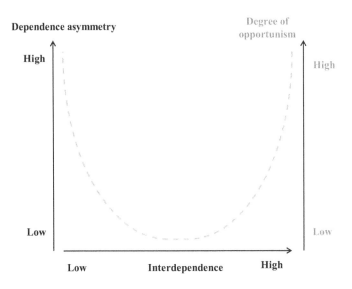

Figure 3.1 Dependence asymmetry, interdependence, and opportunism

considered legitimate by one side but not by the other (e.g., "We are good friends, please hire my nephew, he is a nice guy for the job"). Both deal opportunism and relational opportunism (e.g., non-cooperation with outgroup partners/adversaries) can be reduced by having strong, long-term relationships between distant partners, a strong support for the IT2 paradigm.

A *dilemma* corresponds to a situation necessitating a choice between two equally undesirable alternatives, often because both have uncertain outcomes, resulting in a problem that seems impossible to resolve. A dilemma is internal, often unsaid, unexpressed, unvoiced, kept for oneself, resolved by action (speech is a category of action), based possibly on an arbitrary or random choice to make a decision with generally two alternatives (sometimes more). The crux of a negotiation dilemma is the conditional decision-making: the outcome of one's own decision depends on the attitude and/or decision of the other negotiator. Should the profile of both parties' negotiators be similar (e.g., same age, gender, nationality, culture, profession …) this will generally facilitate the predictability of their behaviour and therefore reduces uncertainty in resolving the dilemma. A direct consequence of the beneficial effects of similarity is that ICBN dilemmas are considerably amplified by cultural dissimilarity.

A lot of minor and successive interactions in negotiation involve dilemmas. There are so many dilemmas that negotiators are only weakly or even unaware of the decision process involved, as well as the other party's reaction which often cannot be directly interpreted. Most of them are related to

communication choices (see Chapter 5), especially when exchanging information; some of these moves are more directly related to strategic issues.

- Disclosing information *or* keeping information secret.
- Disclosing key information in the hope that the other party will recipro-
  cate; however with the latent concern that reciprocation may be fake (it
  would have been better not to move) *or* keeping silent.
- Delivering truthful information *or* lying,
- Reacting to untrue information *or* keeping silent and unknown to the
  lying party that one is perfectly aware of the lie, even if it is a minor one.
- Delivering information that has not been explicitly asked for (or abstain
  from revealing it by omitting what is not requested) *or* not.
- Accepting rather long non-task preliminaries, at the risk of losing useful
  time resources for real, task-related negotiation (*or* not).
- Making concessions (*or* not), and what sort of concessions at what time
  in the negotiation process?
- Threatening with possible litigation (*or* avoiding use of such threats).
- Walking away (*or* not), provisionally *or* definitely, when negotiation
  seems to come to an impasse.

The list is endless. Such small (or, in fact, not so small) moves may come
up at a relatively fast pace, for example several moves in a one-hour face-
to-face negotiation period. In ICBN, the salience of "small" dilemmas is
increased by two complementary issues. First, it is difficult to choose an
alternative communication code given cultural, linguistic, and communication style differences, and sometimes to communicate one's move properly
so that the intent behind this move is clear enough to be properly decoded by
the other side (e.g., concessions made in the hope of reciprocation, however
interpreted by the opponent as a sign of weakness). Second, the other party
may not react as expected and may seem to defect rather than cooperate.
Interpreting their reaction may, however, be hard because of differences in
linguistic and behavioural codes, and in social and cultural cues.

A *conflict* is a struggle between opposing forces, possibly leading to a
battle; this definition underlines the dimension of violence. More generally,
a conflict corresponds to an opposition between ideas, interests, positions,
values, etc. Conflict is almost a synonym of controversy, which highlights
its dimension of cognitive divergence. From a psychological perspective, a
conflict is an opposition between two simultaneous but incompatible wishes,
impulses, sometimes leading to emotional tension, stress, hassle, and/or
worry. The German word for conflict (*Auseinandersetzung*) evokes the image
of people separating from each other, placing themselves against each other.[11]

A clash is often the first open (noisy and visible) manifestation of a conflict, which can however remain underground, unexpressed. Conflict *per
se* is not good or bad. It is generally unpleasant, and conflict avoidance, a
classic negotiation construct,[12] may develop on one or the other side or both

sides because of the unpleasant feelings that it may raise for negotiators. Conflict avoidance results from uncertainty avoidance, impressionability, lack of self-esteem, fear of a loss of face, etc. Conflict is likely to generate stress in a much stronger manner than mere (largely interiorized) dilemmas. Guilt can be generated in non-conflict-prone partners by forcing them into rather harsh disputes in which they feel faulty because of non-congruence with their norm of conflict-avoidance. At the end, manipulated, conflict-avoidant negotiators may tend to concede.

The underlying violence element in conflicts, although bilateral, may be experienced differently by the parties. Conflicts have an objective base in terms of contradicting, possibly incompatible, irreconcilable claims on resources, money, price, strategic objectives, etc. However, the subjective side of conflicts comes in quickly, as well as the likelihood of conflict escalation, with its associated non-rational quarrels and negative interpersonal feelings, thus potentially exasperating a simple rivalry in cornering resources for oneself at the other side's expense. Conflicts may become so harsh that negotiators part ways and decide to stop negotiating even if the deal would have been profitable for both parties. Rational, calculative, often deal-related arguments tend to disappear under the shadow of an uneasy, aggressive, damaged, and in fact unpleasant relationship. A balanced and lucid approach to disagreements and interest divergence may be finally overwhelmed by irrational behaviour, overly negative emotions, anger,[13] and a willingness to take revenge even at a significant cost for oneself, provided that the damage is (or is perceived as) much higher for the "punished" adversary. An assumed and consequent deal orientation can be preferable to a naive relationship orientation to avoid conflict escalation; however, sophisticated relationship management on both sides may also help mitigate conflicts.

Business negotiation is supposed to be non-violent, even if there can be some symbolic violence. Cultural misunderstandings may lead to conflict escalation: differences in values, in social codes, can generate negative emotions.[14] What is – culturally defined – irrational behaviour? We often label the other party as "irrational" when they do not adopt the same type of seemingly rational logic as ourselves. Not accepting that there may exist different types of rationality (e.g., people versus deal rationality, objective vs. subjective rationality, relational vs. calculative rationality) implies that the other party's behaviour and decisions can only be considered "irrational".

Dis-pute dates back to circa 1300, from the Old French *disputer*; that is, "fight over, contend for, discuss" coming itself from the Latin *disputare*, meaning "weigh, examine, discuss, argue, explain". Jeanne Brett (2000, p. 98) explains that conflicts and disputes have perceived goal incompatibilities in common. However:

> Negotiators resolving disputes are determining what can be done about the blocked goal. A dispute is a rejected claim …distinguished from the more general term, conflict … by its explicit nature.

To dispute is used in the Vulgate in the sense of "to argue, to contend with words". Related words are disputable, disputed, and disputing. To dispute may mean: 1) (to) argue, debate, or quarrel about something; 2) to seek to win; or 3) to struggle against, resist. Dispute, as an argument or quarrel, is often used interchangeably with conflict, although in fact disputes are a particular class of conflicts, which represent a more general category. However, argument, speech, and debate, on precise issues, often based on contractual, technical, legal documents differentiate the term from simple conflicts. Disputes (D) are a subset of the more general category of "conflict" (C):

$$D \subset C$$

Disputes are more rational, more strategic on both (or on multiple) sides, more rights-based, grounded on legal and contractual materials (e.g., legislation, draft or previously signed contracts, or preformat contractual documents, such as legal templates of how a particular class of conflict can be solved). Documents help to change conflicts into more rational disputes. People read and write and afterwards try to courteously exchange (make) arguments. They do not only shout at each other (something of an exaggeration). For instance (see Chapter 9, on different types of contracts), a multinational firm (MNF) has been present through a local agent on a foreign market for years. The MNF is happy with this solution in terms of both profits and sales. However, the new policy of the MNF is to develop its presence in foreign markets through subsidiaries rather than local agents. There is a *dilemma*, whether to keep the foreign agent or to follow the new corporate policy. If the contract with this foreign agent is abruptly terminated, the agent overwhelmed by negative feelings may be willing to take revenge (e.g., *conflict*). The agent may decide to go to local courts to seek justice and be compensated. There is a clear conflict between principal and agent, which can escalate to litigation if it is not alleviated by dispute resolution. The rational (and therefore calculative) *dispute* resolution approach is *inter alia* to either properly compensate the agent for the franchise created over years of business or to associate this agent with the newly created sales subsidiary in the form of a joint venture in which he or she can participate.

Dilemmas in ICBN

We have described above what it is to cooperate versus to defect in ICB negotiation interactions. The negotiation process involves micro-moves with the prisoner's dilemma (PD) as the underlying model. I explain below how it applies to ICBN.[15] A dilemma is a unilateral choice situation in a one-shot game/interaction with incomplete information. A number of information cues on the other player (about interests, people, cultures, companies, etc.) in non-anonymous interactions may enable guessing based on subjective probabilistic estimates.

Dilemmas in negotiation micro-moves

Successive micro-moves on each side provide the other side with behavioural information. Most micro-moves are related to language, communication, and culture both in terms of being adopted/decided by one party, and interpreted by the other party, then reciprocated or not. PD-type micro-moves in negotiation are all like cooperation vs. defection (e.g., lying vs. telling the truth, answering questions vs. not answering questions, equivocating vs. replying straightforwardly and precisely, disclosing private information vs. keeping all private information for oneself, making a concession vs. making no concession, reciprocating vs. not reciprocating a collaborative move by the other party, using theatrical emotions to manipulate the other party vs. behaving with self-control).[16] In PD micro-moves payoffs are designed to favour opportunistic behaviour. In the traditional PD setting, the players are often described as being manipulated by a third party (the police investigators) who has a vested interest that they both avow. In real life, negotiators can to a certain extent be almost instrumentalized by third parties.

Conditionality and reciprocation

Micro-moves combine to produce the aggregate negotiation process. As noted above, the prisoner's dilemma sketch applies to negotiation in practice because of the conditionality of moves and the need for anticipation. Many actions, small steps being taken (micro-moves) within the negotiation process may be considered as PDs (C=cooperate; D=defect). For instance, during information exchange: deliver information (C) or keep silent (D); tell the truth (C) or lie (D); use threats: express no emotions (C) vs. feign anger in order to influence the other party (D); or adopt a problem-solving approach and be integrative (C) vs. have a distributive orientation (D). All these moves are influenced by cultural norms for instance because of the fear of being considered weak, indecisive, feeble, or insignificant. They are susceptible therefore to being poorly observed and/or misinterpreted. In game theory, a two-player PD game where each player may either cooperate or defect has the following payoffs:

- T (temptation to defect in order to gain when the other negotiator cooperates)
- R (reward resulting from sharing the benefits of mutual cooperation)
- P (punishment when both negotiators defect)
- S (sucker's payoff for the negotiator who cooperates when the other defects); with:
  (1) $T > R > P > S$
  (2) $R > (T + S) / 2$

What these payoffs mean in practice is rather harsh. Opportunistic behaviour (in the short run) provides a negotiator with the highest gain (T). The return for each negotiator when they cooperate in a *win-win* perspective, R, is lower than the return for a negotiator who defects. P is the loss when both negotiators cheat (e.g., do not deliver true information) in a *lose-lose* perspective. Cooperating when the other player defects, S, is costly. The condition expressed in inequality 2) implies a return for mutual cooperation that is higher than the mean of opportunistic temptation and sucker's payoff, providing more value – in the long run – to cooperation than to defection. This is however a theoretical framework, which I take only as a background metaphor. Observing and ascertaining the nature of the other party's micro-moves in ICBN practice, whether cooperative or defective, is a matter of intuition, interpretation, and perspicacity. In the absence of a clear signal in a move, it is better to abstain from retaliating or rewarding the other party's move.

Iterated PD strategies applicable to negotiation beyond isolated micro-moves

In repeated prisoner's dilemma games, 200 shots and more were played by automatons following some ideal-types of cooperative strategies (i.e., decision rules in an iterated prisoner's dilemma) (Axelrod, 1984). They represent strategies that can be found in ICBN practice.

The *All D* policy of always defecting in a PD corresponds to what can be called unilateralism. It does not mean that it is impossible to reach a joint outcome. Negotiating with unilateralists is possible in a few cases, especially if 1) there is large ZOPA (joint surplus), 2) the unilateralist negotiator has a predictable behaviour, and 3) there is not much interest divergence.

Unconditional cooperation corresponds to a strategy of always cooperating even if the other negotiator defects at times or permanently. This strategy is rare in practice because it is not in the very nature of negotiation. However, it may sometimes emerge when 1) there is strong asymmetric dependence in disfavour of the unconditionally cooperating party, whose survival can only be based on the benevolence of the arch-dominant party; 2) the dominant player does not adopt an exploitative strategy; and 3) both negotiators implicitly agree that unconditional cooperation is the only tenable strategy on the part of the weaker party.

The *Tit for Tat* policy of benevolently cooperating on the first move and then doing whatever the other player did on the previous move (i.e., cooperate if he or she did; defect if he or she defected) has been shown to be the best.[17] What it means for ICBN is clear: a reasonable indulgence at the first encounter is in order. This approach is adapted in case of balanced interdependence and good prospects for joint value creation.

In *Random*, the PD strategy adopted is drawn randomly. It is quite rare in business negotiations. However, it may appear at times in order to confuse the other side, increase their feeling of uncertainty, in the hope of extracting concessions from a blurred adversary (see negotiation tactics in Chapter 8). *Random* may support a strategy of being fuzzy and unclear, hazy and distorted in the dubious expectation that the other party will concede and cooperation will emerge. Randomness may also emerge as an unfortunate consequence of non-managed cultural misunderstandings. Micro-moves cannot be clearly interpreted as cooperative and by default are interpreted as defective based on negative stereotypes.

Tit for Two Tats defects only if the other negotiator defected on the two previous moves; otherwise she or he cooperates. In the background of this strategy are behavioural archetypes such as high forgiveness, tolerance, and indulgence, which can be fairly universal. Such a forgiving strategy can also be justified by down-to-earth deal-related motives such as tolerance for delivery delays when the rest of the deal is quite satisfactory.

A *Friedman* player is never the first to defect but, as soon as the other player defects, *Friedman* defects from then on; that is, no longer cooperates. *Friedman* is fairly universal, and the disappointed party will take revenge by withdrawing and never cooperating again. In ICBN, this may occur when a company has had high expectations of continuous loyalty from its negotiation partner and retaliates by full withdrawal and/or negative action (e.g., a lawsuit, sabotaging the joint business) when they feel betrayed. Loyalty expectations have to be considered seriously as they are not infrequent in the IT2 paradigm and appear, on the contrary, rather bizarre to IT1 negotiators, who should try, however, to deflect the potentially negative consequences of a frustrated party adopting a strict retaliation policy.

In *Tester*, the rule is that the player defects on the very first move to test the other player's response. If the other player ever defects, he or she apologizes by cooperating and by playing tit-for-tat for the rest of the game. Otherwise, he or she cooperates on the second and third moves but defects every other move after that. What is meaningful for ICBN in this PD strategy is that a party may start by provoking the other party and challenge their benevolence. Note that the best solution when confronted with such a provocative test is to nevertheless show a willingness to carry on cooperation by choosing a *Tit for Two Tats* strategy at first.

Basic characteristics of micro-move strategies

Being nice (*Benevolence*) means to play cooperative in the first round (especially, in the absence of any "relational history") and never to be the first to defect. Being nice is normative in IT1 because the other party should be treated in an outgoing, open, and friendly manner in the first encounter.[18] Benevolence at the start of the negotiation is also frequently adopted by IT2 negotiators to initiate Relationship-Building.

Forgiveness/Indulgence implies a propensity to continue cooperation after the other player's defection. It is a highly recommendable attitude in intercultural business negotiations, in particular because perceived defection may not be actual defection due to the misinterpretation of the other party's behaviour (see section on "Uninterpretables", p. 85).

Retaliatory capacity entails the readiness to promptly react to a provocation of the other negotiator (e.g., to a sudden, major, unambiguous, and unjustified defection). Retaliation is frequent between member states of the WTO. When a country's exports are adversely affected by the raising of customs duties, by dumping, or by new nontariff barriers, it takes retaliatory action by establishing countervailing duties or import restrictions. Negative reciprocity (i.e., reciprocating harm by punishment) is a universal behaviour, however practised to different degrees. Proxies of the extent of negative reciprocity at the societal level are, for instance: 1) if and when the death penalty was legally abolished; and 2) the percentage of the population in prisons (with the caveat that culture and nation do not completely overlap). Forgiveness/indulgence is probably more widespread in countries that have legally abolished the death penalty, the pioneering country being Portugal in 1866 (a country for which culture = nation is a reasonable approximation).

Clarity/legibility is an overall positive trait of negotiation moves. If a strategy is too complex, it becomes illegible/unreadable by the other party; unpredictable behaviour is bound to decrease cooperation. However, apparent clarity can also result from blurring tactics (see Chapter 8) as in Chinese Stratagem 29 (*"Deck the tree with false blossoms"*, use artifice and disguise to create and illusion). Note that the intercultural encounter inevitably lowers the *clarity / legibility* of negotiation behaviours and strategies compared with intracultural negotiations.

Echo effects occur when one strategy, faced with a different one, causes systematic repetition of particular positions. There is no such effect in an All-D negotiator being confronted with an unconditional cooperator, because they behave unilaterally, irrespective of the other's moves. There is an echo effect when a tit-for-tat faces an All-D: he or she will start by cooperating and retaliate by defecting in all further rounds. *Echo effects* are the principal cause of conflict escalation, and the consequent snowballing anger and resentment. Escalation processes (positive or negative) are clearly related to echo effects. As a consequence, in ICBN, it may be necessary to interrupt the negative sequence generated by the echo effect through an unexpected positive micro-move that can be interpreted by the other party as a signal of change.

Opportunism at the interface between deal and relationship

Defection and opportunism

Opportunism is simply to adapt action and responses to take advantage of opportunities and circumstances, possibly at the detriment of the other party. Synonyms of opportunism, with both positive (+) and negative (–)

underlying value judgements are: resourcefulness (+), unscrupulousness (–), cunning (+), buccaneering (–), and carpetbaggery (–). Despite some positive aspects, a latent negative value judgement dominates. However, opportunism rarely entails illegal behaviour. Moreover opportunistic behaviour is sometimes difficult to immediately discover and is only later ascertained with an adverse influence on the relationship. For instance, hiding key information is a frequent category of opportunistic behaviour, which enables a party to maintain or even increase information asymmetry in its favour. In terms of the deal and/or relationship model, there are three types of opportunism: deal-related, relationship-related, and opportunism at the interface between deal and relationship.

Deal opportunism (IT1) consists most often in overexploiting information asymmetry in a number of deal-related areas (cost price, actual performance, quality, delivery dates, payment conditions, quality standards, durability), possibly by strategic misrepresentation of key information. Deal opportunism often uses a combination of formal contractual clauses and attributes in product design, services, and warranties which generate *lock-in effects* to be only later discovered by the locked-in party. Other examples of deal opportunism are selling an outdated (or about-to-be obsolete) item (e.g., in technology licensing); hiding key data, stating unrealistic delivery delays (in the absence of delay penalties in the contract); selling/buying when in fact the seller/buyer company is about to declare insolvency and go bankrupt, and will not be able to deliver/pay, however will keep the payment without delivering or keep the item without paying; or goods being delivered in a faraway port and incorrectly arguing that they are damaged (this being difficult to verify) and that their price must be reduced. This is a non-exhaustive list. There are, however, many ways of curbing deal opportunism: most of them are in the realm of checking, verifying, controlling with internationally standardized contract terms (e.g., Incoterms, letter of credit), legally protecting contracts, and using standard international contracts as well as being ready to use efficient litigation procedures (e.g., arbitration).[19] However, the best protection against deal opportunism is to have a trusting relationship; this is not a panacea, however, since relationships can also be abused.

Relational opportunism (IT2) in terms of the iterated (repeated) PD above would consist in credibly simulating a cooperative behaviour during successive moves to abruptly take advantage by defecting when stakes are quite high. This would mean simulating a fake involvement in relationship development when in fact there is no interest in such a process. Chinese Stratagem 8 (*"Openly repair the walkway but secretly march to Chen Cang"*) corresponds to first deceiving the other camp by continuously adopting a conciliating attitude, then assertively putting one's own positions in the forefront. Over-exploiting the relationship may lead a party to 1) reap undue advantages; 2) consider that the partner is there to help and understand however without reciprocating the support; and 3) behave unreliably because there is an excessive sense of the other party's loyalty and it is assumed that they will accept poor behaviour without pulling back.

Opportunism at the interface between deal and relationship is based on 1) using relational assets to try to ignore contractual liabilities; and, conversely, 2) using contractual assets to try to ignore relational liabilities. The renegotiation of contracts is a form of 1) that tends to be easily practised by IT2 negotiators. Their feeling is that the relationship should be strong enough to allow for considering the clauses of the signed contract as nonbinding, at least to be broadly, imprecisely, and even fuzzily interpretable. As we will see in Chapter 7, there is a difference in outcome orientations, in terms of oral (relational, IT2) versus written agreements (deal, IT1), even if negotiation nearly always ends up with a signed contract that is supposed to be the *Law of the Parties*. Standing firm on written contracts and detailed, precisely drafted clauses, threatening with litigation, penalties, and the like to extract compliance is typical of IT1 opportunism at the interface between deal and relationship. This is all the more resented by IT2 partners who bitterly feel caught in a nexus of legal and contractual constraints which they perceive as a betrayal of the relationship and as a sign of the partner's duplicity.

"Uninterpretables" and indulgence in ICBN

In ICBN micro-moves, it is far from always clear (an understatement) whether a move is opportunistic, instrumental, or misleading and is therefore some form of defection, or not. Due to differences in cultural codes (Chapter 2) and communication styles (Chapter 5), some micro-moves may be mistakenly interpreted as being akin to defection. For instance, seemingly hypocritical smiles, unexplained and lengthy silences, sudden and apparently inexplicable anger belong to the category of micro-moves, which I call "Uninterpretables". "Uninterpretables" would be better treated with indulgence in ICBN, because they often do not even need to be interpreted and do not necessarily bear much consequence beyond unease and discomfort. However, susceptibility should remain there, if an "Uninterpretable" persists and is regularly repeated by a party. It is better then to courteously ask for clarification of what this actually means, referring for instance to the other party's culture and language.

Conflict, cooperation, and defection in ICBN

A static view of conflict resolution

Based on the definitions above, a conflict is an opposition between incompatible goals and aspirations, ideas, interests, needs positions, values, etc. There are various types of conflict whether they are based on a divergence of goals, of interests, of positions, of values, of identities, and so on, and/

Table 3.1 Basic orientations in handling conflicts

Negotiator B	Negotiator A	
	Defects *(has no concern for the other party's outcomes)*	Cooperates *(is concerned by the other party's outcomes)*
Cooperates	A Contends – B Yields	Collaboration, Problem-solving
Defects	Conflict avoidance, inaction => withdrawal	A Yields – B Contends => B exploits A

or possibly on a combination and/or a succession of sources and types of conflict. In order to build a bridge between micro-moves and dilemmas (as in the PD) to general orientations in negotiating conflict, that is to conflict resolution (macro-orientations), basic orientations in conflict-handling can be represented as in Table 3.1 based on a combination of Pruitt's (1981) dual concern model and the cooperation/defection choice.

Cooperation resembles any type of behaviour/action that takes into account the other side's interests and concerns; this includes collaboration, reciprocation, open-mindedness, listening, abstaining from opportunism, and problem-solving. This general orientation largely precludes opportunistic moves that may harm the other side's interests. It seems idealistic against the prevalence of self-interest and low other-regarding orientation. However, a general cooperative orientation emerges rather often in the real world. For example, cooperation may emerge between benevolent partners despite asymmetric dependence that could be exploited by the less dependent party. D (Defection) can be seen as any type of behaviour/action that *does not* take into account the other side's interests and concerns; this includes: exploiting and taking advantage of the other party, manipulating, being instrumental, opportunistic, not reciprocating favours, and behaving unilaterally. All things being equal, a cooperative orientation tends to reduce conflict and frequent defection tends to increase conflict. However, defection may sometimes prove quite profitable while not illegal, so that it may make sense to defect in the world of business. Temptation to take advantage of a situation here is the main motivation. A "fair" defection example is letting down a supplier which is near to bankruptcy without being responsible for this difficult situation.

Wade-Benzoni et al. (2002) argue that decision-makers from individualist cultures and decision-makers from collectivist cultures may respond differently to an allocation decision according to its context. Following Leung's (1997) proposition that decision-makers from collectivist cultures placed in dual roles (both allocator and recipient) will prefer equity, they show that Japanese decision-makers, faced with a social dilemma, prefer equality solutions more than U.S. decision-makers. The preference for equality in collectivist cultures (goals of equal outcomes for both parties) is confirmed by Tinsley and Pillutla (1998) who show that Chinese negotiators see equality-oriented behaviours as more appropriate than American negotiators. Furthermore, when briefed with pro-social instructions, Chinese negotiators tend to develop a goal of equal outcomes while Americans are led by the same instructions to the aim of maximising their joint outcome.

The Japanese, the Americans, and the Germans use different models of conflict resolution. The Japanese tend to use the "status model"; that is, social interaction is viewed as governed by status and parties might solicit the advice of higher status figures to solve the conflict. The Germans display a preference for the "regulations" model whereby conflict is solved by applying standardized, universal, and impersonal rules. Finally, Americans prefer the "interest" model whereby parties exchange information on their interests, try to prioritize them, and trade off interests. Another dimension of conflict resolution is whether people tend to avoid or to directly confront conflict. Chinese managers tend to display conflict avoidance whereas Americans tend to develop a competing style. For IT2 negotiators, conflict is a threat to Relationship-Building. Moreover, negotiators who come from more traditional societies, where the dimension of social conservatism is high, tend to be more conflict averse.

Compatible and incompatible orientations in conflict resolution modes

Pruitt's Dual-Concern model may be considered as rather static because it takes into account the concerns of only one player. It also presents a cross-sectional, static view of conflict resolution modes with no moves from one mode to the other during the negotiation process. A "mirror effect" dynamically emerges between the concerns of both negotiators through their strategic orientations to conflict and possible responses to the other party's way of handling conflict (Saner, 2003, 2008).

Apparently incompatible positions in terms of strategies, orientations, and attitudes may lead negotiators to be both competitive and contending. Conflict escalation is likely, especially if they do not move to another position, a negotiator showing more benevolence and this benevolence being (in some way) reciprocated by the other party. Impasse is the likely outcome unless interdependence is so high that it is not a solution. Interdependence is indeed crucial in a bilateral dual concern model. When there is a mismatch (e.g., both being competitive), low levels of interdependence will lead to impasse and exit of either negotiator, while high interdependence will oblige players to move either to a collaborative/problem-solving attitude or to an accommodative/yielding position with a suboptimal arrangement as the outcome and the competitive negotiator winning over the accommodative negotiator.

If both negotiators jointly solve problems this is more difficult to reach in ICBN than in domestic negotiations. If negotiators A and B are avoidant, a consequence of low concern for both their own and the other party's outcomes, they will exit and return to the market if it offers alternatives (see Table 1.5). If both negotiators are accommodative/yielding, cooperative but not assertive, more interested in the other party's outcomes than in their own outcome (possible however rare in business negotiations), there will be little of the positive type of conflict which leads to value creation. Negotiator A's likely outcome will be low joint gains because of a poor exploration of alternatives, and low value creation but a fair division of joint gains. If A or B are accommodative/yielding (cooperative but not assertive), when the other party is collaborative, low levels of conflict will possibly lead to suboptimal joint gains with a winner advantage for the problem-solving party. Avoidant/inactive negotiators faced with collaborative partners will reach a suboptimal arrangement, the avoidant negotiator may withdraw unless persuaded by the collaborative partner not to do so. Finally, avoidant/inactive negotiators faced with accommodative/yielding partners could end with low joint gains, provided that the avoidant/inactive negotiator has not chosen to exit.

There are many bilateral dynamic moves over the negotiation process. Positions may change as the negotiation proceeds and favourably develops. That is why positional negotiation (i.e., sticking to one's position) is poor in terms of maximizing joint outcomes. Inflexibly sticking to a particular position may lead to impasse, deadlocks, exit of one party, joint decision to breach the negotiation, or low joint outcomes due to poor exploration and problem resolution.

Reciprocity, trust, and loyalty

There are three main non-deal related, in fact relationship-centred, ways of curbing opportunism. The deal-related way is to write detailed and – as much as possible – complete and future-oriented contracts and establish ways and means to observe and verify what the other side is actually doing or planning to do, in particular whether they accurately comply with their contractual obligations including quantity, quality, and time. The three non-deal levers for curbing opportunism are: reciprocity, trust, and loyalty.

Reciprocity

Reciprocity is based on successive moves of give and take, rather than taking without giving (i.e., defection). In Chapter 1, the OCR-ACR model offered a good illustration of what *relational reciprocity* is. The OCR (obligational contractual relationship) is based on reciprocated goodwill, favours that need to be reciprocated at some point in time, following comparable benevolence of the other party in previous deals. Reciprocity is a major force in sustaining social norms,[20] it provides a self-sustaining base when applied to economic exchange,[21] and preference for reciprocity can survive under certain conditions even in a population partly composed of opportunists.[22]

It is central in maintaining bilateral reciprocal behaviour that expectations of reciprocal behaviour after a "give" move are met as a basis for curbing opportunistic behaviour. Disillusion when the other party stops the virtuous circle of bilateral, successive reciprocal moves, may damage the relationship. We envisage here the most frequent form, positive reciprocity, where kindness is reciprocated with kindness. However, there are also other forms such as negative reciprocity.[23]

Negative reciprocity (often called strong reciprocity when it is combined with positive reciprocity, forming a "carrot and stick" incentive system) is a costly, unpleasant, and uncertain relational position. It not only requires the sense of feeling blurred, but it also involves negative emotions towards the other party that go beyond the rational. Negotiator A invests in the punishment (e.g., by seriously threatening to withdraw) of negotiator B who did not reciprocate contrary to expectations, or even who demonstrated blatant opportunism. It may be costly for negotiator A, especially in terms of the opportunity cost of the aborted deal; however, negotiator A expects a much larger loss for negotiator B who will probably consider the potential penalty as a reason for changing his or her behaviour towards A. Negative reciprocity may lead to escalation, to exit, or to put the rebuilding of the relationship before deal-related concerns. Prisons are a social and institutional example of negative reciprocity. It costs society, but much more so to the jailed person who is deprived of his or her freedom. Many conflict situations in interpersonal relationships are based on escalating negative reciprocity, for example by depriving oneself of a beloved joint possession, somehow punishing oneself, however hoping that this loss will be much more bitterly resented by the other.

Trust

Trust is neither necessary nor sufficient to reach success in ICBN. It is simply *very useful* and present in a myriad of circumstances in everyday life. No-trust solutions are perfectly feasible (e.g., letters of credit for payments in international trade contracts), especially with trusted intermediaries such as two banks each being trusted by the party they represent and banks being bound by ICC (International Chamber of Commerce) rules for documentary credit.

The no-trust solution (pure deal, IT1 paradigm) involves no relational expectations, no illusions, only rational expectations that the system in which control is substituted by trust will work. And it does work in practice in many cases. Even the worst possible case can be used as the highest probability scenario (e.g., worst case scenario probability tending towards 1) if relying mostly on the relationship (which may be non-existent or fake). No-trust also means no built-in mistrust or distrust, but a state of alert, watchfulness, awareness, and vigilance. This no-trust orientation should be used especially:

- In first ICBN business encounters and first deal ever with a particular trading partner.
- When there is a large potential for opportunistic behaviour, for example taking the goods shipped to a faraway port and not paying for some reason.
- When there is large information asymmetry in ICBN.
- When the partner who is in a position to behave opportunistically is in a fragile national context (weak in terms of political stability, World Competitiveness Report (WCR), and Human Development Index (HDI) indicators, etc.).

Trust is, however, very useful because it 1) reduces the emergence of conflicts, 2) lessens the severity of conflicts when they emerge, 3) sets limits to conflict escalation, and 4) may help in fostering conflict resolution. It also reduces transaction costs, because trusted intermediaries or sophisticated and complex contractual documents are no longer necessary. It also eases the post-agreement implementation of contracts, helps parties face unforeseen events, and curbs cultural misunderstandings to the extent that both parties are less "paranoid" on what they could interpret as faulty actions and intentional misbehaviour from the other side. A distinction can be made between macro-level trust (i.e., broad confidence in a country's institutional, legal, and social system) and micro-trust (in a particular business partner). When macro-trust is low in an unstable and hostile national environment, the need for building an IT2 trusting relationship through negotiation with a reliable local partner is important.[24]

A definition of trust

Trusting behaviour may be defined as action that 1) increases a *trustor*'s vulnerability vis-à-vis a *trustee* whose behaviour is not fully under the trustor's control; and 2) takes place in a situation where the penalty arising from trust being abused leads the trustor to regret the action.[25] Since trusting is about making oneself vulnerable, negotiators should avoid trusting, when not obliged to trust. Trust needs therefore to be based on firm ground: social norms of reciprocity are one of the key explanations why economic actors accept to engage as trustors, despite the risk associated with the opportunistic self-interest of trusted counterparts. The level of trusting behaviour varies cross-culturally (Willinger et al., 2003).

Trust as a fragile asset

Given the role of trusting relationships in limiting opportunistic behaviour, trust is unanimously considered an economic asset in business negotiations. Behaviour in trust games is overwhelmingly considered as a manifestation of the expectation of trusting and reciprocal behaviour: people in general, including negotiators, trust counterparts because they expect that their benevolent behaviour will be reciprocated.[26] However, trust is not only based on shared calculated reciprocal moves over time. It is not what rational IT1 negotiators believe it to be, an emergent property of bilateral compliant behaviour vis-à-vis contract rules. Trust is fragile and needs to be constantly nurtured, cultivated, verified, reprogrammed, repaired, and revamped. Trust is difficult to reach, takes time and effort to build, and is unfortunately easy to destroy. Antonyms such as mistrust and distrust are inseparable from trust.

Trust acts as a lubricant, a facilitating social device in negotiations, particularly in ICBN. However, it is a fragile asset that can be easily damaged, possibly destroyed, by the breach of promises and by opportunistic actions, or by major misunderstandings. When Volvo and Renault wanted to merge in the 1990s, after a long manufacturing collaboration, the final agreement aborted because of the refusal of Volvo's pension fund to accept a golden share for the French public authorities as dominant shareholder. Renault went afterwards in a quite balanced and successful alliance with – at the time ailing – Nissan. In 2017, the Nissan-Renault alliance became the major car manufacturer worldwide.

Trust is simultaneously developed and taken advantage of in micro-moves during the negotiation process. Disclosing private information may increase the trusting relationship and be an opportunity for both parties to start revealing their preferences and utilities in a relatively open manner, without being afraid of it. Often trust-building is normatively (and unilaterally) recommended as if it were a simple matter of benevolence and indulgence. This view of trust may result in lip-service benevolence, superficial empathy, deceptive reciprocal moves, and fake relationship development. The search for trust, followed by a sudden, complete, and abrupt breach of confidence may lead to such distrust/mistrust that it may be even worse than a no-trust situation.

Mistrust means to doubt or to lack confidence in a person, organization, etc. as in "I mistrust his ability to persuade our boss". Mistrust consists for instance in suspicion that the other party has a hidden agenda. Distrust should not be confused with mistrust. Distrust adds adverse expectations to mistrust, as in the sentence "Negotiator A distrusts Negotiator B because A thinks B will cheat him". Distrust is a formal way of not trusting the other party to avoid opportunistic behaviour and the associated risk. Systemic distrust precisely defines obligations and responsibility so that checks and balances can function. The phrase "trust but verify", readily applicable to negotiation, explicitly refers to distrust.

Key factors of trust and trust-based relationships

Three major areas for fostering trusting relationships, *predictability, controllability,* and *interdependence*, are presented in Table 3.2. *Predictability,* that is, being able to foresee, even imperfectly and with some uncertainty, the other party's behaviour and reactions, improves cooperation during micro-moves. Underlying the degree of *predictability* of a target of trust are three factors that are partly universal or can be related either to an IT1 deal and informative perspective or to an IT2 relational and subjective view. *Reputation* is based on objective information, published corporate accounts, audits, rankings, online reputation systems, and so on. It enables one to assess trustworthiness, at least in part. *Similarity* with the other party is based on shared characteristics, especially culture, nationality, language, etc. Such shared characteristics provide ICB negotiators with implicit, often unconscious, joint codes for interaction, in line with the IT2 relational para-digm. Belonging to the same ingroup affords moral links promoting benevo-lent cooperativeness, reciprocal behaviour, and goodwill which are assets in developing and maintaining trust. The third factor is based on the *his-tory of the relationship*. Previous interactions and transactions between the same negotiation partners provide for joint understanding as a basis for mutual trust. It is not only favourable past experiences that foster trust. Past transactions and their implementation may have been fraught with difficulties, complications, and conflicts. However, they (may) have been surmounted and a joint problem resolution capacity has emerged as a poten-tial asset for trusting relationships. In the absence of any relational history, and therefore in a first-time negotiation interaction, it will evidently be more difficult to build trust.

Trust does not preclude control. Paradoxically, *controlling* the other side may have a negative effect on trust due to the implied mistrust or distrust signal it sends, as well as a positive effect, especially in the long run, because it allows the negotiator to assess the partner's trustworthiness. Reciprocal, bilateral control through contract clauses allows observability and verifiability of compliance with precise contractual provisions.[27] Checking whether the other party has accurately fulfilled their obligation is typical of the IT1 doing orientation.

Some form of *Oath* ("my word is my bond") may also appear as a way to control the person who swears on a sacred book (e.g., the Bible, the Quran) or a beloved and respected relative. It is clearly an IT2 type control mech-anism with an ancient, Middle Ages-like background in which the sacred and the profane are not clearly separated. Taking an oath is still formally practised in court settings in Western countries with potentially negative consequences for those who are disloyal to their legal oath. In taking an oath there is an underlying transcendental claim, namely that some supernatural force (e.g., God, destiny, an immanent justice) will punish the betrayer who does not keep a promise. In closed and collusive groups, like the Mafia,[28] it may still be practised; however, only in association with the next control factor, potential *retaliation*.

Retaliation in a mob setting implies the hiring of paid killers and/or taking "hostages"; in a business setting, it is much more peaceful and licit, however in no way less efficient. "Hostages" can be, for instance, dedicated tools (e.g., a sophisticated mould) owned by an industrial company and used by a subcontractor to manufacture parts. Such tools can nevertheless be quickly withdrawn and placed at an alternative subcontracting company because of a lack of reliability on quality, delivery dates, etc. Retaliatory power (in the IT1 style) is built into any sort of contract clause that foresees financial consequences for the non-respect of commitments (e.g., delay penalties) A liquidated damages clause may specify an amount that will be payable as compensation in case of certain breaches of contract (e.g., delivery delay or failure to meet performance guarantees). Another example of non-violent retaliatory measures is to outlaw business persons who have gravely infringed their obligations, corresponding more to IT2.[29] This is possible within traditional ingroup-oriented business communities who retaliate against severe misbehaviour of group members by outlawing them, in a sort of collusive punishment decision. However, this ingroup self-justice is not practicable in most modern business settings which are global and open. Retaliation is only possible through courts, provided that the opportunistic move is unmistakeably against the law, can be documented and proven, and further chastised through a legal sanction.

Interdependence is the third area which influences trust, however in an ambiguous manner, having either a positive (+) or a negative (−) influence on trust. The first key factor (defined in Chapter 1) is the degree of *Concern for the other party's outcomes* (COPO), which is positively related to trust development and maintenance. Understandably, a decent COPO level fosters expectations of reciprocal behaviour and therefore trust. A second positive factor for trust building is the *Perception of joint utility* (+), said differently a subjective assessment of the degree of overlap between each party's interests as well as of the potential for creating value by trading-off items which present different utility levels for both sides. The third factor (dependence asymmetry), that is, low interdependence (see above), can have a serious detrimental effect on trust if it is not managed from a relational perspective by the independent and powerful partner who, however, may need the dependent and relatively powerless partner in the long run, for the sake of diversification and risk reduction.

Loyalty[30]

Loyalty as a moral principle and a relational pattern is contrary to the very nature of business, where flexibility in partnering and the search for the best possible deals is seen as a requisite for survival and profit. This applies to business negotiation in which the consideration of a BATNA and walk-away options are the complete opposite of loyalty. Pure, absolute, loyalty often involves a strong element of vertical, hierarchical, interaction. Loyalty is not in the nature of business because it is at odds with the flexible, egalitarian, and horizontal nature of business behaviour and interactions. Pure loyalty emerges only marginally and it may be only lip-service loyalty. Pye (1986) mentions

Table 3.2 Key factors fostering trust-based relationships

Control area	Factors fostering (or/and damaging) trust-based relationships	Related to...
Predictability	Reputation	IT1
	Similarity: belongingness, moral links, ingroup bonds	IT2
	History of relationships/previous interactions	Universal
Controllability	Contract (observability, verifiability)	IT1 – doing
	Oath ("my word is my bond")	IT2 – being
	Retaliation ("hostages"; outlawing infringers; penalties)	IT1 and IT2
Interdependence	Interest for the other party's outcomes (+)	Universal
	Perception that utility is conjoint (+)	Universal
	Dependence asymmetry, low (–) or high (+)	Universal

the case of Chinese pre-1949 agents of U.S. firms who contacted them after more than 40 years to remind U.S. companies that they still represented them. A competitive market background (i.e., high levels of economic rivalry with many players on both sides) virtually excludes loyalty, because exit options become attractive and plentiful. Loyalty is not really possible except if negotiation partners accept to isolate themselves – at least provisionally – to form a cooperative venture, which remains out-of-market as long as trust and benefits related to exclusive partnerships (e.g., little or no transaction costs, higher social capital) overpower the search for an outside solution.

If loyalty exists in business relationships, it is rarely statutory loyalty, but a "principled loyalty" constantly cared for and nurtured by long-term oriented and highly interdependent business partners. However, loyalty exists in some business relationships, for instance in *single source* procurement (i.e., the supplier and customer are exclusive partners for a particular item, task, and/or service), frequently found in the B2B domain. The Smart vehicles are produced by Daimler-Benz in an integrated factory site where *single source* parts manufacturers have their own dedicated production facilities around the central assembly line of Daimler-Benz. Similar relational designs can be found in other industries such as aerospace and chemicals. Loyalty is then driven by high interdependence, accepted bilateral *lock-in* effects, and the high withdrawal cost for both parties. Many small, often informal negotiations take place within the OCR model presented in Chapter 1. An important ICBN issue is whether loyalty is possible between strangers/foreigners; that is, companies from different cultural and national backgrounds. Both a deal-based approach with many repeated interactions over time, assumed interdependence, and a shared relational conflict-resolution culture may lead global companies to learn to be loyal because it pays (in economic Deal terms) and it is more comfortable (as far as the Relationship is concerned).

Both exit and loyalty are culturally coded in several ways. Exit (i.e., activating one's BATNA) is IT1-coded, not because of the breach in negotiations, which remains possible in any case, but because the exit option is strongly and coldly valued in the IT1 paradigm, just because the best out-of-negotiation alternative happens to be apparently superior to all alternatives considered within the negotiation process. Exit is decided irrespective of the loss in relational assets. Conversely, loyalty as a relational pattern is strongly related to social ties valued by the IT2 paradigm, to the extent that a concept like the BATNA may not sound very appealing to Far East Asians as it seems to encourage negotiators to choose divorce and separation. Negotiation in-between *exit* and *loyalty* appears as the "*Voice*" solution in Hirschman's terms.

Dispute resolution in ICBN

Disputes: A mix of interest divergence and relational conflict

Rights and claims are a central element of disputes, whereas power is potentially more situated in the conflict domain. Deal-oriented dispute resolution is built on a precise (low-context) confrontation of arguments by both sides. IT1 dispute resolution is also interests centred, with privileged routes being exit, third party intervention (e.g., arbitration), and litigation in courts. Conversely, relationship-oriented dispute resolution mechanisms are based on high (sometimes too high) expectations that relational assets will help overcome the dispute and find a mutually beneficial solution. Priority is on repairing the damaged relationship with interests and deal-related debates coming later when the relationship has been improved. Communication styles matter in dispute resolution mechanisms (see Chapter 5).

On the other hand *Relational conflicts* have to do with people and groups of people (organizations) and the clash between their identity characteristics (e.g., nationality, language, personality, gender, profession, see Chapter 6). Relational conflicts are evidenced by non-courteous and in fact non-rational attacks (insults, verbal abuse, and foul language). Symbolically assaulting the other party is the epitome of relational conflicts, especially by challenging their competence, honesty, education, etc.[31]

Often, negotiators, although they would never acknowledge it, feel threatened in their own identity by symbolic assaults from the other side's negotiators, their self-concept, self-esteem, and self-love being challenged. It is largely a subjective extension of interest divergence. Little by little, relational conflicts become partly secluded from objective interest divergence. Conflict escalation, judgement biases, a progressive drift from rational, lucid, and balanced assessment, may result in people trying to punish the other side, even at a cost for them, possibly accepting a lose-lose negotiation. Negotiators may indulge in negative reciprocity, feeling elation at the very prospect that the other side will be punished by losing (supposedly) much more than themselves. Litigation is related to relational conflicts. Escalation in relational conflicts explain why some negotiations end up in revenge seeking, especially in the case of high interdependence, low trust, and negative reciprocity being used on both sides.

As emphasized by Bazerman et al. (2000, p. 297) cross-cultural negotiation research has provided data,

> consistent with the generalization that members of individualist cultures are more likely to handle conflicts directly through competition and problem-solving, whereas members of collectivist cultures are more likely to handle conflict in indirect ways that attempt to preserve the relationship.

Archetypical situation at the boundary of interest divergence and relational conflict

In Table 3.3 we describe four archetypical situations at the boundary of deal-related interests divergence and relational conflict. They are some sort of critical incident, illustrated by examples. Each cell has a suggestive label followed by a question mark. Each archetypical situation tends to progress in the label's direction (e.g., towards a "Deceitful Paradise"), however not inevitably (thus the question mark in each cell). Corrective remedies can be implemented.

A global firm has had a successful and smooth agency relationship with a foreign agent in a local market for years. A high level of deal and relational satisfaction can be observed on both sides. However, the principal, a multinational company, changes its internationalization strategy to fully owned subsidiaries. The relational conflict remains low, possibly non-existent; however the parties have moved from low to high ID. It may also be possible that the local agent will become quite angry, feel betrayed after years of loyal behaviour to the MNF, and a relational conflict will escalate and become high. This is an illustration from moving first from a Deceitful Paradise to a Peaceful Deadlock, and then to a Fertile Inferno, fertile only if remedies are brought.

Table 3.3 Negotiation scenarios combining interest divergence and relational conflict

Relational conflict (RC)	Interest divergence (ID)	
	Low	*High*
Low	1 Deceitful Paradise?	2 Peaceful Deadlock?
High	3 Useless Confusion?	4 Fertile Inferno?

1. Deceitful Paradise?

It seems to be a paradise, an ideal negotiation setting in which there is little ID as well as relational conflict (RC). It can however be misleading, because too much compromise and accommodation, that is, suboptimal solutions/ agreements, may result from overly relaxed exploration of joint solutions whereas problem-solving requires a certain degree of engagement and clash. IJV negotiations in their early phase (or any negotiation with little or no past relational history) display low levels of both ID and RC, with much future orientation. Harsher debates on conflicting goals, resource commitment, implementation and joint IJV management will come later in the post-agreement phase, which may typically degenerate into a *Deceitful Paradise*. What can be done in such a situation? Why is it that ID seems at first so low? The first step is to jointly re-evaluate hard facts behind ID. ID may be underestimated because of a lack of consideration by one or both sides of their own interests (low concern for one's own outcomes in Pruitt's terms). Why is it that RC seems so low? The second step is to jointly re-evaluate RC. Both negotiation camps may be conflict-avoidant (partly a cultural characteristic; see Saner and Yiu (1993) on Swiss conflict-avoidant negotiation style) and reluctant to "play their conflict" properly and resolve it.

2. Peaceful Deadlock?

In this ICBN scenario, interest divergence is high, however relational conflict is low. There is a risk of quietly walking away, exiting, without much consideration for what could have been quite a profitable deal for both parties. The negotiation centres on interests and rights while power is underemphasized. A good example of a potential *Peaceful Deadlock* is one-shot international sales contracts, with a strong market background. Such negotiations may be strongly bargaining oriented, rather short-term, non-relational for both sides therefore with low RC. Exit is the most likely solution if a quick agreement, favourable for the powerful partner, is not reached with low transaction costs.

How can this be resolved? *Peaceful Deadlocks* are typical IT1 scenarios. A little suffusion of IT2 style may prove beneficial with some low-cost relational investment (e.g., face-to-face Skype communication) to establish personal rapport. Alternatively, it is also possible to use a non-conflictual relationship to explore IDs, tone them down, and argue about differentiation to escape the trap of selling mere commodities.

3. Useless Confusion?

International sales contracts that are potentially profitable for both sides, albeit with a high relational conflict, are an illustration of the *Useless Confusion* scenario. The conflict rather than being related to ID which is low is due to RC, a lack of affinity and fit between partners, as well as cultural misunderstandings. The market background is a global bilateral oligopoly for highly specialized technological components, and the negotiation partners are long-term oriented and interdependent. In this scenario, interest divergence is low. This would logically command a quick and satisfactory agreement for both sides. However, relational conflict is excessive, overdone, often starting from a lack of personal affinities or large cultural differences, and the emphasis on the relationship is too high. In the example above, it could be that long-term partners face an unexpected and unforeseen negative event creating a harsh present conflict. Trust seems to be broken; conflict escalation takes places mostly because of RC. Finally, negotiators part ways despite first-rate past and future deals. The moral of the story: Overemphasis on relationships may create confusion.

What can be done in such a situation? *Useless Confusion* is a typical IT2 scenario when intercultural communication and personal chemistry do not work. The general recommendation is then to be deal oriented, adopting an IT1 perspective. Go back to the basics and manage the relational aspects with a matter-of-fact, firm, however courteous and open style. De-escalate RC by showing or simply suggesting that parties follow a non-rational avenue and that there is much to be done to reach higher levels of joint outcomes. Mediation, conciliation, and third parties may help in *Useless Confusion* situations (see below).

4. Fertile Inferno?

The *Fertile Inferno* scenario can be illustrated by the case of a labour negotiation between a multinational mining company (MMC) and its local workers in a period of 1) deep depression of raw materials, ore, and metal prices, and 2) negotiation of a four-year collective labour agreement with employees as is usual in the mining industry. MMC has large inventories of ore and metal ready for sale. It has strategically increased its inventories to face a possible hard strike lasting up to four months. Mining employees have also prepared the confrontation by progressively creating a strike fund.[32] Negotiation has started however from widely divergent base positions on salary increases, work conditions, number of working hours per week, holidays, etc. In this scenario, both interest divergence and relational conflict are at their maximum, possibly leading to severe conflict escalation. Mining employees start a strike and establish pickets to bar non-striking workers belonging to the *"yellow"* union. The police intervene and there are violent skirmishes. Finally, MMC decides in favour of a lock-out and the site is provisionally at a standstill. After two weeks of semi-hostile confrontation, some talks restart and it takes an additional three months to reach a final four-year labour agreement.

The *Fertile Inferno* scenario may also correspond to a misbalanced deal (i.e., one negotiation partner is exploited by the other, taking most of the surplus, claiming a lion's share of the value created), with little or no socialization, due to lack of preliminaries in a first time encounter. In the *Fertile Inferno* scenario, both IT1 and IT2 matter and should be used as simultaneous conflict resolution paradigms. What to do? The advice here is to first repair the damaged relationship in order to rebuild minimal trust and empathy, then start joint problem-solving to reach an agreement on the deal.

Interpersonal and/or inter-organizational relationships and conflicts

Conflicts and disputes may be interpersonal, between individual negotiators and/or inter-organizational, between the companies looking for an agreement. Interpersonal conflicts are based on personality, lack of personal affinities, value divergence, and sometimes *cultural hostility* (examined in Chapter 6). Inter-organizational conflicts are of a different nature because actual interests, rights, and power are likely to be played in a more distant, rational, and strategic manner, top executives generally being experienced negotiators.

Organizations (represented by the CEO, a senior VP, or a team of top executives) most often give negotiation mandates to individual negotiators, who may be senior managers, however not in a position to close the deal without referring to their principals, that is, they negotiate *ad referendum*. Negotiation mandates consist in instructions on the deal, on aspiration levels, out-of-negotiation alternatives to be considered, and – possibly – recommendations to adopt a particular negotiation style. Mandated negotiators are supposed to follow instructions as much as possible because they are in a vertical (hierarchical) interaction with their principals. If they feel that one of their instructions is not going to be properly respected, mandated negotiators should refer to their principals for advice and further instructions. Relationships between organizations are in no way equivalent to those of the mandated negotiators. Possible situations range from no conflict between organizations but a harsh interpersonal conflict between their mandated negotiators (or the opposite situation) to conflicts at both interpersonal and inter-organizational levels. The interaction between mandated negotiators and the organization they represent is *vertical*, with a subordination link for the mandated negotiators vis-à-vis their organization.

Conversely, interactions between negotiators or an organization are *horizontal* interactions, between peers, non-hierarchical, between equals, with the caveat that power and dependence differentials may reduce the equality assumption. Figure 3.2 shows also that, in a few rare cases, there may be interactions and a relationship between a negotiator on one side and the organization on the other, for instance because he or she is a former employee and/or has already cooperated with them in the past. That is why, before starting any ICBN, it is worthwhile to search for the *geography* of

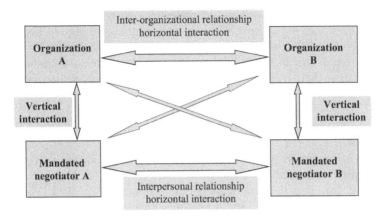

Figure 3.2 Organizations and mandated negotiators: Vertical and horizontal interactions

relationships between organizations and individual negotiators; that is investigate all six possible bilateral contacts, even if simply to conclude that they are non-existent.

Third parties and alternative dispute resolution (ADR)

Third parties can be brought to the negotiation table, provided that both parties agree on their presence, their potential contribution to the process, as well as their compensation (e.g., who pays for the service delivered by third parties? Which party do they serve and/or represent?) The first third party category provides the parties with technological expertise (e.g., experts, especially technical experts), legal counselling (e.g., lawyers), and/or support for overcoming language and communication barriers (e.g., interpreters/translators) in multi-lingual business negotiations. Technical, scientific experts are sometimes brought to the negotiation table to help parties fix some facts (e.g., assess the value and/or the implementability of a technology) as well as consultants especially for auditing facilities or accounts in acquiring a company. Their real skills, impartiality, possible conflicts of interest, as well their attitude to confidentiality issues must be thoroughly checked and monitored.

The second type of third party category is directly involved in various aspects of the negotiation process, in what is often referred to with the acronym ADR, that is, alternative dispute resolution (see Chapter 7).[33] Sometimes conflict is so harsh between the parties that some people on each side do not want to talk to each other. Going back to the negotiation table provisionally seems very difficult because the conflict is overplayed. Different types of facilitating third parties may be introduced.

Conciliator – Conciliators enter the scene when parties do not talk to each other and/or they are both aware that the negotiation cannot proceed without outside intervention. The conciliator, the weakest form of ADR third party, first meets with both parties separately. She tries to have the parties start or restart a negotiation process when only one party is ready to negotiate and the other party is not. She may, in an effort to resolve their conflict, discuss and suggest possible solutions.

Mediator – Mediation is a form of ADR that goes beyond mere conciliation, since the mediator actively assists the parties in negotiating a settlement to their dispute. However, a mediator is not like a judge: She cannot impose a solution on the parties. Mediators go beyond conciliation and make formal offers to both parties, helping them to explore win-win alternatives and suggest possible bilateral concessions to reach agreement, if possible. Mediation is frequent in small-stakes, domestic, non-business negotiation, however rare in ICBN.

An *Arbiter* is nearer to a judge; however, arbitration is a private, out of court ADR. The parties decide in advance that arbitration will lead to an award with which they agree to fully comply, even if it does not correspond with their expectations. Contrary to conciliation and meditation, which are used generally for domestic and small size dispute resolution, arbitration is a well-established and widely used means to end disputes in international business. Arbitration clauses are often included in contracts negotiated at an international level, with different arbitration bodies, the most well-known being the ICC.[34] Most countries have signed and ratified an international convention on the recognition of arbitration sentences by local courts. The enforcement of arbitration decisions is therefore not an issue. The cost of arbitration is relatively high and is sometimes a useful limitation for a company willing to enter an arbitrage procedure. Often, companies, rather than entering in costly out-of-court litigation prefer to negotiate a settlement of the dispute on an amicable basis.

The most frequently used ADR method in ICBN is arbitration. Arbitrators make the final decision if parties cannot reach an agreement but have agreed for the arbitrator to settle in their names. Arbitrators generally start with a conciliation phase, and, if unsuccessful analyse the case from a legal standpoint, however introducing the pragmatic view of balancing obligations and benefits for both parties (in the style of the old British *remedies of equity*).

Two other types of third parties must be mentioned: observers and agents. It is rare for neutral, non-participant observers such as academics, journalists, and the media in general to be invited to attend negotiation sessions. The private and confidential aspect of business negotiations precludes such involvement unless the benefits are obvious and they are indeed rarely clear. Agents and any form of business intermediaries can be invited to participate in some way in the negotiation. However they have their own interests which they bring to the negotiation table with much ambiguity. Imagine a large real-estate deal, where the real estate agent is present, recruited and paid by the seller. It may be in the vested interest of the real estate agent to support the claims of the buyer for a price discount, because the deal will be closed very quickly, minimizing his or her workload and therefore maximizing the return. This may be true, even if he or she separately negotiates a lower fee with the seller. Agents and intermediaries never represent a party but themselves. The general issue before introducing third parties is, which side does a third party represent, beyond the fallacy of being paid by and actually serving an organization, and beyond the ostensible helpfulness and dedication towards that organization (see Chapter 7).

Conclusion

To sum up, at the "atomic level" negotiation is composed of a series of – often unnoticed – micro-move dilemmas about whether to cooperate or to defect. These dilemmas, when poorly managed by one or both sides may further aggregate into relational and/or deal conflicts, in which cultural differences increase the risk of misunderstandings leading finally to conflict escalation. Conflicts *per se* are not good or bad; they are the very nature of negotiation and conflict/dispute resolution is its *raison d'être*. The level of opportunism is related to a combination of interdependence and interest divergence. Some generic relational strategies (reciprocity, trust, and loyalty) as well as a more general concern with the relationship can curb opportunism at the interface between deal and relationship through dispute resolution approaches which blend the IT1 and IT2 paradigms.

Notes

1 On conflict and disputes in construction contracts see Fenn et al. (1997).
2 See Lytle et al. (1999) on the strategic use of interests, rights, and power to resolve disputes.
3 Despite the very useful distinction between interests, rights, and power, there are significant overlaps between the three categories (see Chapter 8).
4 See Usunier (2011) and Usunier et al. (2017) on the role of language in cross-cultural business research.
5 Online B2B marketplaces enable companies to get electronic access to global markets and promote their products and services globally by posting product offers and reaching customers worldwide. See Myler (2016).
6 For more information about this successful partnership of more than 40 years, see www.cfmaeroengines.com/press-articles/safran-and-ge-celebrate-40-year-partnership/
7 Van Zandt (1970) shows that intercultural negotiations between Americans and Japanese are six times as long and three times as difficult as intracultural negotiations between Americans.
8 On how behavioural interdependence and social exchange interact, see Scanzoni (1979).
9 See Jones and Lim (2012).

10 Williamson (1975, p. 255); see also Hodgson (2004).

11 Etymologically, conflict comes from the Latin verb *confligere*, derived in the early 15th century from the Latin *conflictus*, past participle of *confligere*, meaning "to strike together".

12 On conflict handling styles and conflict avoidance, see Pruitt and Rubin (1986), Kirkbride et al. (1991) for China; Thomas (1992), Pinkley and Northcraft (1994), Elsayed-EkJiouly and Buda (1996) for the Middle East; Morris et al. (1998) comparing the US, China, India, and the Philippines; Kozan and Ergin (1999) about Turkey and the UK (2010); for an illustration of the Swiss conflict-avoidant style, see Saner and Yiu (1993).

13 See Kumar (2004) and Barry, Smithey Fulmer, and Van Kleef (2004).

14 See Kumar (1997).

15 The limits of game theory should however be noted, especially for ICBN. See Sebenius (1992), about challenging conventional explanations of international cooperation and epistemic communities.

16 On the influence of culture on cooperation in the prisoner's dilemma, see Wong and Hong (2005); on experiments in 15 small-scale societies using other experimental games (ultimatum, dictator, public goods), see Henrich et al. (2005).

17 See Axelrod (1984).

18 See Kolb and Williams (2004).

19 For a detailed presentation of alternative dispute resolution, in particular arbitration, see Rudd and Lawson (2007, pp. 207–222). They are also briefly summarized in this chapter.

20 Fehr and Gächter (2000).

21 Kranton (1996).

22 Guttmann (2000).

23 See Fehr and Gächter (2000). Gächter and Herrmann. (2009).

24 See Grayson et al. (2008) on micro versus macro-trust. Macro-trust in a national environment can be assessed through the *Global Competitiveness Report* indicators. See: www.weforum.org/reports/the-global-competitiveness-report-2017-2018.

25 Lorenz (1988, p. 197). Vulnerability should be understood as involving both opportunist and non-opportunist actions of actor B (*trustee*) which bear negative consequences for A (*trustor*), especially in case of incompetence.

26 The level of trusting behaviour differs cross-nationally. It is measured either through question 24 in the *World Value Survey* (Inglehart, 2004); that is, "Generally speaking, would you say that most people can be trusted or that you need to be very careful in dealing with people?". Trust scores are based on the percentage answering "yes" to this question (for national scores of trust see: www.worldvaluessurvey.org/WVSDocumentationWVL.jsp). Another avenue for measuring trust levels is the investment game (Berg et al., 1995). Northern Europeans for instance have been shown to trust more and to be more trusted than Southern Europeans (Brülhart and Usunier, 2004). Only small differences in trust levels have been observed among Chinese, Korean, Japanese and U.S. subjects (Buchan et al., 2002; Buchan et al., 2006). Trusting others and being considered as trustworthy are two different issues: Fershtman and Gneezy (2001) have shown for instance that Ashkenazic Israelis were considered significantly more trustworthy (i.e., better trustees) by both Ashkenazic and Sepharad

Israelis. Trust has been shown to be based on rational expectations of reciprocal behavior and not mere altruism (Brülhart and Usunier (2012).

27 On observability and verifiability, see Brooks (2015).

28 See Gambetta (1988) and Bigoni et al. (2016).

29 See Greif (1994) on an historical comparison of trust regulated by loyalty to the group (the Tunisian Maghribi merchants) versus an open trust generating system based on contracts and the possible intervention of third parties (the Genoese merchants).

30 We use here the concepts of Albert O. Hirschman (1970) in *Exit, Voice, and Loyalty.*

31 Reactions will differ in affective vs. neutral cultures (Trompenaars, 1993).

32 A strike fund is a reserve set up by a union ahead of time to provide strike pay or for other strike-related activities.

33 On ADR, see Carnevale et al. (2004), Maude (2014, pp. 264–276), and the report on dispute resolution of HBS-PON (2012) accessible at www.pon.harvard.edu.

34 For ICC standard arbitration clauses, see: www.iccwbo.org/products-and-services/arbitration-and-adr/arbitration/standard-icc-arbitration-clauses.

4 Cultural time orientations in negotiation

Time is money.

(English proverb)

Let the plum tree wither in place of the peach tree.
(Chinese Stratagem 11, meaning "sacrifice short-term
objectives to the long-term goal")

Herb Cohen recounts a negotiation with Japanese business partners:

> Instead of beginning negotiations right away, they first had me experience Japanese hospitality and culture. For more than a week I toured the country from the Imperial Palace to the shrines of Kyoto. ... Every evening for four and a half hours, they had me sit on a cushion on a hardwood floor for a traditional dinner and entertainment. Can you imagine what it's like sitting on a hardwood floor for all those hours? ... Whenever I inquired about the start of the negotiations, they'd murmur, "Plenty of time! Plenty of time!"
>
> Cohen (1980, p. 94)

Time-based misunderstandings in international business is a classic topic which has drawn much attention and given rise to a lot of anecdotes, most of them relating to appointments, punctuality, and the diverse concepts of time-related courtesy across cultures. Synchronization is always difficult; even when the basic time codes seem to be shared by people or by organizations, there still may be some significant variations related to the particular time systems of individuals, or the specific temporal cultures of organizations. Complex negotiation, such as in the case of international turnkey operations, requires a synchronization process which is heavily loaded with precise, linear time; meeting the dates is strongly emphasized and delay penalties are assigned to lateness in the realization phase.

Among all the dimensions of culture which have a significant but almost invisible impact on business negotiations, time patterns are probably the strongest. Time illustrates the invisible nature of culture particularly well: business negotiators wear watches, use a planner, and agree that it is standard practice to fix dates and deadlines; that is, they seemingly share common beliefs about time management. Yet, beyond this apparent uniformity, they behave quite differently in terms of planning and scheduling tasks. In fact, time permeates the whole of business negotiation, both the starting phase and the process, and finally also the outcome of the negotiation, at least in terms of durability of the business relationship. Taking time explicitly into account in international business negotiations makes all the more sense when one realizes that there are differences in the representation of time and how the patterning of time consistently differs across cultures. As the example from Cohen shows, there are substantial differences in the very beginning of business negotiations, and that is why use of time in the starting phase is dealt with: getting to know each other, scheduling the process and making appointments. The negotiation process itself involves a series of tasks that are either directly time-related (planning tasks for instance) or are embedded in time, such as time pressure in the bargaining process which may result in one party unnecessarily yielding for reasons of perceived time pressure. When discussing substantive clauses dealing with plant construction or common operations, the partners plan, define dates and deadlines, and possibly set delay penalties. This chapter explains how this common planning process is often flawed by the uneven temporal cultures of the partners, sometimes making the negotiation of common planning an illusion rather than a reality. Time may also be viewed as an outcome of the negotiation; interpretations vary as to the extent to which the signing of a contract is seen as actually concluding the negotiation process. Finally, advice is offered for using time shrewdly in international business negotiations. Although examples in this chapter are taken from a great many countries and cultures, the major contrast is between Western temporal models (linear, economic time), mostly those of Americans and Northern Europeans, and Eastern Asian time patterns (cyclical-integrated time), especially Chinese and Japanese, as East Asian nations are now obvious challengers of the Westerners in terms of business efficacy, given their rise in world trade.

The influence of time on intercultural business negotiations

An isolated round of negotiation for selling aircraft can take place over some months (the negotiation time itself); several such "rounds" may be necessary for signing a particular contract between an airline and a plane manufacturer that will extend over the next five years, including maintenance and possible change for a new version of the plane (venture time). These two time frames are generally embedded in a much longer relationship between the airline and the aircraft company, which may have been continuous over the last 25 years (time frame of the exchange relationship). Time aspects of negotiation have their initial basis in the actors: How long will they negotiate, from start to finish? Will they participate up to implementation? What

Table 4.1 Time in intercultural business negotiations

Starting the negotiation	Time for preliminaries (getting to know each other)
	Setting the agenda/scheduling the negotiation process
Time in the negotiation process	Making appointments and setting deadlines
	Managing temporal clash in ICBNs
	Temporal clashes between negotiating organizations
	Time pressure in the bargaining process
	Timing of concessions
Relationship time frame	Long-term orientation favouring an integrative orientation
	Making plans together: planning construction and resources; dealing with deadlines and delays
	Discrepancies in the partners' temporal cultures
Time as an outcome variable	Relationship versus deal: continuous versus discontinuous view of time
	Written agreements as a timeline for negotiation

is their own cultural background as far as time is concerned? How does the negotiation fit with their personal agenda, as individuals and as members of organizations, with their degree of occupation and the possible scarcity of their individual time? Time is related to *the structure of negotiation*: parties may set a common agenda, plan and organize negotiation on the base of precise time schedules or, on the contrary, they may prefer an informal style of negotiation in which time is seen as a constraint rather than a key resource. Time may also influence *negotiation strategies* in as much as future orientation seems a prerequisite for developing an integrative strategy. Time works also as a *process variable*, influencing negotiation phases, the appointments between the parties, and the rhythm of negotiation, its pace, speed, and its rituals. Finally, time is embedded in the kind of outcomes sought by the parties, whether a deal, with strict time boundaries, or a relationship which is hoped to extend into the long term. Table 4.1 presents the different aspects of time which must be considered in international business negotiations when they involve people from different cultural backgrounds.

A temporal framework involves three separate categories with a set of interrelationships between these categories: conceptions of time (based mostly on culture), mapping activities to time (related to both situations and tasks), and actors relating to time (i.e., their individual beliefs, behaviour, and adjustment).[1] Time management in international business negotiations is a complex issue as shown in Figure 4.1. First, time is both a process and an outcome variable. Second, individual negotiators have their own attitudes to time and time management which result from their personality traits.[2] Last, negotiators belong to particular national/cultural groups in which they have been educated; consequently, they have developed a view of what time *is* and how it should be managed in terms of *synchronization with others* in the native group. Synchronization, which from the

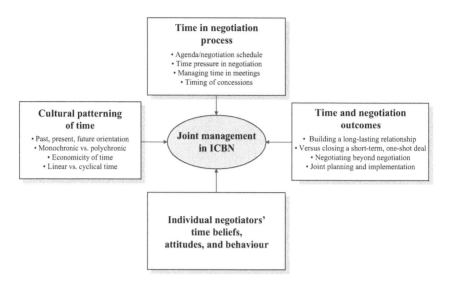

Figure 4.1 Determinants of time management in ICBN

Greek means developing a common time frame, is the key learning process through which people develop beliefs, attitudes, and behaviours related to time management. In negotiators' native cultures, there are modal beliefs and behaviour as to setting dates, dealing with delays, and managing time in meetings. Time-loaded negotiation activities display both cultural and individual variability and they are influenced by situational variables in the negotiation process, such as the amount of time available for talks or some inescapable deadline (e.g., the date of the opening ceremony for the Olympic Games).

The next section insists on cross-cultural differences in time patterns. However, it should always be kept in mind that there are also individual and situational determinants of negotiators' time. For example, an American negotiator whose cultural background emphasizes time scarcity, may nevertheless display patience and a sense of timelessness, if he or she has plenty of time available and the company has not put him or her under pressure to close the deal promptly.

Cross-cultural differences in the patterning of time

Most business concepts are time-based: actualization, investment choice, product life cycle, sales forecasting, or the planning of new product launches, to name but a few. Normative time in marketing and management seems indisputable, and its very nature is rarely questioned: it is perceived as linear, continuous, and economic. However, time, in a cross-cultural perspective, is probably the area where differences are both the largest and the most difficult to pinpoint, because assumptions are very deep-seated; and formally, we adopt a common model of time. People's relationship with time changes with respect to periods of history and the level of human development, according to the technology available for measuring time, to the emphasis given to natural and social rhythms, and to the prevailing metaphysical views. Each vision of time (*Zeitanschauung*) corresponds to a vision of the real world, its origins, and destiny (*Weltanschauung*). Time manifests itself prominently through its social functions in that it allows people to have a common organization of activities and helps to synchronize individual human behaviour. Encyclopaedic approaches to the concept of time show that never has one time pattern eliminated a previous one. Each new time pattern superimposes itself on the one that previously prevailed. As a consequence, individual time perceptions may result from adding or mixing different basic patterns of time. Most of the literature in cultural anthropology considers time perceptions as cultural artefacts.

Dimensions of time orientations

Table 4.2 shows time-related cultural assumptions, which correspond to four common problems:

1) To what extent should time be regarded as a tangible commodity (economicity of time)?
2) How should tasks and time be combined? (Monochronic versus polychronic use of time).
3) Should time be seen as a single continuous line or as combining multiple cyclical episodes? (Linearity versus cyclicity of time)
4) What are the appropriate temporal orientations: towards the past, the present, and the future?

There is some overlap between the prevailing solutions to these four questions. However, the four basic time assumptions need to be considered in order to acquire a substantive view of what is a cultural model of time (e.g., the Japanese *Makimono* time in Figure 4.2).

Economicity of time

Time may be seen as external to us and, as such, be treated like a tangible commodity. The concept of economic time is based on accurate time reckoning, dependent on precise dating and defined duration. It results in people trying to use their time as wisely as possible, scheduling, establishing timetables and deadlines. Measurement of parking meter time by units of 7.5 minutes or sport performance in hundredths of a second is typical of economic time being precisely measured and bearing direct and explicit financial

Table 4.2 Time-related cultural differences

Basic problem/Cultural orientations	Contrasts across cultures
Is time money? (a) Economicity of time (tangible time)	Time is regarded as a scarce resource or, conversely, as plentiful and indefinitely available.
How to schedule tasks (b) Monochronism versus polychronism	Only one task is undertaken at any (preset) time, following a schedule ("agenda society"), versus dealing simultaneously with different tasks, actions and/or communications (polychronism) for convenience, pleasure, and efficiency.
Is time a continuous line? (c) Linearity (L) versus cyclicity (C) of time	Time is seen as linear-separable, cut in slices (L) versus the emphasis on daily, yearly, and seasonal cycles (C).
How should we emphasize past, present and future? (d) Temporal orientations	The focus in negotiation may be on future common achievements, past, present, and/or future relationships, or present conflicts and trade-offs
(i) towards the past	People with high past orientation consider the past as important: resources must be spent on teaching history, visiting museums, and referring to tradition and past works. The basic assumption is that people's roots are implanted deep in the past and no plant can survive without its roots. Converse for low past orientation.
(ii) towards the present	People with high present orientation consider that they basically live "here and now". Although not always enjoyable, the present must be accepted for what it is: the only *true* reality we live in.
(iii) towards the future	People easily and precisely envisage and plan their future. They are project-oriented, prepare for the long-term, appreciate the achievements of science, and so on. For them the future is inevitably "bigger and better"? Converse for low future orientation.

consequences. Many European countries, as well as the United States, are emblematic of the "time-is-money" culture, where time is an economic good.[3] Since time is a scarce resource, or at least perceived as such, people should try to achieve its optimal allocation between the competing ways of using it. Norms tend to be very strict regarding time schedules, appointments, and the precise setting of dates and durations in a society where time is strongly felt as economic. Needless to say, attitudes towards money and the money-value of time are inseparable from business negotiations. Economicity of time has a general impact on buyer-seller interaction: "undue" waiting is experienced as a waste of scarce resource and the time spent negotiating together is always balanced with the potential return of the deal.

Monochronic versus polychronic use of time

Hall has described two extreme ideal-types of behaviour in task scheduling, which he calls M-time (monochronism) and P-time (polychronism). Individuals working under M-time do one thing at a time and tend to adhere to preset schedules.[4] When confronted by a dilemma (e.g., a discussion with someone that lasts longer than planned), M-time people will politely stop the conversation, in order to keep to their schedule. In M-time societies, not only the start of a meeting but also its finish will be planned. P-time, on the other hand, stresses the involvement of people who do several things at the same moment, easily modify preset schedules and seldom experience time as "wasted". P-time may seem quite hectic to M-time people: "There is no recognized order as to who is to be served next, no queue or numbers indicating who has been waiting the longest" (Hall, 1983, p. 47). P-time people are more committed to persons than to schedules. When confronted with a conflict such as the one described above, they prefer to go on talking or working after preset hours and break their schedule, if they have one. Mexican negotiators, coming from a polychronic culture, often move from one issue to another, discuss many issues simultaneously, overlap in conversation and ignore turn taking in talks, and interrupt the negotiation for unrelated events.[5] In contrast monochronic American negotiators organize issues sequentially and prefer to work on one issue at a time. In general, Hall has described Americans as typical M-time people whereas Japanese, Chinese, and Middle-Eastern people are typical P-time people. John Graham recalls a negotiation with Russians about the sale of gas turbines, which took place in the pleasant and neutral ground of the French *Côte d'Azur*. However, the Soviet negotiators suddenly become tough and demanding. He explains why:

> Why had the Soviet attitude turned so cold? Because they were enjoying the warm weather in Nice and weren't interested in making a quick deal and heading back to Moscow. The call to California was the key event in this negotiation. Our people in San Diego were sophisticated enough to allow our negotiators to take their time. ... Finally, during week four, the Soviets began to make concessions and to ask for longer meetings. Why? They couldn't go back to Moscow after four weeks on the Mediterranean without a signed contract.
>
> (Graham, 2003, p. 46)

The PERT (programme evaluation and review technique) programming method is an example of a typical "agenda-culture", where M-time is the central assumption. PERT is based on graph theory, and has an appealing U.S. "management science" look: the technique is based on the starting and finishing dates of each individual task and the constraints across tasks (especially those which need to be finished before other tasks can be started). The algorithm calculates the "critical path", that is, the succession of articular tasks which have to be realized without delay if the total completion time is to be minimized. It explicitly aims to reduce a universe of polychronic tasks (they really take place simultaneously, which is part of the problem) to a monochronic solution (the critical path). Management methods, basically originating in the United States and Europe, favour pure monochronic organization. They clearly push aside polychronic attitudes, which tend to make plans and schedules rather hectic. When it comes to delays and being "on time", precise monochronic systems give priority to meeting dates and commitment to schedules.

To illustrate sources of tension between people who have internalized different time systems, Edward Hall (1983, pp. 53–54) takes the example of a monochronic woman who has a polychronic hairdresser. The woman, who has a regular appointment at a specific time each week, feels frustrated and angry when she is kept waiting. At the same time, the hairdresser also feels frustrated. He inevitably feels compelled to "squeeze people in", particularly his friends and acquaintances. The schedule is reserved for impersonal people such as this woman, but since he does not know them personally, keeping to the schedule is not important to him. The distinction between M and P-time is important for business negotiations, in as much as the parties will have to discuss issues, write down clauses, and schedule their meetings.

An empirical comparison of conflict resolution models in Japanese, German, and American cultures, shows that Americans are more polychronic than German and Japanese negotiators who do not differ significantly from each other. Another study shows that, contrary to what was to be expected based on Hall's views, French people are not more polychronic than Americans.[6] Similarly, other negotiation researchers, studying how managers from the United States and France negotiate delivery delays in international business, find that French negotiators are more oriented than Americans toward "quantitative time" (i.e., Hall's M-time). These findings seem to partly disconfirm Hall's assertions about M and P-time across cultures.[7] This is consistent with the classification of Ott (2011, p. 433) who distinguishes between three time cultures: "Linear-Active" (e.g., U.S. and Northern Europeans), which broadly corresponds to M-time, "Multi-Active" (e.g., Latin Americans, Southern and Eastern Europeans, Arabs and Africans, Indians), which broadly corresponds to P-time, and "Reactive" cultures (mostly East Asians), which displays a flexible attitude to time.

Palmer and Schoorman (1999) distinguish three different dimensions in Hall's M-/P-time: time use preference, context, and time tangibility. Time use preference refers to narrowly defined polychronicity; that is, the extent to which people prefer to engage in multiple tasks simultaneously. It is now well-documented that Americans display strong tendencies to polychronicity *sensu stricto*.[8] A second aspect of Hall's contrast of M- and

P-time is the interaction with context: M-time is univocally associated by Hall with low context communication, while P-time is directly associated with high context communication. Negotiators being part of the context, P-time cultures give priority to people over tasks. The third element is "time tangibility" (i.e., "economic time"); that is, time being viewed as a commodity. Time use preference, high or low context, and time tangibility are partly disconnected. Individuals may display a behaviour where low context and multitasking combine with a tangible view of time. Many businesspeople are time tangible *and* multitasking, privileging fuzzy temporal adjustment in ICBN.

Linearity versus cyclicity of time

A strongly economic view of time, when it is combined with monochronism, emphasizes the linearity of time. Time is viewed as being a line with a point at the centre, the present. Each portion of the line can be cut into slices, which are supposed to have a certain money value. Basic religious beliefs play a key role in supporting such a linear view of time: Christianity has a one-shot interpretation of worldly life, and people do not live twice (as in the James Bond film title). People wait until the final judgement for enjoying reincarnation. On the contrary, Asian religions, including Hinduism and Buddhism, assume that, on the death of the body, the soul is born again in another body. The belief in regular reincarnation, until a pure soul is allowed to escape the cycle and go to *nirvana*, radically changes the nature of time in a specific life: it is not all the time I have got, it is simply one of my "times" across several lives. For most Asians, cyclicity is central to their pattern of time: the *nirvana* is the final release from the cycle of reincarnation, attained by extinction of all desires and individual existence, culminating (in Buddhism) in absolute blessedness, or (in Hinduism) in absorption into Brahman. Naturally, patience is on the side of the people believing in cyclical reincarnation of the soul. For the Christians, it is more urgent to achieve, because their souls are given only one worldly chance. But, as the New Testament puts it clearly, those who do right, even in the very last moment, will be considered favourably...

Another element which favours a cyclical view of time is the degree of emphasis put on the natural rhythms of years and seasons, the sun and the moon. So-called "modern" societies are then largely opposed to "traditional" ones, in as much as modern means technology, mastering nature and, to a certain extent, the loss of nature-related reference points. The Japanese are known for having maintained a strong orientation towards nature, even in a highly developed society. Their floral art of *Ikebana* or the emphasis on maintaining a contact with nature, even in highly urban environments, are testimonies to their attachment to the natural rhythms of nature. Even within a country, the relationship to nature influences the model of time adopted by urban in contrast to rural people.

Elements of cyclicity are based mostly on metaphysical assumptions or on astronomical observations, but they also include some arbitrary divisions, which are more social than natural. The duration of the week is a good example of the social origins of the reckoning of time cycles. In a classic article, Sorokin and Merton (1937) give the following illustrations of the variability in the number of days of the week, through anthropological observation, underlining that time is conventionally rather than naturally determined:

> The Khasi week almost universally consists of eight days because the markets are usually held every eighth day. … The Muysca in Bogota had a three-day week; many East African tribes a four-day week; in Central America, the east Indian Archipelago, old Assyria (and now in Soviet Russia), there is found a five-day week…and the Incas had a ten-day week. The constant feature of virtually all these weeks of varying length is that they were always found to have been originally in association with the market.

Elements of cyclicity of time have therefore three main origins: religious assumptions about reincarnation of the soul; natural rhythms of years, seasons, and days; and the social division of time periods which is more arbitrary, less natural and "given", than we assume. Time is naturally both linear and cyclical, and culture has complex time patterns which combine both views, as shown on p. 117 by the example of Japanese *Makimono* time. It is important for business negotiations that linear time emphasizes *discontinuity*; a point on the timeline such as the signing of a contract or the start-up of a plant is perceived as opening a totally new period of time. Conversely, cyclical time favours a more integrative picture of the universe, a stronger sense of the *continuity* of events.

Temporal orientations: past, present, future

The perception of time also tends to be related to temporal orientations vis-à-vis the arrow of time. As stated by Kluckhohn and Strodtbeck (1961, pp. 13–15):

> The possible cultural interpretations of temporal focus of human life break easily into the three-point range of past, present and future… Spanish-Americans, who have been described as taking the view that man is a victim of natural forces, are also a people who place the present time alternative in first position… Many modern European countries … have strong leanings to a past orientation … Americans, more strongly than most people of the world, place an emphasis upon the future – a future which is anticipated to be "bigger and better".

Being past-oriented means that people emphasize the role of the past in the explanation of where we are now. Europeans are typical of this assumption, as are some Asian people. They will tend to restore old buildings, invest in museums, teach history at school, etc. It does not mean that temporal orientation to the past is only based on cultural assumptions. It also depends on individual psychological traits.[9] Furthermore, in societies undergoing a rapid process of economic change, past orientation is often provisionally underplayed.

Present orientation is the most logical assumption, in terms of quality of life at least. It means that people favour the "here and now", believing that the past is over and the future is uncertain, theoretical, and difficult to imagine. Religion may play an important role in pushing people towards present orientation, if it emphasizes that only God decides about the future. In terms of temporal orientations, the Arabic-Muslim character has been described as fatalistic, rather short-term oriented, and not future oriented.[10] As stated by Harris and Moran (1987, p. 474):

> Who controls time? A Western belief is that one controls his own time. Arabs believe that their time is controlled, to a certain extent, by an outside force – namely Allah – therefore the Arabs become very fatalistic in their view of time... most Arabs are not clock watchers, nor are they planners of time.

Future orientation is naturally related to the view that people can master nature, but also to the view that the future can in some way be predicted or at least significantly influenced; future orientation is reflected in languages. In societies where future orientation is strong, it is backed by the educational system and by an "imagination of the future" supported by reports on scientific breakthroughs and technological developments. Language reflects (and pre-shapes) how people envisage the future. Time vocabulary and tenses tell a lot about the linkage between language and time representations. For instance, the English/U.S. word *deadline*, if literally understood, seems to suggest that "beyond this timeline, there is a danger of dying", providing a built-in sense of urgency to a date agreed upon. The word *deadline* is used as such in many languages, because it conveys a typically Anglo-American sense of time commitment, not to be found in other languages.

Combined cultural models of time: The Japanese Makimono time

Economic time usually goes with linear time, monochronism and future orientation, and it is our "modern" time, near to Robert J. Graham's concept (1981, p. 335) of the "European-American (Anglo) perception that allows time to have a past, present and future, and to be sliced into discrete units and then allocated for specific tasks". From this view, time can be saved, spent, wasted, or even bought, just like money. Graham has tried to represent a synthesis of time perception dimensions, not only as a set of different perceptual dimensions, but also as complete temporal systems. He contrasts "Anglo" time, which he describes as being "linear-separable", with the "circular-traditional" time of most Latin-American countries. This perception arises from traditional cultures where action and everyday life were not regulated by the clock, but rather by the natural cycles of the moon, sun, and seasons. Graham proposes a third model, "procedural-traditional", in which the amount of time spent on the activity is irrelevant, since activities are procedure-driven rather than time-driven. This system is typical of the American Indians, and to a large extent it also typifies African time. Graham's "procedural-traditional" time is hardly a "time", in the Western sense.

But it is not that simple: some people may share different cultures and move from one time model to another, depending on the other people involved and the particular situation, using different types of "operating cultures".[11] As Hall (1983, p. 58) states, "The Japanese are polychronic when looking and working inward, toward themselves. When dealing with the outside world ... they shift to the monochronic mode... The French are monochronic intellectually, but polychronic in behaviour".

A naive view of Japanese temporal orientation would lead one to assume that the Japanese are simply future oriented. In fact, a specialist in Japanese business, Robert Ballon,[12] argues that the Japanese are neither future nor past oriented. To him, the Japanese are present oriented and focused on the here and now. Hayashi (1988, p. 2) explains the difficult attempt at finding cross-culturally equivalent terms by asserting that: "Many kinds of Japanese behaviour are extratemporaneous", meaning that they are not time-based. Hayashi explains further what he calls the *Makimono* time. In their model of time, the Japanese tend to posit the future as a natural extension of the present. Japanese are basically people working with a cyclical view of time, based on their Buddhist background which believes that souls of dead people transmigrate to newly born human beings, in an eternal cycle. "In Japanese cultural time, the past flows continuously toward the present and also the present is firmly linked to the future. In philosophical terms, we might say the past and the future exist simultaneously in the present".[13]

Therefore, the linear-separable model of time, found in Western cultures, does not predominate in Japan. The notion of continuity is central to Japanese time, just as the notion of discontinuity is central to Western models of time. A Japanese definition would say "the present is a temporal period that links the region of the past with the world of the future".[14] Both the notion of continuity and the arrow of the future targeted *towards* the present are central in the *Makimono* time pattern (Figure 4.2). Coming back to Cohen's experience cited at the beginning of this chapter, the Japanese concern to have him learn what they are reflects a preoccupation with continuity: if he is to make deals with them he has to understand their past.

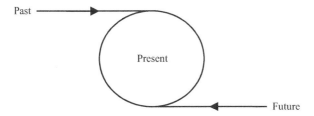

Figure 4.2 Japanese *Makimono* time pattern
Source: Hayashi (1988, p. 9)

Starting the negotiation: Preliminaries, agenda, and schedule

Time for preliminaries

The role of spending time on establishing personal relationships, especially in Asia and South America, is noted by most negotiation authors, both academics and practitioners.[15] There is a series of reasons why a personal relationship is needed: establishing the context of communication;[16] acquaintance with the other person's being part of the necessary context; a less strict separation between personal and professional spheres than in the West; and the importance of personal status that creates the need to spend time in exploring who is who with some discretion, in order not to offend partners. This is all summed up in the recommendation that an American negotiator will be well-advised to develop personal relations away from the negotiation room: "The usual intense and rather dry approach to doing business must be supplemented with a social relationship. The Japanese are accustomed to the use of entertainment as a means of becoming better acquainted and of developing goodwill".[17]

The cultural time concept of Americans, strongly economic, partly explains why spending time to build personal relations is implicitly seen as bad. Time being seen as a resource not to be wasted, spending time on non-business matters, on non-task-related issues is experienced as a violation of their cultural norms. "Non-task sounding", that is, establishing rapport and getting to know each other, the first phase in Graham's four-phase process of business negotiations,[18] not only needs a relaxed sense of economic time but also some past orientation: seeing Japanese shrines, or learning the basic about Zen or Ikebana, the Japanese floral art. The Japanese feel that an understanding of their past is necessary for understanding them as negotiation partners today.

Setting the agenda and scheduling the negotiation process

These tasks are considered in most of the negotiation literature as necessary for the second step in Graham's four-stage model: task-related exchange of information. An agenda is a schedule and list of items to be discussed during the negotiation process. In many cultures the very notion of "agenda setting" is unheard of: cutting the process into pieces in advance and allocating time lots to each "task" is, at best, theoretical. Hall's differences between monochronic and polychronic are relevant for the scheduling of negotiation. An agenda-oriented negotiation team, with a strong belief in the value of monochronic time, tends to try to negotiate clauses sequentially, whereas the other party, polychronic, may skip from one issue to another, coming back to points which had apparently been already settled, because they tend to negotiate globally. Graham and Herberger (1983) call it "One thing at a time": Americans usually attack a complex negotiation task sequentially, that is, they separate the issues and settle them one at a time. As emphasized by a report of the United States Institute of Peace (2002, p. 5) about U.S. negotiating behaviour:

> Americans tend to subscribe to a view of negotiation as a linear process, a sequence of stages, that typically begins with prenegotiation, advances to the opening moves of the formal negotiation, continues through a probing middle phase, and culminates in an end game and a binding agreement.

Making appointments and setting deadlines: Managing temporal clash in ICBN

Time in the negotiation process

Partners from different cultures may be working together to develop a low-cost operation, or a new R&D project, or distribution and sales facilities, depending on the objective of the joint venture. In such settings, issues to do with time will inevitably arise, both at an everyday level, simply in order to meet at the same time, and at a deeper level, that of assigning a common time frame to business operations. Trompenaars recounts a story on an international meeting between IT1 and Singaporean and African (IT2) negotiators who arrive late (2.20 p.m.) at the meeting scheduled at 1.50 p.m. This excerpt illustrates the clash of temporal cultures when negotiating, both at the individual and at organizational levels.

> All except the American, Dutch and other north-west European representatives complained that these [time intervals determining bonuses and merits] were far too frequent. To Johnson and his Dutch and Scandinavian colleagues the frequency was obviously right...The manager from Singapore said: "Possibly, but this go-for-the-quick-buck philosophy has been losing us customers. They don't like the pressure we put on at the end of the quarter. They want our representatives to serve them, not to have private agendas. We need to keep our customers

long-term, not push them into buying so that one sales person can beat a rival".

(Trompenaars, 1993, p. 115)

Different time perspectives, be they organizational or cultural, result in temporal clashes. The conflicts that result from the inability to merge different ways of dealing with time may be located at an individual level; that of business people interacting with foreign partners and negotiating with them. Temporal clash at the level of individual interaction results from differing answers given to the following questions: how is somebody treated when he or she arrives half an hour late for a negotiation session? Do sessions have a finishing time in addition to their starting time? Is time also structured during the meeting by setting an agenda and a definite time limit for discussion on each point?

To illustrate the synchronization problem at work, let us take the example of a French business meeting versus a meeting in the United States (a fairly polychronic versus a fairly monochronic culture). In France, some people come a quarter of an hour late, and some half an hour. Not only does the meeting not start on time, but those people who were on time have to wait for those who are late. Rarely do people who are late apologize. Some, not all, simply explain why they were late. It is not rare that, when somebody arrives quite late, most other people stop their discussion and spend five or ten minutes explaining to the latecomers what has been said up to now (fortunately, the content of French meetings is generally easy to summarise!). Moreover, contrary to the U.S. meetings, French meetings are almost never assigned a finishing time. This means that quite often, if there are several successive meetings, the reason why some people arrive late is that the previous meeting was late and finished one or two hours after the (more or less vaguely and implicitly) agreed finishing time.

Temporal clashes between negotiating organizations

Temporal clash in negotiation may also be based at an organizational level, that of companies trying to design some sort of common venture, through a merger, an acquisition or a joint venture. There are many instances where the failure of an international alliance has been attributed to lack of cultural fit, or conflict between the two cultures; temporal clash based on culturally different time patterns is also a cultural clash. In the case of a French-Indian joint venture,[19] the French partner, a world leader in specialized equipment goods with one plant in France and two in the United States, was willing to enter the Indian market with a 5–6 year time horizon for pay-back. India limits foreign ownership to 40% and sets strong red tape on foreign partners' route to JV formation. Finally, it was decided to invest in two stages. In the first stage IJV was supposed only to assemble imported parts. In a second stage, it was due to increase local manufacturing. But, in fact, communication misunderstandings added to delays in some governmental authorizations and, finally, financial difficulties related to expected large orders that did not come led the two partners to a typical temporal clash. The Indian partner interpreted the situation as a lack of long-term commitment on the French side and asked for a direct progression to the second stage. Having a much shorter horizon than that needed to overcome the problem, the French company refused. Finally, the IJV slowly came to a halt because neither of the two partners wanted to take responsibility for officially discontinuing the venture.

Time-based tactical moves: Exerting time pressures in the bargaining process

The effect of time pressure is contingent on the accountability of the negotiator:

> When negotiators are not accountable to a constituency, time pressure results in less competitive interaction and a higher proportion of agreements. In contrast, when negotiators are accountable to a constituency, time pressure results in more competitive interaction and in a higher proportion of impasses.
>
> (Mosterd and Rutte, 2000, p. 241)

Suffice it to say that international business negotiators are generally accountable to a constituency, the CEO or top-level executives in their organization. As a consequence, the effect of time pressure often translates into more competitive behaviour, the use of harder tactics (involving demands and threats), and a greater propensity to break negotiation talks.

The place where the negotiation takes place has an obvious influence on time-scarcity. Those who are "at home" can monitor their regular business tasks while participating in the negotiations. Those who have left their home country to negotiate at their partner's location can for many reasons, both professional and personal, be impatient to go back. The pressure of "wasted time" can be easily used against those who have both an economic pattern of time and are far from their home base.

As such, the expression "to waste time" has little meaning for many cultures, especially for most African cultures.[20] One may lose something tangible, like a ring or a pencil. But in order to waste and lose time, time should be a thing or, at least, it would be necessary to be able to separate time from the events with which it is inextricably bound up, making it difficult to equate abstract time with a monetary unit of measurement. For instance, within their culture, the Bantu people of the southern part of Africa know nothing comparable to a linear Newtonian time, in which events take place. There are events, and each one of these events carries its own desire and its own time. Time cannot be wasted or lost, because time has simply to be lived or experienced, whatever may be the way to experience it. No one can steal time, not even death.

The same tranquillity in the face of time may be seen in the Orient, compared with the Occidental anguish and guilt about time that might be wasted or lost. Several authors in the field of international business negotiations note that time pressure is strongly felt by American negotiators, whether they negotiate with the Chinese[21] or with the Japanese.[22] American negotiators are eventually forced to yield by their representation of time, potentially wasted or lost if it is not optimally allocated. When this logic is pushed to its extreme, it may result in total inefficiency. People spend their whole time thinking of possible alternative uses of their time and calculating which of these alternatives offers the best marginal return. As noted by Adler (2002, p. 219):

> Americans' sense of urgency disadvantages them with respect to less hurried bargaining partners. Negotiators from other countries recognize Americans' time consciousness, achievement orientation, and impatience. They know that Americans will make concessions close to their deadline (time consciousness) in order to get a signed contract (achievement orientation).

Pressure can be exerted on economic-time-minded negotiators by postponing the beginning of the negotiation, delaying meetings, keeping the end of negotiations a secret, etc. Herb Cohen gives a classic example of how the Japanese manipulate their Western partners' excessive time consciousness. The Japanese negotiator asked him when he arrived at Tokyo airport:

> "Are you concerned about getting back to your plane on time?" (Up to that moment I had not been concerned.) "We can schedule this limousine to transport you back to the airport", I thought in myself, "how considerate", Reaching my pocket, I handed them my return flight ticket, so the limousine would know when to get me. I didn't realize it then, but they knew my deadline, whereas I didn't know theirs.
> (Cohen, 1980, p. 94)

However, urgency has a two-sided value. As noted by careful observers of American negotiation style,[23] "Americans are not always looking at the clock". They may use their own self-defined deadlines to put the other party under pressure. They may also let diplomatic negotiations stretch out for years when there is little interest in the American media for the issue under discussion.

Timing of concessions

The pattern of timing of concessions tends to differ whether people tend to settle one issue and proceed to the next or whether they negotiate more globally. Certain cultures, like the Chinese and the Japanese, tend to make fewer concessions through the earlier stages of the negotiation process, because they have a much longer non-task sounding phase, needing more time to establish the relationship and obtain information. In Asian cultures, negotiators will discuss all issues prior to making any concessions and begin with mutual concessions only when they perceive that the end of the negotiation is in sight.[24] U.S. executives tend to offer concessions throughout the negotiation process, seeing the "give and take" process as having to start early and to lead to reciprocal and balanced concessions. The difference in the appropriate view of what are "timely concessions" (continuous versus last moment, "cherry-on-the cake" concessions) can lead to misunderstandings between the partners. If two parties use different approaches to the timing of concessions (linear, segmented versus holistic and global concession making), the process may lead to frustration and distrust, because both parties are confused about the willingness of their counterpart to concede and tend to underestimate the other party's good will.[25]

As noted above, time pressure can be seen as a legitimate tool to be used for extracting last-minute concessions from the other party. Exploitation of time pressure can be resented by the party which is taken advantage of. However, this party should probably have prepared some minor but noteworthy concession to be offered in such a case.

It has been noted that, in highly bureaucratic contexts, negotiators will use the argument of the complexity of their organizational process and the consequent necessity to refer to various bodies in order to delay concessions. However, negotiators from such countries also need to bring back something to their superiors and, as noted by John Graham (2003), the timing of concessions can be inverted when these negotiators come close to their deadline. They run short of time and, if they are negotiating in a costly place, their organization will not allow them to stay longer and, ultimately, they risk being blamed by their superiors if they go back empty-handed. This leads them to concede.

Time frame of the relationship between negotiation partners

Negotiations strategies: Long-term orientation as favouring an integrative strategy

The adoption of an integrative strategy is facilitated, *inter alia*, by the ability to envisage the future; this permits the discovery or "invention" of new solutions, which enables both partners to overcome the problem of the fixed size of the "territorial cake". Its size is limited in the very short term and it is only by envisaging what the future between the negotiation partners could be that it becomes feasible to adopt a more expansive view of the "common cake". The nature of international transactions often imposes it: business is fairly continuous over several years, and therefore implies a very strong buyer-seller interdependence. The performance level depends largely on the extent and the quality of the collaboration between the partners.

Negotiators' time horizon when forming international strategic alliances influences their strategic behaviour in negotiation. It is a well-established result that expectation of future interaction with cooperation partners affects current behaviour: in a last round with no future interaction, negotiators use harder tactics and are more prone to defection and exploitation than to cooperation. Rao and Schmidt (1998) have studied how time horizon influences the cooperative frame; they found that the correlation is 0.38, significant at the 0.01 level. Furthermore, American alliance negotiators with longer time horizons tend to limit the use of hard tactics in negotiation and to be more rational in their approach to alliance negotiation.

The value of long-term orientation is often better understood by the Asians for whom a new fifth dimension has been added to Hofstede's (2001) four dimensions. A research team based in Hong Kong and initiated by Michael Bond has designed a questionnaire called CVS (Chinese Value Survey), which has been administered in 23 countries.[26] It is based on basic values as seen by native Chinese social scientists. A new dimension was discovered through the CVS. Bond coined the term "Confucius dynamism", to emphasize the importance of Confucius' practical ethics, based on the development of long-term relationships, and valuing (1) the stability of society based on unequal relationships, expressing mutual and complementary obligations; (2) the family as the prototype of all social organizations; (3) individuality; (4) virtuous behaviour towards others, which consists of treating others as one would like to be treated oneself; (5) virtue, with regard to one's tasks in life, which consists of trying to work hard and being patient and persevering.[27]

Making plans together: Coordinating and planning common ventures

In many international negotiations planning a common venture, the steps of construction of a turnkey plant, or the implementation phases of a joint venture or licence agreement, need explicit reference to dates, deadlines, and the sequencing of interdependent tasks; that is, planning. Planning is such a basic function of management that it is extremely difficult to admit that there are other models of time from those on which it implicitly rests. Naturally, it would be naive to consider that business people have purely traditional time patterns, such as those described earlier. In fact, complex patterns of time-related behaviour may be used by people sharing several cultural backgrounds, one of them being the original in-depth background, the other(s) being much more superficial. Furthermore, the native cultural background may be undervalued because it is supposed to be "inefficient" or it is unknown to foreigners. Accordingly, people belonging to non-linear/economic time cultures often have a tendency to imitate the cultural way of life that they tend to regard as the "best". It might result in buying a superb watch as an item of jewellery or a diary because it is fashionable. But the functional behaviour which is in line with the watch or the diary will not be adopted. After these objects have been bought, they lose their cultural value as practical tools of the economic/monochronic/linear/separable time pattern. People involved in this type of cultural borrowing might prove unable to take any appointment seriously. They will probably experience difficulties in following any preset schedule.

The fallacies of borrowed time patterns in intercultural negotiation

Ideal and actual temporal behaviour

Ideal patterns of time and actual temporal behaviour may differ widely for negotiators who apparently use their partners' time culture rather than their own. The idea of possible discrepancies between ideal patterns and actual behaviour was expressed by the anthropologist Ralph Linton:

> All cultures include a certain number of what may be called ideal patterns... They represent the consensus of opinion on the part of the society's members as to how people should behave in particular situations ... comparison of narratives usually reveals the presence of a real culture pattern with a recognizable mode of variation ... it [the ideal pattern] represents a desideratum, a value, which has always been more honoured in the breach than in the observance.
>
> (Linton, 1945, pp. 52–54)

Dor Bahadur Bista, in the case of Nepal, highlights the conflict between time-based behaviour related to foreign education and the traditional influence of fatalistic beliefs on the lack of future orientation and sense of planning. He comments about the many Nepali students who graduate abroad and come back in positions of authority as planners of development projects:

> Control is placed in the hands of the planner. But fatalism does not allow this kind of control, and is inherently antithetical to pragmatic thought... the new values that they bring back with them immediately confront fatalism and are typically defeated by it... After forty years of planning and an accumulation of foreign trained graduates, Nepal, then, still has little manpower to effectively bridge the disparities between the culture of the foreign aid donors and that of their own.
>
> (Bista, 1990, pp. 137–138)

Hidden language of time

In everyday management behaviour (appointments, scheduling, meetings), it is quite probable that we face a high level of cultural borrowing: actual time behaviour of economically successful countries like the United States or countries of northern Europe have been imported by other nations as ideal patterns.[28] It is, for instance, very clear that in Latin-European countries, the PERT technique, which is designed for the scheduling of interrelated tasks, has been implemented mostly for its intellectual appeal. In France, where many managers and top executives have been trained as engineers, there has been a great interest in this scientific management technique. Real project planning in France and Latin-European countries very often works with high discrepancies relative to PERT dates: French people tend to be intellectually monochronic but actually behave in a polychronic manner.[29]

Sometimes people even use two completely different systems in parallel. This somewhat contradictory situation is most easily recognized by looking at the construction of some turnkey projects in developing countries. At the beginning, during the negotiation process, and on signature of the contract, everybody seemingly (and also sincerely) agrees about using an economic time/ monochronic pattern. In fact, the partners share the same belief, but it is an ideal pattern on one side and the actual behaviour on the other. There may not even be discussion about it: obviously it is the right way to proceed. But afterwards, extreme confusion appears when the project is being implemented.

Relationship versus deal: Continuous versus discontinuous views of time

Time as an outcome variable

Many Western negotiators consider that a signed contract places a clear-cut temporal limit upon the negotiation process. It is stopped and the implementation phase starts, based on the precise contractual outcomes: time-based clauses and agreements. As noted by Ghauri and Fang (2001), the Chinese prefer a broad agreement setting general joint principles and are reluctant to enter into precise details as to the assignment of responsibilities for definite tasks. Consequently, signing the contract cannot be the final point for negotiation.

Cultures which have a cyclical and integrative view of time have an underlying concept of negotiation in which it is only one round of a recurrent relational process, with little sequencing compared with people holding a linear/separable view of time. This is to be found also in the outcome orientation, where the timeline of negotiation is less important to people with a cyclical/integrative view of time: to them, a signed contract is no real reason not to pursue the negotiation process further. Eiteman (1990, p. 62), reporting on American executives' perceptions of negotiating joint ventures with Chinese managers, notes the comments of a negotiator for a major U.S. firm that: "the bargaining (with the Chinese) never stopped after the original agreement was signed and business actually started". And the president of this firm, located in Beijing, remarks that "production operations were nothing more than a continuation of the frustrations of the original negotiating sessions, with previously agreed upon points always changed by the Chinese". In fact most Chinese negotiators attribute success to negotiation activities involving Relationship-Building. For them failure occurs when either they have not established a relationship, or they have done it, but it is not perceived as a good one. As a consequence, Chinese negotiators appear as less task-oriented than Americans: "the approach of getting to the business at hand immediately is regarded as rude and impolite, which affects negotiation outcomes and subverts long-term relationships".[30]

Written agreements as a timeline for negotiations

There are two different ways to look at the influence and function of the written agreement on the time span of the exchange relationship. Those favouring written-based trust-building tend to see a written agreement as a very definite break in the exchange relationship, embedded in "written" time, based on dates, deadlines, and delay penalties, all of them task-centred rather than relationship-centred. It completes a phase during which potential relations have been carefully discussed and explored. It establishes a strict contractual code, which has then to be implemented with punctuality and timeliness. Written words, sentences, and formulas have to be strictly observed. If a party feels free to depart from what has been written down, the Damoclean sword of litigation will hang over the parties.

Those favouring oral-based, personal trust consider the signing of a written agreement as an important step, but only one of many in a continuous negotiation process. The negotiation process was active before signature and will be active afterwards. A continuous negotiation process, where the contract is only one step, is seen as the best basis for maintaining trust.

As stated by Edward Hall (1960, p. 94):

> Americans consider that negotiations have more or less ceased when the contract is signed. With the Greeks, ... the contract is seen as a sort of way station on the route to negotiation, that will cease only when the work is completed. The contract is nothing more than a charter for serious negotiations. In the Arab world, once a man's word is given in a particular kind of way, it is just as binding, if not more so, than most of our written contracts. The written contract therefore violates the Moslem's sensitivities and reflects on his honour.

Managing time shrewdly in ICBN

Temporal adjustment in intercultural business negotiations

With increased international interaction it would be naive to assume that negotiators do not adjust in business negotiations when they come from culturally alien temporal cultures. Furthermore, when getting acquainted with each other they tend to develop a common time frame where each party has its own contribution. The common venture being negotiated also has an influence on the progressive building of a shared temporal culture.

Very often the starting model for time management in the negotiation process will be a classic monochronic one, involving agenda setting and a precise planning of the talks. Both parties, wherever they come from, tend to consider this model as the best one from a normative point of view, since it is the dominant normative model in business. However, as argued by Slocombe (1999), time management has three facets which may be complementary or, at times competing:

- Beliefs: the extent to which people in a particular time-culture believe it is the right way to do things.
- Attitudes: to what extent people prefer to be engaged in a particular way of managing their time and synchronizing themselves with others.
- Behaviour: what time management they actually practise and implement, possibly in discrepancy with both their beliefs and attitudes.

Most negotiators have a certain ability to adjust to a polyphasic behaviour. Consequently intercultural business negotiators will evolve from normative assumptions to real-world adjustment. They will partly renounce their beliefs and attitudes as to what is appropriate and develop a form of behavioural adjustment which takes into account what works and what is acceptable to the other side as a way of working together. I outline below a likely adjustment process in terms of the three dimensions of M- versus P-time (tangibility, polyphasia, and low versus high context).

Tangible time will remain tangible because the negotiations process tends to lend credit to the view that time is a scarce resource, especially at start and finish periods. Talks are always longer than foreseen. Additional issues arise as the negotiation proceeds, and a reasonable level of contending (with some confrontation on both sides) is time consuming. Negotiators have an idea (even if vague) of the "time budget" they are going to allocate to a particular negotiation. Even though they do not calculate a precise amount of time (e.g., in hours or days) dedicated to a particular negotiation, they have a sense that negotiation is extending way beyond what was scheduled to happen and beyond implicit deadlines as to the wished end for the negotiation process. Consequently, even negotiators who do not feel a sense of urgency (i.e., people with time rather intangible) tend to adjust to a more economic-minded view of time. Time tends to become more reified, commoditized, and therefore economic, when, being partly consumed, it is perceived as becoming scarce. The general direction of adaptation will be from time intangible to time tangible views of the negotiation process.

Those coming from monotasking (monochronic *sensu stricto*) cultures may start the negotiation by imposing some typical devices of monochronic cultures: an agenda where each issue is clearly delineated and its discussion precisely scheduled. However, monochronic negotiation partners, when confronted with polychronic partners (*sensu stricto*) will be forced to give up the precise planning of the negotiation process; they will not be even able to defend it as a reasonable procedure for going further. As a consequence, negotiations processes between polychronic and monochronic people tend to develop according to a polychronic way of mixing issues and debating several topics at the same time. Moreover, multitask orientation and polychronicity are frequent among managers, even in supposedly economic time-minded cultures such as that of the United States.[31]

Multitasking is a natural evolution of the negotiations process. It is likely that monochronic negotiators perceive polychronicity as negatively related to coordination and teamwork.[32] However, polychronicity has to do with fuzzy and unorganized synchronization, and although not satisfactory for negotiators with strongly ingrained beliefs that only linear and organized processes are efficient, polychronicity may at times liberate the creative exploration of joint solutions. Polychronicity can also be positively associated with achievement striving but also positively correlated with impatience and irritability.[33] Polychronic behaviour allows the reduction of role overload for negotiators who have to face the discussion of multiple issues at the same time (especially in the phases of information exchange and persuasion), and in this sense it may help them monitor their level of stress. This positive effect may even overcome the negative impact on stress for monochronic persons of being forced to adopt a polychronic approach to the negotiation.

Moreover, when in the middle of a smoothly and satisfactorily proceeding negotiation, business negotiators may feel that they still have plenty of time available, thereby reducing their perceived time urgency. As a consequence, they may provisionally experience a sense of timelessness[34] which helps them adopt a more polychronic and less time tangible approach to business negotiations. However, as we will see later, the feeling of timelessness, caused by people being stimulated and rewarded by the task and forgetting about time, schedules, and deadlines, ceases when negotiators actually run out of time and when their high workload forces them to adopt a more monochronic approach.

Negotiators may begin from low-context premises, especially if one party comes from a low-context culture and drives their counterparts into a quick jump into the discussion of issues at stake without spending enough time to get acquainted and create a common context *at the start*. However the level of joint context in communication will increase with the sharing of information, with common knowledge about issues at stake and progressive acquaintance of people around the negotiation table. As a consequence, the level of usable, common context for both parties increases and they are more likely to adopt higher context communication as the negotiation proceeds. To sum up: even if a negotiation round starts between classic monochronic and classic polychronic partners, it is likely to progressively shift to a more synchronic mode (tangible, multitask time combined with relatively high context communication).

Finally, it is also common practice that parties follow a more monochronic approach in the last phase of a negotiation round which deals with the drafting and signing of a detailed contract. Drafting each clause is a particular task to be performed and even though parties may sometimes jump from one clause to another because they are interrelated, mono-tasking will be dominant. Furthermore time becomes urgent at the very end of a negotiation process since negotiators have generally spent more time on talks than initially foreseen. Based on a laboratory experiment involving 26 groups, Waller et al. (1999) have shown that time urgency reduces a group's polychronicity. At the very end of a negotiation process, time-urgent group members will increase the level of monochronicity in group work and this has been shown to have a positive effect on efficiency with the primary task.

Some rules for managing time in international business negotiations

In short, the international business negotiator should follow some basic rules:

1) Take time for adequate preliminaries: getting to know the other party is most often crucial. More time is needed than in domestic business negotiations, since cultural as well as personal knowledge have to be acquired. However, don't get fooled by your partner exploiting you by overextending initial socializing and thereby reducing time available for task-oriented negotiation.
2) Control your time: do not get trapped by your own cultural time model; that is, try to be aware of it. If needed, be prepared to renounce a negotiation, because the stakes are too low, or send lower level, less expensive executives. If possible, negotiate at home where you have a competitive advantage over your foreign partner in terms of time control.
3) Never tell the other side when you are leaving because this gives them control over your time.
4) Allow yourself plenty of time, and even more: patience is an asset for negotiation and it is destroyed by time pressure. In the US-Vietnamese peace talks in Paris, the Vietnamese were at a time advantage because they had rented a villa with a two-and-a-half year lease, whereas the Americans rented hotel rooms on a week-to-week basis.
5) Do not get fooled by the other party seemingly sharing your time pattern: try to set realistic dates and deadlines and, if needed, plan softly, introducing time slack, allowing for delays to be absorbed without ruining the economy of the whole venture. Remember: better plan modestly and realistically than go into enormous delays that ruin the credibility of the whole planning process.
6) Accept temporal clash to the extent possible. Before participating in a negotiation, learn the basics about the behavioural norms in your partner's culture concerning appointments, punctuality, and planning.

7) Wait for the negotiation process to extend beyond the signature of the deal. For most cultures there is no clear timeline defined by the signing of a contract; the most important time frame is that of the relationship, not that of a particular deal.

Notes

1 Ancona et al. (2001).
2 Usunier and Valette-Florence (1994, 2007).
3 Usunier (1991).
4 Hall (1983).
5 Foster (1995).
6 Tinsley (1998) uses the IPV polychronicity scale from Bluedorn et al. (1999) to assess the degree of polychronicity of negotiators coming from the three cultures under review. See also Conte et al. (1999).
7 Prime and Bluedorn (1996) and Potter and Balthazard (2000).
8 See Kaufman et al. (1991), Bluedorn et al. (1999), and Kaufman and Lindquist (1999).
9 Usunier and Valette-Florence (1994, 2007).
10 Ferraro (1990).
11 Goodenough (1971).
12 Robert Ballon quoted in Hayashi (1988).
13 Hayashi (1988, p. 10).
14 Hayashi (1988, p. 18).
15 Hall (1983), Pye (1986), Graham and Sano (2003), Hawrysh and Zaichkowsky (1990); Li and Labig (2001).
16 Hall (1976).
17 Burt's comments (1984, p. 7).
18 See Graham and Lin (1987).
19 Knittel and Stefanini (1993).
20 Usunier and Lee (2013).
21 See Pye (1982, 1986), Tung (1996), Graham et al. (2014).
22 See Graham (1981), Graham and Sano (1989), Graham et al. (2014).
23 USIP (2002).
24 Simintiras and Thomas (1998).
25 Schuster and Copeland (1999).
26 Chinese Culture Connection (1987).
27 Pye (1986, p. 79).
28 Usunier (1991).
29 Hall (1983).
30 Li and Labig (2001, p. 356).
31 Palmer and Schoorman (1999).
32 Benabou (1999).
33 Conte et al. (1999).
34 Mainemelis (2001).

Part two

People and processes

5 Intercultural communication for business negotiations

Smaller offences are always better neglected.

(Adam Smith, 1790, p. 33)

IT1 Deal-oriented communication is necessarily more factual, explicit, and depersonalized (ideally impersonal), because it is assumed that 1) facts and interests may be blurred by relationships between people and by their subjectivity, and 2) decontextualized communication is always preferable in business. This type of communication provides clarity and a joint understanding of what has been agreed upon, as opposed to fuzziness and contradicting interpretations. Conversely, in the Relationship-oriented IT2 model, it is assumed that people (influenced by identity cues such as nationality, culture, language, age, gender, personality, status, personal and family connections, and so on) and their relationships are at the very centre of the negotiation process, generating a strong need for contextualized communication. Relationship-Building communication styles are more implicit, fuzzier, and more interpretive than Deal-Making communication styles, at the possible expense of clarity. This chapter elaborates on the role of particular languages in shaping the style of verbal communication, especially how low-context cultures (IT1) and high-context cultures (IT2) differ in terms of explicitness and the contextualization of messages. The role that non-verbal communication plays in ICBN cannot be ignored. However, because non-verbal communication is culturally coded in rather diverse ways, a pragmatic solution is mostly to avoid the don'ts and adopt the local dos in as much as one is able to mimic foreign ways. The chapter concludes on issues related to language choice both in speech and writing, the role of interpreters, and how to avoid communication misunderstandings during ICBN.

Information exchange: Messages, channels, context, and coding-decoding processes

Communication and negotiation

Negotiation and communication are deeply intermingled because parties need to exchange information to explain their needs, positions, and proposals.[1] Negotiators also try to persuade and influence the other side through communication. Feedback is required to check if messages have been properly understood by the receiver. Progressively, each party more or less precisely understands what the other camp is ready to accept. Parties tend not to easily disclose what could be considered as private (confidential) information. As a consequence, the communication process in negotiation is partly impaired by the necessity to hide one's cards. The negotiators repeatedly exchange messages to progressively align independent and competitive goals into what is assumed to be a cooperative objective.[2]

During the negotiation process, a large number of messages are exchanged between the parties. The message format is important for the information exchange to succeed and for avoiding communication misunderstandings, for instance when a party says "yes" but actually means "no". High-context messages need to be decoded, interpreted. They cannot be taken at face value. In a very low-context communication style, a "yes" always means "yes". The emphasis put on the role of context in communication derives from Edward T. Hall, an American anthropologist.[3] The communication mode that first springs to mind is the verbal mode. Phrases and words in a single language have (more or less) a precise meaning; in any case, we live with the necessary assumption that words and their combinations have a particular meaning, and that the listener gets a clear message from the speaker. This assumption allows us to avoid the time-consuming task of constantly verifying that the message received is the same message as that which was sent. Even in an exchange that is primarily verbal, part of the message is non-verbal: gestures, gesticulations, attitudes, etc. The issue then is to know to what extent non-verbal/implicit messages (which will be discussed in the next section) mix with verbal/explicit messages. Communication integrates feedback mechanisms to verify or improve the clarity of messages. In many cultures, the accuracy of the communication process needs to be checked by various means, including repetition, paraphrases, interruption, and questions.

The first stage in a communication process is for the emitter to design a message. This process involves verbal and non-verbal signs and signals that are intended to convey the message though a communication channel (e.g., face-to-face, by phone or email). The receiver should have the capability to assign proper meaning to what has been sent, which is a major difficulty in ICBN because negotiators do not share the same linguistic and non-verbal codes between senders and receivers. Semantic understanding (related to meaning *per se*) as well as psychological interpretation (i.e., meaning is transformed by emotional attitudes manifested by the sender and decoded by the receiver) must be constantly checked. In ICBN, it is likely therefore that the clarity of communication will be impaired by noise in the communication process.

Reasons for voluntarily sending distorted messages in negotiation

Negotiation communication (NC) is not an ordinary, everyday information exchange. It is impossible to put (lay down) your cards on the negotiation table, to straightforwardly and openly expose positions, needs, interests, as well as confidential information (e.g., cost and price information, strategic alternatives, preferred options). This would be a one-sided integrative move, however potentially disastrous if the other party does not reciprocate (see Chapter 3) by revealing their own cards. They would take advantage of information asymmetry to claim most of the value thus created. It is never advisable to disclose all or a large part of your hand (e.g., one's cards, including trumps) because it reveals needs and preferences and offers an avenue for the other party to assess your reservation price.

At the same time, paradoxically and contradictorily, it is necessary to progressively disclose information to explore joint solutions, promote problem-solving, and create value. Like in a card game, the objective of each player is to win in a process of alternating tricks won by one side, then the other. Self-disclosure is therefore prudent; its pace is slow and progressive and accelerates when the final agreement is nearing. At the beginning, self-disclosure is often dissimulated, sometimes voluntarily misleading (e.g., claiming a fake, unverifiable BATNA), in order to shuffle cards, at the risk of spreading confusion and causing misunderstandings, which are in fact preprogrammed in NC. This is evidently worse in ICBN communication since the parties do not share the same code. Without exaggerating, it may result in distorted, confused, and contorted NC, later creating a need for clarification and to defuse and soothe misinterpretations and mix-ups.

In the forms of content-related communication in the Shannon and Weaver model, the fair exchange of true information is called *representative communication*.[4] The intention of the sender is to send a clear and unequivocal message, which may nevertheless be partly misunderstood due to noise and/or inadequate decoding. However, there may be many reasons why negotiators send voluntarily distorted, sometimes unclear, and at times misleading messages. This is true for negotiation in general as well as for ICBN. The unwillingness to disclose one's position explains why parties do not straightforwardly reveal their preferences for fear that reservation price, needs, priorities, and expectations can be rather accurately guessed by the other party. NC is partly "masked" communication because hiding or disguising key information is standard behaviour in negotiation. *Instrumental communication* is often used, that is an attempt at manipulating the other party by delivering information which is not false *per se*, but mostly aims to influence. Emitting instrumental communication targets persuasion rather than mere information. Expectations of the party emitting instrumental communication as to how the (possibly quite distorted) message will be decoded by the other party may not be met because of a lack of understanding of how the other party will decode the message due to differences in communication style.

Beyond mere instrumental communication lies *strategic misrepresentation*; that is, knowingly delivering "non-true" and manipulative information. A party may, for instance, convey false information on the value they assign to a particular "good" in the negotiation or on key data (e.g., lying on delivery dates or on quality). Cultures do not put the same value on communication attitudes such as frankness, speech openness, and instrumentality. Lying or dissimulating information may be perfectly acceptable in some cultures (more IT2) and frowned upon in others (more IT1), although practised everywhere and at all times. Lying entails a wide range of communication from mere omission (e.g., hiding key information), minor lies, to actively deceitful communication (e.g., forging accounts). The greatest prudence and caution is called for.

Contextual cues in ICBN communication

Context and contextual cues are important in ICBN communication. Often in ICBN, the decoding of communication (messages) requires the understanding of the context in which these messages have been emitted. Contextual cues in ICBN are largely related to *being* and the IT2 paradigm. They are associated with personal characteristics (e.g., age, gender, status, role, race, physical appearance such as tallness, stoutness, clothing, body odour) and location in space and time (e.g., social background, place, time). Contextual cues are idiosyncratic (i.e., particular to each culture and its insiders), therefore difficult to embody in a set of general rules, and render communication complex and somewhat uncertain for outsiders. That is why a clear, explicit, non-distorted information exchange (rather in the IT1 style, doing, action-oriented, rather unconcerned with the negotiation partner's personal characteristics) must be as decontextualized as possible.

When negotiators from different cultures communicate, they exchange elements of non-verbal communication (e.g., gestures, eye contact), part of what Edward Hall (1959, 1960, 1976, 1983) calls context, which is used in the decoding of implicit messages. The analogical components of verbal messages, such as a way of saying "yes" that makes it mean "no", profuse thank yous that contain a meaning other than their "digital" content precisely because their excess is also part of the context.

The cultural context of communication styles

Communication styles differ according to whether messages are sent in a direct vs. indirect manner and whether negotiators are talkative or listeners. Communication styles also involve choosing what is considered as relevant information as well as ways to compress them into a message that may be either broad or narrow, context-bound or context-free, and based on hard fact or general principles. Similarly, the tendency to disclose information, and the preference for asking questions as opposed to providing answers, are all embedded in communication styles. Involuntary messages are every so often emitted by negotiators through their personal characteristics of age, size, weight, sex, dress, and so on. These characteristics are encoded in the culture of the speaker, and decoded by the listener using their own cultural programme. Cues for interpretation are provided by the circumstances of the conversation, including where and when it takes place, and the meeting atmosphere.

Verbal communication styles embrace such elements as tone of voice, frequency and nature of conversational overlap, speed of speech, degree of apparent involvement in what one says, emphasis on talking versus emphasis on listening, digressive and indirect speech styles, etc. These are marked by cultural norms which implicitly define what is, supposedly, "good" communication ("good" meaning appropriate between members of the cultural community in so far as they share the same code).

There are four areas where communication style is strongly culture-bound:

1) Communication style reflects a self-concept. In cultures where the self-concept is strong, one may expect a communication style based on talking and self-assertion; where, on the contrary, self-suppression is valued, a modest and listening communication style is more likely.

2) Communication styles reflect a view of what is appropriate interaction. The Latin style of interruption is a lot about showing interest. Southern Europeans often find themselves speaking when others have not finished their sentence. Negotiators with Anglo-Saxon, Germanic, or Nordic communication styles may feel uncomfortable about what could seem an impolite overlap or even a rude interruption, even though it is really well intended. In Latin cultures, interruption and overlap show empathy with the other speaker and shared interest in the topic. Furthermore, Southern Europeans are (or they believe they are) able to speak and listen at the same time.

3) Communication styles also reflect the appropriate emphasis respectively put on talking and listening, according to cultural norms. Japanese top executives often behave like a "sphinx": they are almost pure listeners. One of their key roles is to listen to people. With some exceptions, Japanese bosses often display a mediocre talent for making public speeches and appear to be poor spokespersons. Whereas the Japanese tend toward a "two listeners" communication style, the Latin cultures tend toward a "two speakers" communication style. In Japan, silence is in fact valued as a full element of communication. It conveys messages, which, although implicit, may be interpreted through contextual factors. In a novel entitled *Shiosai*,[5] the Japanese writer Yukio Mishima features a young fisherman, Shinji, who takes his salary back to his mother, a widow with another younger son. Shinji's salary is the family's only resource. Mishima (1954, p. 57) recounts:

> Shinji liked to give his pay envelope to his mother without uttering a word. As a mother, she understood and always behaved as if she

did not remember it was pay day. She knew that her son liked to see her looking surprised.

4) Many messages are included in silent communication, and remain "unsaid". In general, European and American negotiators tend to fear tacit and unspoken messages much more than Asians do. Understanding the communication behaviour of the other side is important, irrespective of whether the value judgement put on it is positive or negative, because it facilitates sharing meaning. Silence may be experienced positively, as a moment for listening (especially to what is "not said"), or negatively as a sign of possible damage in the interaction flow, as wasted time, or even as a sign of potential animosity. In the same way, conversational overlaps may be seen as diluting the clarity of exchange, mere impoliteness of the overlapper, or a lack of interest in what one says. Conversely, it may be interpreted as a sign of empathy, a quick time-saving feedback, or even a necessary sign for pursuing the conversation.

The rules for achieving "good" communication are therefore largely cultural. The feeling that the flow of messages is going smoothly between negotiation partners is based on their ability to avoid messages that would be altered, confused, or incomplete. The value judgement on "good" or "bad" NC, appropriate or inappropriate NC, is largely based on unconscious cultural standards, negotiators implicitly agreeing or disagreeing on appropriate rules of communication. In an intercultural situation, negotiators have to allow themselves the informal opportunity to discuss and establish the rules of their communication (i.e., what is called meta-communication). Edward Hall comments on what friendship means and involves in the United Sates compared with other countries/cultures.

> As a general rule, in foreign countries friendships are not formed as quickly as in the United States, but go much deeper, last longer and involve real obligations. For example, it is important to stress that in the Middle East and Latin America your "friends" will not let you down. The fact that they personally are feeling the pinch is never an excuse for failing their friends. They are supposed to look out for your interests. Friends and family around the world represent a sort of social insurance that would be difficult to find in the United States.
>
> (Hall, 1960, pp. 90–91)

Low- and high-context communication styles: Explicit versus implicit messages

Contextualizing messages as an element of communication style

Negotiators in the IT1 paradigm tend to use a precise and decontextualized communication style. Conversely, negotiators in the IT2 paradigm tend to use a more implicit and context-bound, communication style. The meaning of contextualized or decontextualized is illustrated by many examples in Chapter 3 and in this chapter. However, between these extreme positions, there is an infinite variety of combinations. The first distinction in language-based communication is whether the messages sent by the speaker are explicit; that is, can they be taken literally rather than interpreted "in context". Setting messages "in context" would imply that what is literally said has to be in some way reinterpreted using various cues taken from the context, particularly the cultural context of the speaker.

Message format and information exchange

In most cases, communication is dependent on its context: who says it, where, when, and how it is said. Contextual factors may change what actually seems to be said literally.

Although Edward Hall does not precisely define what a message "context" is, it entails *inter alia*: location, people involved (age, sex, dress, social standing, etc.), and the background of the talks (e.g., at the workplace, in a showroom, during a round of labour negotiations, during a sales visit). For Hall:

> a high-context (HC) communication or message is one in which most of the information is either in the physical context or internalized in the person, while very little is in the coded, explicit, transmitted part of the message. A low-context (LC) communication is just the opposite; i.e., the mass of the information is vested in the explicit code.
>
> (Hall, 1976, p. 91)

Context influences communication without the participants even being aware of it. Cultural prejudices may intervene in decoding messages from a young negotiator such as unconscious questioning as to whether this young person deserves trust. The association between age and credibility, for instance, differs according to culture, from positive, to neutral or negative, therefore biasing the information exchange. A major element of context is the knowledge, acquaintance, and familiarity with the negotiators on the other side, and whether or not this personal relationship is a condition for seriously negotiating business. Personalization is required for IT2 negotiators whereas it is better for IT1 negotiators to somewhat depersonalize the communication process.

Context brings together the sum of interpretation mechanisms that originate within a culture and allow the message to be explained. In HC communication cultures (e.g., South America, China, Japan, and the Middle East) the message is largely implicit. Key interpretive information should be derived from the physical context (e.g., place, setting) and the social context (i.e., people: status, age, gender, and so on). Conversely, in LC communication (e.g., Germany, Scandinavian countries, and the United States) messages are explicit, containing information which, at the extreme, could be assigned a binary, digital value (Yes = 1, No = 0).[6] Low-context communication cultures favour explicit, context-free messages, which can be more easily coded in a univocal manner than communication from HC cultures where messages are implicit and need contextual knowledge, particular to a definite culture, country, and language, to be decoded by the receiver.

An important consequence for ICBN is that both sides' communication style needs to be assessed first, based on nationality, culture, and language. If both sides derive from a LC culture, communication can be assumed to be precise and explicit. If one negotiating party is more comfortable using a LC style but the other side has a HC style, the LC negotiators should ask precise questions, verify interpretation, and validate joint understanding. If both sides use HC communication, but come from different areas of the world (e.g., Japan and the Middle East), negotiators have to be aware that contextual codes are not shared. A certain degree of preparation is needed, on the part of at least one of the parties. Communication may at times be uncomfortable and indistinct. Patience, courtesy, and other-regarding orientation help achieve proper information flow.

Thought patterns in LC cultures are linear and emphasize rationality and logic, while HC cultures communicate in a more non-linear way with less apparent emphasis on linear rationality.[7] LC cultures are more information-based, and employ direct, textual, factual, and analytical arguments when negotiating. Conversely, in Japan, which is considered a typically high-context culture, additional information beyond a written format is preferred. As Hall (1976, p. 103) emphasizes, in LC communication, "most of the information must be in the transmitted message to make up for what is missing in the context". LC communication therefore tends to emit clear and univocal content, all of which do not require interpretation. Messages in LC communication are arguably more transparent; they have more explicit information content than HC messages, which require more interpretation and person-to-person interaction.

It has been stressed that HC communication is more sophisticated and allows more complex information processing. As Edward Hall (1976, p. 117) argues, "Internal contexting makes it possible for human beings to perform the exceedingly important function of automatically correcting for distortions or omissions in messages". LC communication proceeds in a different way, first by reducing distortions and omissions in *sent* messages as much as possible, making messages linear, articulated, explicit, simplified, however easy to understand in the absence of contextual clues. LC communication provides the lowest common denominator for intercultural communication between negotiators in a way that may not be always fully satisfactory, because it often looks "minimal". It does, however, provide a more secure basis for, and an easier path towards, mutual understanding. This largely explains the dominance of English as the typical LC business language and therefore the *lingua franca* of international business and intercultural business negotiations.[8]

HC communication tends to be more indirect, ambiguous, and understated than LC communication, which rather openly and precisely expresses facts and intentions.[9] The risk for LC negotiators is to appear naive and far too ready to disclose information because of their direct and explicit communication style. HC communication requires more contextual cues, some of which are related to the business partner (e.g., gender, age, ingroup, education, status), leading to more personalized business communication. However, HC communication has its strengths: it does better reflect the complexities of ICBN most of which are culture and context-bound. The IT1 LC communication style, while it is convenient for clearly organizing facts and information, is weak for other aspects of negotiation which are clearly context-bound and therefore impoverished or even obliterated by the near disappearance of contextual cues.

LC cultures and explicit communication

Low-context and explicit messages are almost "digital" and could be translated into simple computer units (bytes). Compliance with rules and dates is deeply associated with LC countries. Appointments are one example of explicit messages that in low-context cultures must be taken literally. An example of a LC seller's explicit message to a potential buyer is: "I can offer you a price of $140 per package of 12, to be delivered in cases of 144 within five weeks". LC cultures with explicit communication are the U.S. and Canada, together with the Germanic cultures (Germany, Switzerland, and Austria), Scandinavian countries, Australia, and New Zealand (see Table 5.1 for a detailed list of country HC-LC scores).

High-context cultures: A more diffuse communication style

In many cases HC negotiators prove reluctant to be direct and explicit: Language may explain part of it, as explained on pp. 149–51. Politeness and rules of address may forbid *being* too explicit, as it may be considered rude. Roles (e.g., buyer-seller, subordinate-superior, agent-principal, sex roles, etc.) may prescribe a deferent and listening attitude that is not conducive to straight and explicit expression.

In LC cultures, people tend to focus on specific issues and address their counterpart in a specific role (as a buyer for instance), not really impersonally but with a precise view of what the person in front of them has to *do*. Conversely, in HC cultures, people generally address broader issues and easily move between roles in their counterpart (e.g., as a private person, as a buyer, as a potential friend). A diffuse communication style should not be paralleled with "confused" communication, but it is clear that communication with HC negotiators may at times appear complicated to negotiators from LC cultures. HC cultures, according to Hall, include Latin America, the Middle East, China, and Japan. In Japan, context plays a significant role. For example, addressing others perceptibly shifts in register between more than 20 subtly different forms according to the age, sex, and social position of the conversation partner, as well as the speakers' relative positions in the social hierarchy (pupil/teacher, buyer/seller, employee/employer). The word "no" practically does not exist in the Japanese vocabulary. A "yes" in certain circumstances can actually mean "no". Keiko Ueda (1974) distinguishes 16 ways to avoid saying "no" in Japanese. The range of possible solutions varies from a vague "no", to a vague and ambiguous "yes", a mere silence, a counter-question, a tangential response, exiting (leaving), making an excuse such as sickness or a previous obligation, criticizing or refusing the question itself, saying "No, but…" or "Yes, but…", delaying answers ("We will write you a letter") and making apologies. The virtual absence of "no" in Japan manifests itself in email contacts. A German manager comments:

> "I know that Japanese people are very, very polite and never say "No"… So, I encourage them to say "No" when they mean no. And I double-check with them to make sure when they say "Yes" they mean yes". Nuances in the tone of voice are lost in emails, so when dealing with important issues with Japanese associates, the German manager always follows up with a phone call.[10]

Negotiators from HC cultures need a fairly good understanding of and acquaintance with a conversation partner. Impersonal negotiations (such as coming for a short meeting to discuss a deal, rapidly getting to the heart of the matter, and insisting on quickly closing the deal) will make a person from HC cultures ill at ease and impede negotiation. Kim et al. (1998) found that people from HC cultures (i.e., China and Korea) are more socially oriented, less confrontational, and more complacent about life than people from a LC culture (i.e., U.S.).

Occasionally, some cultures which fall in the midrange may shift from an explicit/specific to an implicit/diffuse communication style, and vice versa. The United Kingdom and France are examples of such a tendency. The British practice of "understatement" values complicity between people at the expense of clarity. French has often been considered as a good language for diplomacy because it can be alternately vague and precise, according to the kinds of words and style chosen. Sometimes French can be written with very precise words, with simple sentences (subject verb complement), but it can also, if the occasion demands, be styled in a very vague manner, starting with long dependent clauses describing circumstances and possibilities.

HC-LC communication styles exhibit different levels of correspondence between ideal behaviour (e.g., what is said or promised) and actual behaviour. In the HC style, communication is more personalized; however with expectations from an HC negotiator that the personalized relationship may

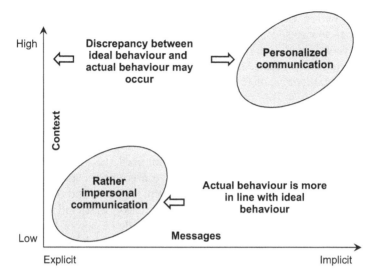

Figure 5.1 Communication styles and discrepancies between ideal and actual behaviour

be used for "repairing" some confusion about the preciseness of commitments (e.g., delays, deadlines, delivery provisions) and – sometimes – a relative lack of reliability of the HC partner in performing tasks as agreed by contractual provisions. As a consequence, the HC partner allows a certain "margin of error" between what has been said, more or less explicitly, and what is actually done, in the hope that the personalized relationship will afford benevolence and tolerance. Conversely, LC negotiators are used on average to more precisely and more firmly stick to what they have promised to do. LC commitment is to deeds rather than to people (see Figure 5.1). This may be a source of tension in international negotiations (English, 2010).

Limitations of Hall's high/low-context cross-cultural communication framework

Despite a widely shared acknowledgement of Hall's pioneering contribution to the field of intercultural communication, a number of critiques have been addressed regarding his HC-LC framework.[11] First, it has been characterized as an all-encompassing framework which was anecdotally derived. Hall (1959, p. 186) himself proposed the broad-brush statement that "Culture is communication and communication is culture". As a consequence, Hall's framework may appear as a simplistic description of both culture and communication. As emphasized by Goldsmith: "the high/low-context distinction … does not provide an account for normative judgements of how individuals respond to context-specific communicative dilemmas".[12] A further critique of Hall is related to the implicit assumption that culture is univocally associated with national groups,[13] at the risk of ignoring cultural differences within nation-states, especially those that display large ethnic and/or linguistic diversity (e.g., India). This limitation is all the more important as globalization has been intense over half a century (i.e., since the publication of Hall's *Silent Language*, in 1959), and within-country diversity has increased while cross-country diversity has diminished. Therefore, language diversity should be taken into account along with HC-LC communication styles.

It has also been said that Hall's conceptualization of culture tends to be operationalized as a dichotomous variable. However, both Hall's work and further references that have operationalized the HC-LC concept are much more nuanced, enabling us to derive a country classification in five categories from low to HC with low/medium, medium, and medium/high as intermediate categories (see Table 5.1). One reason that Hall's contribution is somewhat caricatured may come from the title of one of his chapters in *Beyond Culture* (i.e., "Contexts, High and Low"), which induced readers to believe that it is a purely dichotomous divide. It may also be that Edward Hall is too often referenced on the basis of secondary sources, without primary reading of the source texts.

A critique of Hall is his lack of explicit reference to language structure. Hall even rejects what he calls "the linguistic code" as unrelated to the HC-LC framework, as if "linguistic codes" were completely comparable and as if all languages required the same level of context for messages to be interpreted. Hall was also influenced by the view of linguistic relativity (i.e., the Sapir-Whorf hypothesis[14]), however without digging much into linguistic issues. The reason may be that Hall was also deeply influenced by psychoanalysis and emphasized the non-verbal, unconscious side of communication,[15] at the expense of the verbal side, which tends to be favoured by linguistics.

Non-verbal communication in ICBN

Essentials of non-verbal communication

A lot of communication is unconsciously, unintentionally, unwillingly sent through non-verbal language (NVL). Mehrabian (1971) estimated that 93% of total communication was conveyed by NVL. Such NVL messages are also almost unconsciously decoded by the other negotiator. NVL communication should be taken into account, especially if discovering late (but not too late) that something has gone wrong because of inadequate NVL. NVL is subtle and tacit. Most involuntary emotional expressions cannot be deliberately managed. A very few non-verbal cues can be managed such as vesture; however, physical appearance cannot be managed: a negotiator cannot change her or his age, height, (physical) build, face (unless with make-up), etc. A person's dress style, being shaved or unshaved, can be "decided", but it could easily be interpreted as bizarre, possibly offensive if for instance an American negotiator adopted the dress style of his Saudi counterparts. Calculated actions in terms of non-verbal behaviour, beyond their rare feasibility, are bound to fail when body language conveys different messages for both sides according to situations and circumstances, for instance kissing between men and/or women as a sign of friendship.

Body language and non-verbal communication

Since much of what is exchanged in communication is only implicitly meant, tacit rather than explicitly verbalized, non-verbal communication is largely used as an interpretative framework, which allows people to try to overcome some shortcomings of verbal communication.

Communication through gestures (body language)

Body language is an infinite source of differences and misunderstandings. A Muslim considers a person sitting with their shoe-soles turned at their counterpart an insult.[16] Ways of greeting people differ greatly between cultures. While the French have the custom of shaking hands the first time they meet a person each day, many cultures (e.g., Australia, the USA, the UK) use handshakes much less. In Japan, a bow is the appropriate manner of greeting. In certain large Japanese department stores there are hostesses whose sole job is to bow to each customer who comes into the store. Anyone who has observed bowing rituals in Japanese railway stations or airports is struck by their complexity, the number, depth, and synchronization of bows being accurately codified. As Ferraro (1990, p. 73) notes:

> In fact it is possible to tell the relative social status of the two communicators by the depth of their bows (the deeper the bow, the lower the status) ... The person of lower status is supposed to initiate the bow, and the person of higher status determines when the bow is completed.

A challenge in intercultural communication is to understand what hand and/or head gestures mean in a particular culture, especially if physical contact and proxemics are involved. Moving the head up and down means "yes" in most Western European countries, but it means "no" in Greece and Bulgaria, and moving the head from left to right is a sign of negation for some and affirmation for others. In many Western countries it is considered a gesture of affection to pat a child on the head, but in Malaysia and many Islamic countries the head is considered to be the source of spiritual and intellectual activity and is therefore sacred.[17]

Various forms of non-verbal communication involve physical contact: some groups kiss (the cheek, lips, hand, foot), take a person by the arm, clasp the shoulders, pinch the cheek, shake hands, tickle, stroke, give a little pat, etc. These gestures, running over into the realm of familiarity and sexual conduct, are subject to extremely diverse codes of use. The kiss, regarded as normal between Russian men or Arab men, who also hold hands in the streets, may appear shocking to Anglo-Saxons. Ferraro recounts his own experience while conducting field research in Kenya, walking with a key informant who was also a close personal acquaintance:

> As we walked side by side my friend took my hand in his. Within less than 30 seconds my palm was perspiring all over his. Despite the fact that I knew cognitively that it was a perfectly legitimate Kikuyu gesture of friendship, my own cultural values (that is, that "real men" don't hold hands) were so ingrained that it was impossible for me not to communicate to my friend that I was very uncomfortable.
>
> (Ferraro, 1990, pp. 85–86)

The significance of NVL communication codes is complex. It would be overly simplistic to oppose people who are reserved in their physical contact (e.g., Anglo-Saxons) to those who are more liberal. For instance, men and/ or women kissing each other in public when meeting may seem shocking in some cultures in which physical demonstration of friendship should be kept private. Dancing, which is part of many cultures' social gatherings, may seem indecent to some and perfectly innocent to others.

Facial expressions and communication with the eyes

Laughing and smiling, winking and blinking, frowning and knitting one's brow express communication. A smile can be a sign of satisfaction, of agreement, of embarrassment ... or even no sign at all. Certain cultures may consider the spontaneous expression of attitudes and emotions by a facial expression to be normal. The reverse is true in other cultures, particularly in some Asian countries where it is considered desirable not to display emotion. This has given rise to the impression that Asians are inscrutable and stoic. According to Morschbach (1982, p. 308):

> Self control, thought of as highly desirable in Japan, demands that a man of virtue will not show a negative emotion in his face when shocked or upset by sudden bad news; and, if successful, is lauded as *taizen jijaku to shite* (perfectly calm and collected) or *mayu hitotsu ugokasazu ni* (without even moving an eyebrow) ... The idea of an expression-less face in situations of great anxiety was strongly emphasized in the *bushido* (way of the warrior) which was the guide-line for samurai and the ideal for many others.

Direct visual contacts, such as looking someone straight in the eyes, or, conversely, looking away, or lowering the eyes, or turning them away when they meet someone else's eyes, are all given specific meanings in different cultures. This is proof that the same conduct (innocent as it may be) can be arbitrarily given opposite meanings. Arabs often look each other straight in the eyes because they believe that the eyes are the windows of the soul and that it is important to know the heart and soul of those one is negotiating with. By contrast, Japanese children are taught in school not to look their teacher in the eyes, but to look at the level of the neck. When they become adults, it is considered a sign of respect to lower their eyes when with superiors. Europeans have a tendency to look people straight in the eyes; like the Americans and Australians, they tend to associate a lack of honesty with someone who looks away, and see it as a potential signal of an unfriendly, defiant, impersonal or inattentive attitude.[18] A lack of eye contact for the Americans is a signal that something is amiss. For American executives, the lack of eye contact is not only disconcerting but also reduces their perceived bargaining performance.[19] Dealing with unknown communication styles, especially non-verbal ones, is not an easy task. Comprehensive understanding of local cultural interpretations of body language requires one to stay long enough to learn. One can avoid NVL gestures when there is fear of being misunderstood.

Interpreting the other party's non-verbal language

The locally "adequate" NVL behaviour is learned during childhood, through rearing and education; it translates into a profoundly ingrained physical demeanour. Awareness begins with the capacity to *unlearn* by discovering the cultural relativity of one's own non-verbal communication behaviour. *Unlearning* is a condition for the learning process to take place. If NVL is assumed to be relative, the interpretation of the other party's non-verbal language poses serious challenges in terms of awareness, knowledge, and adjustment. The relativistic view is that diversity (and therefore incomplete communicability) exists in NVL.

Conversely, if NVL is assumed to be rather universal, very deep, and unconsciously decoded in a rather consistent manner across cultures, then the interpretation of NVL seems rather straightforward.[20] However, whether considered a universal or relative form of communication, there are drawbacks to non-verbal communication both for the emitter and for the receiver. It is quickly and unconsciously expressed, sending multiple messages in an instant. Messages must be rashly interpreted, in a fraction of a second, which increases the odds of misinterpretation. NVL is sometimes difficult to decode. It cannot be stored, reproduced, and (hardly) discussed. NVL may be ambiguous (e.g., nodding, face expression, posture), possibly misleading, and even deceitful. Furthermore, NVL is not easily manageable communication because it is spontaneous. It is hardly possible to willingly and credibly emit NVL with a reasonable expectation that the other party will not perceive it as fake, forged, lacking in sincerity, and possibly hurting the emitter's credibility.

NVL as a communication means cannot be used in the dark or at a distance (unless using Skype or FaceTime), when negotiators cannot be observed. Contrary to spoken and/or written verbal language, there is no corpus for interpreting NVL meaning: no dictionaries, no convenient instrument such as *Google Translate*, no storage of NVL information, no printing and diffusion of knowledge, no transformation of NVL into digitalized information as is the case for verbal language (VL) with voice recognition and character recognition (OCR). This is the reason for the huge dominance of VL over NVL, its massive superiority, despite the claims of NVL partisans.[21]

When trying, however, to manage one's own non-verbal language as a communication tool in negotiation, in the IT1 paradigm (e.g., doing oriented, self-control, as exposed in Chapter 3), contextual cues are often perceived as being "manageable", and negotiators think that they may simulate or pretend, without being "discovered". The IT2 *being*-oriented negotiator, more relativistic and pondering that NVL is largely unconscious and deeply programmed (i.e., negotiators cannot change their NVL: "it *is* as it *is*"), tends to think that self-control and developing an artificial behaviour have limitations. Contextual cues in NVL are not perceived as really "manageable". You may simulate and pretend; however the chances are high that you will be "discovered". There are three types of solutions when one is confronted with unmanageable, if not uncontrollable, NVL. They are valid for both IT2 and IT1 negotiators (assuming that they are subject to the over-optimistic illusion of being able to control NVL).

- Behaving in an unconstrained manner and freely adopting one's own culture's NVL, however without exaggerating the trait.
- Suppressing NVL as much as possible because it is unmanageable: behaving like a Sphinx, inert and almost stone-like, listening, avoiding facial expressivity, blocking gestures, etc.
- Trying to identify near universals in NVL and using them only, avoiding body language that may be offensive to the negotiation partner.

The best solution is probably to behave naturally, without trying to suppress body language and NVL, while simply avoiding offensive NV messages (at least as perceived in the target culture, and as far as negotiators can be aware or become conscious of their being unpleasant to the other party). This can be based on a don'ts list and on interviewing cultural insiders before negotiating. Also avoid over-interpretation; let all participants behave freely and spontaneously. Nobody should be made to feel guilty for unintentional mistakes. Most NVL and body language will simply reflect how negotiators spontaneously behave given their cultural background learned in childhood and early socialization, and in fact mirror their natural behaviour and their true character. If offended, react like the *impartial spectator* and the *prudent man* of Adam Smith: ignore the NVL "offence" if minor and obviously unintentional, and avoid any over-reaction that would lead to purely subjective (i.e., strictly non-rational) conflict escalation.

The role of language in ICBN communication

Cross-cultural communication is also inter-linguistic communication (across natural languages) in three ways: 1) Through the direct use of a joint communication language; 2) through interpreters, when negotiators speak different languages and have chosen to use such intermediaries in the hope that interpreters will enable negotiators to clearly communicate in their native language or through translators for written, in particular contractual, language; and 3) through the influence of language-related mindsets on communication style and negotiation behaviour. What I mean by "language" is not any general communication code (e.g., the language of arts) but natural, national languages spoken by a group of people, with a vocabulary, a grammar, and a syntax, both spoken and written. The French language has two words for the English word language, *langage* (the general category of communication codes) and *langue*, which corresponds to the English (mother) tongue or (native) language.

Languages and HC/LC communication styles

The contextuality of communication is partly related to whether a national language itself expresses ideas and facts more or less explicitly. The Japanese language, for instance, is in general less precise (less explicit) than English or French: personal pronouns are often not explicitly expressed in Japanese, and the number of tenses is smaller, especially compared with English, French, or German. In Japanese, both spoken words (that is, sounds) and written words (based on *kanji*, or pictograms, and syllabaries such as *Katakana* and *Hiragana*) often have multiple meanings, so that the listener needs some kind of contextual clarification. Sometimes, Japanese people write the *kanji* (ideographs) briefly on their hand to clarify what they are saying.

Naturally it would be false to broadly say that certain languages are vague and others precise. The real world is more complex. This has to be strongly nuanced when one looks more carefully at the structure of the language. German, for instance, has many verbs that have quite different meanings according to the context. Examples arise just by consulting a German–English dictionary. For instance, the verb *absetzen* means, according to the context, to deposit or deduct a sum, to take off a hat, to dismiss an official, to depose a king, to drop a passenger, to sell goods, to stop or pause, or to take off (a play). The same holds true for the Finnish language: even though the Finns, like many northern Europeans, have a reputation for their explicitness in communication, Finnish has a very special language structure which renders context useful in communication. Finnish (part of the Finno-Ugrian languages, really only shared with Estonia and Hungary) uses 16 cases which virtually replace all the prepositions used in other languages. Even proper nouns can be declined using these cases, transforming one or two syllables at the end of the word.

Languages share a common objective; that is, to convey meaning in an appropriate way from people to people. But they achieve it differently, relying to varying degrees on precise words, structured grammar or, in contrast, on contextual indications of how ambiguous meanings should be made precise. English is a precise and fairly context-free language. This holds especially true for "international English". The *lingua franca* of international business is context free, rendering it a bit impoverished, however precise at the same time.

Hall's theory of LC-HC communication cultures is based on his background as a cultural anthropologist, on his field studies of American Indian cultures, and his pioneering work with U.S. diplomatic services. It is related to other cultural patterns relating to time (monochronism-polychronism), relationships, and interpersonal distance. Hall seems not to view language as strongly related to HC-LC communication styles when he states: "The problem lies not in the linguistic code, but in the context, which carries varying proportions of the meaning. Without context, the code is incomplete since it encompasses only part of the message".[22] However, later in the same chapter, "Context and Meaning" (Chapter 6), Hall writes about the linearity of language (with the English language implicitly in mind) and gives many examples related to the U.S. decontextualized legal system (e.g., in U.S. courts: "Answer the question, Yes or No", p. 107)". On the other hand, Hall gives HC examples based on the Chinese language and writing system as an art form as well as on the way French courts tend to contextualize trials, French communication culture being a HC-LC *mélange* (Hall's terminology). However, being a cultural anthropologist, not a linguist, he seems to overlook how deeply language structure is related to the HC-LC divide. Many Asian languages use no gender, little or no personal pronouns, do not conjugate verbs, and provide locutors with a relatively undersignified text, which requires much information from the context for the message to be understood by the receiver.[23] Similarly a semi-HC language such as French avoids repetitions of the same word for the sake of elegance and therefore uses synonyms or pronouns at the direct expense of preciseness and clarity. Meaning is supposed to be understood from context. French people communicating in English must forget the sacred rule they have learned not to repeat words, especially in writing. The – supposed – synonyms are misunderstood by English speakers (readers) who do not understand why different words are used for the same concept. In very HC languages like Japanese and Chinese, gender and number as well as person are often understood from the context. The subject, especially "I", will often be omitted in Japanese, while in Chinese verbal forms will not change with time, gender, or person. Conversely LC languages are often over-coded (redundant) to make messages even more explicit. When a German locutor says "*Ich mache*", the first person singular is both in the personal pronoun *Ich (I)* and in the ending *(e)* of the verb which applies only to the first person singular in the present and active tense. HC-LC communication styles are partly related to language structure. Indo-European languages on average favour low- to medium-context communication, while many Far East languages such as Chinese, Japanese, Thai, or Vietnamese favour HC communication.

Communication in LC languages, especially English, is more universal because it requires fewer contextual cues to be understood. Context as defined by Hall is essentially qualitative and related to five disparate categories of events: subject or activity, situation, status, past experience, and culture (Hall, 1976, p. 87). In HC communication the challenge is not only that it is more context-bound, but also that the context is specific to particular cultures and languages. As a consequence, it may be more difficult to communicate across different HC language-cultures[24] than for an HC person to communicate with people from LC language-cultures. HC communicators need *their* native language because it tends to be strongly associated with particular contextual cues, familiar to them. However, these contextual cues are unfamiliar to communicators from other HC cultures. HC communicators may feel uneasy communicating with other HC business people (i.e., also HC communicators, however not within *the same* context) while they may paradoxically feel more comfortable interacting with LC communicators. For HC business communicators, it may be easier to adapt to LC communication style rather than to multiple and divergent HC styles. Conversely, LC communicators often tend to assume that language is relatively neutral and instrumental.[25] Because LC communicators are used to relatively precise and explicit messages, they tend to perceive translation and interpretation as a matter of technique for which dictionaries provide good lexical equivalence. LC communicators tend to assume that language professionals, both interpreters and translators, can do a fair job at reconstructing clear texts in a number of foreign target languages.

Language differences and ICBN communication

Communicating across languages, being understood (and possibly being misunderstood) is a real challenge. For most people, there is a big difference between spoken (oral) and written communication (e.g., contracts, letters, documents and brochures, mail). The respective emphasis on oral versus written language is important in ICBN (see Chapter 7).

Another aspect of language use is whether people prefer direct versus indirect communication. Reluctance (or apparent reluctance) to be direct has several culture- and language-related motives:

- A fear of conflict or breach of harmony. Negotiators, by being too direct, may be resented as aggressive, possibly provocative and/or confrontational.
- A mindset issue: some negotiators need to set the *big picture* and the context first, allude to general principles, past experiences, and events and get to the point only later.
- Directness in negotiation, especially in the preliminaries may be perceived as disrespectful, especially in vertical interactions and in hierarchical, high power distance societies.

When such motives are present, the cultural habit is deeply ingrained to express oneself through indirect language forms for fear of being resented as impolite and/or quarrelsome. Figure 5.2 distinguishes four speech styles based on linguistic structures, the logical sequence of thoughts, grammar, and rhetoric. Speech styles differ from direct (e.g., Northern Europeans, Americans), semi-direct (Latin languages) to semi-indirect style (e.g., Arabic-Middle East) and indirect (e.g., East Asians), privileging linear or circular communication patterns, single or parallel thought development, with or without digression. All get to the point through different "speech routes".

The disadvantages of indirectness (mostly an IT2 communication feature) are sometimes badly felt by IT1 negotiators using a direct communication style. However, they must display patience and prudence, politely inciting the negotiation partner to be more matter-of-fact, to avoid unnecessary digression, repetitive illustrations and trying to speed up the process of getting to the point.

Language skills, mono- and multilingualism are practical issues for ICB negotiators. However, negotiators are rarely chosen for their talents in speaking foreign languages. Multilingual negotiators with full proficiency in several important languages are quite rare. The most frequent situation is that of originally monolingual negotiators who use English as an International Language (EIL) as a joint language beyond their respective

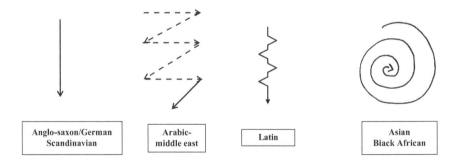

Figure 5.2 Direct and indirect speech styles
Source: adapted from Kaplan (1966)

native languages. This is in line with the arch-dominance of English as the typically LC business language and therefore the *lingua franca* of international business.[26] However, verbal communication in English, between non-native speakers may pose problems in understanding words (due to different accents), sentences (because the foreign language syntax is unduly introduced in English), and key negotiation concepts, making it hard to avoid communication misunderstandings and therefore to reach a mutually profitable agreement. That is why the deliberate and conscious choice of language is necessary in ICBN as well as the introduction of interpreters.

Language choice and the role of interpreters

An integrative approach assumes that negotiators focus on seeking and sharing information. Communication has been shown to generate greater cooperation even among negotiating partners that display strong tendencies toward self-interest.[27] The language used for a particular negotiation is therefore of some consequence: the myth that any language can be translated into another language often causes English to be chosen as the central negotiating language and/or to hire interpreters when proficiency in English is too low.[28] In the case of Sino-Foreign joint ventures some years ago, few Chinese people were capable of speaking a foreign language, and all oral communication between a Chinese party and their foreign partners had to pass through interpreters: "When a third person is involved no genuine, direct communication between two people can take place. In other words, 'heart-to-heart' talks are unlikely to take place".[29] Furthermore, due to poor translation, it may be that only 30–40% of the actual content of what was said in Chinese is conveyed to the non-Chinese speaking negotiation partners, resulting in the discarding of good ideas and suggestions made by the Chinese.

There are semantic differences in the words used and many misunderstandings can arise from ignoring the precise meaning of key concepts central to the negotiation;[30] Adachi (1998) gives the example of noticeable differences in the use of the word "customer" by Japanese and American negotiators. Cultural connotations and contextual cues used to decode messages are a crucial aspect of conversation that needs careful attention in order to understand the meaning beyond the mere translation of words.

When messages are exchanged, the degree to which they should be interpreted has to be taken into account as well as the cross-cultural differences in linguistic styles, involving the use of silence or conversational overlap.[31] For instance, in Japan silence is a full form of communication. Research by Graham has reported twice as many silences in Japanese than in American[32] interaction. Western companies often have the impression that they "do all the talking" while their partners from Japan, China, or South Korea keep silent or ask questions. Low-context negotiators, such as

Americans, have a tendency to be explicit, precise, legalistic, and direct in communication, sometimes being forceful and even appearing to be rude to the other party.[33] In an empirical survey of Japanese and U.S. negotiators, Adair et al. (2001, p. 380) show that direct and indirect communication patterns are consistent with Hall's theory of low versus high- context communication:

> The U.S. negotiators relied on direct information to learn about each other's preferences and priorities and to integrate this information to generate joint gains. They were comfortable sharing information about priorities, comparing and contrasting their preferences with those of the other party, and giving specific feedback to offers and proposals. The Japanese negotiators relied on indirect information, inferring each other's preferences and priorities from multiple offers and counteroffers over time.

Negotiators must be ready to hear true as well as false information, discourse based on facts as well as on wishful thinking or pure obedience to superiors. Frankness and sincerity are culturally relative values: they can be interpreted as mere naivety, a lack of realism, or a lack of self-control in speaking one's own mind. Furthermore, waiting for reciprocation when disclosing useful information for the other party makes little sense in an intercultural context. Frankness and directness in communication are a substantial value to the Americans and to a lesser extent to the French, but not to Mexicans in formal encounters, or to Japanese at any time.[34]

The extent of how formal or informal a negotiator should be is a particularly difficult issue. A contrast is regularly made between cultures which value informality (e.g., American) and those that are inclined to be more formal (most cultures which have long historical roots and high power distance). "Informality" may be thought of simply as another kind of formality, and the "icebreaking" at the beginning of any typical U.S. meeting between unknown people is generally an expected ritual. It is more important to try to understand what kind of formality is required in which circumstances with which people. Outside of formal negotiation sessions, people belonging to seemingly quite formal cultures can become much more informal.

In ICBN, interpreters may serve a crucial purpose as transposers of meaning. They may translate better from one language to another than in the reverse direction, and this will depend not only on their native language, but also on a personal leaning that they may have towards one party. It is also necessary to make sure that they are truly loyal to the party that has hired them. It may be advisable to hire several interpreters when the business at stake justifies it. Sussman and Johnson (1993), based on a qualitative analysis of critical incidents provided by professional interpreters (in German, French, Japanese, and Spanish), highlight three major roles for interpreters: editor, cultural coach, and monitor/checker. In their view, international executives should be informed consumers of interpretation services. Executives conducting business through the services of an interpreter should hire an interpreter with proven or accredited skills and try to avoid using multiple interpreters since the use of many interpreters results in confused and protracted business transactions. It is also necessary to determine whether the interpreter should be a passive or an active participant taking on more than the strict interpreting role.

Accepting the Whorf–Sapir hypothesis (i.e., that language shapes worldviews, perceptions, and communication) implies that business people from different cultures not only communicate in different ways, but also perceive, categorize, and construct their realities differently.[35] This therefore supposes being in a "state of alert" in communication, a readiness to accept that words, even those that are translated with no apparent difficulty, offer only an illusion of sharing in the same vision of reality. It is necessary to retain as many foreign words as possible in their original form, thereby keeping culturally unique concepts. Asking questions to interpreters and/or to negotiation partners enables one to retrieve precise meaning of words or expressions and to identify shared meaning.

For instance, in the examination of contract clauses, it is necessary to try to extricate the true meaning of each clause, starting from the perspective that they are never exactly equivalent. This is true even in the case where a dictionary seems to (falsely) indicate that an English term is a strict equivalent of a French term, used *verbatim* in contracts written in English, such as *Force Majeure* versus *Act of God*.[36]

How to avoid communication misunderstandings during the negotiation process

Sources of communication misunderstandings in ICBN

Negotiation partners (or opponents, according to whether the cooperative or the competitive side is privileged) often do not share the same cultural and linguistic background and/or a similar communication style. Misunderstandings between the negotiators may come up over their differences of opinion as to what is truly important (e.g., interests, positions, rights, facts, feelings and empathy). As outlined in previous chapters, negotiators from HC/diffuse communication cultures prefer spending time chatting about life in general with the very purpose of getting to know their negotiating partner. Those from LC/specific communication cultures, on the other hand, prefer to get straight down to business, avoid wasting time on chatting, and proceed directly to rational talk on the issues at stake.

Messages may be coded in a rather LC communication style and subsequently decoded by HC communication receivers, or vice versa. This adds a further challenge in terms of *intercultural* business communication. As argued by Haworth and Savage (1989, p. 231), explaining their channel-ratio model of intercultural communication:

> The ratio of explicit to implicit information in the channel is cultur-ally and contextually determined, and intercultural communication problems may be analyzed in terms of mismatches between the channel ratios of the participants.

The channel-ratio model of intercultural communication emphasizes the importance of "knowledge" and the overlap in the phenomenal fields of the sender and receiver. Knowledge includes the body of facts, skills, and experiences the individual has acquired through cultural conditioning, as well as knowledge of the other party, which Hall (1976) considers critically important. Each culture has a characteristic division of the channel in terms of explicit (E) and implicit (I) information. Thus knowing that specific infor-mation will not be made explicit by a participant from a low E/I culture (i.e., HC) requires that additional information has to be gathered outside the channel.

A number of ICBN communication misunderstandings are related to differences in conversational style: conversational overlap, listening versus talking, hard versus soft address, the different ways to alternate talking and listening and/or to deal with what seems embarrassing silence. The solu-tion is first to become aware of communication style differences and then to develop Adam Smith's *impartial spectator* view, free of value judgements about a disturbing communication. Finally, conscious and deliberate adjust-ment is necessary: for instance, being ready for unusually long silent periods; accepting silence as a non-threatening behaviour; using silence to reciprocate for silence; asking questions rather than answering a barrage of questions from the other side; accepting being interrupted by over-lappers, how-ever courteously and firmly asking to be allowed to utter a full statement; accepting that *conversational style* may be merely conversational and not a sign of rudeness.

The lack of skills (or at least overestimated communication skills) attributed to the other party in a global EIL environment is now a major source of communication misunderstandings. There are both advantages and drawbacks in the use of EIL in ICBN: while it provides a joint low-context language, apparently facilitating communication, it also tends to conceal a lack of English proficiency and to promote mix-ups, errors, and finally confusion. This is a tricky issue since "less talented" negotiators may frown upon being directly addressed on this issue (and potentially lose face). Slowing down the pace of communication, re-phrasing, clarifying, playing language games (e.g., mixing words in different languages) are solutions to this problem. For tackling poor intercomprehension, negotiators may also track key concepts (e.g., business, legal, and financial) that may exhibit cross-cultural variance, and ask interpreters and translators for clarification.

A problematic issue related to the discrepancy in language skills is to choose a language for the contract. This language may be imposed on the other party through linguistic domination. The contract language issue is examined in Chapter 7.

The *respective role of verbal and non-verbal communication* and the relative emphasis put on each form of language (VL and NVL) is another source of communication misunderstandings. The best solution is to rely mostly on VL, especially when NVL is difficult to decode. The *Degree of engagement* in what is (or has been) said, should never be overestimated. A proverb says that promises only engage those who listen to them. Consequently a major source of communication misunderstandings is the respective role of written documents and speech (see Chapter 7). Understandably IT1 negotiators are wary of purely verbal commitments and ask for agreements to be put in detailed documents. However, as is shown in further chapters of this book, they should remain cautious about the binding value of such written engagements. A final remark is that communication misunderstandings in ICBN generate stress and emotions, which are themselves part of the messages. Emotions may target instrumental communication, a negotiator trying to send emotional signals (real or feigned) that may generate a feeling of guilt or shame in the counterpart. In neutral cultures there is less need for emotions because suppressing emotions is the norm; negotiators from low emotional expressivity cultures may try to remain uninfluenced by manipulative emotions. However, Kumar (2004, p. 103) notes that the expression of negative emotions by IT2 collectivistic negotiators stemming from a violation of relation norms (i.e., severely hurting the relationship) by their partner is mediated by the ingroup-outgroup distinction:

> ... the presence of negative agent-based emotions will almost surely compromise the possibility of attaining a negotiated agreement. It is also worth noting that the specific behavioral response to the violation of relational norms by the opposing negotiator depends upon whether or not the opponent is a member of one's in-group or out-group. Collectivists may be less hesitant to respond in an aggressive manner to individuals who are not members of their in-group vis-à-vis individuals who are.

Courtesy and apology in ICBNs

Courtesy, politeness, and related marks of civility and respect are found across all societies; however they are coded differently. The common aim is to acknowledge status and position as well as to send preliminary positive signals of considerate behaviour to the other party's negotiators. However, this willingness to appropriately behave, while having a universal core, also obeys to local customs, at times leading negotiators to involuntarily offend their counterpart(s). An apology may then be required. The objective of apologetic statements and behaviour is to stop possible conflict early after an incident that could lead to conflict escalation. Courtesy and apology in ICBN stand at the interface between HC communication and NVL. The degree of formality has to be considered: A common practice in the U.S. is to automatically address others by their first name. The same is true in Iceland and Canada, as well as Australia. In more formal countries, such as Germany, Austria, Switzerland, and Sweden as well as many Asian countries, it is better not to address new contacts by their first names unless invited to do so. The meaning and function of apologies varies cross-culturally. The Japanese for instance apologize more frequently than Americans, especially when they do not bear responsibility for what they apologize for. Americans apologize because they feel guilty for some action and want to acknowledge responsibility. In both cases, the function of apologies is to repair possible damage to the trusting relationship caused by misbehaviour. However apologies for competence (i.e., task-related, doing and IT1) violation are more effective for Americans while apologies for integrity (i.e., people-related, being and IT2) violation lead to greater trust repair for Japanese negotiators.[37]

A core set of courtesy rules exists in ICBN. Politeness and courtesy are based on linguistic indirection used to show social consideration, by not being direct.[38] Thus, politeness is always HC communication in any culture. The set of universal rules is mostly in the form of don'ts, such as not spitting at a person or slapping another's face. However, the degree of contextuality varies according to language and culture. The word *courtesy* is derived from the word "court", meaning the residence of a king or emperor. It emphasizes the kind of noble behaviour that enhances self-respect through the respect of others. Most languages have such a word. German, for instance, has the word *höflich* (polite), based on the German word for court, *Hof*. Foreigners are forgiven much provided they are not arrogant and they show consideration for their hosts, even if they may be ignorant of their customs. Modest, though firm, behaviour facilitates the acceptance of cultural mistakes by the other party.

If you are considered an offender, ask for clarification. If needed present apologies, without pushing regrets so far that your position in negotiation would be undermined. Communication rules can be especially sensitive when problems occur. For instance, there are two forms of apology in Japan,[39] the *sunao* apology, which is a sort of gently submissive apology given with good grace, and a sincere form of apology, which is more from the heart. These apologies are codified in Japanese conduct manuals, which provide many readily usable apologetic expressions. Conversely, most Westerners tend to favour direct, spontaneous, and non-formulaic apologies, in which sincerity is conveyed through original expressions. It is easy to find *savoir-vivre* manuals which describe local norms of courtesy and apology as well as to ask for insider information. However, apologies should be kept in the

limits of what is strictly necessary for avoiding misunderstandings and conflict. Beyond a certain threshold, over-apologetic statements may harm both
the credibility and the positions of an ICB negotiator.

Mindsets: Big picture versus micro-focus orientation

Content issues in ICBN relate to information exchange and to arguments
and persuasion. Differences in mindsets are reflected in the weight
attributed to general causes, broad principles, all-encompassing ideas,
versus down-to-earth, programmatic, and pragmatic statements that are
nearer to implementation issues. Ways of reasoning and making arguments
stereotypically oppose Big Picture versus Micro-Focus orientations, for
instance, when a party starts by discussing broad principles when the
other side is willing to proceed with a clear and focused agenda of clearly
defined, down-to-earth, and practical issues When negotiators do not
share common "mental schemes" – a similar *mindset* – it may be difficult
for them to solve problems together. They need to share some joint views
of the world, especially on questions such as: What is the relevant information? How should this information be sought, evaluated, and fed into
the decision-making process?

An important distinction in the field of cross-cultural psychology contrasts
ideologism with pragmatism. As Triandis suggests[40]:

> Ideologism versus pragmatism, which corresponds to Glenn's univer-
> salism versus particularism, refers to the extent to which the information
> extracted from the environment is transmitted within a broad frame-
> work, such as a religion or a political ideology, or a relatively narrow
> framework. This dimension refers to a way of thinking, an important
> element of the "mindset".

People differ in their ways of relating thinking to action: while "ideologists"
think broadly and relate to general principles, "pragmatists" concentrate on
focusing on detailed and precise negotiation issues that are to be solved one
by one, sequentially. "Pragmatists" prefer to negotiate specific clauses, in
a sequential manner. Conversely, "ideologists" favour arguments that promote a "global way of thinking", preferring to establish general principles,
package deals, and a more holistic type of agreement (i.e., a broad and loose
memorandum of understanding rather than a detailed and precise contract).
Triandis hypothesizes that complex, traditional societies will be ideologist,
whereas pluralistic societies, or cultures experiencing rapid social change,
will be pragmatist. Such a distinction between ideologists and pragmatists
may be traced to the differences between a legal system of *common law*
(mainly English and American) and a legal system of *code law*. Whereas
common law favours legal precedents set by the courts and past rulings

(cases), *code law* favours laws and general principles. Code law aims to formulate general principles so as to embody the entire set of particular cases in an all-inclusive system of written rules of law.

The "ideologist" orientation, which is to be found, for instance, in Southern and Eastern Europe, leads negotiators to try to establish principles before any detailed discussion of specific clauses within the contract begins. Ideologists prefer and promote globalized negotiations in which all of the issues are gathered together in a "package deal". Conversely, the pragmatist attitude corresponds to attitudes found in Northern Europe and the United States. Pragmatism demands that an outline of the scope of the existing problems be drawn before solving each problem one after the other. Pragmatists focus their thoughts on the factual aspects of the transaction (deeds, not words; evidence, not opinions; figures, not value judgements). They want to achieve tangible, identifiable outcomes, which means they have to be realistic.

Ideologists use a wide body of ideas which provides them with a formal and coherent description of the world: Marxism or Liberalism for instance. Every event carries meaning when it is seen through a broad intellectual framework. On the other hand, the pragmatist attitude first considers the extreme diversity of real world situations, and then derives its principles inductively. As emphasized by Fisher (1980, p. 50), pragmatic Americans may resent an ideologist culture, such as France, when conducting intercultural business negotiations.

> The French assign greater priority than Americans to establishing the principles on which the reasoning process should be based. Once this reasoning process is underway, it becomes relatively difficult to introduce new evidence or facts, most especially during negotiation. Hence the appearance of French inflexibility, and the need to introduce new information and considerations early in the game. All this reflects the tradition of French education and becomes the status mark of the educated person.

Ideologists tend to resent pragmatists in ICBN as being too interested in trivial details, too practical, too down-to-earth, too data oriented, and unable to look at issues from a higher standpoint. Conversely, pragmatists resent ideologists in ICBN for being too theoretical, lacking practical sense, and concerned with issues that are too broad to lead to implementable decisions. In the first stages of the negotiation process, the differences between ideologists and pragmatists may create communication misunderstandings that will be difficult to overcome during subsequent phases. Indeed, developing common norms will be difficult in itself, although it is necessary if both partners want to be able to predict the other party's behaviour. A frequent comment in such situations will be: "One never knows what these people have in mind; they do not accept facts; their behaviour is largely unpredictable".

Arguing and being persuasive in negotiation: Data, theory, speech, and virtue

Galtung (1981) contrasts what he calls the "intellectual styles" of four important cultural groups: the "Gallic" (prototype: the French), the "Teutonic" (prototype: the Germans), the "Saxonic" (prototype: the English and the Americans), and the "Nipponic" (prototype: the Japanese). Saxons[41] prefer to look for facts and evidence that result in factual accuracy and abundance. They are interested in "hard facts" and proof, and do not like what they call "unsupported statements".

Galtung compares the Saxonic style with the Teutonic and Gallic styles, which place theoretical arguments at the centre of their intellectual process. Data and facts are there to illustrate what is said rather than to demonstrate it.[42] However, Teutonic and Gallic intellectual styles do differ in the role that is assigned to words and discourse. The Teutonic ideal is that of the ineluctability of true reasoning *Gedankennotwendigkeit*; that is, perfection of concepts and the indisputability of their mental articulation. The Gallic style is directed towards the use of the persuasive strength of words and speeches in an aesthetically perfect way (*élégance*), words having an inherent power to convince.

Finally the Nipponic intellectual style, imbued with Hindu, Buddhist, and Taoist philosophies, favours a more modest, global, and provisional approach. Thinking and knowledge are conceived of as being in a temporary state, open to alteration. The Japanese "rarely pronounce absolute, categorical statements in daily discourse; they prefer vagueness even about trivial matters … because clear statements have a ring of immodesty, of being judgements of reality".[43]

These distinctions make sense for two phases in the negotiation process: task-related exchange of information (i.e., influencing how facts and evidence are valued), and persuasion and concessions (e.g., to what extent negotiators value speech, discourse, and intellectually articulated arguments versus the utterance of outcome-oriented, practical statements). A party's commitment and self-conviction, especially in the final phase of negotiation, have to be filtered and prudently assessed based on its intellectual style. Discrepancies in both factual and persuasive argumentation patterns are hurdles in ICBN. For the clarity of reciprocal understanding, arguments need to be equivalent in both the statements and the inferences. Solutions for LC negotiators communicating with HC negotiators include repeating the message, clarifying and asking for clarification, trying to understand, and/or using culture-free, logical arguments (i.e., logically valid statements).

Choice of communication channels for ICBN

There are many communication channels available for ICBN: face-to-face talks (mostly oral), exchange of email with their text and attachments (written communication), conversation by phone (oral again, with no visual NVL exchange except with Skype, FaceTime or WhatsApp), exchange of letters (written, formal communication), or negotiation by action (e.g., companies that compete through price or advertising in the hope of finally calming down the lose-lose competitive game). All these communication channels can be seen as substitutes, judged on their compared efficiency in conveying information and facilitating problem-solving and agreement. However, rather than substitutes, they should be considered as complementary in terms of message content and feedback performance as well as for improving clarity by using different channels for particular segments of ICBN communication.

Following the World Wide Web and Internet revolution of the last 30 years and the extensive use of computer-mediated communication, especially email, there has been an increasing use of global electronic media in negotiating international deals.[44] Contrary to traditional face-to-face negotiations, email does not offer non-verbal feedback that is available when communicating through other media. Electronic communication though can be very useful for dispersed negotiations, when matters have to be discussed without incurring the high costs associated with face-to-face, cross-border negotiation of very distant partners. Chinese and American managers prefer face-to-face over computer-mediated negotiation. However, neither the Chinese nor the Americans, negotiating intraculturally, perceive that there is a significant difference between email-based written negotiations and the same negotiations on a web-based discussion thread, even though the latter method seems to allow for more continuous interaction.[45] Culture has been shown to affect non-face-to-face communication as is the case with negotiation through email.[46] Finally, email communication is often mixed with face-to-face encounters; emailing is widely affected by prior personal acquaintance with the people involved. If negotiators have started with some face-to-face exchange, computer-mediated negotiation will be largely facilitated and communication misunderstandings arising from the "dry style" of emails may largely be avoided.[47]

For HC communicators who need more direct, face-to-face socialization to create personal acquaintance, digital Internet communication is not a substitute for face-to-face communication. As emphasized by Samiee (1998, p. 423): "HC cultures revolve around personal contacts and, as the Internet is a relatively impersonal medium, attempts to automate processes and transactions are not likely to be well received". One may in fact question whether cultures that prefer an implicit communication style easily accept communication over the Internet.[48] The potential reluctance to use digital communication in HC communication cultures could be explained by more emphasis on oral communication whereas LC cultures are more at ease with written-only communication. Rosenbloom and Larsen (2003) examine the relationship between culture and channel communication in business-to-business negotiation by comparing fax, phone, email, and written communication between partners from HC and LC countries. They find that email communication is more common within culturally similar partners than between channel partners with high cultural distance. Phone communication, on the other hand, is much more frequently used by partners with high cultural distance than by partners with low cultural distance.[49] Communication technologies converge; however languages, communication styles, and meanings conveyed through electronic channels remain different. The Internet is indeed far from immune to the language-based difficulties wrought by HC versus LC cultures. For instance, MacLeod (2000, p. 37) notes:

> Sentences written in Japanese need to be formal, whereas an informal tone is suitable for the U.S. Translation also throws up questions of length. Each page of English may need up to two pages in German. In some Asian languages, not only are the characters larger than in English, they also read from right to left.

HC languages are the ones that are growing most rapidly on the Internet, including Chinese and Arabic. The top languages in millions of users in June 2017[50] were English (985), Chinese (771), Spanish (312), Arabic (185), Portuguese (158), Indonesian (157), Japanese (118), French (108), and German (85). When automating contact and negotiation, for instance through B2B websites, the Internet allows marketers to customize information targeted at different cultures. This should include both verbal and non-verbal content that is congruent with specific cultures.[51] The use of a visitor's language symbolizes respect for the culture, increasing the potential bond. Non-verbal content should also be adapted, for instance, by incorporating local values and symbols into the site, based on the visitor's location. Finally, email communication is important because it conveniently conveys LC communication. Negotiators need to be conscious of the receiver's cultural background, as evidenced by the following comment by a manager:

> You should be very careful [in emails] not just start out in a cold business-like manner with some cultures ... If I am dealing with the Dutch, I don't have to be so careful; I can just get right to the point in my email. If, on the other hand, I am dealing with our Chinese or Latin American friends, I am always more careful about how I begin my message to them. I build up to the topic by saying things such as, "I hope you are doing well. We haven't talked in a while. I just wanted to take a minute to chat with you about something that came up".[52]
>
> (Woodward, 1999)

Active listening: A solution for avoiding cultural misunderstandings

Listening is always easier than talking because it apparently involves less effort and mental activity. However, the mere listener may fall into passivity and possibly be considered a pure eavesdropper. Active listening is a solution to avoid passivity and shunt the negative interpretation of snooping. Active Listening (AL), a technique created by Carl Rogers, can be used in intercultural business negotiations to cultivate a collaborative relation with the opponent. AL is based on empathetic, genuine, and non-judgemental attitudes. Open-mindedness is a key asset for AL, the final aim being to enable the other side to freely, openly, and completely express its needs, preferences, and priorities. The active listener should avoid any preconceptions and prejudices. Active listeners show constant availability to being attentive and refraining from interrupting. Open questioning, asking clarifying questions, and tentatively rephrasing the partner's statements without distortion help make AL a collaborative conversational tool rather than a passive approach to negotiation. As emphasized by Saner (2008, pp. 176–177):

> Moreover, active listening and requests for clarification strengthen the conviction that the agreement sought is in fact attainable. While the less experienced negotiator will skirt around tricky or unclear points, for fear of jeopardizing the agreement, the professional [negotiator] is thinking about the possible problems of practical application while the negotiation is still going on.

Table 5.1 Classification of countries according to their degree of low- versus high-context communication style

Low	Low to Medium	Medium	Medium to High	High
Denmark	Australia	Croatia, Cyprus	Algeria	China, Hong-Kong
Finland	Austria	Czech Rep., Estonia	Bolivia	India, Indonesia, Iran, Japan
Germany	Belgium	France, Greece	Brazil	Koweit, Lebanon
Luxembourg	Canada	Italy, Lithuania	Egypt	Macau, Malaysia
Netherlands	Israel	Poland, Romania	Morocco	Nigeria, Pakistan
Norway	U.S.	Slovenia	Peru, Russia	Philippines, Singapore
Sweden		South Africa	Saudi Arabia	South Korea, Syria, Taiwan
Switzerland		Spain, U.K.	Turkey	Thailand, UAE, Vietnam

Source: adapted from Usunier and Roulin (2010)

Notes

1 See Putnam and Roloff (1992) and De Moor and Weigand (2004).
2 Pruitt and Rubin (1986).
3 Hall (1959, 1960, 1976, 1983). See Bluedorn (1998) for an in-depth interview with Edward T. Hall. Hall advised diplomats, and later on, business people in ICBN. Hall (1914–2009) was fascinated by foreign cultures, sometimes showing a certain prejudice in their favour, and perhaps against his American native culture.
4 See Angelmar and Stern (1978).
5 Mishima, Yukio (1954), *Shiosai* (English title, *The Sound of Waves*).
6 High- and low-context communication cultures have been described and analyzed by Edward Hall (1960, 1976, 1983).
7 Kaplan (1966).
8 Charles (2005), Louhiala-Salminen, Charles, and Kankaanranta (2005).
9 Gudykunst et al. (1996)
10 Hans Boehm, managing director of the German HRM Association quoted by Woodward (1999, p. 15).
11 See Rogers, Hart, and Miike (2002).
12 Goldsmith (2001, p. 528).
13 Ess and Sudweeks (2006); Goldsmith (2001).
14 see Carroll (1956).
15 Rogers et al. (2002).
16 See some body language differences on: www.helpguide.org/articles/relationships-communication/nonverbal-communication.htm, retrieved June 10, 2018.
17 See Harris, Moran, and Moran (2004); for a quick fact sheet on proxemics (i.e., cultural attitudes related to interpersonal distance), consult: www.cs.unm.edu/~sheppard/proxemics.htm.
18 Harris, Moran, and Moran (2004).
19 Hawrysh and Zaichkowsky (1990, p. 34).
20 A universalistic view of NVL is proposed by Semnani-Azad and Adair (2011) in comparing the display of "dominant" non-verbal cues (DNVCs) between Canadian and Chinese negotiators in combination with gender differences. Three DNVCs are assumed to be universally valid: 1) using more physical space, 2) adopting a more relaxed posture, and 3) expressing more negative emotions. The display of DNVCs is supposed to vary cross-culturally, however without real empirical support, suggesting that DNVCs vary across cultures.
21 "Next time you hear someone say: 'Did you know that 93% of our communication is actually delivered by non-verbal means?' Tell him to say that nonverbally". Source: www.study-body-language.com/Verbal-and-non-verbal-communication.html#sthash.UMWH0F77.dpbs accessed 12 November 2017.
22 Edward Hall, *Beyond Culture* (1976, p. 86).
23 In Japanese, a verb has no ending to indicate person or number; there is no article used with nouns in most cases; one and the same form of a noun may mean both the singular and the plural form; and subject and object are often omitted if they are understood from the context (Association for Overseas Technical Scholarship, 1975).
24 "Language-cultures" refer to countries where the national culture is deeply associated with a particular language (e.g., China and Mandarin, the U.S. and English, France and French, Germany and German).
25 Sussman and Johnson (1993).

26 Charles, 2005; Louhiala-Salminen et al., 2005.
27 Wade-Benzoni et al. (2002).
28 Brannen and Salk (2000, pp. 473–475) give a detailed account of how language
    use is negotiated in the case of a German-Japanese joint venture in which English
    was the official language.
    When a Japanese or German was confused or needed help, they would confer
    with members of their same cultural group in their mother tongue. This was
    done solely to expedite matters and clarify issues rather than as a means of
    excluding one or the other group from decision-making.
    A German manager commented on the joint use of English, German, and
    Japanese as follows (p. 474):
    The work language is English. But, during discussion, they would sometimes
    speak Japanese and I thought this was a good thing because you know your own
    language better and can understand better and can discuss things more precisely.
    One has to be tolerant ….
29 Hoon-Halbauer (1999, p. 359).
30 See Usunier (2011).
31 George et al. (1998).
32 Graham (1985).
33 USIP (2002).
34 Fisher (1980).
35 See Sapir (1929) and Carroll (1956).
36 To investigate the equivalence/non-equivalence of terms, take two dictionaries
    and look in each of them at the translations in both directions. The Langenscheidt
    compact dictionary translates *Act of God* as *Force Majeure*, but it translates
    Force Majeure as *overpowering circumstances*. Other dictionaries translate
    Force Majeure as "*circumstances outside one's control*". The next step is to con-
    sult a lawyer to clarify legal meanings and consequences. *Force majeure* is used
    verbatim in English language contracts.
37 Maddux et al. (2011); see also their literature review on cultural differences in
    the meaning and functions of apologies.
38 Morand (1996).
39 Sugimoto (1998).
40 Triandis (1983, p. 148); see also Glenn (1981).
41 As Galtung states (1981, pp. 827–828) when he describes the intellectual
    style of Anglo-Americans, "…data unite, theories divide. There are clear, rela-
    tively explicit canons for establishing what constitutes a valid fact and what
    does not".
42 "Discrepancy between theory and data would be handled at the expense of
    data: they may either be seen as atypical or wholly erroneous, or more signifi-
    cantly as not really pertinent to the theory" (Galtung, 1981, p. 828).
43 Galtung (1981), p. 833.
44 For a review and discussion of non-face-to-face negotiations, see the section
    entitled "The case against face-to-face communication in bargaining" in
    Bazerman et al. (2000, pp. 295–296).
45 Potter and Balthazard (2000).
46 Ulijn et al. (2001): based on a study involving 20 participants, Ulijn et al. use
    speech act theory and psycholinguistic analysis to investigate the possibility to
    bring business people from different national cultures together via low-cost

email negotiation. However, they seem to remain sceptic about the use of non-face-to-face channels to support intercultural negotiation.

47 Parlamis and Geiger (2015) show the limitations of email negotiation through qualitative analysis of email transcripts.

48 Ulijn et al. (2000) investigate the impact of Internet communication technologies on interactions among national, corporate, and professional cultures. Full electronic negotiation systems have been proposed, such as INSPIRE (Kersten and Noronha, 1999). Kersten et al. (2002) find a number of cultural differences between managers from Austria, Ecuador, Finland, and Switzerland when they negotiate electronically.

49 Rosenbloom and Larsen (2003).

50 See "Internet world users by language: Top 10 Languages", *Internet World Stats*, Source: www.internetworldstats.com/stats7.htm, accessed 21 November 2017.

51 Luna, Peracchio, and de Juan (2002).

52 As an example, Woodward (1999, p. 15) quoted Jeanne Poole, manager of international HRM benefits and systems for PQ Corp.

6 Negotiation styles
Gender, personality, profession, and organization

> When I endeavour to examine my own conduct, when I endeavour to pass sentence upon it, either to approve or condemn it, it is evident that, in all such cases, I divide myself, as it were into two persons; and that I, the examiner and judge, represent a different character from that other I, the person whose conduct is examined into and judged of. The first is the spectator, whose sentiments with regard to my own conduct I endeavour to enter into, by placing myself in his situation, and by considering how it would appear to me, when seen from that particular point of view. The second is the agent, the person who I properly call myself, and of whose conduct, under the character of a spectator, I was endeavouring to form some opinion. The first is the judge; the second the person judged of. But that the judge should, in every respect, be the same with the person judged of, is as impossible that the cause should, in every respect, be the same with the effect.
>
> (Adam Smith, 1790, p. 101)

This chapter serves as a counterpoint to IT1 and IT2 ideal-types of Deal-Making and Relationship-Building. Negotiators may behave rather differently from what could be expected based on the ideal-types related to cultural belonging and nationality. This is because 1) their own personality may be far from the modal personality in their culture/nationality, 2) their professional culture may dominate over other behavioural cues and lead to profession-based attitudes in negotiation (e.g., lawyers are rather distributive in general; aerospace industry negotiators are long term and relationship oriented), and/or 3) the organizational culture of their company may translate into a stronger Deal-Making or Relationship- building orientation in ICBN. This chapter first addresses how individual negotiator characteristics influence ICBN, and second it outlines the role of gender, age, and race in ICBN. The chapter then discusses how the professional background of negotiators influences their ICBN behaviour followed by an examination of the impact of organizational culture on ICBN. The chapter goes on to examine judgement biases which may affect individual negotiators in ICBN, including cultural hostility. The two last parts respectively deal with negotiation teams and offer Chinese and Greek "symbolic resources" for negotiators to strategically orient their behaviour in ICBN.

How individual negotiator characteristics influence ICBN

Based on a simulated negotiation, it has been shown that individual differences between negotiators (e.g., positive beliefs about negotiation, conflict handling style, intelligence and creativity, personality traits, gender, age, and physical attractiveness) account for almost half of the variation in individual outcomes (46%).[1]

Individual and organizational cues, credibility, complicity, and joint rationality

Individual negotiator characteristics influence ICBN because they are embedded in sociodemographic cues such as gender and age.[2] They are visually detected and at the same time culturally decoded along various dimensions, including *credibility*, softness vs. hardness, etc. They also correspond to roles (e.g., sex roles in general contaminating the perception of female negotiators; age roles such as the traditional expectations vis-à-vis older negotiators in a particular culture). Non-visible individual cues cannot be straightforwardly noticed, such as nationality, educational background/profession, or organizational affiliation. However, they can be retrieved by informally asking questions and retrieving information. Negotiators respond positively to any signs of interest that others show towards them. Negotiators on each side may share common details such as age or education. This is likely to generate some preliminary forms of *complicity* and *connivance*. However, there is no absolute guarantee that connivance will result from sharing common details, especially if cultural codes concerning a particular characteristic (e.g., age, education or gender) significantly diverge. Furthermore, these interpretations, when in a negotiation context, may be unstable, unpredictable, ambiguous, and even paradoxical. This can be due to stereotypes being suddenly "jostled", revised, and even reversed, because of complex two-way or three-way interaction effects between different individual negotiator characteristics (e.g., age and gender; gender and education; education and age; gender and organizational membership; age and gender, and education). For instance, a young female manager with a powerful role as purchasing manager for a large organization may suddenly become a highly credible negotiator, because locally prevalent (undesirable) gender stereotypes are overpowered and overturned by role, power, and organizational aspects. Ambiguity and stereotypes in interpreting individual negotiator characteristics progressively vanish with relationship development over time, whether in a particular negotiation round or over successive negotiations. While *credibility* is a prerequisite for being taken seriously in ICBN, *complicity* is not. In the absence of any *complicity*, parties can develop joint rationality based on objectivity, reflexivity, cultural awareness, avoidance of stereotypes, and circumvention of judgement biases, much in the style of Adam Smith's *Impartial Spectator* and *Prudent Man* in his *Theory of Moral Sentiments*.

Who is seen as a credible negotiation partner? By whom?

Credibility affects perceived authority and trustworthiness. A lack of credibility may result in lower concern for the less credible party's outcomes, undermine the problem-solving orientation even when initiated by the less credible party, and finally encourage an opportunistic, contending, and distributive attitude. Misunderstood credibility is a poison.

The credibility issue is largely bilateral, interactive, built on a mirror effect as in the *Theory of Moral Sentiments*. Perceiving one's own lack of credibility when confronting another party may undermine self-esteem, and result in a somewhat self-fulfilling prophecy where the non-credible negotiator unconsciously behaves as he or she is perceived rather than as he or she actually is. Credibility is perceived by the other side according to cultural codes. A negotiator who is credible in a particular cultural context may be much less credible in another.[3]

Self-concept, self-image, and credibility

Triandis (1983, p. 147) has emphasized three dimensions of the self-concept which may have a strong influence on the cultural coding/decoding process of credibility: 1) *self-esteem*, i.e., the extent to which negotiators think of themselves as very credible or not; 2) *perceived potency*, i.e., the extent to which negotiators view themselves as powerful, able to accomplish almost any task; and 3) *perceived activity*, that is, to what extent a negotiator sees him or herself as a doer, an active shaper of the world.

Since negotiators generally live in homogeneous cultural settings (i.e., monolingual countries or regions within a country with a dominant culture, religion, and shared values), they are used to sharing the same cultural codes. But when negotiators come to ICBN where they do not share the same codes, establishing credibility/trust may unexpectedly become a problematic issue. For example, somebody may be seen as a credible negotiator at "home" because he or she displays a low self-concept profile (e.g., modest, patiently listening to partners, speaking little and cautiously). If his or her counterpart considers that a credible negotiator must imperatively exhibit a high self-concept (e.g., showing self-confidence, speaking arrogantly, not paying much attention to what the other is saying), a credibility mismatch is likely.

A classic example is the misinterpretation by Soviet leader Nikita Khrushchev of President John F. Kennedy's credibility. This was one reason for the serious Cuban missile crisis in the early 1960s. Kennedy and Khrushchev had held talks in Vienna, after the unsuccessful invasion by U.S. soldiers resulting in the Bay of Pigs defeat. During their meeting, young President Kennedy openly recognized that the attack had been a military and political mistake, which he regretted. Khrushchev saw this acknowledgment as testimony of Kennedy's naive frankness and lack of character.

Khrushchev erroneously inferred that it was conceivable to gain advantage by installing nuclear missiles in Cuba targeted at the United States. This led the world to the brink of nuclear war between the two superpowers. The events which followed showed that Khrushchev had been wrong in evaluating Kennedy's credibility. Ultimately, Kennedy showed great firmness and negotiation skill.

Khrushchev's mistake may be explained by differences in the cultural coding of credibility. Whereas in the United States, reaching a high position while still young is positively perceived, Soviet negotiators associated age with the ability to carry responsibilities. Moreover, the admission of a mistake or a misjudgement is positively perceived in the United States. U.S. communication ethics value frankness and honesty based on the belief that individuals may improve their behaviour and decisions by taking into account the lessons of experience. On the other hand, in the Soviet Union at that time, admitting that one had made an error was rare. It generally implied the very weak position of people subject to the forced confessions of the Stalinist trials.

Decoding-encoding signs of credibility

Personal credibility is unconsciously decoded through physical traits. Being tall, for instance, may be perceived as a sign of strength, energy, and character. Being corpulent may be considered a positive credibility sign in societies where famine is recurrent. Where malnutrition is a reality for part of the population, being well nourished and even fat is instinctively associated with wealth and power. These credibility signs are however relative. Weight, height, age, and sex cannot be considered adequate criteria for selecting negotiators. Negotiators may be aware of their partners' credibility codes, but unwilling and in fact unable to meet their criteria. Promoting one's own credibility does not involve, for a negotiator, changing oneself.

Each of the following individual characteristics plays a role in early credibility: age, sex, height, corpulence, face, tone and strength of voice, self-esteem, perceived potency, perceived activity, etc. This profile mostly influences credibility in early contacts and during the exploration phase.

Gender, age, and status in ICBN

Gender issues in ICBN

The place of women in society has greatly changed over the last century. Women have long been denied some basic rights, such as voting, and in many societies the place of women is still very different from that of men. Until a few years ago, the electoral status of women was still not completely equal to that of men even in advanced countries like Switzerland, in very traditional cantons (Appenzell). For a variety of roles and capacities in society, women are dependent on men, mostly economically. They are kept in the role of pure home-keepers, not allowed to work outside the home, and often not permitted to go shopping or manage the family budget, as in some traditional Muslim countries. Worldwide differences in the self-concept of women and the concept held by men of women are striking.

The influence of gender in negotiation is far from simple, very complex in fact, because of interaction effects with other key negotiator characteristics and negotiation variables. There are differences between gender (as a sex attribute), the gender aspects of personalities (e.g., "masculine women" and "feminine men"), gender culture (e.g., position in society, interactions, and sex roles construed by local cultures), and feminine culture (feminine vs. masculine cultures).[4]

Negotiator gender may be a problematic issue in societies which do not grant an "equal" place to men and women, and tend to consider women as inferior human beings (e.g., India, or in Pearl Buck's novels in China where a newborn child is called a "small slave" if female). Half of the talents are virtually lost, which might explain why societies which have promoted gender equality do on average better in GNP/capita and HDI (Human Development Index). Women are the most necessary gender because of their dominant role in procreation (especially in times of artificial insemination).

However, there is a paradoxical effect of gender on negotiator credibility in ICBN, which may reach summits. Even in societies where gender equality is not the rule (e.g., India, Saudi Arabia), women may reach top positions in government (e.g., the late Benazir Bhutto in Pakistan, Sirimavo Bandaranaike in Sri Lanka, Indira Gandhi in India, Sheikh Hasina in Bangladesh). There is a sort of paradoxical role reversal; when a woman becomes highly credible there is an over-proportionally positive escalation of her negotiation position.

Gender is probably the most important cultural difference, because of the definite roles and self-concepts imposed on boys and girls by culture, education, and socialization. In *Male and Female*, Margaret Mead (1948, pp. 7–8) puts it in the following terms:

> In every known society, mankind has elaborated the biological division of labour into forms often very remotely related to the original biological differences that provided the original clues... Sometimes one quality has been assigned to one sex, sometimes to the other ... Some people think of women as too weak to work out of doors, others regard women as the appropriate bearers of heavy burdens ... In some cultures women are regarded as sieves through whom the best guarded secrets will sift; in others it is the men who are the gossips.

The role of gender in negotiation has been mostly studied in the U.S. context, highlighting that female negotiators, on average, tend to ask for less, to be somewhat conflict avoidant, to be less assertive than men, and to be concerned with preserving the relationship (i.e., a favourable disposition for ICBN). In fact it is a relatively traditional elaboration, underlining in fact why Western societies are still battling against gender biases and discrimination. However, American research on how women negotiate in comparison with men is a good starting point. Moreover it is not exclusively based on how male negotiators view female negotiators, but also on how female negotiators view themselves as negotiators, and/or how females construe (view, believe) they are viewed as negotiators by male negotiators.[5]

The weak status of women in the other party's society may be a problematic issue. However, this is far from being always the case. If multinational, multicultural, and global teams negotiate face to face with a gender-diverse composition on each side, gender may play a limited role. The effect of gender on negotiation behaviour and on perception by the other party is moderated by other individual, contextual, and organizational variables: age, personality, social class, family background negotiation role (e.g., buyer vs. seller), organization, asymmetric dependence, market background, more or less "feminine industry" (cosmetics versus industrial B2B), and clear empowerment of negotiator versus mandate negotiator, as well as circumstances such as for a female negotiator to be accompanied by a male subordinate (and letting it be known).

Other favourable circumstances include: a female negotiator being the owner of the business, her status as a key executive, and her professional recognition manifested by various credentials, diplomas, and known achievements. The general advice for female negotiators in ICBN, when confronted with a gender-biased party, is to search for the favourable leverage points noted above and confront the rest.

Cross-cultural differences in attitudes towards younger/older people and age credibility

A general difference is that traditional societies tend to consider older people as more credible (probably because of their life experience) whereas the West values younger people for their open-mindedness, flexibility, and creativity in negotiation.[6] Generally speaking older people are less integrated than before in families, now with more nuclear families, less extended families, more emphasis on impersonal (non-family) care for the elderly, etc. However, there are still large differences across societies in terms of placing value on age and experience and these can be extended to the domain of business.

Age in young negotiators may be associated with inexperience, lack of seriousness, and a still mild character, or, in contrast, with open-mindedness, creativity, ability to change things, and to undertake new projects. Naturally these contrasted qualities are present in all young people of all cultures. What is more interesting is how a certain culture values older people (e.g., East Asia, Africa) or younger people (e.g., the United States). The probable reason for such differences is that qualities typically found at a particular age are implicitly perceived as more congruent and favourable for the overall development of society. Emphasis on age is associated with other cultural orientations such as power distance. It is also related to the dominant family models prevalent in a particular society: where the family is nuclear and the family structure fairly weak, the authority image linked to parent roles will also tend to fade away, as will the positive emphasis on older negotiators. Where, on the contrary, the extended family is dominated by a patriarch, his role and status will favourably influence his credibility as a negotiator (at least as perceived by his own side).

On average, "modern culture" values younger people because changes are extremely rapid (e.g., TV advertising revolves around young blondes, shaggy-haired surfers, or yuppie-like professionals), whereas in "traditional culture" the elderly have traditionally been considered as a source of wisdom and guidance for the community, their age being consequently valued. A consequence for ICBN of differential age valuation is that the choice of negotiators could be partly done according to their age, when the implied status and power of older negotiators is favourably perceived in the partner's culture (and vice versa for younger negotiators). Mixing different age classes in a negotiation team may also make sense to sidestep stereotypes, both positive and negative, related to age.

Compensating for low credibility

Rather than adjusting to negative stereotypes and prejudiced views related to negotiator characteristics, it may be decided that it is preferable to confront stereotypes by playing against prejudices and biased views of credibility. For instance, leveraging on one's organization size and reputation may largely compensate for lower personal credibility. Credibility may also be leveraged by expertise, market power, a favourable role position, a managing position despite being a relatively young executive, or simply the sagacity of imposing oneself despite unfavourable credibility stereotypes. Do not hesitate to let the other party know what your position, responsibilities, and the extent of your decision-making power are within the organization. Previous experience, diplomas, etc. may also impress the prejudiced party with whom it is not required to be too shy and modest. Do not hesitate to boast a bit, even if you are a bit reluctant given a reserved and non-arrogant personality. Women may also bring to the negotiation table a male colleague who is a subordinate and clearly signal it. Younger negotiators may show up with supposedly more experienced negotiators who are at the same hierarchical level.

Professional background and ICBN behaviour

Negotiation styles are impacted by professional culture.[7] The professional background of individuals has a significant influence on their negotiation behaviour. Below I tentatively outline how lawyers, engineers, economists, accountants, etc. focus on certain aspects of negotiation according to their educational and professional backgrounds. This interacts with their role in negotiation (expert, mandated negotiator, buyer versus seller, etc.). Negotiation behaviour may differ in terms of:

- Pure self-interest (economists) versus concern for the other party's outcome.
- Importance of the law, of rights (as in the interests, rights, and power [IRP] model); e.g., lawyers.
- Importance of norms and professional practices (e.g., medical schools training).
- Importance of hard facts versus judgement or preferences (e.g., engineers).
- Sensitivity to individual personality and interpersonal interactions (e.g., psychology, foreign language training).
- Power orientation (e.g., maybe political sciences, sociology).
- Distributive (e.g., lawyers) versus integrative orientation.

The case for profession-based affinities in ICBN: Shared education

Professional mindsets are built through educational background but also through a sense of belonging to alumni networks of highly reputed graduate schools and universities (e.g., top schools in different countries, Ivy League, etc.). If professional background is shared, negotiators will have joint references, similar ways of framing issues, and comparable thinking and problem-solving patterns. Shared professional-educational background enables negotiators to bridge a number of differences. Shared membership in academic and professional associations, being Harvard or more generally Ivy League alumni, will make joint understanding easier in ICBN. Because of such shared characteristics, negotiators from different camps may feel that they are members of the same professional-educational ingroup, even though their ingroup identity is not based on concrete cues such as kin, blood, or ethnic group but based on occupying the same abstract territory defined by academic disciplines, professional training, and shared practices.

Membership-based territoriality corresponds largely to Western *doing* cultures. Here, an outgroup orientation is valued as concerns people. What negotiators have done up to now is indicated by their curriculum vitae (CV). An interview guide in countries where affirmative action compliance is important generally considers it discriminatory to enquire about applicants' age, citizenship, marital status, and birthplace. This information is not only legitimate in *being* cultures, it is essential to ascertain who the applicant is. Membership-based "abstract territoriality" is mostly based on professional achievements, evidenced by diplomas, membership in professional bodies, being an alumnus of an Ivy-League university, and so on. The epitome of such abstract ingroups is represented by the "golden boys". For them insider trading is fraud, showing that the use of their natural ingroup advantages is viewed as evil. The space of "golden boys" is a mix of top MBA schools, noisy trading floors where financial deals are negotiated and closed, and belonging to a club of global traders constantly connected worldwide. We can only imagine the profound differences between the New York "golden boy" and the lay Bengali farmer.

Business school graduates or those holding the title of doctor in Germany belong to these "modern groups" that are based on *doing* and competence rather than *being*, age, sex, and national, cultural, or ethnic ingroup membership. It is assumed that access to membership is organized on a non-discriminatory and objective basis and that it is in the interest of society as a whole because the "best people" do an "excellent job". However, even in a *doing* framework, relational competence never disappears in favour of pure professional competence. Managing relationships is still an important part of the *doing* competences.

Paradoxically, when abstract territoriality is very strong, it largely re-creates primitive ingroup behaviour, but based on different criteria. Even the world of academia, which is very outgroup oriented in terms of gender, nationality, religion, and age, is very ingroup oriented when it comes to doctoral degrees and the journals where people publish. It is therefore essential to have a look at the CV of other negotiators (to the extent that information is accessible through the Internet and social networks) and check whether they have global, multi-local, or purely local experience. Certain professions, occupations, and interests are naturally global (e.g., aerospace engineers) while others are more rooted in the local scenes due to language, the regulations of education, diplomas, and access to professions. Employee representatives and trades unions are generally entrenched in local labour regulations, the local language, their history and style of industrial relations, etc. This may explain the relative inability of trades unions to negotiate and build a transnational alliance (despite the existence of some transnational bodies such as the European Trade Union Federations). Local workers' interests clash against each other as soon as they are competing for new industrial jobs or fighting against the transfer of manufacturing activities in a low-cost country.

Lawyers in ICBN: A problematic case

Lawyers are classically introduced in a negotiation when drafting the contract and fine-tuning its legal aspects. However, when unilaterally introduced by a single party early in the negotiation process, it may signal mistrust to the other side, especially in traditional IT2 cultures, which often associate lawyers and legal issues with litigation (and not the avoidance of future litigation as is often the case for IT1 negotiators).

Furthermore, lawyers may tend to be distributive because their negotiation strategy centres only on the perceived interest of the party which they represent.

Lawyers have a normative orientation, legal texts being largely rules, with some flexibility in applying and interpreting them (thus jurisprudence), however with the underlying view that it is important to analyse texts, and define who is right and who is wrong. Especially lawyers representing only one party tend to display a bias that their party is "right" and the opposing party is "wrong". Lawyers have to and want to justify high fees. Therefore they generally try to show that they are bringing useful contributions (possibly in USD amounts), although this may be mostly by drawing the attention of their principals to advantageous dispositions and clauses for the adverse party and recommending that they battle them off. This may translate into distrustful and possibly hostile attitudes toward the other party and their own lawyers seen as radical opponents as in a court trial.

The mindset of lawyers and specialists in legal studies implies thinking in terms of rules, obligations, and rights as entitlements, legal constraints, damage, torts, etc. Consequently, lawyers value claims and a distributive and hard approach in favour of their principals. It is entirely different from the mindset of negotiators who value interests, flexibility, value creation, problem-solving, and tractable solutions.[8]

What makes lawyers really dangerous for IT2 negotiators is that they introduce a threat of litigation, a sense that the relationship is distrustful, insincere, hypocritical, about to break, a very poor sign for future joint work especially at the implementation level. An IT2 party may even decide to withdraw and breach the negotiations when an IT1 party brings in their lawyers early in the negotiation process and, worse, without warning them prior to negotiations. Although some lawyers have an international background with legal training in international business law, many lawyers remain local. Law and legislation are always local to a large extent. Legal practice therefore largely remains multi-domestic and not global, with some strictly local legal professions such as notaries. Although some notaries develop cross-border competence, most remain strictly locked into their national language and legal and institutional systems. When drafting ICBN contracts, a solution is to introduce lawyers who have an economics or business training in addition to their international contract law background with ICBN experience.

Organizational culture and intercultural business negotiations

A long-term versus short-term oriented organizational culture explains why an organization may negotiate in ICBN with a Relationship orientation despite coming from an IT1 country-culture or conversely adopt a rather Deal-oriented stance in negotiation despite coming from an IT2 country-culture.

Organizational design reflects corporate culture, especially a more or less centralized management system. If decisions are made by executives in key positions this will impact the degree of delegation for a mandated negotiator.[9] Narrowly defined negotiation mandates should by and large be the rule for highly centralized organizations, with regular if not continuous reporting to principals and steady validation by them. Conversely, decentralization and the practice of delegation and subsidiarity will result in clear mandates giving to the mandated negotiators enough leeway to negotiate according to their instructions without constant reporting to and endorsement by their principals. Decision-making style has also to be taken into account; either individual decision-making reflects the inputs of one individual or collective decision-making requires that the entire group of people concerned with the negotiation be consulted and that a supervisory committee must approve the agreement.

An organization may also value flexibility and reactivity when confronted with changing circumstances (ad hockery) or value strong commitment to decisions and planning. Whether ad hoc responses or elaborate plans are created in the face of changing situations has to be considered especially when implementing negotiated contractual arrangements. Organizations may have more or less simple or complex rules, translating into more or less elaborate procedures and structures, informal vs. formalized procedures. It is important to assess whether detailed, formalized procedures and complex forms vs. simple and rather informal procedures are needed to justify actions.

An organization with a strong external emphasis on satisfying customers/ clients will be in general easier to negotiate with. Conversely, a rather self-centred organization with a strong internal emphasis will tend to focus on internal organizational activities such as meetings and reports. This is likely to make their negotiation behaviour less reactive, less empowered, and less concerned with their counterparts' outcomes.

Whether an organization mostly values cooperation or competition between its members has an overall influence in adopting a distributive (competitive) versus integrative (cooperative) orientation when negotiating with other organizations. Whether peers are considered as competitors for scarce resources or trusted colleagues in a common cause may also impact the general coherence and consistence of a negotiation team. An organizational culture may be more or less people-oriented, especially according to the emphasis put on being competitive in accomplishing tasks and dedicated to organizational "work" (important for IT1) or on a social focus displaying concern for the personal and social needs of people (in line with IT2).

A "hire and fire" type of HRM system may result in a preference for "expendable negotiators", replaceable *ad libitum* sometimes in complete ignorance of the other party's relational needs. This may cause significant frustration in the IT2 negotiation partner if they have built a relationship and need to start from scratch with an unknown negotiator on the other side, especially if she or he has not been briefed by her or his forerunner. IT2 negotiators will feel more at ease with IT1 negotiators when their HRM system values stable employment (P&G style).

In loyal organizations where people stay for a rather long period of time, it is likely that negotiators will develop a thorough knowledge of organizational expectations and therefore know what they are expected to do. This is especially true for negotiation mandates and for agent-principal relationships, where stable employment facilitates the understanding of role expectations, job definition, and the clarity of mandate and instructions from principals to mandated negotiators. Conversely, negotiators from short-termist, hire and fire employers may ignore how they are expected to behave and how their efforts contribute to the accomplishment of organizational objectives.

Organizational cultures (OCs) should be taken into account for both negotiation sides, assessing the fit between OCs. A last remark: for a negotiator, organization reputation may supplement relatively weak personal credibility.

Individual negotiator's cognitive and affective biases

When reading the judgement biases literature especially as concerns negotiation the question springs to mind: Are negotiators their best enemies? Framing effects, judgement biases, positive illusions and overconfidence, and all sorts of both cognitive and affective biases affect ICBN behaviour.[10] The next question is: How do you remain rational in negotiation? Judgement biases seem to be pretty universal; however, a certain degree of optimism and self-confidence remains necessary for a negotiator. Most "illusions" at the very source of judgement biases are paradoxically drivers of energy and enthusiasm in ICBN. They should be accepted and reflexively understood as being part of human cognition; however, kept under the control of a matter of fact and realistic evaluation of situations, interests, and people. Moreover, what is most often called "judgement biases" corresponds to human failures in following the IT1 normative model of calculative rationality.

Impact of framing effects on negotiation

Framing effects result from information being presented in a particular way. Framing effects influence how a negotiator cognitively reacts to a choice situation. Information may be presented as a loss or as a gain, as certain or uncertain. A frame results for instance from an initial reference and its perception (e.g., present salary). On average, people tend to avoid risk when a positive frame is presented but seek risk when a negative frame is presented. Which issues are susceptible to be framed in some way? The present situation or status quo can be framed positively or negatively. How can frames be manipulated to generate a framing effect that is favourable to a party in the negotiation? Negotiators who want to use the framing effect define issues at stake in a way that is likely to close a deal, reach consensus, or win an argument. First offers contain a framing effect particularly when they are excessively high, because they anchor the negotiation (see Chapter 8).

In *Negative Framing* (e.g., the present salary when applying for a new job) any concession made against negotiation goals is perceived as a loss by the negotiator or her principals. Conversely, in *Positive Framing*, any improvement over the present situation is perceived as a gain by the negotiator or her principals. Research[11] shows that negatively framed negotiators tend to make fewer concessions and to less frequently reach an agreement than positively framed negotiators.

To illustrate framing effects, let us take the example of a repeated price negotiation, between a purchaser and a supplier. The market background has changed since the last encounter six months earlier; a downturn in a cyclical market has driven market prices down and the buyer's power position has significantly improved over the previous upturn period, which was favourable to the seller due to a supply shortage. A negatively framed negotiator (seller) would consider any price decrease as a loss over the previous situation, and be reluctant to concede rebates. Conversely, a positively framed negotiator, considering the new market price level would view any price above this level to be a bonus. Note, however, that mere common sense indicates that a "double bias" attitude brings negotiators to a more realistic assessment of the situation. In order to defend one's own position it may be useful to simulate negative framing. Conversely, a "positive frame" is helpful for the negotiator to close a deal at the end. In fact, positively framed negotiators tend to perceive negotiated agreements as fairer and more balanced.[12]

Framing effects partly depend on social norms, fairness, and the perception of equity. Equity judgements and social norms are important in negotiating agreements, especially in negotiations between labour and employers, because of the underlying view that distributive justice commands a fair and equitable distribution of joint outcomes. Equity judgements can be affected by framing effects.[13] Take the case of a slightly profitable company located in a region where the industry base is declining and unemployment is high. Most workers want to stay in the region and are therefore willing to keep their jobs within the company. A net salary cut is considered inequitable by respondents, whereas a nominal gain which does not, however, cover inflation appears more acceptable. In *Situation 1* presented with a *negative frame* (salary cut), there is no inflation. The company decides to cut this year's salaries by 7%. 62% of the respondents consider that, in this situation, the company has not made a fair and equitable decision. Conversely, in *Situation 2*, annual inflation is 12%. And the company decides to increase this year's salaries by 5%. In this positive framing situation, only 22% of the respondents consider that, in this situation, the company has not made a fair and equitable decision.[14]

Superiority and positive illusions, overconfidence, and wishful thinking

Judgement biases are generated by a number of illusions, an illusion being a false appearance or a deceptive impression of reality. Illusions may be about oneself, about circumstances, about likely outcomes, about being able to impose oneself and/or manipulate the other side. Illusions tend to distort the appreciation and evaluation of basic features in the negotiation setting, and thereby to significantly affect behaviour and strategies. The *Superiority Illusion* is based on an inflated, non-realistic self-image (e.g., "I am smarter, more honest, more talented, more clever, more creative and fairer than most others"). Feeling superior may result from high self-esteem and/or perceived potency (see above) due to a combination of cultural and non-cultural factors (e.g., being an alumni from a top school, being very wealthy and powerful, belonging to a top family in a socially stratified country). Note that many of these subjective superiority cues may be unfamiliar to the other side in ICBN. It may also be that the ego-inflated negotiator ignores similar "superiority cues" in the other side's negotiators and irritates them by not acknowledging that they are peers. Superiority illusions typically lead to overconfidence and a lack of prudence and reserve in asserting one's own positions. Adam Smith's *prudent man* avoids superiority feelings.

Positive Illusions (over-optimism) are frequent in many life situations: when presented with probabilities based on large populations, individuals tend to significantly underestimate for instance the probability of being affected by cancer or overestimate the likelihood of not having a serious car crash.[15] The misapprehension behind positive illusions has to do with a self-serving evaluation of one's behaviour and capacities vis-à-vis others (e.g., being more health conscious and more physically active, being a better and more prudent driver than others). Over-optimistic negotiators tend to *underestimate* the probability that they will experience *negative events* such as the other party withdrawing or winning the case to its advantage. They tend also to *overestimate* the probability that they will experience *positive events* in the future such as successfully closing a negotiation or having a smooth and easy post-negotiation phase with no hurdles when implementing the ICBN contract. Those more likely to experience Positive Illusions (over-optimism) are (probably) more HC-IT2 because they allow for more discrepancy between desired and objectively foreseeable outcomes than LC-IT1 negotiators (see Figure 5.1).

Wishful thinking (WT) and *Overconfidence* have a strong impact on judgement in negotiation because they induce negotiators to largely underestimate conditionality and uncertainty in future outcomes. Wishful thinking entices us to believe that situations will always turn to our advantage. Wishful thinking is a self-serving bias: it is always tempting for a negotiator to believe that his or her subjective confidence in his or her judgements is reliably greater than the objective accuracy of those judgements.

Overconfidence biases result from a miscalibration of subjective probabilities and occur particularly when confidence is relatively high. Negotiators may be overconfident in themselves, in the likely occurrence of favourable outside events, in a favourable fate, or in the very assumption that being very confident brings about positive developments. The French saying *impossible n'est pas français* (i.e., impossible is not a French word) or "We can do it" (American wartime slogan designed to boost morale) typically promote overconfidence.

Although overconfidence and WT are very near, overconfidence is one, however not the only, antecedent of WT. High self-esteem and perceived potency (useful to a certain extent, despite the risk of fostering superiority illusions) may lead negotiators to overestimate the accuracy and reliability of their judgements; that is, to underestimate errors in their evaluations. Other factors also play a role in WT: unrealistic enthusiasm, positive illusions, and deceitful circumstances (e.g., a strong hierarchical stance – such as in high power distance cultures – that infuses in the subordinate an exaggerated sense of "must do"). WT cannot be transferred to the realistic and bilateral setting of a negotiation, because the other party is unlikely to "buy in" what they consider at best as illusions.

It is a speculative hypothesis that low power distance IT1 negotiators might be less prone and inclined to overconfidence and WT in negotiation, due to a more realistic, low-context, and explicit assessment of subjective probabilities. Conversely, it may be that in rather high power distance societies, IT2 negotiators with a more fuzzy (high-context) view of reality are more WT prone. The worst case, for relatively high ranking, status-minded IT2 negotiators from high power distance societies, would be that their overconfidence may have been constantly reinforced by submissive subordinate behaviour. They may tend to *subjectively* transfer their innate sense of superiority related to hierarchical power (however only within *their own* organization and culture) to negotiations with external and independent partners who are in no way subordinates but peers.

The last form of judgement bias in negotiation results from the *illusion of control*, which is a tendency to overrate one's ability to control events that are not completely controllable because outcomes cannot be fully influenced.[16] Most negotiators believe that they have more control on the outcomes of their actions than they actually do, even for purely random events such as throwing dice.[17] In my view, negotiators are more likely to display illusions of control when they come from a master-of-destiny oriented culture (LC-IT1).

Loss aversion and avoidance or acceptance of sunk costs

It seems a priori rational to accept one's mistakes and to draw a clear end line as to their possible negative influences on future outcomes, rather than going on and on in the hope that the situation will improve. *Sunk costs* are related to feelings of regret for having to abandon resources that may later appear as wasted. The metaphor is that of valuable resources disappearing in a sink. Sunk cost escalation is often caused by the optimist illusion that things will improve in the near future. Some companies go bankrupt by continuing on the wrong course just because they do not want to write off huge amounts of money that may mistakenly have been spent. Poor investment in shares or bad purchases should for instance be considered sunk costs (SCs). However, loss aversion may lead an investor not to sell shares in the hope that their value will later increase. If optimist expectations are not fulfilled by the "invisible (and largely unpredictable) hand" of the market, he or she may finally lose more money than if he or she had decided to sell them earlier recognizing the sunk costs in the investment decision. In negotiation, a lot of time and effort are devoted to talks; however, it may appear that the best possible negotiated agreement is clearly under the BATNA. If negotiators want to remain rational, they have to admit *from the start* that all the costs involved in negotiating the deal are potential *sunk costs*. We tend to positively re-evaluate the quality of our past decisions to reduce the inconsistency between our behaviours or decisions and their actual outcomes (cognitive dissonance). Cognitive dissonance plays a role in favouring solutions which avoid the clear acknowledgement of SCs. When there is such a gap, some of our beliefs must be altered to eliminate the painful *dissonance* and artificially build greater cognitive consistency.

To illustrate the issue of SCs in negotiations, let us take the example of a minority shareholder position negotiated with another company. Negotiation seemingly led to a bargain for the acquirer, USD 5 million, because the acquisition target was a heavily indebted loss maker. (Dubious) strategic motives were the main reason for acquisition and not profits. Positive illusions were at work (e.g., "*we* will do better than *they* did"). Framing effects also played a role (e.g., "the situation cannot be worse; there is ample room for improvement") as well as the illusion of control despite a minority position that did not guarantee full decisional power. It later appeared that the acquirer only had a 40% share, an uncomfortable position where they have to take their share of the burden of debts. No competitor was there to acquire the ailing target, a bad omen for the future. The unfortunate acquirer is now obliged to regularly compensate for the continuing losses, since the acquired company would run out of cash and go bankrupt.[18] No bank is ready to grant additional loans. Even debt restructuring is difficult and at a very significant interest rate premium. Finally, the acquirer is obliged to cash out 40% of the monthly USD 2.5 million, that is, it pays USD 1 million per month. After less than a semester, the acquisition has cost more in accumulated losses than its acquisition cost.

Why are SCs so difficult to accept for both individual decision-makers and organizations? First it is always difficult to acknowledge and accept one's own mistakes or a great change in circumstances and/or market situation. It is even trickier to acknowledge responsibility for a poor decision and the resulting SCs, when others have previously questioned and challenged the decision. Accepting SCs goes with an acknowledgement of individual or collective responsibility, a possible loss of face for the people involved in making a poor decision. Furthermore they risk punishment such as being fired or losing their reputation. Often people and organizations wait as long as possible to recognize SCs.

Cultural hostility and the risk of non-rational conflict escalation

Cultural hostility, largely a subjective and affective rather than a cognitive bias, may be a problematic issue in ICBN. Sometimes it is one-sided at first, only one party latently displaying cultural hostility toward the other party. It is rare that cultural hostility is openly expressed (e.g., as in some of U.S. President Donald Trump's statements); rather, it is suggested by contemptuous remarks and behaviour. It ends up being bilateral, the bashed party retaliating by attacking the other party country and culture with demeaning and depreciative comments at the risk of non-rational conflict escalation. Cultural hostility derives from prejudices and negative stereotypes about the other party, generally at a broad and aggregate level: prejudices about their country, their culture, their language, their religion, their political system, their ethnic orientation; the list is endless. I call it cultural hostility, because it is based on a clash of representations and values, sometimes more perceived than actual, and the self-shock effect (i.e., feeling one's own identity questioned, and possibly threatened, when observing unfamiliar cultural behaviour and norms).

Underlying contentious issues of cultural hostility in ICBN may be race and racism. Country bashing on the other hand results from contempt for particular aspects of countries, for example, low purchasing power, strong inequalities, generalized – small and large – corruption, poor political systems (lack of a free political scene, dictatorship), pitiable local arts and crafts, etc. Cultural hostility may result from negative stereotypical perceptions of the local culture (e.g., the caste system in India), from complaints on the local standards (e.g., food, hotels, road safety) accompanied by suggestions that it is better in one's home country. Cultural hostility results in gratuitous statements that vex the other party. When negotiating in ICBN, demeaning remarks about local workers, corruption and ethical standards, or political instability should be avoided. Negative feelings related to bashing (e.g., contemptuous remarks and value judgements) pile up when clearly perceived by the party targeted by cultural hostility. Therefore, avoid the negatives even when the other party mentions them. Be extremely prudent; do not feel invited to comment in the same negative direction. Natives only feel allowed to criticize their own country. Even they would mind if you were to back and support their criticism.

Cultural hostility is not straightforwardly affirmed; rather it is mixed in information exchange, persuasion, and communication. The image of a number of countries (e.g., Russia, China, Iran) in Western media is pretty poor: undemocratic, if not dictatorial, lack of reliability of public infrastructures, absence of Western-style governance, uncertain legal and contractual systems, and the like. Western IT1 negotiators are literally invited to make negative value judgements on a number of countries that offer excellent business opportunities and are tough, however reliable, business partners.

Racism is often confused with cultural hostility. Racism precedes cultural hostility, but cultural hostility does not necessarily imply racism. Negotiators may be hostile to those from another culture, without being racist. Racist theories have been progressively abandoned over the last two centuries, although, the differing intellectual capacity among negotiators of different races or ethnic groups is still being discussed.[19] In contrast to racism, cultural hostility does not imply prior prejudices as to who is inferior or superior according to race or culture. Culture is part of a person's heritage and identity. There is a strong affective dimension, when a person's cultural values are threatened. This emotional response may result from individual interactions with negotiators whose cultural values are quite different. This may lead to feelings of unease, difficulty in communication, and lack of empathy. A defensive response may develop, in terms of minor and unconscious cultural hostility.

Not only territorial conflicts but also economic competition may cause cultural hostility, especially when combined with cultural differences. For instance, some negative feelings toward the Japanese in the United States were generated by media reports of the large trade imbalance in disfavour of the U.S., combined with Japanese protectionism. Cultural hostility directed at economically successful nations is often a fairly ambiguous feeling, where admiration and envy for the other's achievements go along with contempt for many traits of the envied people and an unwillingness to understand the root causes of the other's success. Cultural hostility is sometimes amplified by language and communication problems. Intercultural misunderstandings between negotiators may stem from a lack of competency in the other's language, or from the natural tendency to adopt defensive stereotypes. This often results in a snowballing cultural hostility. How should cultural hostility be defused? The best solution is to avoid negative comments on the other party's country and culture and, when on the receiving end of culturally hostile messages, to politely and unemotionally send a matter-of-fact message on their non-relevance for the negotiation at hand.

How to become more rational in negotiation

Rationality in negotiation is based on adopting the attitudes of Adam Smith's *Impartial Spectator* and *Prudent Man* in his *Theory of Moral Sentiments* (see citation in the epigraph for this chapter). Prudence is thought of by Smith as a part of the Character of Virtue that helps moderate the individual's excesses. The epigraph in this chapter explains the self-critical nature of his *Impartial Spectator*, being divided into two persons, first an *examiner and judge* and second an *agent* engaged in practical action.

Prudence requires that negotiators must be prepared not to reach an agreement. Factually list and review your alternatives, both within and out of negotiation; and objectively assess what you will do if negotiation fails. Accept the risk of sunk costs if walking away without a signed deal.

Assess whether the negotiation partners are likely to walk away without a negotiated deal or if they are rather looking to build a relationship. If mostly deal-oriented try to consider their own alternatives if they decide not to reach an agreement. It is however difficult to "put yourself in their shoes" and to bridge information asymmetry. The *Impartial Spectator* accepts uncertainty and subjective probability assessment when assessing the other party's options.

There are multiple issues at stake in a negotiation. Real negotiation issues may vary for both parties and/or the relative importance may differ. In ICBN, a key concern is to clearly identify whether the dominant issue is Relationship-Building or deal closure. On more detailed issues, assess the relative importance of each negotiation issue for your own camp in comparison with that of the negotiation partners.

Provided that a negotiator constantly remains an *Impartial Spectator*, constantly accompanied by a self-critical spectator of his or her actions as an agent and a *Prudent Man* or a *Prudent Woman*, he or she may reasonably and prudently indulge in slight over-optimism, because a certain degree of enthusiasm provides stamina in negotiation. However, the negotiating agent should remain cautious since a positive and realistic imagination of the future is needed. As for the *Prudent Man* or *Prudent Woman*, they should absolutely refrain from any cultural hostility towards their business partners, if only because of enlightened *self-interest*. When confronted with framing effects, either as a "framed" or a "framer", prudent negotiators should play on both sides of the frame, both the negative and the positive, trying to develop an objective and impartial view of both losses and gains.

Negotiation teams: Multiplicative versus additive castings

Single negotiator versus negotiation team

In case of an individual negotiator, the first question to be raised is whether she or he has all the necessary skills to negotiate. A single negotiator may have competence and credibility problems if she or he does not possess all the skills needed *in situ*. Negotiation stakes may be low and it might be a repetitive type of agreement for which a general framework has been agreed upon during a previous negotiation round. If the negotiation is only about fine-tuning details such as delivery dates and quantity, an individual negotiator can do a good job provided that there is no misbalance in numbers between the parties. It is always unpleasant for an individual negotiator to face a team. This is exactly how job interviews take place. Applicants most often face several interviewers who ask questions and try to see who the prospective employee is and to make sure of her talents as well as her fit with the position. This is an uneasy situation in which the lonely negotiator may have a hard time reacting quickly enough to defend his position. The recommendation is clear: team negotiators, not a single negotiator, should be sent to confront another team.[20]

Other issues should be addressed such as the level of a negotiator within his organization, whether he or she has a mandate or is a full-fledged negotiator. Status minded partners from high power distance societies often dislike being confronted with (what they perceive to be) lower status people as opponents in negotiation, especially if they are principals in their own organization and the other negotiator is mandated by her superior/principal who does not appear, except very late in the process. At least the perception of a status gap may lead status minded negotiators to consider that they are not taken seriously. In fact their self-esteem is questioned and this may result in a loss of face (especially for IT2 negotiators).

If choosing a negotiation team, the issue is the same as with an individual negotiator; that is, which pack of skills is required for the team? A negotiation team is costly and diverse. As explained below, the "casting" should build on complementarity and be rather homogeneous (precise). Team members should fine-tune their positions, possibly distribute roles and decide on how to communicate both within the team and with the other team. This should be done before entering into face-to-face negotiation with the other party to reduce the risk that a negotiation team will appear exceedingly divided.

Replacing a negotiator may be necessary for some reasons (e.g., she or he left the company or was assigned to a different position). Some recommend having an "expendable person", a negotiator who is non-indispensable as an individual person, and can therefore easily be replaced by someone else. This is common in the IT1 perspective, in which people are unimportant ("separate people from problems"). In the IT1 perspective, expendable, replaceable persons oblige IT2 partners to start from scratch with new players on the opposite team, at the risk of a personal chemistry clash. This change in negotiator(s) may be problematic if unannounced and unmanaged. Socialization has to be restarted from zero and some characteristics of the new negotiator may be problematic for IT2 partners (e.g., members of unequal status). The people-based part of the relationship is lost, at least temporarily, especially if the former negotiator was positively perceived by the other side. The new negotiator may miss the history of the negotiation and the experience of how it previously developed. A diary of the negotiation and a transmission of experience from the former to the new negotiator are necessary. Finally, clearly announcing the change in persons, providing clear explanations, and giving some cues to the other party about who the new negotiator is may be a simple matter of courtesy; at the same time it is quite useful to ease the negotiation process.

Team negotiation: Multiplicative versus additive castings

When an organization builds a team, it looks for functional and skill complementarity between the members. A team has a casting side like in movies.[21] In order to save on costs, famous movie stars being very expensive, the producer and the director may be tempted to save on some assignment by hiring to-be-stars rather than box office superstars. The key issue is compensation vs. non-compensation of talent heterogeneity. The assumption underlying the additive casting is that average team quality is based on an arithmetic mean of their talents. However, an untalented and inexperienced negotiator may not display the mix of flexibility and firmness necessary for ICBN, and spoil the efforts of otherwise talented team members. Other team members have therefore to "fight" against his or her awkwardness and waste effort to regain lost ground. A multiplicative casting, in which average team quality is based on a geometric mean of individual talents, seems nearer to the reality.

Team negotiation: Composition and dynamics

In international, complex negotiation, such as turnkey contracts and joint ventures, it is often the case that each side is represented by a team of negotiators (e.g., three or more) rather than by individual negotiators. These teams are chosen on an ad hoc basis, representing for instance different divisions of the company and/or functional areas. Complementarity is assumed, while (overlooked) individual differences within the negotiation team (NT) may in fact be considerable in terms of nationality, language, culture, or business-related aspects, like experience with the company. Differences in status within the team and within the organization they represent, in expertise, in roles, and in language and communication skills, may create internal conflicts within the team and undermine the NT efficiency. Team members are supposed to serve the corporate interest. However, they may have conflicting priorities and preferences; that is, diverging opinions in terms of how they view the negotiation process, its purpose, and the types of outcomes to be attained. In a study of 45 negotiation teams, Jeanne Brett and her colleagues[22] found that for the companies "the biggest challenge came from their own side of the table" (Brett, Friedman, and Behfar, 2009, p. 2).

The influence of the team context varies both when teams are culturally homogeneous and when they are culturally diverse. Gelfand et al. (2013) show that, due to harmony norms, collectivistic Taiwanese teams tend to negotiate significantly suboptimal outcomes, lower than for Taiwanese solo negotiators. Conversely, individualistic U.S. negotiator teams outperform solos in negotiation, suggesting that IT1 individualists are paradoxically better able to take advantage of individual differences by mitigating competitiveness with team cooperation (this being probably related to the very strong emphasis on team work in the American culture). Comparing U.S. and Japanese cultures, Von Glinow et al. (2004) show that emotional conflict is heightened in multicultural teams by communication challenges related to language and linguistic differences. The appropriateness and the meaning of "talking" differ according to cultural background. Questions emerge such as whether and how to engage in talking together about the conflict, to the extent that non-talk alternative to conflict resolution may be desirable.

Stakes must be high – negotiating in teams involves higher costs, increased complexity, and the risk of uncoordinated behaviour sabotaging a party's position. A NT may be monolithic (from the Greek etymology, like a single, solid stone) as opposed to non-monolithic, when individual negotiators allow themselves to openly diverge, or even have a real disagreement at the negotiation table, in front of the other party. An aligned sense of purpose and coordinated behaviour are reasons why it would be better for the NT to be monolithic, but these arguments are only scratching the surface of the issue. Paradoxically enough, a non-monolithic NT can be an asset for effective negotiation, provided the homework has been done by the team members beforehand.

Heterogeneity in the NT is likely to increase if the team members represent different divisions of the same company, different subsidiaries, and/or different functional areas. However, it is even trickier when they come from different organizations which are assembled in a negotiation consortium. A key issue in team negotiation is therefore team work is addressed and planned vs. unaddressed and vs. unplanned. Brett, Friedman, and Behfar (2009) suggest different avenues for addressing NT divergence.

- They recommend exploring potential conflicts by plotting out each NT member's priorities, preferences, and interests.
- Divergences in data interpretation should be uncovered and solved in favour of a joint understanding of key issues and information.
- Different team members have different constituents and should negotiate purpose and priorities with their internal mandates to be able to align with other NT members.
- The negotiation to come can be simulated by the team members, to confront their personalities, communication styles, and possible conflicts. Role playing may lead them to assign roles within the NT (Who is who? Who does what?) to coordinate and maximize their influence on the opposite party.
- Because face-to face communication is quick and does not allow private information exchange within a NT, it is advisable to have some tricks for discrete intra-team communication, like having agreed-upon body language to signal a number of messages.

Continuity in the composition of the NT is important, especially if the process extends over a relatively long period of time. If a NT member has to definitively leave the negotiation table, for instance, because of a new assignment, a diary of the negotiation will help the new NT member to enter the process. She should be offered the possibility to follow the steps described above.

Heterogeneity and diversity in the NT, far from being a liability, is an asset when it is properly managed; that is, when a common sense of purpose has been pre-negotiated. Communication coordination is of utmost importance for team negotiation. As a final note, there is a possibility that cross-NT (cross-team) affinities sometimes appear in IBN. A team member on one side feels empathy, based on sympathy, shared kinship, or personal attraction with a member of the opposite NT. Unexpectedly, negotiators may share a common language, education, or similar life experiences which lead them to cross-team complicity. This may extend to being more concession prone, more susceptible to disclose information, etc. One may wonder whether this emerging connivance should be considered a threat or an opportunity. If properly managed by the NT, that is, openly unveiled and discussed within the team, it may become an asset, especially when the team includes bi-cultural negotiators (Kern et al., 2012).

Personality, emotional/cultural intelligence, and ICBN skills

Skills required from ICB negotiators[23]

The key skills required from an ICB negotiator are patience and flexibility. Patience helps negotiators both create and claim value in negotiations, because they do not fear spending time on exploring alternative solutions and later claiming their fair share of the joint outcome. Ideally, ICB negotiators must be active listeners, calm, and able to master their emotions. Courtesy and respect for the other party's cultural codes (e.g., *Ningensei* described on pp. 192–194), as well as intercultural communication skills should be added to this list. Authority should be shown without being commanding or pushy; role authority as well as personal empowerment can be displayed, however avoiding the display of a misplaced hierarchical stance which is at odds with the horizontal, egalitarian setting of negotiation.

Opportunistic behaviour is partly a cultural and personality trait. Some negotiators feel unashamed not to respect their commitment and not to fulfil their agreed-upon obligations. Resistance to provocations such as lying and non-respect of commitment is another key skill for ICB negotiators, who should avoid interpreting too much especially when the other party's behaviour is ambiguous and equivocal. An apparent lack of commitment may be due to unforeseen events and circumstances that the other party hides for fear of being ashamed and losing. Similarly, circumvent the propensity to think of the opposing party's personality as naive and lacking stamina, when in fact their cultural norms value a modest and unassertive self-profile. Empathy, language proficiency (or at least sensitivity to language issues), and ability to disentangle deal and relationship are other key ICBN skills.

Cultural intelligence[24] and emotional intelligence can be developed either though training or by recruiting adequate ICB negotiators.[25] Emotional intelligence, according to psychologist Daniel Goleman (Goleman, 2006), involves not only the awareness of one's own and the other party's emotions but also the ability to empathetically understand how emotions on both sides interact and combine together. Emotional intelligence feeds the ability for active self-control (i.e., not only pure emotional restraint) and the capacity to regulate one's own mood and behaviour in a way which will positively transfer to the other side's capability to regulate their own emotions. However, as emphasized by Earley and Mosakowski, cultural intelligence differs from emotional intelligence (2004, p. 139):

> Cultural intelligence is related to emotional intelligence, but it picks up where emotional intelligence leaves off. A person with high emotional intelligence grasps what makes us human and at the same time what makes each of us different from one another. A person with high cultural intelligence can somehow tease out of a person's or group's behavior those features that would be true of all people and all groups, those peculiar to this person or this group, and those that are neither universal nor idiosyncratic.

Cultural intelligence is related to the ability to delay judgement, possibly suspending it for some days, and actively retrieving new cues for understanding, persistence when facing hostility or incomprehension, and thinking before acting.

Personality and negotiation styles

An introductory caveat is in order: Do not try to be someone else. However, it is tempting to change some aspects of oneself in the hope of becoming a better negotiator. Therefore, it makes sense to try to understand one's own personality traits based, for instance, on the Meyer/Briggs personality type inventory (MBTI). The MBTI opposes personalities on four polar dimensions: Extroversion vs. Introversion, Sensing vs. Intuitive, Thinking vs. Feeling, and Perceiving vs. Judging. Extroverts seem more adapted as negotiators because of their sociability and orientation to the outer world. However, introverts may be good listeners and keep a strong focus on their interests. Sensing negotiators are facts oriented, practical, and precise, while intuitive negotiators privilege the big picture, metaphors, and innovation. Thinkers are logical and objective (much like in the *logos* orientation described in the next section), while Feelers are more subjective in their approach to negotiation. Perceiving negotiators place the emphasis on information seeking, data-gathering, and understanding situations, while remaining highly flexible. Finally, Judgers are concerned with controlling events and planning action.[26]

A first direction for improving one's performance in negotiation is to adopt a negotiation style which fits with one's personality. It is beyond the scope of this book, dealing with culture and negotiation rather than personality and negotiation, to comment at length on the issue of choosing a negotiation style. However, a number of negotiation books offer detailed insights.[27]

A second direction is to choose (if possible) negotiation situations that correspond to one's own personality traits. Some competitive personalities may be more adapted to one-shot deals, short-term and bargaining-oriented, in which their hard sell talents will triumph. Conversely, more collaborative and long-term oriented personalities may feel more at ease with the ICBN Relationship-Building type of negotiation described throughout this book.

Symbolic resources for ICB negotiators

Developing empathetic persuasive skills is an essential aspect of personality in negotiation, especially in ICBN. I present below three frames which may help ICB negotiators to assess their own styles, building on strengths and trying as much as possible to offset weaker points. The first guiding frame is of ancient Greek origin, Aristotle's Rhetoric building on *ethos* (morality), *pathos* (empathy), and *logos* (rationality). The second set of recommendations is based on four Confucian behavioural principles, originally Chinese, however shared by the Japanese under the name of *Ningensei*. The third general framework is based on the symbols expressed in the Chinese five element system, Water, Wood, Earth, Fire, Metal (*Wu Xing*). The combination of strengths and weaknesses expressed in each element and in their interactions (each element generating and moderating other elements) is a useful symbolic resource for the self-assessment of one's own skills in ICBN.

Argumentation and persuasion Greek-style

The Rhetoric of Aristotle, with its three components of *ethos*, *pathos*, and *logos* is a nice guiding framework for developing persuasive skills, because it is an essential aspect of negotiation.[28] I call it a symbolic system because it roughly corresponds to IT1 Western categories of morality, sympathy, and rationality. The first component in Aristotle's Rhetoric is *Ethos*. Ethos is the Greek word for "character". Not only is the word "ethic" derived from ethos but many other words use this root. Ethos corresponds to the moral sense in a personality (i.e., the capacity to address moral issues as questions rather than ready-made normative answers as to what is good or bad). Personal goodness and benevolence are part of ethos (rather like the Confucian *Rén* as well as the Japanese *Amae* explained on p. 194). Ethos conveys a message on the negotiator's credibility and character which contributes to his or her power of persuasion. By ethos, Aristotle meant credibility, authority, and legitimacy.

> We believe good men more fully and more readily than others: this is generally true whatever the question is, and absolutely true where exact certainty is impossible and opinions are divided … his character may almost be called the most effective means of persuasion he possesses.
>
> Aristotle (McKeon, 2001, p. 1329)

The second persuasion engine is *Pathos. Pathos* is a broad concept relating to "suffering" and "experience" and also more generally to feelings and emotions. The words pathology, empathy, sympathy, and pathetic are derived from the Greek *Pathos*. It refers to emotions in general and to the emotional connection between the negotiator and her counterpart. Other-regarding orientation in the form of positive pathos is a key component of persuasion skills. *Pathos* is defined by Aristotle in the following way, insisting that a negotiator's own emotions, both positive and negative, can be used to persuade negotiation partners by appealing to their emotions. "Secondly, persuasion may come through the power of the hearers, when the speech stirs their emotions. Our judgments when we are pleased and friendly are not the same as when we are pained and hostile" (Aristotle in McKeon, 2001, p. 1330).

The third component of Aristotle's Rhetoric as the art of persuasion is *Logos*. Aristotle defines the appeal to logic and reasoning to convince in the following terms. "Thirdly, persuasion is effected by the speech itself when we have proved a truth or an apparent truth by means of the persuasive arguments suitable to the case in question" (Aristotle in McKeon, 2001, p. 1330).

Logos is the Greek root of many facts, science, logic, and rationality-based words in English (e.g., logical, therefore convincing). Speech, reasoning, and discourse, both oral and written (presentation as well as books and articles), are central in *Logos*. Facts and statistics, scientific proof, data, evidence as well as historical and literary sources are the typical means used by *Logos* to generate a sense of truthfulness and inevitability in the arguments made by a negotiator. Persuasion is effected by a logically articulated, rational speech which "proves" the truth of arguments used in negotiating.

Aristotle's rhetoric framework has limits; however, it draws our attention to the need to use all three pillars of persuasive skills as well as the necessary balance between them. ICB negotiators may assess their natural tendencies and abilities in mobilizing *ethos*, *pathos*, and *logos*. For instance, rights-oriented negotiators who combine logos and ethos should be careful to develop also *pathos*, the second pillar of persuasive skills, if they do not want to appear as insensitive and dry.

Other-regarding orientation East Asian-style

Confucian thought focuses on the cultivation of virtue and the maintenance of ethics. Some of the basic Confucian ethical concepts and practices include *rén, yì, lǐ,* and *zhì*.[29] The IT2 emphasis in these concepts is more on moral and social behaviour than on logic and rationality as in the Western Aristotelian (rather IT1) framework described above. This set of moral guidelines for human interaction is found in most East Asian countries. The Japanese concept of *Ningensei* exemplifies the same four interrelated principles of Confucian philosophy: *jen, i (amae), li,* and *shu* (Goldman, 1994).

Rén (仁), meaning "benevolence" or "humaneness", is at the heart of human behaviour when people manifest compassion toward other human beings. Benevolence and empathetic behaviour related to *Rén* entails active listening, caring for the views of negotiation partners, and looking for their feelings and true intentions. However there are pitfalls to possibly excessive other-regarding orientation. In terms of the Dual Concern Model (Chapter 1), *Rén* may translate into disproportionate concern for the other party's outcomes. In the IT1 paradigm there should be a balanced consideration for the needs of both sides.

Yì (義/义) consists in remaining righteous and cultivating a moral disposition to do good. Confucian *Yì* called *i* by the Japanese, also termed *amae*, is concerned with group welfare by directing human relationships to the common good. According to Goldman (1994, p. 33), "The *i* component of *ningensei* surfaces in Japanese negotiators' commitment to the organization, group agendas, and a reciprocity (*shu*) and humanism (*jen*) that is long-term, consistent, and looks beyond personal motivation".

The Confucian *Lǐ* (禮/礼) is a system of ritualized behaviours and propriety norms that governs individuals in everyday life. *Li* codes behaviour in a precise and formal manner, and is supposed to smooth the interpersonal and social expression of *jen, shu* and *i*. The Japanese *meishi* ritual of exchanging business cards can be considered as typical of *li* coded etiquette.[30] However, codes corresponding to formal manners differ across cultures. They need not necessarily be imitated by cultural outsiders unless they have a practical purpose (such as the *meishi* ritual) in the non-task sounding negotiation phase. The comprehension of alien social interaction codes in ICBN commands respect, however, not imitation. *The Confucian principle* of *Zhì* (智), or *Shu* in Japanese, is based on a norm of generalized reciprocal behaviour essential in Relationship-Building. It obliges the individual to refrain from actions and behaviour toward others that would be unpleasant if directed to oneself. This mirror game allows one to understand what is right and fair, or wrong and unfair in both one's own and others' behaviours. *Zhì/Shu* is a practical protective device in Confucian philosophy which negatively considers individual failure to sustain the moral values of *rén* and *yì*. Similarly the Japanese equivalent of *Zhì*, *Shu*, emphasizes the importance of reciprocity for the cultivation of human relationships. *Shu* is an affective and intuitive means of coding messages and involves "belly communication" when negotiating.[31]

The five Chinese elements in ICBN: Generating integrative collaboration[32]

In the Chinese philosophical tradition, five basic elements (*Wing-Xu*) compose our world: *Wood* (*mu*), *Fire* (*huo*), *Earth* (*tu*), *Metal* (*jin*), and *Water* (*shui*). Each element has a symbolic meaning and their balance is important for the negotiator. The five elements are traditionally regarded as the foundation of everything both in daily life and natural phenomena. They have their own character and can generate or destroy one other. Each of these five elements gives a symbolic force to the negotiator, who should use it shrewdly since each element 1) generates another symbolic element and 2) is moderated and counterbalanced by still another symbolic element (see Figure 6.1).

Wood relates to vegetation and flowers and expresses beauty and benevolence. *Wood* articulates destiny, representing lavish, brilliant, blooming, flourishing aspects. In negotiation, *Wood* stands for the richness and quality of negotiators' arguments.

Fire represents features related to strength or softness, to power and influence, as well as to bravery and forcefulness. *Fire* is related to the sense of commitment and to the sense of propriety. In ICBN, *Fire* provides negotiators with stamina, respectability, and good manners.

Earth fundamentally represents a link to material life and to the real world. *Earth* is related to depth, fidelity, and honesty. The *Earth* provides the status, rich or poor, and represents the birth and growth of everything. In ICBN, the *Earth* element corresponds to both a deep sense of the real issues at stake and a rather realistic attitude.

Metal is associated with both righteousness and practical decision-making. *Metal* determines the life span, longevity or failure, and foretelling (i.e., predicting, forecasting) dangers and difficulties, penalties and dead ends. *Metal* is also associated with prudence. In ICBN, *Metal* governs the ability to predict possible negative events, to be precise in drafting contracts, and to value justice, righteousness, and honesty (e.g., ethical standards). The *Metal* element provides the negotiator with strength and the ability to reach a decision that is applicable in practice and profitable for both sides.

Water relates to imagination and wisdom. Because of its liquid, fluid, and agile nature, *Water* promotes talents and represents aptitude and brightness, as well as an agile and accurate mind. In ICBN it is susceptible to lead to strong ability to invent creative solutions, to be flexible (e.g., not be stuck in the middle or adopt a positional stance). *Water* also relates to the ability to clarify complex situations and intricate negotiation issues.

The five elements provide ICB negotiators with symbolic resources that guide their involvement in the negotiation process. However, going too far in pursuing the path indicated by a first element results in generating the next element on the *Wu Xing* circle, possibly fostering its negative side, which then requires a third element to intervene as a moderator, and re-balance the "triangle". That is why the *Wu Xing* is based on a circle and five arrows inside, between a first element, a second element generated by the first, and a third element which generates the first element and acts as a moderator of excesses in the second element (see Figure 6.1 and Table 6.1).

Compared with the Western four element system, *Earth*, *Air*, *Fire*, and *Water*, two human-transformed elements (*Wood* and *Metal*) exist in the Chinese elements which do not occur in the Western – purely natural – framework. One element (*Air*) exists in the Western framework that does not exist in the Chinese elements.

Water supplies the negotiator with the power of imagination and agility of mind. In turn, *Water* generates (i.e., nourishes) *Wood* which stands for the richness and quality of arguments, problem-solving abilities, and the creative exploration of joint solutions. However, making arguments (excessive *Logos*) should not be at the detriment of decision-making. *Wood* needs a counterbalancing element which it finds in *Metal*. *Metal* penetrates *Wood* by cutting, sawing, drilling, nailing, screwing, etc. Excesses in the *Wood* element are moderated by the practical decision-making orientation in *Metal*.

Wood-based argumentation generates (i.e., feeds) *Fire*, that is, possibly too strong commitment at the risk of a lack of self-control. Trying hard to convince the opponent, being passionately committed to one's goals

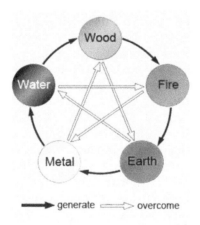

Figure 6.1 Interactions between the five elements in *Wu Xing*

Source: adapted from: "The Five Elements (Wu Xing)" available at www.travelchinaguide.com/intro/astrology/five-elements.htm, accessed 27 January 2018

Table 6.1 The five Chinese elements and negotiation behaviour

Element 1 generates...	... Element 2, which is...	... moderated by Element 3
Water (imagination and creativity)	*Wood* (brilliant, blooming ideas)	*Metal* (practical decision-making)
Wood (brilliant, blooming ideas)	*Fire* (commitment/ propriety/power)	*Water* (imagination and creativity)
Fire (commitment/ propriety/power)	*Earth* (material life/ deal-fidelity)	*Wood* (brilliant, blooming ideas)
Earth (material life/ deal-fidelity)	*Metal* (practical decision-making)	*Fire* (commitment/ propriety/power)
Metal (practical decision-making)	*Water* (imagination and creativity)	*Earth* (material life/ deal-fidelity)

should not translate for a negotiator into a lack of self-control. However, *Fire* is moderated by *Water* which quenches *Fire*. Excessive commitment can be moderated by the *Water* element bringing brightness, wisdom, and a flexible mind.

Fire, related to the sense of commitment, generates *Earth* (i.e., *Earth* is a crusty surface produced by the cooling of magmatic *Fire*). The risk with *Earth* is that negotiators become so solidly fastened, that they turn out to be too single-minded and possibly stubborn. Therefore *Earth* is moderated by *Wood*, the underlying symbolic image being that *Wood* parts *Earth* (e.g., tree roots breaking up soil and even rock). *Wood* in the form of roots or trees can prevent *Earth* erosion. Single-mindedness and excessive resolve related to the deep-seated *Earth* element should be curtailed by coming back to more sophisticated, diverse, and creative arguments; that is, by breaking up a too solid and steadfast position. This is especially true for positional negotiation.

Earth, which represents the link to material life and to the real world, generates *Metal* since its soil contains ore and minerals. *Metal* commands practical decision-making, deal-orientation, and risk and danger conscious-ness. However, too much *Metal* may result for a negotiator in excessive deal-orientation, narrow-focused and mean practicality, and a counterproductive obsession to make things work. Being overly concerned with possible nega-tive events and their unpleasant consequences are the possible undesir-able aspects of the *Metal* element for a negotiator. *Metal* needs a balancing element, which it finds in *Fire*. *Fire* melts *Metal*. The strength and robustness of *Metal* should be used by the negotiator, however moderated by *Fire*, to avoid becoming a cold-hearted decision-maker, lacking *Pathos* and empathy.

Metal, associated with practical decision-making, generates *Water* (i.e., *Water* runs off of *Metal tubes*). *Water* (imagination and creativity) is moderated by *Earth* (linked to material life and pragmatism) because cre-ative ideas should as much as possible remain realistic. *Earth* absorbs, dams or muddies *Water*. Creativity should find down-to-*Earth* limits.

Conclusion

A balanced self-orientation in ICBN requires reflexivity, moderation, patience, and prudence. Be yourself, try to remain sincere and genuine, however prudent and impartial. Do not try to be someone else. This may imply difficult trade-offs between being yourself and wearing a mask, which may be to some extent necessary in some social situations. The paradoxical recommendation of "negotiating rationally in an irrational world"[33] does not apply to the world of ICBN, which is far from being irrational. Rather rationalities broadly differ between an IT1 calculative, economic, and utilitarian rationality and an IT2 relational, group, and identity-based rationality.

Notes

1 Elfenbein et al. (2008).
2 See Maude (2014, pp. 213–216) on individual negotiators' characteristics, Jeong (2016, pp. 185–188) about psychological/individual idiosyncrasies, and Hernández Requejo and Graham (2008, pp. 130–137) about key bargainer characteristics. How five strong negotiator personalities interacted in the Congress of Vienna negotiations in 1815 is presented by Dupont and Audebert-Lasrochas (2013, chapter 6).
3 See Foster (1995, pp. 219–234) on the importance of rank, status, and position in ICBN.
4 See Hofstede (2001, pp. 279, 350) for discrepancies between gender, gender roles, and feminine culture. See also Kolb and McGinn (2008) and Kolb (2009) on negotiation and gender as well as gendered negotiations.
5 See Kolb and McGinn (2008). My own, unpublished, empirical observations using the Kelley's (1966) game over more than 20 years, and comparing the average profit of male and female negotiation students, is that male fare slightly better than female students; however, the difference is not statistically significant and changed over recent years in favour of female students. Furthermore the standard deviation of outcomes is significantly larger for women, suggesting that some women tend to be influenced by their traditional sex role in negotiation while others are not.
6 Globally, the generational divide has been on the increase over the last 50 years due to rapid technological change, increased individualism and affluence, and changes in family models and values (see Hernández Requejo and Graham, 2008, pp. 96–97).
7 For more on the difference between professional and national culture see Lang (1993), Salacuse (1998, 1999), and Sebenius (2002).
8 See Menkel-Meadow (2001).
9 On decision-making styles across cultures and the role of organizational culture in ICBN, see Fisher (1980, pp. 27–36), Foster (1995, pp. 290–291), Kalé (2003, pp. 78–80), and Jeong (2016, pp. 191–193).
10 On judgement biases in negotiation see Bazerman et al. (2000); on cognitive biases across cultures, see Thompson, Neale, and Sinaceur (2004), Morris and Gelfand (2004), and Caputo (2013).

11 Bazerman and Neale (1992), Neale and Bazerman (1992), Bazerman et al. (2000), Bazerman (2002).

12 Bazerman and Neale (1992).

13 Kahneman, Knetsch, and Thaler (1987) have shown that equity judgements can be affected by framing effects.

14 This scenario is taken from Bazerman and Neale (1992, p. 118), based on the Kahneman et al. (1987) study on the influence of framing effects on fairness judgements. However, I found weak confirmation of this result over 15 years with Swiss negotiation students.

15 There is a huge literature on positive illusions on relationships, whether simply close, marital or romantic, on one's own mental health, etc. Far from being only self-deceptive, positive illusion may also bring a number of side benefits.

16 The effect was named by psychologist Ellen Langer and has been replicated in many different contexts.

17 Bazerman and Neale (1992).

18 For instance, Etihad Regional had faced the huge losses of its German subsidiary Air Berlin for years. At the end of 2017, Etihad Regional accepted its investment in Air Berlin as *sunk costs* and Air Berlin went bankrupt.

19 Research studies show that the *inter-individual* variability of genetic characteristics is much larger than the *inter-racial* variability (Segall et al., 1999). In other words, genetic differences *among* Europeans or *among* Africans are much larger than the genetic differences *between* Europeans and Africans.

20 For different approaches to team negotiation, see Bazerman and Neale (1992, Chapter 14, pp. 126–139), Hernández Requejo and Graham (2008, pp. 136–137), Saner (2008), Maude (2014, pp. 134–138, 216–218), Baber and Fletcher-Chen (2015, pp.148–151), Graham, Lawrence, and Hernández Requejo (2014; Chapter 6, pp. 75–91 on "Getting the team right").

21 See Elberse (2007), Alchian and Demsetz (1972), and Caves (2000).

22 Behfar, Friedman, and Brett (2004), Brett, Friedman, and Behfar (2009).

23 For a detailed presentation of intercultural competency issues, see Rudd and Lawson (2007, pp. 153–173). See also Bazerman and Neale (1992, pp. 105–115) on negotiation, learning, experiences and expertise.

24 See Earley and Mosakowski (2004).

25 Key bargainer characteristics are examined in Hernández Requejo and Graham (2008, pp. 130–137). The issues around negotiator selection and training are treated in Maude (2014) chapter 6, pp. 129–154, and in Foster (1995, pp. 275–277).

26 Kalé (2003).

27 Cellich and Jain (2004) in chapter 3 (pp. 43–52) describe typical negotiation styles and offer advice as to how to select one's own negotiation style based on a 35 statement Personal Assessment Inventory (pp. 50–51). G. Richard Shell (2006), in his landmark book, *Bargaining for Advantage*, provides advice both for collaborative people (who need to become more assertive, confident, and prudent) and competitive negotiators (who need to become more aware of other people and of their legitimate needs) in two different sets of seven "tools" adapted to each negotiation and personality style. Maude (2014) mentions extroversion, and risk-seeking vs. risk avoiding as personality characteristics that may have an influence on performance. He also usefully highlights the

role of interpersonal attractiveness, that is, the degree of fit between individual personalities, as having a positive impact on cooperation in negotiation. See also Wheeler (2013).

28 See Weiss (2015).
29 https://en.wikipedia.org/wiki/Confucianism
30 Goldman (1994).
31 In Matsumoto's (1988) words.
32 My thanks to Professor T.K. Peng from I-Shou University, Kaohsiung, Taiwan for cultural insider validation.
33 Title of Bazerman and Neale's (1992), Chapter 18.

7   The intercultural business negotiation process

Besiege Wei to rescue Zhao.

(Chinese Stratagem 2, i.e., avoid a head-on battle with a strong enemy, and instead strike at his weakness and attack the opponent's vulnerabilities)

Chapter 7 first presents classical phases of the negotiation process according to the IT1 model, centring mostly on the face-to-face part of the process. Phases are generally based on the linear, rational, sequential, planned approach (setting agenda and schedule), settling one point after the other. Against this approach, a Relationship-oriented IT2 party may display a preference for non-planning as a favoured route to Relationship-Building and further Deal-Making, adopting a holistic approach, a package deal, no sub-agreement being considered as closed before the whole is agreed upon. This can border on chaos when the IT2 party decides to significantly question particular aspects of the deal (e.g., price) in the very last moment before signing, leaving the IT1 party with a painful sense of being unduly exploited. The chapter discusses the role and length of preliminaries, necessarily longer and more personal when a relationship is primarily sought after. The challenge of unprepared negotiators is examined, especially when the other party comes fully prepared, having properly done their homework. Two types of post-negotiation are examined. First, finalizing the deal, from an apparent (oral) agreement to an explicit (written) contractual arrangement, with all sorts of opportunistic moves related to oblivion, interpretation, and particular readings of what has been said earlier. Second, post-negotiation occurs after the contract has been signed. For IT1 negotiators, a deal signed should be implemented as the law of the parties; it is a sacred piece signalling detailed and explicit commitment. Each clause should be carefully respected. Conversely, for IT2 negotiators, the relationship is paramount and should enable the contracting parties to ICBNs to overcome obstacles, misunderstandings, and unforeseen events during implementation. IT2 negotiators consider signing a contract as important, but as a simple milestone in the negotiation process, in no way its actual end. They rather view implementation as a continuously extended negotiation process. That is why litigation may occur in ICBNs with a wide discrepancy on how the threat of legal action and/or actual litigation is perceived. Perfectly legitimate for IT1 negotiators, getting a legal third party, arbitrator or judge, involved may be resented by IT2 negotiators as a breach of the relationship. The last section reviews the third parties that can intervene in ICBNs (experts, interpreters, mediators, conciliators, arbitrators).

Preparing, planning, and scheduling versus deliberate improvising and ad-libbing

Stage 1 – Preparing for negotiation

In books about negotiation following the IT1 paradigm, preparing for negotiation is strongly recommended. However, it is not so clear in negotiation practice if negotiators prepare that much and follow the normative recommendation of the negotiation literature. Like Hamlet's "To be or not to be", a key question in ICBN is "To prepare or not to prepare". Excessive preparation has downsides: it is unilateral and may bring the parties to the negotiation table with rigid and incompatible expectations as to the outcomes and therefore a lack of flexibility in adjusting their positions. Parties should not prepare to such an extent that negotiation is already "closed" when it starts. Preparation remains unilateral, even though one may take into account the other party at this stage (e.g., by anticipating their concerns, needs, their probable positions, interests, rights, power, likely goals, reservation price, BATNA). Parties may also try to assess more interactive negotiation variables such as interdependence, negotiation style, etc. All this is, however, susceptible to partial or even complete disconfirmation after face-to-face negotiation has started. That is why it is tempting to underprepare and remain open to quick learning at the start of the face-to-face negotiation process. Paradoxically, there is a need to prepare and a risk of over-preparing. In general, at least one or the other or both parties come prepared (this being the normative stance). However, for a host of reasons they may come rather unprepared, because of time pressure, uncertainty in assessing the other party's needs and interests, conditionality of expectations, or any action-oriented norm (e.g., "act first/think later"). As the negotiation proceeds, parties must be ready to experience linearity *or* chaos, a structured agenda and schedule as a preferred route to Deal-Making *or* non-planning as the favoured path to Relationship-Building. Although preparation is clearly useful, it must be anticipated that the other party may come prepared, half-prepared, or unprepared.[1]

Information gathering as a preliminary step before the negotiation process itself

Ideally (IT1), in the pre-negotiation stage, parties attempt to understand each other's needs and assess likely demands. They also prepare by looking at alternatives, and gathering information on aspects of the future deal. There are different levels of information gathering.

The first level deals with macro-environment information, in particular general facts on the national and business context of the negotiation partner. This entails both broad social and economic indicators, as well as info on political stability, recent political changes, and more fine-grained material on the local culture (novels, music, etc.), which will provide an initial understanding of the potential partner's context. HC-IT2 negotiators will generally consider cultural information more important than LC-IT1 negotiators who are prone to consider that business negotiation is culture-free. The macro-environment information also comprises local infrastructure, the business environment, foreign exchange legislation, taxation schemes, the legal system, import duties, stay and work permits, and any local regulation that may influence deal negotiation. This information has to be considered in terms of both opportunities and constraints.

Second, publicly available information based on secondary sources should be systematically searched from published data such as corporate accounts, the Internet through search engines, and corporate intelligence companies such as Moneyhouse, Dun & Bradstreet, and Kompass, providing information on the potential partner for minimal search costs.

Third, private information should be gathered as much as possible. Information asymmetry is related to private information, which is supposed to be proprietary to each party. It is, however, possible to obtain private information by interviewing executives, customers or suppliers, provided that they are willing to disclose what they know. The market background and the competitive scene for each side are easy to describe. A look at competition on both sides will provide the first clues on the advantage related to market power (e.g., buying power or a quasi-monopolistic position) and the alternatives for each negotiation camp.

Fourth, some information may be on the fringe of publicly available and private information because not all is said in what is publicly accessible (e.g., corporate financial situation, annual accounts especially in the case of a publicly listed company). Similarly, information on competitors and relationships (e.g., joint projects) with these competitors can be retrieved officially, leading to an evaluation of the other party's alternatives; however, the details of where concurrent talks/negotiations stand are difficult to obtain publicly. Information asymmetry is reduced to strictly private and confidential information if the homework consisting in gathering publicly available information has been properly completed.

Strictly private and confidential information on the other party is difficult to retrieve by official means, unless the other party accepts being audited or detectives are hired, and/or unofficial means are employed (e.g., industrial spying). A simpler solution for information gathering in the negotiation preparation phase is to ask for private information from the potential partner, and consequently be ready to reciprocate by delivering one's own private information. The usual caveats about truthfulness, opportunism, and instrumentality apply to this kind of reciprocal exchange. One way to verify truthfulness, opportunism, and instrumentality is to ask the other party for private information which can be verified because it has already been otherwise retrieved. Moreover, refusal to disclose private information is often information *per se*, because there is suspicion that the other party may voluntarily hide a critical situation such as a large proportion of doubtful debts in the accounts receivable or a tight production schedule that will inevitably result in jumbo delivery delays.

A useful tool to assess our level of information and the (probable) level of information of the other side is the Johari's window (Figure 7.1). The horizontal axis features what is (un)known from available information. The vertical axis features what the other party knows (does not know) through information given to them. The "Arena" corresponds to common knowledge. It is important to have a clear sense of the nature and the extent of shared information. Conversely, the "unknown" area corresponds to what both partners do not know. Cooperative information exchange would typically target an increase in the "Arena" zone and a decrease in the "unknown" area. For the rest, it is advisable for a party to increase the "Façade" zone and decrease the "Blind Spot" zone in order to generate favourable information asymmetry. This is true at any step of the pre-negotiation, negotiation, and post-negotiation processes.

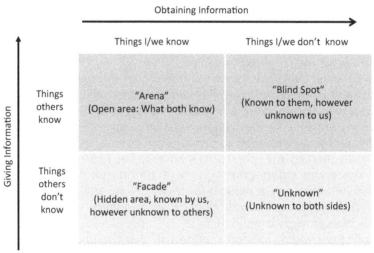

The Johari Window: Giving information reduces the "Facade" zone while obtaining information reduces the "Blind spot" zone

Figure 7.1 Johari's window
Source: adapted from Luft and Ingham (1961)

Retrieving key information on factors influencing the negotiation interaction

Key information should be retrieved as concerns the future inter-action: dependence levels for both parties, accordingly interdependence, as well as the strategic orientation of the potential partner (e.g., based on previous interactions they have had with other companies). In addition, parties have to define their goals and expectations, reservation price, as well as the alternatives (ATNAs and BATNA), the needs and interests at stake on both sides including the potential gains or losses on significant issues, and finally the organizational and strategic fit between parties.

Further it is necessary to ascertain the main aspects of the Deal and to define the problem to be solved. This starts with establishing a list of the issues at stake, ranking them from the least to the most contentious. For all issues, it is advisable to define what one is ready to accept as well as to guess-timate what the other party is probably ready to accept or not, rating the acceptability of solutions for each side on a scale from desirable to unaccept-able with intermediate positions. Negotiators willing to adopt a structured and numbered approach can do so for their own side and for the prospective partner, however in a speculative manner, based on the information previously gathered. The example below provides a non-exhaustive list of issues for an international project sale:

- Form of contract for a project sale: turnkey versus BOT (Build-Operate-Transfer).
- Reservation price.
- Local subcontractors.
- Delay penalties.
- Variable price/fixed price.
- Possible trade-offs and value-creating options.
- Other topics considered important, for instance role distribution between team members.

Predefined strategy versus basic interests

In the IT1 normative orientation it is recommended that parties should come to the negotiation with a predefined strategy based on their expectations; however with the caveat that such a strategy is unilateral. It is therefore preferable to draft a simple list of basic interests, which works as a series of thresholds for what is acceptable or unacceptable. Basic interests, beyond fixing "reservation" price or positions for calculative or strategic issues, also outline walk away options, margins of manoeuvre, possible concessions and their extent, as well as the planned use of particular tactics.

Drafting basic interests should be done with the view that most moves in negotiation are conditional on the other party's reaction. "Thought experiments" such as, "What do we do if they do not accept this?" enable a more realistic approach to the confrontation of positions. Because of conditionality, the advice to "Put yourself in their shoes" appears easier to say than to do. Is it truly realistic and feasible to envision oneself in the role of the other party? What if their negotiation behaviour ends up being the exact opposite of what has been painfully imagined? A better, in fact paradoxical, motto would be "Try to put yourself in their shoes but do not forget to remain in your own shoes". Some negotiators may be reluctant to speculate about what they consider to be undesirable alternatives. Open imagination of the future means that relationship-oriented negotiators would have to put themselves in the shoes of the other party who is ready to breach negotiation and walk away, contrary to their values and goals which centre on Relationship-Building.

When outlining expectations, goals, and basic interests, a central question is whether each side separately prepares (the most frequent situation) or if, at some point, both parties decide to jointly prepare the negotiation. There must be an informal agreement on pre-negotiating together, which enables parties to disentangle pre-negotiation meetings from real face-to-face negotiation, which will come only later. Preparing negotiations from this cooperative perspective makes it easier to come up with mutually beneficial alternatives.

A frequent IT1, normative piece of advice is for a party to take the lead in planning and managing negotiations in a linear and LC style by being proactive and even a bit pre-emptive on setting a detailed agenda and a preset schedule for the coming negotiation. This is intended to build up relative power, especially vis-à-vis IT2, more spontaneous and HC style negotiators. However the IT2 party may not feel obliged by constraints to which they pay lip service. As a conclusion, it should be stressed that while it is clear that preparing for negotiation is by and large useful, there are limitations to preparation. It remains questionable and uncertain who has a decisive advantage over the other in ICBNs, whether the over-prepared party or the under-prepared party.

Linearity vs. chaos, agenda and schedule vs. non-planning

An IT1 party may try to impose their own linear, organized, and "clean" route to Deal-Making. However, despite the agenda and schedule being controlled and promoted by the IT1 party, when confronted with an IT2 party a rather chaotic process may emerge. For IT2 negotiators face-to-face negotiation is necessarily contextual and rather unplanned, considering that this is their preferred route to Relationship-Building. The models of the negotiation process presented below should be taken with much care as they are rarely found in the real world: 1) phases may overlap, 2) one party may decide to go back to an earlier phase, and 3) phases correspond to a linear-reconstructed time model, in which a task must be finished for the next task to start.

Five-phase model of ICBN

The traditional (IT1) model of negotiation comprises four phases.

1) *Non-task sounding*: activities which can be described as targeting the development of an interpersonal rapport and aiming for each party to become better acquainted as well as learning key characteristics of other negotiators (e.g., age, nationality, education, status, previous experience).[2]
2) *Task-related exchange of information*: at this stage, negotiators more precisely indicate their interests, needs, and preferences and supply the other side with (more or less true) information on situations, facts, and data, which underlie their positions.
3) *Persuasion*: parties try to modify the subjective utilities expected by the other party by using argumentation and different persuasion tactics.
4) *Concessions and agreement*: preparing the final, precise draft of the agreement which is often the outcome of a number of reciprocal concessions, of a "small steps" policy, and the end product of a series of sub-agreements.

As noted above, this model should be viewed with caution. Although the four major types of activities are meaningful, this conceptual framework, with its strictly successive phases, is based on a linear, Anglo-Saxon time perception. It may not be verified in practice.

The proposed ICBN model includes a pre-negotiation (before discussing the deal) and a post-negotiation phase (i.e., after contract signing, during agreement implementation).

• *Stage 1: Preparing for the negotiation* (alone or together) and/or *preliminary talks*; this phase of the negotiation process is described on pp. 202–206. If preparation is not unilateral but includes preliminary informal talks, this activity can be also be part of the negotiation process as early bilateral exploration of needs, stakes, fit, power, alternatives, possibly tentative offers, etc. This may lead to aborted negotiation.
• *Stage 2: Relationship-Building* – This phase is face-to-face and a full part of negotiation, especially in the case of a first encounter, when the parties are not acquainted. The *non-task* value judgement needs to be removed since it implicitly suggests that this phase is not really useful for Deal-Making.
• *Stage 3: Task-oriented negotiation*, generally includes face-to-face talks (i.e., information exchange, persuasion to change the other party's utility and preferences, making and accepting concessions to come as close as possible to an agreement). Here activities that are in different phases in the traditional model are placed in only one phase because the linear succession of information exchange, then persuasion, then

concessions – and agreement – is unlikely to happen in ICBN in so orderly a manner. It is most often mixed: concessions can come very early as well as persuasion attempts, in fact before information exchange has even been completely performed. It is important to admit that a lack of time and effort spent on preliminaries or information exchange result in mixing activities all over the negotiation process. Especially when parties start early with persuasion and forget to properly exchange information and explore solutions.

- *Stage 4: Finalizing the agreement* – from an oral to written agreement (contract). This phase, in which the apparent verbal agreement has to be transformed into a precise contract often leads back to renegotiating several aspects of the deal.
- *Stage 5: Post-negotiation*, implementing the deal beyond its signing as a continuously extended negotiation process – this is also an addition to the traditional model, in favour of the IT2 perspective that negotiation never really stops. Post-negotiation is discussed on pp. 213–216.

Stage 2: Relationship-Building

Getting to know each other may include "wine and dine" activities, non-business related exchanges such as talking about personal backgrounds, life experiences, family issues, local customs, and so on. In an IT1 perspective, this may be seen as irrelevant to serious business negotiations, overly personal, unnecessarily touching on strictly private matters, and even dangerously subjective. Relationship-oriented preliminary activities done together to socialize are perceived as tourism, holiday and leisure, not the kind of task and job for which the negotiator is paid. It may instil a feeling of guilt in an IT1 negotiator for whom it is an unfair use of his or her pay. That is why in the IT1 perspective, *Non-task sounding* should be shortened as much as possible and kept within strict time limits.

In the IT2 perspective, it is a meaningful and necessary part of the negotiation process as Relationship-Building preliminaries, rather than a relatively dry deal-oriented *non-task sounding*. This is understood as imperative when meeting for the first time. However, in case of a corporate relationship history involving several negotiations between both camps, this phase will take on a different turn, for instance by welcoming newcomers and getting acquainted with them as well as by exchanging on events and changes since the last negotiation round. In the case of a very first encounter, "Informal talks" may also serve to investigate whether it is worth going on in a lengthy and arduous negotiation that may not lead to agreement. These "Informal talks" are already part of the negotiation process.

For IT2 negotiations, Relationship-Building is normally not intended to investigate the degree of conflict and power, dependence, etc. in order to judge if it is better to walk away soon before going further into the negotiation process. However, IT1 negotiators may try to transform this

Relationship-Building phase, at least in part, into preliminary "informal talks" on the deal itself. By mixing Relationship-Building preliminaries with informal deal-oriented talks, parties will check the initial situation in terms of: 1) perceived level of cooperation or conflict, 2) actual power, dependence, and interdependence, 3) whether the goals on both sides are realistically compatible, 4) the expected benefits of cooperation, and 5) whether the relationship can be established or not. However, misunderstandings at an early stage in the negotiation process due to lack of, or misfit in too short, preliminaries (e.g., based on mere icebreakers and jokes in English) may result in aborted negotiations.

Stage 3 – Task-oriented negotiation: Information exchange, persuasion, and concessions

Often called "face-to-face" negotiation in the traditional business negotiations literature, it is mostly but not necessarily always face-to-face, since emails, traditional post mails, and video-conferences as well as phone conversations can be combined.

Information exchange

What is generally meant by information exchange in negotiation is that parties give truthful information and provide evidence, reciprocating when receiving representative information (IT1). Ideally, this is the best solution to jointly define the problem based on each party's needs and expectations (provided that they are prepared to reveal them) and to foster problem-solving. Alternatives have to be investigated and gauged by each side against its preferences (again provided that parties are ready to reveal them). This requires not only open-mindedness but also a willingness to take risks. As noted above, it is often argued that the negotiation process is dominated by the partner who organizes the agenda (IT1). However, this may not be true as the other side might not feel obliged to follow an agenda that has been forced upon them.

IT2 negotiators, rather than starting negotiations by setting a detailed, linear agenda in which particular issues will be discussed, and presumably agreed upon, one after the other, prefer to have a general discussion setting a framework and broad principles for the relationship. In fact, the IT1 tendency to negotiate supposedly independent aspects of the deal step by step is not always a way to ensure success. Because issues are often interconnected and need to be contextualized, IT2 partners will not respect a corseted agenda and will feel uneasy with the absence of a more general understanding on joint interests, which is likely to foster cooperation at the start. The advantage of sequentially negotiating, one issue after the other, may be that it enables one to simultaneously discuss both the contentious and the non-contentious sides *within* each issue and make trade-offs at each step. However, a number of small trade-offs on isolated issues often misses the "big picture" opportunities of value creation by trading *across* rather than only *within* issues. This is why IT2 negotiators are – legitimately – wary of micro-negotiations with sub-agreements, much in the IT1 style.

Persuasion and concessions in ICBNs

Persuasion is instrumental communication because it aims at changing the other party's positions (e.g., their preferences, their utility for a particular item, their willingness to take risks, and/or to make concessions). Arguments and manoeuvres for influencing the other side are successful only if there is sufficient comprehension of the other party's position, based on a rational conjecture of their reactions to persuasive arguments and manipulative tactics. A party may react adversely to negative persuasive statements such as threats or warnings (see Chapter 8) and this may in the end backfire on those who voiced such statements. Rationally anticipating reactions enables parties to avoid non-credible and unscrupulous persuasion attempts. Presented in Chapter 5, the technique of active listening enables a negotiator to suggest that he or she is respectful and sensitive to the arguments of the party he or she patiently and actively (not passively) listens to. An active, empathetic listener can at times utter a few strongly persuasive arguments because he or she has reached a high level of credibility just by listening attentively. Moreover, active listening enables a thorough understanding of the other side's viewpoint and of its most powerful arguments. Consequently, it assists the active listener in fine-tuning his or her own persuasive arguments, especially when considering alternative solutions. Conversely, persuasion in the form of continuous and active instrumental communication (not so infrequent with some IT2 negotiators) may backfire by giving the impression of non-credible manipulators rather than rational negotiators. Persuasive tactics are considered in great detail in the next chapter.

Concessions can start at any time in the process. Such questions are in order for conceding: When? What, that is, on which issues? Should concessions be systematically reciprocated in a give-and-take manner? Do we search for additional concessions when the agreement already seems to be satisfactory? When does one stop asking for concessions? When should the negotiator stop conceding to the other party? The next chapter presents tactics for extracting concessions from the other side. Making concessions early may not be a good idea, whatever the negotiation paradigm or circumstances. Such entry concessions can be apparently motivated by the hope of improving the relationship. They consist in unilaterally yielding on some aspects of the deal, without even being asked to do so. The first rule should be to make concessions on the basis of give and take signals. At intermediate stages in the process, negotiators often send conditional signals indicating that they are ready to move by making concessions. Potential concessions can be phrased in a conditional-reciprocal manner such as "If you agree to ... we will seriously consider conceding on ... (another issue)".

There is a difference between calculative concessions (they can be measured as a price and/or a money amount) and strategic concessions, which cannot be evaluated in accounting terms. They can be traded off against each other; however, it is important for the party receiving the strategically valuable advantages (e.g., long-term access to resources, markets, knowledge) to check whether they do not pay too high a monetary price for this strategic advantage. On the other hand, concessions in the form of compromise with successive small calculative steps may result in missing the key value creating options, which are often related to the strategic big picture.

When an agreement seems acceptable, just because the ZOPA is large, does that mean that we should agree, when in fact further negotiation efforts would perhaps increase our share of the surplus zone? Value claims, that is, asking for concessions that increase one's share of the pie, should be made only when there is a clear suspicion that the joint outcome is not fairly distributed. When value creation seems to be complete and value distribution appears to be fair, it is advisable not to ask for further concessions. Confronted with a take-it-or-leave-it offer, it is prudent to avoid settling under pressure, that is, global yielding behaviour under the pressure of some kind of blackmail (see Chapter 8 on tactics for extracting concessions).

Stage 4 – Finalizing the agreement: Discovering disagreement behind apparent agreement

Converting an informal deal from an apparent oral agreement into an explicit contractual arrangement is called "post-negotiation" by some. However, it is an integral part of the negotiation process, since drafting the contract almost inevitably leads to re-discussing and renegotiating issues that previously seemed to be completely agreed upon. Stage 4, finalizing an agreement, very much corresponds to a situation of bilateral monopoly. Much time, effort, and money may have been invested to reach this point. High *sunk costs* would appear because of a breach of negotiation at the end of the process. Lost opportunities would possibly lead to unpleasant feelings of regret in the future. In short, backing out is difficult for both parties. However, they are not really in full, precise, and fixed agreement. There are still after-thoughts, unclear points, issues that have been voluntarily kept unspecified or ambiguous, and semi-agreed upon issues that are in dire need of final elaboration. This will become clear when trying to reach an explicit contractual arrangement and discovering with some discomfort that the oral agreement is only apparent.

Drafting a contract in ICBN is much about renegotiating what seemed to have informally been agreed upon. Contracts, although practised worldwide and extremely useful in and of themselves, are very much part of the low-context communication style described in Chapters 2 and 5. Because the agreement is put down on paper and signed by each party, there is a commitment for joint actions, and rights as well as obligations on both sides. Contracts are made to deal with such casualties as failing memory in oral agreements, a party not keeping their promises, deceitful agreements based on communication misunderstandings, and different perceptions and comprehension of what has apparently been (orally in most cases) agreed upon. Moreover tricky implementation issues which were previously envisioned often emerge when drawing up the contract.

There are four main purposes in drafting a written contract:

- Sub-agreements in the form of contracts clauses or articles can be stored and consulted later so that remembering is not an issue as in oral agreements, the details of which can be easily forgotten by one party.
- If their phrasing is precise and explicit (i.e., low-context), clauses are supposed to circumvent misunderstandings in the future as to the interpretation of respective obligations.
- The contract summarizes detailed commitment on both sides; it is "the law of the parties".
- The contract has therefore a legal value and can be brought to a judge or an arbitrator in case of formal litigation.

While being a solid and concrete base representing the joint understanding, a contract paradoxically should have some built-in flexibility either to deal with expected events (e.g., delivery delays) or to take into account unforeseen changes in the future.

Drafting a contract is not a simple formality such as putting an arrangement on paper in commonly agreed upon language, phrasing, and wording. Due to the difference in preciseness and explicitness between oral and written agreements, it is likely that parties will be obliged to go back to previous phases of the face-to-face negotiation process, when in fact they were convinced there was full agreement. Ambiguity in clauses may be intended or unintended; *bona fide* partners may have a hard time disentangling mere inadvertence from hidden intents.

In drawing up a contract, the language used matters, not only the national language(s) that are chosen to have legal forces, but the different linguistic versions of the same contract, which pose translation and conceptual equivalence problems.[3] In order to limit painful and disappointing renegotiation when drafting the final contract, discussion should be summarized after each session of oral negotiations, by writing memos of negotiation sessions or keeping concise minutes of meetings. Memos or minutes will be checked by each party for agreement at the beginning of the next negotiation session. Summarizing and testing joint understanding enables parties to develop a shared comprehension of what they have agreed upon. Ideally, talks should be recorded and transformed in a format that allows parties to accurately check what has actually been said. Transcripts based on audio-recording (possibly using Audacity or Media Player) have much value in allowing a passage from oral to draft-imperfect written form that can later be rewritten in final form.

A "good" outcome (an oral and relational arrangement) does not necessarily lead to a "good" (written-contractual) agreement and vice versa. A good outcome may generate perceived satisfaction on both sides and provide a relational and strategic framework for the deals to come. Conversely, an apparently good agreement may not lead to good outcomes at the implementation stage, especially when some clauses cannot be put in practice and/or lead to misbalanced situations and contentious issues (e.g., inapplicable delay penalties, unrealistic performance obligations). However, a well-drafted agreement contains detailed economic dispositions as to how the deal will be practically implemented. While being necessarily incomplete, the contractual agreement must anticipate circumstances, hardship, and unexpected events and foresee how they will be jointly treated by the signing parties. Ultimately, parties may walk away before signing, one or both of them activating their BATNA. An agreement may fail in the final phase of drafting the contract.

Stage 5 – Post-negotiation: Negotiating the deal beyond its signature

Renegotiation vs. litigation

The post-negotiation phase may be considered very differently by IT1 and IT2 negotiators. Broadly stated, for IT1 negotiators the deal is the outcome and the contract terms must be strictly complied with, irrespective of which party is concerned. Even a very detailed and comprehensive contract (sometimes more than 100 pages long) remains a low-context document. The high degree and the strict nature of commitments relate to the letter of contractual materials to which parties should constantly refer in case problems arise at the implementation stage. An IT1 party may feel deeply threatened by the other party being non-compliant and/or willing to renegotiate a clause previously agreed upon and signed. It latently means that all the efforts spent in drafting the contract seem like a pure waste of time. Renegotiating a particular joint commitment also seems like a door opened on complete renegotiation. Therefore, the IT1 negotiator's willingness to renegotiate a closed deal is very low especially if his or her expectation is that it will lead to a much less favourable situation compared with the present signed contract. An astute (and culturally sensitive) IT2 negotiator may send signals that he or she is ready to pay for what the renegotiation item is asking for. An astute (and culturally sensitive) IT1 negotiator may send signals that he or she is ready to renegotiate some aspect of the deal provided that he or she is not at a loss because of this renegotiation. However, cultural misunderstandings are going to lead to conflict escalation if IT2 negotiators, after asking for renegotiation and being repudiated, bluntly decide not to comply with the contractual terms and impose their point of view in the hope that the other party will yield. After several conflictual exchanges and after threatening to go to court, the IT1 party may decide to choose litigation as a preferred answer for conflict resolution.

Negotiating beyond negotiation – ICBN stage 5 – is the typical IT2 solution. As seen in Chapter 4, the timeline of negotiation is not abruptly interrupted by signing contracts. Since the outcome orientation is relational and people-based, it is expected by IT2 negotiators that the IT1 party will be able to renegotiate as part of a continuous negotiation process. The threat of litigation is understood by the IT2 negotiator as inflicting major damage to the relationship; however not to the extent that he or she will decide to comply with the letter of the contract. It may have become difficult, even virtually impossible, to comply with and respect clauses because of unforeseen circumstances and unexpected events. If brought to court by the IT1 party, especially if the IT1 claims have significant chances of being accepted by the judge or the arbitrator, the relationship is dead and there is little or no way to come back to a joint understanding.

In fact renegotiation is related to the threat of litigation in a complex and ambiguous manner because of interdependence. When implementing the contract, parties are highly interdependent. It is difficult to change partners, to step out of the agreement because implementation costs have already been incurred on both sides. For instance, if a purchasing company is in dire need of parts produced by a subcontractor, the purchaser cannot easily shift supply to another subcontractor due to dedicated equipment and customized design. In construction contracts and public works it is quite frequent that costs explode and delays pile up. When a strict deadline is there (e.g., for constructing a stadium for the Olympic Games which has to be ready by a fixed date), the future owner is so tightly bound to the contractor that they have to grant additional funding far beyond the agreed upon price. The future owner often renounces the delay penalties to have construction finished by the deadline and avoids (worst of all) obliging the contractor to declare bankruptcy. It is in fact too late to switch to another partner. The future owner is locked in a situation, frequent in public works and turnkey plants, in which it is no longer possible to back away. Finding an alternative partner may be extremely costly, if not impossible. Wishful thinking and unexpected events may lead to an underestimation of contract feasibility. In these examples, the parties are strictly tied and renegotiation is imposed by real world constraints. The short French game and counting-out rhyme[4] well expresses the reality of being so closely tied up:

I hold you, You hold me
By our little goatee.

The first one of us two
Who will laugh
Will get a wee slap!

The incompleteness of contracts sets strong limitations to a purely legalistic deal-orientation in the IT1 style. When negotiating, future contingencies cannot be foreseen; unforeseen events may emerge after signing the contract. In the *incomplete* contracting approach, the possibility exists for parties to engage in constructive renegotiation later. However this view of contracting (much in line with the IT2 paradigm) has not dominated over traditional IT1 contract law.

When important changes occur in the environment where the negotiated contracts have to be implemented, such as a revolution, a coup, or a major economic downturn, contracts need to be renegotiated. The *winner's curse* (see Chapter 9) is a typical case when contracts cannot but be renegotiated. Unforeseen circumstances and events, which typically correspond to *Act of God*, *Force Majeure*, or *Hardship* clauses often command renegotiation. Last, in the IT2 paradigm, the relationship has priority over the deal and its weaknesses should be repaired by *bona fide* partners in a collaborative relationship beyond the formal written contract. Ambiguity, incompleteness, and unforeseen circumstances do not necessarily lead to open conflict at the post-negotiation stage, precisely when parties consider that they are still negotiating beyond the formal agreement.

Differences in outcome orientation

Oral versus written agreements as a basis for trust

The debate over oral versus written agreements as a basis for trust between parties is often clipped into two stereotypic sayings: "Get it in writing" versus "My word is my bond". For cultures where "my word is my bond", trust is a personal matter, and is people-based. In the "get-it-in-writing" mentality, trust is more impersonal, based on contracts, rules, and compliance. There are reasons, beyond the mere incompleteness of contracts, which explain that the legalistic IT1 approach to contracts can fail. There is a potential dissymmetry in interpretations of clauses in any negotiated agreement; mainly due to misunderstandings and divergent interpretation of obligations on both sides, to language problems, etc. Sometimes negotiators agree, however on different bases and they may not see the divergence. The agreement may also be perceived differently in terms of the stability of the exchange relationship, and the accuracy and explicitness of exchange provisions. Even "prospective writing", that is, envisioning and foreseeing all possible events, difficulties, and conflicts that may arise in the future, may be a problem between the parties. "Prospective writing" aims at reducing the incompleteness of contracts by sketching probable (however not certain) prospective difficulties *now* and drafting together joint solutions in future-oriented, problem-solving clauses designed for worst-case scenarios. This kind of "imagination of the future" may be in fact subjectively perceived by IT2 parties as the very proof that these negative developments are quite likely to occur and that a *bona fide* relationship is not considered a real asset for solving problems related to unforeseen (and unforeseeable) events.

In written agreements, there is always sophisticated dialectic interplay between trust and distrust/mistrust. It would be naive to believe that profits, especially difficult-to-forecast future accounting profits of each party, are the only possible outcome of the negotiation process. The main reason for profits not being the sole possible outcome is that they are never certain. Basic differences in outcome orientation are generally hidden from the negotiation partners, amplifying misunderstandings. Another reason is that many cultures are relationship- rather than deal-oriented: they prefer a "gentleman's agreement", a loosely worded statement expressing mutual cooperation and trust between the parties, to a formal Western-style contract. For instance, the most critical element of preparation for a negotiation with the Japanese is drafting an opening statement which seals the start of a relationship, in which the Western side may have the opportunity to seize the moment and set the tone for the rest of the negotiation.

Agreements are achieved by negotiation and by signing written contracts. In the United States, more than 1.2 million lawyers help people negotiate and litigate within the framework of written agreements. There are 281 lawyers per million inhabitants in the United States, versus 33 in France and a tiny 7 in non-litigation oriented Japan.[5] Contracts are not everywhere considered "the law of the parties". ICB negotiators rely on a mix of oral/informal understanding and written/formal contractual agreement.

Asymmetry in the perceived degree of agreement

Exploring, maintaining, and checking the bases for trust is a more complex process. It entails various possibilities. First an agreement may be non-symmetrical. A agrees with B, but B does not agree with A. Either B wishes to conceal their disagreement or there is some sort of misunderstanding, usually language-based. Second, negotiators agree, but on different bases, and they do not perceive the divergence. They have, for instance, quite different interpretations of a clause or some kind of non-written agreement. Although much may be written down, some concerns remain unwritten and implicit. What is unwritten and implicit may seem to one party evidently in line with a written clause, but not to the other party. Moreover, if they do not confront their interpretations, they have no opportunity to become aware of the divergence. Third, the agreement may not be understood by both parties as having the same degree of influence on: a) the stability; and b) the precision and explicitness of the exchange relation.

Written documents as a basis for mutual trust between the parties

As noted above, unsaid distrust and/or mistrust dominate at the beginning in written agreements. It is implicitly assumed that such dis-/mistrust is natural and needs not be mentioned. This has to be reduced in order to establish trust. In the IT1 perspective, trust is not achieved on a global and personal basis but only by breaking down potential sources of distrust in concrete situations which may hamper common action. Trust is built step by step, with a view towards the future. Therefore real trust is achieved only gradually. Trust is largely deprived of its personal aspects. Thanks to the written agreement, the parties may trust each other through joint (impersonal) rules, although they may not trust each other as people. Trust is taken to its highest point when the parties sign a written agreement.

On the other hand, IT2 cultures that favour oral agreements tend not to hypothesize that trust is constructed by the negotiation process. They see trust more as a prerequisite to the negotiation of written agreements. Naturally, they do not expect this prerequisite to be met in every case. Trust tends to be mostly personal. Establishing trust requires that people know each other. That is probably why many Far Eastern cultures need to make informal contacts, discuss general topics, and spend time together before they get to the point, even though all this may not appear task-related. Subsequently, the negotiation process will be lengthy because, people being supposed to trust each other from the start, the negotiation process should not damage or – worse – destroy trust, which is the basic asset of their exchange relationship. They will avoid direct confrontation on a specific clause, and therefore globalize the negotiation process. Global friends may be local foes, provided trust as the basic asset of the negotiation process is not lost.

In the IT1 paradigm, contract-based trust written agreements follow the basic underlying logic: First, mistrust is the starting assumption (although never explicitly stated, because it is unpleasant and rude); the challenge of trust building is then to progressively undermine the reasons for distrust and thus develop bases for trust. Trust is built incrementally, by isolating potential sources of opportunistic behaviour and distrust and rather openly discussing contentious issues and touchy situations; the highest level of trust between the parties is reached when they sign the contractual documents. Questioning written and signed clauses (worse: not respecting them) is considered as a breach of law by one party which justifies entering into litigation for the other.

Conversely, in the IT2 paradigm, that of oral agreements and people-based trust, negotiators do not start from the assumption that trust will be built during the negotiation process; trust (sometimes more simulated than real) appears as a prerequisite to negotiation. Trust finds its main source in real flesh and blood people, not in abstract and intellectual texts. Direct confrontation on a clause is avoided as much as possible; negotiators tend to globalize negotiations (*package deal*). As noted above, the formal signature of an agreement is not the actual timeline (end) of the negotiation, but rather an important step in a continuous negotiation.

The cultural status of written materials is ambiguous. That one should always "get-it-in-writing" is not self-evident. The contrary idea may even impose itself ("if they want it written down, it means that they don't trust me"). Traoré Sérié explains, for instance, the respective roles of oral communication (spoken, transmitted through personal and concrete communication, passed on for generations by storytellers) and written materials (read, industrially printed, impersonally transmitted, with no concrete communication) in the African culture.

> Reading is an individual act, which does not easily incorporate itself into African culture. Written documents are presented as either irrelevant to everyday social practices, or as an anti-social practice. This is because someone who reads, is also isolating himself, which is resented by the other members of the community. But at the same time, people find books attractive, because they are the symbol of access to a certain kind of power. By reading, people appropriate foreign culture, they get to know "the paper of the whites".
>
> (Traoré Sérié, 1986, quoted in Ollivier and
> de Maricourt, 1990, p. 145)

Legal traditions and attitudes towards litigation

Different attitudes towards litigation

Litigation is a normal route for those favouring written-based agreements as the ultimate means of resolving breaches of contract. The oral and personal tradition (IT2) is less susceptible to remedy conflict by litigation, because litigation has major drawbacks for them:

1) It breaks the implicit assumption of trust.
2) It breaches the required state of social harmony, especially in the Far Eastern countries, and may therefore be quite threatening for the community as a whole.

For instance, IT1 negotiators introducing lawyers early in the negotiation process is interpreted by IT2 negotiators as a sign of distrust, a clear preference for litigation over negotiation, and a denial of the one-to-one relationship by bringing outsiders to the negotiation table. Adler explains the case of a Canadian negotiator in Egypt whose Egyptian counterpart did not show up at their meeting intended to write contract details with their respective lawyers.

At issue was the perceived meaning of inviting lawyers. The Canadian saw the lawyer's presence as facilitating the successful completion of the negotiation; the Egyptian interpreted it as signaling the Canadian's mistrust of his verbal commitment. Canadians often use the impersonal formality of a lawyer's services to finalize an agreement. Egyptians more frequently depend on a personal relationship developed between bargaining partners for the same purposes.

(Adler, 1986, p. 162)

In the perspective of "prospective writing" outlined on p. 215, IT1 negotiators introduce lawyers as facilitators for prospective problem-solving with the utmost positive consequence, in their view, that the likelihood of future litigation will be massively reduced. For IT2 negotiators lawyers are confused with attorneys and therefore litigation oriented. Lawyers may therefore be perceived as a vivid testimony of both distrust and lack of willingness to engage in a *bona fide* relationship. As David states:

The "good judge", whether Chinese, Japanese or Vietnamese, is not concerned with making a good decision. The "good judge" is the one who succeeds in not making any award, because he has been skillful enough to lead the opponents to reconciliation. Any dispute, as it is a threat to social harmony, has to be solved by a settlement through conciliation. ... Law as it is conceived in the West is seen as good for barbarians, and the occupation of lawyer, in the limited extent that it exists, is regarded with contempt by the society.

(David, 1987, p. 89, my translation)

These remarks by a specialist in comparative law give a good idea of the differences of litigious tradition between the Far East and the West. In the field of contracts, the Western saying "the contract is the law of the parties" dominates the practices of international trade. But this is, in part, window-dressing. When negotiating internationally, a set of written contracts is always signed. This is not to say that people choose either oral or written agreements as a basis for trust. The real question is rather: how should the mix of written and oral bases for trust, as they are perceived by the parties, be interpreted? People do not deal with conflicts in the same way. Negotiating together requires a capacity to envisage different ways of managing disputes. Not only differences in rationality and mental programmes, but also differences in time representations, may lead to a partner "who thinks differently" being considered a partner "who thinks wrongly".

The utmost caution is recommended when interpreting the bases of trust, whether written documents or oral and personal bonds. Even for IT1 negotiators, who prefer to "get-it-in-writing", a number of business deals, sometimes large ones, are based on an oral agreement between two key decision-makers. It would be a mistake to believe that personal relationships do not exist in places where written contracts are generally required.

Essentials about litigation and arbitration in ICBN

In the IT1 Deal perspective, litigation is a not a standard, desirable part of the negotiation, but it is a real world solution to harsh conflict and impasse especially when walk-away options do not exist any longer. Litigation provides for a joint outcome, decided by a judge or an arbitrator, when parties are deadlocked in their conflict. The perspective of litigation can and in fact should be incorporated into the negotiation process. It could even be seen as a desirable outcome for an opportunistic negotiator if litigation leads to damages and compensation in his or her favour that are even more profitable than the deal itself would have been, had it worked smoothly.

There is no unified legal framework, globally applicable for contract law. Public International Law (PIL) covers relationships and litigation between sovereign States related to international treaties, territory and border issues, recognition of sovereign States, belligerency, war, etc. The ICJ (International Court of Justice) in The Hague (Netherlands) exclusively deals with PIL conflicts between nation-states. Companies and individuals have no access to ICJ. There is no international court judging disputes between companies and/or natural persons, with limited exceptions.[6]

Each country has its own international private law (IPL) which defines a set of rules for determining which national law applies when a natural person (e.g., a foreigner) or a moral person (e.g., a foreign company) is involved in a dispute. Local judges must be ready to apply foreign laws. The application of one or more foreign laws involves significant complications related to collecting foreign legal texts in their source language, organizing translation in the local language, as well as understanding the spirit and the letter of foreign laws. A dispute in private international law, for various reasons, may be pending before a court in two different countries, for instance because each party has introduced an action against the other in his or her home country (problem of the exception of *lis pendens*). The exception of *lis pendens* is an objection against the admissibility of the claim; however there are solutions out of this dilemma prescribed by international conventions.[7] Litigation, whether relating to personal (e.g., marriage, divorce) or to business matters (e.g., contracts), requires long court trials whose outcome is uncertain. Five years seems short to obtain an award. The foreign judgment must often be enforced in a different country, on the basis of an *exequatur*; that is, a legal document issued by a local authority that permits the enforcement of a right. A judgment rendered by a foreign court may not be enforceable unless it is accompanied by a judgment of *exequatur* given by a local court. Most developed countries have concluded a convention on the enforcement of foreign judgments which allows them to enforce them locally, unless the foreign award includes provisions which completely contradict the law of the country where it is to be enforced.

Fortunately, parties to international contracts are allowed to choose the law of any State as the law applicable to their contract. Most ipl local legislation uses the rule of autonomy for contracting law. The law expressly or implicitly referred to by the parties to the contract is the *governing law*. The principle of party autonomy in international contracts implies that parties are free to enter into contracts and to determine their contents, as well as to choose the law of any State as the law applicable to their contract. In general, it is better however that the *governing law* be connected with the basic features of the contract such as the law of the country where the contract will be implemented, or classical laws for particular industries, for example the oil industry or banking.

Rather than attributing jurisdiction to local courts, international companies most often choose the way of *International Commercial Arbitration*. Arbitration is recognized by international conventions. It is much faster than national courts; however it is a rather costly procedure. The ICC offers arbitration procedures, which are the most frequently chosen by negotiators and their advisory lawyers. However, there are other arbitration bodies such as the arbitral courts in Geneva or Stockholm, or ICSID (International Convention on the Settlement of Investment Disputes).[8]

Arbitration starts with a mediation phase; then each party chooses a judge and both choose a third. The arbitration court applies the law chosen by the parties (possibly including a judgment in equity) and makes an award, which is likely to *exequatur*. In practice arbitral sentences are almost always followed by the parties and are susceptible to *exequatur* like the judgements of national courts.[9]

If arbitration is chosen by the parties they should write a compromissory clause providing for the submission of a matter or matters to arbitration.[10] A clause of provision for possible disputes stating that the parties will share the costs of litigation is useful if not necessary. Legal language must be chosen for the contract; that is, the only version lawfully valid for easing joint interpretation and avoiding misunderstandings about legal concepts, especially at the implementation stage (*langue qui fait foi* [governing language]). The language to be used in the arbitration proceedings has also to be designated providing a common framework for legal procedures and practices. In arbitration procedures, like in national courts, parties have to designate the governing law taking into account the contract's features and the potential impact of differences in legal systems (e.g., Continental European *Code Law* versus British and U.S. *Common Law*). A jurisdiction clause[11] assigns litigation to a national jurisdiction or to an arbitral court (e.g., ICC). However, some Islamic countries impose the Sharia laws and local courts. Contracting parties also have to be aware that in federal countries, such as in the United States, the governing law must be that of a particular state (e.g., Indiana or Texas for an oil-related contract).[12]

Litigation as part of the negotiation process

Potential litigation is part of the negotiation process. Damage money granted by a court to a party may result from challenging the negotiation process and/ or outcomes in court (especially when implementing the signed agreement). Such unexpected events have to be considered beforehand, that is, when negotiating and before signing any contract. An unscrupulous negotiator may hypocritically keep silent when finding out what he or she considers as a nice opportunity for profitable damage litigation. The prospective litigator will hide his or her intention, secretly assign a probability distribution to the outcomes of a trial (damages awarded) against the other party, and weigh benefits against litigation costs. For instance, the to-be-acquired company in a takeover negotiation may involuntarily leave some key information undisclosed, sincerely assuming that the potential acquirer is cognizant of such information. The to-be-acquired company would have been ready to disclose information if the other party's negotiators had asked for it. There is room here for the acquirer to later sue the acquisition target. Generally speaking, hidden negotiation intentions (never voiced, underground, tacit) of gaining money through litigation should be unveiled and taken into account, however not discussed with the prospective litigator who should remain under the illusion that his or her ploy will go on undiscovered.[13]

Examples of hidden negotiation intentions abound such as negotiating just to "test prices" (e.g., in real estate, B2B...), considering the agreed-upon price as information for setting future reservation price, and then withdrawing by pretending that one is no longer willing to sell. In negotiations for know-how licences, the prospective licensee may enter into a fake negotiation with the patent holder and potential licensor just to gather key technology information and then withdraw. However a non-disclosure agreement may help in limiting such indelicate behaviour (see Chapter 9). Another example of opportunistic behaviour that may be on the fringe of taking the indelicate party to court is the sudden and abusive breaking off of negotiations (*rupture abusive des pourparlers*). This legal negotiation concept exists in some countries, for instance France and Germany. Abrupt termination of negotiation talks may be considered "abusive" when a party terminates *negotiations* in *breach* of this duty of loyalty and good faith. The terminating party may be held liable for an abusive breach of negotiation talks.[14]

The type and amount of damages granted by local courts is a significant incentive (or conversely disincentive) for deciding to litigate. In the Unites States *punitive damages* may be awarded in addition to actual damages; they are considered punishment for a defendant's behaviour that is particularly harmful as well as exemplary reparations intended at deterring both the particular defendant and other potential infringers. In most countries, only damages related to actual and/or subjective losses inflicted are awarded by the local courts, resulting in much lower amounts than in the United States (e.g., the magnitude may be one to ten). *Punitive damages* are a major incentive for tort litigation.[15]

How *lawyers* are compensated by plaintiffs is another major incentive (or conversely disincentive) for deciding to litigate. In the United States, attorneys, especially for tort law, can be compensated by a percentage fee based on the damages awarded to the plaintiff who therefore has no fees to pay, especially no initial down-payment of lawyers' fees.[16] In many countries, contingency fees are either forbidden or simply not practised by lawyers. A major disincentive for litigation is that it is costly from the very start. Often the threat of litigation is a way to negotiate and force agreement. The party that risks having to pay damage will rationally compare the estimated amount with what it would probably cost them if negotiating an out-of-court settlement, later endorsed by the judge.

Questions to be addressed as concerns third parties in general

Third parties may help in the negotiation process. Third parties are there provisionally; their involvement is limited to specific aspects of the negotiation process; they do not appear in all negotiation sessions. However, from the negotiation process they learn a significant amount of private/proprietary information that they should not disclose. They may represent an aid for improving the flow of communication (e.g., interpreters). They can play a go-between role especially in a foreign, alien context such as agents, middlemen, and intermediaries (however, not without ambiguity). They may facilitate the deal and increase the clarity and the completeness of the written contract (e.g., lawyers, notaries). Negotiation facilitators act as third parties involved in alternative dispute resolution (ADR). Rarely, outside observers attend the negotiation process. This may be the case for academics who do negotiation research based on in-depth case studies or consultants who advise the parties on how to best manage the negotiation process. Non-participatory observation requires strict constraints: acceptance by parties, absolute non-intervention, impartiality, and full confidentiality and discretion. There are a number of common questions valid for any third party involved in an international negotiation:

- Who do they actually, rather than formally, represent?
- Is their own interest really in line with (that of) the party they are supposed to represent?
- By whom are they paid? (Possibly: do they secretly receive side payments from the opposite camp?) Are they paid by one party? By the other party? By both parties?
- Are they susceptible to favour their own interests over those of the party they represent?
- Is there a risk of information leakage? Is the confidentiality of negotiated matters guaranteed by a non-disclosure agreement or by a confidentiality clause?

These questions are particularly meaningful in an ICBN context because third parties may not share the same nationality, language, values, and interests as the party who hired them. Opportunistic behaviour is more likely when no similarity cues are shared, and therefore no ingroup feeling is there to generate scruples and curb opportunism.

Agents and agency contracts are analysed at greater length in Chapter 9 (Negotiating different types of contracts). Middlemen or intermediaries in foreign countries, as independent organizations, have their own interests, their own agenda, their own view of the negotiation process in which they are partly involved. No loyalty, even the tiniest bit of fidelity, can be expected, unless a real relationship has been built over time with the intermediary. If they betray some contractual dispositions, local courts will be very reluctant to sentence them to damage money. A sponsor in Saudi Arabia, a middleman imposed by Saudi Law, to be chosen by foreign companies on an official list, can be trusted only after several successful interactions, and when an interpersonal relationship has been built over time. The same holds true for agents and dealers in foreign markets when involved in negotiation processes. The case of notaries and real estate agents is the most representative of this issue: lack of loyalty must be assumed unless relational assets, outside of short-term economic interests, alleviate the agent's opportunistic behaviour. It is never clear who real estate agents really represent. They are supposed to be under contract with the vendor, but their best interest is to sell as quickly as possible, and they often tend to end up representing the buyer.

Concluding remarks

An ICBN process is on average less linear and organized than messy and improvised. The IT1 need for planned and scheduled negotiation, for preparedness and clarity, may at times be unsatisfied. It is however not a preference for disorder and confusion that leads other (IT2) negotiators to prefer a spontaneous and improvised process; it is rather the underlying conviction that the personal alchemy in Relationship-Building can only occur in reasonably natural and unstructured interaction.

Notes

1 On chaos and improvisation in negotiation, see Wheeler (2013).
2 For models of the negotiation process, see Graham (2003) and Jeong (2016).
3 Usunier (2011).
4 Translation on www.mamalisa.com/?t=es&p=2464. There seems to be no English equivalent of this French counting rhyme.
5 See www.tentmaker.org/Quotes/lawyers-per-capita.html and www.bostonglobe. com/opinion/2014/05/09/the-lawyer-bubble-pops-not-moment-too-soon/ qAYzQ823qpfi4GQl2OiPZM/story.html.
6 The standardized rules of the ICC (International Chamber of Commerce), especially the Incoterms, and the European Court of Justice in Luxembourg, dealing only with matters related to EU law, are the most notable exceptions.

7   The general power of the tribunal to hear the claim is not contested, but the special situation that a claim on the same cause of action is pending before another forum is alleged to preclude the tribunal from asserting jurisdiction.

8   "The International Centre for the Settlement of *Investment* Disputes (ICSID) is an ad hoc tribunal established pursuant to UNCITRAL Rules to arbitrate International *Investment* Agreements and provide foreign investors with a means for redress against states" (https://en.wikipedia.org/wiki/International_arbitration).

9   "An *exequatur* is a legal document issued by a sovereign authority that permits the exercise or enforcement of a right within the jurisdiction of the authority. The word is a form of the Latin verb 'exequi', which denotes 'let it be executed'"

10 For details about the ICC Arbitration Clause see: www.acerislaw.com/icc-arbitration-clause-international-chamber-commerce/

11 Through a jurisdiction clause, the parties agree to the courts of a particular country taking jurisdiction over their disputes. A jurisdiction clause may be either "exclusive" (i.e., only the specified courts will have jurisdiction) or "non-exclusive" (i.e., the parties may litigate in other courts).

12 For standard international contracts, see: www.contractstemplates.org/international-contract-template, or type "international sales contract template" into a search engine.

13 See Watkins (2007) on the failure of the Daimler-Chrysler merger. More generally on the role of cultural differences in international mergers and acquisitions, see Stahl and Voigt (2008), Marks and Mirvis (2011), and Langosch and McCarthy (2017).

14 See Bourgeois and Martinez-Tournalia (2015).

15 "Punitive damages are considered punishment and are typically awarded at the court's discretion when the defendant's behavior is found to be especially harmful. Punitive damages, or exemplary damages, are damages intended to reform or deter the defendant and others from engaging in conduct similar to that which formed the basis of the lawsuit. … Punitive damages are often awarded if compensatory damages are deemed an inadequate remedy" (https://en.wikipedia.org/wiki/Punitive_damages).

16 Lawyer fees may be charged in a number of ways, including contingency fees, hourly rates, and flat fees, or a combination of them. Contingency fees, based on a percentage of a client's recovery, are not allowed in many countries. Contingency fees encourage litigation because the plaintiffs pay no fees if the claim is unsuccessful.

8 ICBN strategies and tactics

Steal the beams and change the pillars.
(Chinese Stratagem 25, i.e., change the rules
which they are used to follow)

A negotiation strategy is not only about (one's own) needs and goals but also about how to reach them (implementation) and how to deal with the conditionality, uncertainty, and (progressive) discovery of jointly profitable solutions. Goals are self-centred, unilateral in an individual task. However, in a typically shared, bilateral task, goals can only be conditional, depending on how the other party reacts, this being especially true in ICBN. Goals are related to outcome stakes (e.g., financial benefits, impact on corporate strategy, possible sunk costs, setting a precedent for future business, accountability to stakeholders, urgency to reach an agreement, and possible options). Not only is goal compatibility required for reaching a joint outcome but also compatibility in negotiation approach, which is less than guaranteed in an ICBN setting.

What is strategically the most important is first to understand the features of the negotiation to be held. An appendix at the end of this chapter, building on this and previous chapters, gives a detailed list of all the basic aspects of a negotiation.

This chapter first deals with how to develop interest-based strategies (a rather universal concept) and implement them through negotiation tactics that enable one to reach goals without damaging either the relationship or a mutually profitable deal. I set the limits of typical IT1 strategic frameworks for negotiations such as the IRP model (Interests, Rights, and Power) or "Principled" negotiation. Coalition building in multiparty ICBN is examined next. The design and the preparation of an ICBN strategy are based on strategic and cultural analysis (see checklist at the end of this chapter). Negotiation tactics (first offer, opening, persuasion tactics, especially when they are *hardball* tactics) are presented in the light of their impact on both deals and relationships. The last part discusses avenues for countering hardball tactics.

Basic negotiation strategies

A distinction is often made between tough (or hard) versus soft strategies with an underlying view that tough is exclusively deal-oriented and soft is mainly relationship-oriented. Other frameworks for categorizing negotiation strategies have an intermediate position between the soft and tough poles. Sometimes this framework contrasts a more rational, reasonable, and purely interests-oriented strategy, called "principled negotiation" by Fisher et al. (2011). However, if we take each normative element and adopt a critical view, "principled negotiation" appears as a poor candidate for universal negotiation behaviour because it is too rational and overly simplistic. The IT1 (deal-oriented) versus IT2 (relational) paradigm is meaningful for designing ICBN strategies, however only in combination with objective market background, interdependence, and relational factors.[1]

Tough strategy

Synonyms for *Tough* highlight different facets of such a negotiation strategy: its harsh side (e.g., rough, hard, strong, and hard-hitting) and the risk associated for the party confronted with this strategy (e.g., threatening, dangerous). A tough (strategy) negotiator describes the other side as a competitor, rival, adversary, opponent, opposed party, enemy, foe, etc., emphasizing antagonism and opposition. A neutral label would be "participant". Tough strategies are stereotypically viewed as distributive, only concerned with one's own outcomes (in terms of the Dual Concern Model, see Chapters 1 and 2). A tough party is ready to exit if needed, is non-concessive, and possibly exploits the other side, manipulating, being instrumental at best, abusing, misusing arguments, circumstances, and situations, and is fixed-pie oriented with a tendency to opportunism. How can a tough strategy exist (and work) in the real world? The answer is: Only when and if certain basic conditions are met:

- There are strong information and power asymmetries in favour of the tough partner.
- A non-competitive market background, few price references, rather a monopsony (if buyer is the tough party) or a monopoly (if seller is tough), or possibly a bilateral monopoly.
- Low interdependence because of unbalanced dependencies (the tough strategy party is not very dependent on the other party, generating low interdependence).
- The tough side is short-term oriented (bordering on the deal-only paradigm).
- There is large availability of alternative negotiation partners.
- The potential partner has no or a weakly defined BATNA.
- The tough side exerts strict dominance over the other party.

Tough strategy negotiators play rather unconditionally, behaving as unilateralists. A strong limitation to the adoption of such a negotiation strategy is that all, or at least most, of the basic conditions mentioned above must be present for the tough strategy to be successful. If the two camps simultaneously use a tough strategy, a no deal outcome, even a profitable one, is likely … unless they choose to soften their positions.

Soft strategy

Soft is a very broad adjective; it has many meanings, with synonym adjectives emphasizing a relaxed style (e.g., lax, easy, easy-going), indulgence and forgiveness (e.g., lenient, forgiving, indulgent), a lack of structure (e.g., spineless), and a readiness to yield (e.g., undemanding, concessive). The latent negative value judgements related to food and taste[2] and to character (*inter alia* feeble-minded, bendable, easily impressed), fortunately combine with more positive traits such as compassionate, gentle, kind, sympathetic, or tender. Taken together, rather negative value judgements underlie the soft strategy concept in negotiation, corresponding to the description of a weak person or personality rather than that of a soft strategy. Typical stereotypes about the soft strategy comprise an excessive, abusive concern with creating and/or maintaining the relationship at any price, and a tendency to blindly trust the other side. Soft negotiators are assumed to yield because they are more interested in the other party's outcomes than in their own (in terms of the Dual Concern Model): they would be so concessive as to accept one-sided losses to avoid conflict and reach an agreement. Additionally, they are supposed to prefer listening (latently considered passive) rather than talking (officially considered active), and are open to representative communication even if the other party uses instrumental communication. How can a soft negotiation strategy ever exist in the real world? Again, only when certain basic conditions are met: in short the opposite of the conditions described for the tough strategy, in particular a high level of dependence on the other party (who may or may not adopt a tough strategy), and strong pressure to reach an agreement even if it is not directly profitable.

Mixed, reciprocal, and/or obligational strategies

Mixed, intermediate strategies, by far the most frequent in ICBN, are based on reciprocal moves and reciprocal behaviours over time (as defined in Chapter 3). Reasons for adopting a mixed strategy are numerous: repeated interactions, high interdependence level, B2B negotiation with a long-term focus, and a possible exclusive relationship on both sides (*single source – single customer*). Reciprocal strategies make sense in strongly cyclical markets (e.g., chemicals, iron and steel, cement), where market power changes over time according to industrial cycles (e.g., high/low market power for sellers/ buyers in market upturns and vice versa in downturns). Either negotiation partners sign long-term contra-cyclical contracts or a cooperative behaviour of the powerful player towards the weaker one is later compensated by the other player when market power has shifted in his or her favour.

As outlined in Chapter 3, reciprocity can be direct (give and take between A and B) or indirect (in *upstream reciprocity*, A helps B, then B helps C because he has received help from A; in *downstream reciprocity* because A has helped B, C helps A). Direct reciprocity is understood differently in IT1 and IT2. In the IT1 paradigm, *reciprocity* is *formalized*; that is, favours as well as expectations of reciprocal behaviour from the other party are codified, tabulated, based on proportionate give-and-take moves, and built on categorized and catalogued favours and counter-favours. Such niceties are listed, ordered, systematized, monitored, and checked for balance between each side. The time frame of reciprocation is relatively short (e.g., less than one year, when not immediate).

The IT2 paradigm privileges *obligational reciprocity*. Favours and concessions are only loosely related to expectations of reciprocal behaviour from the other party. They are not precisely codified and tabulated. Give-and-take moves do not need to be proportionate. The time frame of reciprocation is long (years, possibly 10 or 20 years). *Obligational reciprocity* is relatively informal. Favours and counter-favours are not openly monitored by either party nor checked for "proper" balance. However, *obligational reciprocity* is not a paradise. Too loosely defined reciprocation obligations and horizon that is too long term may pose problems such as a *misbalance* in reciprocal obligational performances and the opportunistic exploitation of relational debts (never repaid). Indirect reciprocity[3] assumes a belief in the transitivity of relationships (e.g., the friends of my friends are my friends) and is practised in business networks. Such beliefs are justifiably low in the IT1 paradigm and high (at least higher) in the IT2 paradigm. Note that both forms of indirect reciprocation are found in social and economic networks as well as in coalitions. They are not immune to collusion effects and the discriminatory exclusion of outsiders.

We can therefore contrast two kinds of mixed negotiation strategies. The first (IT1) is self-determined, well defined, based on calculative goals, with the major tenet of principled negotiations (i.e., "separate people from problems"). Progress in negotiation is based on formalized reciprocity moves, quick reciprocation, and a strict balance between give and take. The second mixed strategy (IT2) favours broad, *shared* goals, a partnership/relationship orientation, allowing for flexible adjustment to the other party's own needs and preferences. It is based on *obligational reciprocity*. The IT2 strategy is more open, more incremental, and better takes into account uncertainties in intercultural communication than the IT1 strategy.

The IRP model in an intercultural negotiation perspective

Each negotiation has a certain playground, which is centred more on interests, on rights, and/or on power. There are also combinations of these basic elements. For instance, negotiations based on interests tend to avoid positional confrontation, while negotiations focusing claims on rights and/ or on power would easily fall into the trap of positional/territorial/fixed pie negotiation.

Interest-based negotiations

It is the central tenet of *Principled negotiation* to rationally focus on interests (assumed to be essential in problem-solving and value creation) rather than positions (supposed to lead to distributive and win-lose negotiations). Consequently the advice is to separate people from problems. *Interests*, as in the well-known concept of *self-interest*, are a multifaceted construct with an economic-utilitarian facet (e.g., benefit, gain, good, profit), a more affective/ relational side (e.g., affection, attraction, regard, sympathy), and two more neutral facets (attention, concern, curiosity; and activity, hobby, pastime, etc.). What Fisher et al. (2011) have in mind is clearly the utilitarian side as is the case in *self-interest*. It is true that *self-interests* may have a large overlap zone. In Fisher and Ury's view, this overlap zone may be further increased by exploring mutually profitable solutions.[4]

However, this is problematic in ICBN. As shown in the above semantic exploration of the interest concept, it is extremely difficult to disentangle people from problems, especially in the IT2 paradigm. Even deal-oriented IT1 negotiators when engaged in problem-solving will inevitably (and to a large extent unconsciously) mix sympathy-based interests with purely utilitarian interests. In the IT2 paradigm, it is impossible to separate people from the problem as the relationship is paramount. Being soft on people and tough on deal-related issues is misunderstood in IT2 as an irreconcilable and somewhat hypocritical attitude. Being soft with people may be considered insincere if being at the same time tough on deal related issues.

Rights-based negotiations

Rights are entitlements based on legal and contractual texts, be it patents, trademarks, corporate statutes, collective labour agreements between unions and employers, such as *Tarifvertrag* in Germany or *conventions collectives* in France and a large number of continental European countries, or labour contracts in the mining industry. Rights-based negotiation between management and employees covers such issues as salary scheme, qualifications, working conditions, rules concerning hiring and firing employees, rules concerning the right to strike or not to strike (for instance by relinquishing the right to go on strike against a pay rise over some years, e.g., a four year period). They are locally negotiated, within the framework of national company law, labour laws, contract law, industrial property rights, and so on; that is, all legal dispositions that cover any issue related to corporate activity, be it with employees, shareholders, customers, and/or any stakeholder in the business.

Rights-based negotiation consequently covers a broad array of topics and a variety of situations, within and between companies, and involves an intercultural dimension when the parties differ in terms of country/culture, which is often the case in the mining industry. A party may want to formally change joint rules in a rights-based agreement when the other party needs to build a trusting relationship. Distrust may occur because of a lack of a common mindset and the fear of losing some key "privileges" obtained in the past. These rights are often understood by the party that sits on them as a protection against an even weaker position in future negotiations.

Rights-based negotiations frequently tend to be positional and confrontational. In most cases concrete threats can be used by each side (e.g., a strike and lock-out in industrial relations negotiations; going to court against a supposed patent infringer). In pure rights-based negotiations, conflict escalation is frequent and can be very harsh. The market environment has a significant influence on the outcome of rights-based negotiation, in case of market downturn, industry overcapacity, especially for raw materials, oil and mining, since it weakens the employees' position vis-à-vis employers. The macro-environment (e.g., local communities and public authorities) support for the local party is likely and often occurs, however with the limitation that public authorities in the host country are more or less aware that it may lead the MNF to disengagement.

Trade-offs can be difficult to envisage, because of clogged positions, which seem a priori irreconcilable. Imagination is blocked and creative solutions are sometimes frowned upon as potential traps, leading a party that would accept a change in the rights schedule to lose much and win very little in return for its concessions. Conflict intensity in rights-based negotiation may increase with high uncertainty avoidance on the employee side. In this sense, the advice of principled negotiation to focus on interests rather than positions appears rather sensible.

Power-based negotiations

Power also is a concept with multiple facets; the first is the capacity to achieve (e.g., ability, capacity, capability, competence), the second facet is associated with forcefulness (e.g., energy, force, strength, vigour), and the third facet relates to hierarchy and dominance (e.g., authority, right, command, control, dominance, domination). Power is rather obviously culture-dependent, at least in the dimension of Power Distance examined in Chapter 2. Power is also largely culture-free in as much as economic power relationships are influenced by a large number of deal-related variables: 1) market background, respective size of organizations, financial strength, part (percentage) of each party in the total business (sales figure, total purchases) of the other party; 2) objective factors underlying power asymmetries (see appendix): information asymmetries, role-related asymmetries, differentials in expertise, in leadership, in prestige; and 3) differences in out-of-negotiation alternatives, commitment, legitimacy, risk-taking ability, and capability to reward/coerce the other party.

The cultural dimension of "Power Distance" has been somewhat artificially transferred from a vertical-hierarchical setting (i.e., superior-subordinate relationships) to the horizontal-egalitarian setting of negotiation. The simple fact that there is a power differential between parties does not automatically translate into exploitative and authoritarian power abuse by the powerful partner vis-à-vis the less powerful party. Power *per se* is essentially different from the actual use of power. When mitigated with benevolence, power can be used to influence rather than coerce, to guide rather than force, and to give energy and determination to the weaker party. Paradoxically, there can be (not always however) a protective and benevolent orientation in power use, in particular when the powerful party wants to develop a sense of affiliation in the weaker party, especially because they are a reliable and trustworthy partner.

How power is played in different cultures is worth careful consideration. A French *rapport de force* (i.e., confrontational power demonstration on both sides),[5] is not the rather subtle use of *power* in the UK, or the German *Macht* which basically expresses objective dominance. Power-orientation has, however, the disadvantage of fostering positional negotiation, when the powerful party is exploitative, does not make a reasonable use of its power, and claims the lion's share of the value created by negotiation (Lytle et al. 1999). The weaker party has no choice but to defend its position and centre on its own claims. Power orientation sets strong limits to "Principled" negotiation in ICBN. "Principled" negotiation with its *doing* orientation, utilitarian rationality, self-control, and its ability to objectively assess situations, is a nice solution for IT1 negotiators. However, it tends to exclude both power and people, which does not make much sense in ICBN.

IRP combinations in an ICBN setting

The distinction between Interests (I), Rights (R), and Power (P) as bases for negotiation is rather meaningful, however somewhat artificial, because there are overlaps between I, R, and P. I, R, and P are not completely disconnected categories. In industrial relations negotiations, there is much overlap between interests (e.g., wages, holidays), rights (e.g., legal and contractual conventions between labour and employers), and the exercise of power through strikes and lock-outs. Similarly, talks about a takeover or a merger between two companies mix interests and power. Furthermore according to local contexts, parties may be more rights-oriented, more power-oriented, or they can focus on their interests, rather than their rights or their power position. Table 8.1 shows how negotiations are likely to develop according to how each party (P1 and P2) is oriented in terms of I, R, and P. Note that principled negotiations are possible when both parties are mostly interests-oriented, and conditionally if one party or both accept to play down either rights or power.

Table 8.1 Forms of negotiation according to IRP combinations

Party 2	Party 1		
	Interest-based	Rights-based	Power-based
Interest-based	"Principled Negotiation" (PN) for P1 and P2	"Dialogue of the deaf", unless P1 understands that they can swap rights against other advantages	PN if P2 accepts to play down power to promote joint interests
Rights-based	"Dialogue of the deaf", unless P2 understands that they can swap rights against other advantages	"Legal Negotiation": a debate over legal and regulatory arguments dominates the process	Confrontation between action, threats, and change (P1) versus rules and status quo (P2)
Power-based	PN if P1 accepts to play down power to promote joint interests	Confrontation between action, threats, and change (P2) versus rules and status quo (P1)	Confrontational Negotiation, unless both P1 and P2 accept to defuse the power conflict

Coalition building in multiparty ICBN

In multiparty negotiation, compared with dyadic, face-to-face negotiation, there is a possibility to build coalitions to gather and bring together resources to influence the negotiation process and outcomes. Coalitions aim at increasing power and influence, when the main interests and/or rights are shared (and why not identity in IT2 style) and there is not too much divergence for the rest (in terms of relationship history, shared values, etc.). Coalition building is a form of strategic move in negotiations, especially needed in multiparty negotiation when parties are too numerous to be represented on a purely individual basis.[6]

A negotiation, even a simple two-party negotiation, always implicitly targets coalition building. Generally dyadic arrangements exclude potential partners or outsider parties, which are finally kept out of the particular agreement. However, coalition building explicitly occurs when there are more than two parties, up to more than 100 as in WTO Multilateral Trade Negotiations between sovereign states. The EU is a coalition of 28 nation-states according to Article 24 of the General Agreement on Tariffs and Trade (GATT) treaty, which allows regional integration in the form of a Free-Trade Zone or a Customs Union (as is the case for the EU).[7] Coalitions result in interest groups and "like-minded" alliances of countries. Coalitions appear in international trade negotiations, in collective bargaining in local negotiations between trades unions and employers and/or in any multiparty negotiation. After a certain threshold, in terms of membership size (companies, countries, unions, etc.), coalitions become quite large and communication between their members needs to be formally organized, as well as the decision-making processes that may include voting systems, arbitration, and random decision procedures. Coalitions are not monolithic parties: their interests rarely are fully convergent. Members of coalitions and subgroups first need to negotiate among themselves before entering the main negotiation. Membership in a coalition is voluntary and a member may decide to withdraw. However, participation in a coalition enables members to uphold shared interests.

Types of coalitions

In large, multiparty negotiations, the number of parties may reach more than 150 (e.g., in WTO Multilateral Trade Negotiations). This book, being centred on business negotiations, generally focuses on two-party, bilateral negotiation. However, even in a two-party setting, one or both camps may be non-monolithic,[8] especially when teams rather than individuals negotiate face-to-face. In non-monolithic team negotiations, a pre-negotiation within teams is necessary to adjust their positions, take the true measure of differences in opinions and/or style, and possibly distribute roles (see good guy – bad guy tactic on p. 246). A different case is the multiparty setting which starts with three independent parties. When negotiation is multiparty and multi-issue, it may become quite complex. Coalitions have their dynamics, especially because there is rivalry between coalitions for attracting members of other coalitions. Individual actors may increase their positions by competitive proposals to join one coalition or the other. Common sense indicates that in a three-party setting, two parties, A and B, may join their interests with regard to the third, party C, and therefore become dominant. However, interests of parties A and B may not be fully aligned. Both A and B may share joint interests with C on particular topics and issues. By playing astutely between A and B, C, playing the role of spoilsport, can question their coalition, and possibly become either A or B's ally and exclude the third. A number of key characteristics influence coalition stability.

- The degree of heterogeneity in terms of preferences, needs, and positions.
- The degree of heterogeneity in terms of interests, rights, and power.
- The degree of heterogeneity in terms of power (e.g., some members may represent large organizations, countries, etc. while others are comparatively, small or even tiny); more influential members may take on a role as coalition leader(s). Some leading players (e.g., India, Mexico, Indonesia, and Brazil at WTO) may represent smaller ones in a coalition.
- The *affectio societatis* (i.e., like-mindedness, social capital) built over time between coalition members.

A coalition is not only defined by those who participate in it but also by those parties who are not members of the coalition or even parties against which the coalition is organized. For example, the international coalition of national employer federations (e.g., UNICE in Brussels for the EU countries) is more powerful than coalitions of national trades unions from several countries (employees). At the global level, coalitions of employees are represented by the International Trade Union Confederation (ITUC), the Trade Union Advisory Committee to the Organisation for Economic Cooperation and Development (OECD), and ten global union federations (GUFs). The absence of ideological like-mindedness among trades unions and the cross-country competition for jobs through manufacturing delocalization probably explain this scattered coalition landscape for employees. Even if difficult, building coalitions to increase power and reach efficiency is of key strategic importance.

Heterogeneities in power and size and the stability of coalitions

Consensus building in coalitions (if they are stable and not fake) creates consistency and convergence between the interests and goals of their members. However, what is in the best interest of a coalition is not necessarily the best solution for all (that is, for outsiders, minorities, and for social welfare). Often coalitions assemble heterogeneous parties in terms of size, financial power, people represented, etc. For example, large companies and small and medium-size businesses most often represent separate coalitions. However, they coordinate their efforts, especially when opposed to unions or negotiating with public authorities. Inequalities in power, size, and influence are an enduring reality of coalitions. Smaller players have to join together, sometimes in sub-coalitions, when they want to have a say in important multiparty negotiations, where their influence otherwise would be quite small. By being a member of a sub-coalition within the larger coalition, they at least have information on, if not a direct say in, the negotiation process. This allows access to interest groups, collective bargaining, and/or multiparty negotiation. The presence of inequalities of all sorts generates a need for social norms regulating the access and the working of coalitions. Perceived fairness, based on procedural and/or distributive justice, and perceived inequalities are based on (more or less shared) normative assumptions providing a fertile ground for internal debates within coalitions between unequal members. Negotiators hold different perceptions about equity according to situations. When negotiations are multiparty and multi-issue, the diversity of, and compatibility between, perceptions of equity have to be considered. Furthermore, what is equitable for me is not necessarily acceptable for others (hence, a need to be reflexive). The following conditions, when met, increase coalition stability:

- Joint interests (large common denominator) overpower possible interest divergence.

- No (or little) free-riding and free-riders in the coalition, few or no spoilsports, few or no completely self-interested negotiators; leaders in the coalition can peacefully coexist.
- Joint learning of coalition members over time (e.g., WTO and multilateral negotiations).
- Ability to internally negotiate and find solutions to minor differences in positions.
- Strength of opposition to and differentiation from other coalitions (oppositions unite).
- Sufficient resources to organize the working of the coalition (staff, communication, meetings, travels, etc.) and to properly manage the representation of members, their involvement, and the consensus-building process.

As noted above, confederations of trades unions are not a very stable and strong type of coalition. Conversely, industry associations are more stable and influential because they meet the conditions above.

Shifting from negotiation to alternative collective decision-making methods

Negotiation may be considered as an alternative collective decision-making method, alongside voting, random decisions (e.g., throwing dice), or delegating the joint decision to a third party (e.g., arbitration). The majority rule is often used as an alternative decision-making method for complex negotiation with too many parties. Voting can also be considered an initial step in creating coalitions. It is simple and expedient. In a purely cooperative group, voting may lead to an optimal outcome. In a purely competitive group, it may be the only way to avoid a dead end. However, in groups with mixed motivations (both competitive and cooperative), the most frequent case, it may lead to sub-optimal outcomes (Bazerman and Neale, 1992). There are, however, significant drawbacks to majority vote. First, it does not take into account the diversity and the degree of individual preferences on multiple issues. Second, it does not take into account the needs, interests, and positions of minority groups/parties. Third, majority vote does not facilitate exploration and learning about preferences which lead to an optimum outcome. Blind majority vote may, when naively implemented as if it were a unanimous decision, result in ignoring large minority interests. In the political domain, rights-based negotiation is absolutely needed to offset the risks related to majority vote, essentially for protecting the basic interests of minority groups.

The advice therefore is quite clear: Avoid the majority rule in multiparty, complex negotiation (unless there are too many people, e.g., thousands or millions). The unanimous rule is sometimes more efficient, however not always. It frequently leads to reaching an impasse, a quite probable outcome in the case of unanimous vote. The unanimous rule, because of the risk of one or two negotiators blocking any decision, often leads to the search to avoid a dead end through negotiation. At the end, the preferred solution is that which avoids a veto, which is not necessarily the optimal joint solution.

The relative power of negotiation, majority vote and unanimous decision-making can be empirically investigated based on a negotiation simulation[9] between five managers representing different departments. They have to share a limited budget between three items for which they have different utility levels. Managers have their own payoff information for each particular solution.

The conclusion is: better negotiate than vote. Negotiation is (on average) superior to voting. The grand mean for 75 groups in my negotiation class from 2006 to 2017 is 284 for negotiation, near the optimal joint outcome (300), and 221 for both majority vote and unanimous vote.[10] Majority vote results in the lowest joint utility scores compared with both negotiation and unanimous vote. Unanimous vote and the very demanding rule that a single veto may hamper the decision, leads to the risk of heading into a dead end and to sub-optimal outcomes. As usual in political systems, outcomes are somewhat sensitive to voting procedures. If people vote sequentially, particular items will probably be retained, while a distributive justice norm could emerge. Heading into a dead end is then likely and previous votes could be questioned. Parties could also choose to vote on a package deal (incidentally the voting procedure itself needs to be negotiated), which is a better solution to avoid impasse in unanimous voting.

Negotiation is superior to voting because it enables participants to consider creative alternatives, which satisfy most individual interests and maximize the joint outcome. The general recommendation is to avoid replacing negotiation by voting as much as possible. When voting is not necessary, use negotiation and voting as complements rather than substitutes! Combining negotiation and voting may in fact be a good idea.

Opening tactics

Opening options

Opening options in ICBN are related to local bargaining customs, to the ZOPA, to anchoring effects, and to the spread of everyday bargaining as well as to role expectations in particular cultures. Opening tactics become more complex with multi-issue negotiation since it is generally difficult to estimate a reservation price. Opening options (i.e., who declares a price first and which price to offer) are related to the decline of traditional bargaining activities in most IT1 countries. In most of these countries, the compulsory display of price tags imposed by regulation especially in B2C sets a legal norm: sellers are obliged to explicitly (low-context) make the first offer, and they generally make a take-it-or-leave-it offer which reduces the transaction costs related to information search and negotiation. Some bargaining still exists for equipment goods and for some large ticket items in consumer durables; however the base price is stated by the seller. In IT2 countries, *souk* bargaining practices and the frequent absence of price display by sellers imply more complex and implicit (high-context) rituals for the exploration of an exchange price. Bargaining is good hands-on training for business negotiations. Negotiators from IT1 countries, where bargaining is legally controlled, may be at a disadvantage compared with negotiators from IT2 countries because of the lack of hands-on experience based on everyday bargaining in local markets. In traditional bargaining, when prices are not displayed, the bargaining ritual and practice is that the seller (who perfectly knows what the item is worth) will wait as long as possible for the buyer to make an offer. Price and quality comparison across competing offers is always useful. Nobel laureate V.S. Naipaul (1981, pp. 145–146) reports on bargaining in Pakistan for renting a jeep with the help of his local guide Masood.

> Masood asked me to stay out of the way, and not to speak English, while he bargained .... He said they had asked for 750 rupees; he thought they would settle for 700; [Masood tells them he will go to the bazaar find another jeep]. A man came out of the office. He asked for 650. Masood paid no attention. He said to me grimly, in English, "Let us go to the bazaar". We walked through the bazaar .... a man was hosing down a beaten-up jeep; he asked for 900 rupees. So we went back to the government office and settled, not for 650, but for 700.

Traditional views of opening tactics

Who makes the first offer and at what level? The basic choice is to make a strong and high or a soft and concessive ("fair") first proposal nearer to what should be considered a "fair" price. The first offer is important because of its anchoring effect (i.e., it sets an initial reference that will influence the whole price negotiation process). It has been empirically shown that the level of the first offer has a significant, however minor, influence on the final price (Galinsky et al., 2005) and that negotiators should make the first offer to achieve better gains (Gunia et al., 2013), this being true irrespective of both culture and power differentials. However, the first counter-offers matter also. If a high first offer is answered, in fact negatively reciprocated, by a correspondingly low counter-offer, a large part of the anchoring effect is lost. Roles (e.g., buyer versus seller) are important. In the IT1 paradigm, it is more or less expected that the first offer is a seller's obligation. In the IT2 paradigm, it is clearly more open: there is no clear expectation as to who makes the first offer. Some [IT1] references on the first offer, explaining its advantages and drawbacks and its risks, comment that "Common wisdom for negotiations says it's better to wait for your opponent to make the first offer. In fact, you may win by making the first offer yourself".[11]

The choice in terms of opening tactics is often expressed as *Lowball/ Highball* (first offers). Highball consists in starting with extreme demands; that is, an unreasonably low (high) opening offer, later followed up by only small and slow concessions if the other negotiator has not decided to walk away. A *sine qua non* condition for high first offers in ICBN is indeed the absence of a clear reference for market prices. The negotiator facing such strong initial demand should avoid letting his or her own expectations be anchored; that is, influenced. As noted above, a possible response is to reciprocate by a similarly extreme counter-offer which largely offsets the anchoring effect, and obliges the other negotiator to strongly reconsider his or her opening offer. A good response for dealing with Lowball/Highball is to ask for a more reasonable opening offer instead of making a counter-offer. Another response is to explicitly show both awareness of and displeasure with such a tactic, and threaten to leave the negotiation. The main reason for not making the first offer in ICBN is role related; local customs may dictate that the buyer, respectively the seller, should make the first offer. Saner (2008, p. 60) uses a nice metaphor about strong openings, artillery, and negotiation.

> He who aims high (but not too high!) shoots far. This simple rule of artillery is equally true for negotiation. A strong demand sends an arrow far into the enemy's rank and thus demarcates the framework for the negotiation. … If we point the cannon higher, the shot will not go as far as it might. Thus it is useful to have a realistic estimate of one's own position. We need to utilize our range to the full, but if we aim too far, we will not hit the target, but merely waste our energy.

Prices and price lists: Leaving a margin for manoeuvre

Negotiating prices can start from an official price list, especially in case of multiple items being traded. The setting of prices must address the unique deal and relationship of the buyer. Often B2B negotiators start with a higher list price in markets where it is necessary to leave a margin of discretion. At the beginning it is uncertain who will give way and concede: the seller or the customer. Who will be the first to make concessions, either because of market dominance or because of yielding norms internalized within a particular society? At least four items play a major role:

1) The initial power position of each party.
2) The degree of urgency for either the buyer or the seller to close the deal.
3) The negotiation margin: whichever price is initially announced, it must leave room for further negotiation. It may be in the vendor's interest to

propose a high initial price in order to leave the customer some room for manoeuvre. When the buyer is supposed to obtain a discount, his or her negotiation performance has to be validated by superiors. In such cases, a buyer's task is first and foremost to obtain a price rebate. Ironically, the seller does a favour by opening the negotiations with an exaggerated price (see Box 8.1).

4) The economic process by which buyers and sellers progressively adjust price; for instance, in the case of auctions and competitive bidding situations based on a tender offer, a bidding price that is too high would eliminate the bidder from the shortlist of pre-selected candidates.

Box 8.1 Price levels and the buyer/seller relationship

Scenario 1

The seller wishes to offer a fair price from the start, close to the final price, expecting that it will win over the customer. This is meant (IT1) to convince the buyer of the seller's honesty, openness, and genuine desire to do business at a reasonable price. If the customer shares these (European and American) values and decides to cooperate, an agreement is quickly reached.

Scenario 2

The same seller offers the same near-to-final price, as a sign of goodwill towards the buyer. The buyer who comes from a different culture (IT2, say India or Pakistan) is embarrassed. Rather than a low price, his boss expects him to obtain the greatest possible discount from the seller. His role centres on obtaining rebates rather than on the price level itself. The announced price, close to the final price, leaves almost no room for rebate negotiation. With no grounds to negotiate, dissatisfied buyer and seller will walk away.

Scenario 3

The IT1 seller announces a much higher initial price. In doing so, he or she leaves room for negotiation right from the start so as to allow the IT2 buyer to demonstrate skill in a mutually beneficial bargaining exercise. This enables parties to increase the long-term value of their social relationship. The agreed price is close to that of Scenario 1. The buyer being interested mostly in rebates and the seller in price level, both can achieve greater satisfaction than in Scenario 1.

Information and persuasion tactics

Content-related tactics

Content-related tactics address how best to communicate for problem-solving, especially in the exploration phase, whether negotiation should be agenda oriented or not. IT1 negotiators tend to prefer an ordered and closed (finite) list of topics to be sequentially discussed within a definite time frame (schedule). Topics are meant to be sufficiently independent to be negotiated sequentially, that is, separately. In the IT2 paradigm, negotiation topics are assumed to be interconnected. They come as they emerge from spontaneous communication, this being meant to free creative problem-solving from the corseted framework of an agenda. As far as negotiation issues are interconnected, it is somewhat debatable to treat them in a purely sequential manner. Issues that offer a potential for value creation should be treated at the same time to facilitate trade-offs. Calculative issues, based on money, costs, etc. that seem be discussed in isolation may in fact hide connections within a broader, strategic picture. Value creating trade-offs across individual objects often require a strategic approach, especially when negotiation topics are at the interface between deal and relationship (e.g., jointly hiring top executives for a joint venture or a merged company).

A typical IT1 tactic would be to take the lead in preparing the agenda. This is not necessarily the best possible idea. This comes with many caveats, especially that an agenda prepared by one party may be considered as non-binding by the other, especially if they have accepted the agenda with some reluctance, not only for its content but also because they do not agree with the very concept of *agenda*. Taking the lead would be a typical IT1 attitude. However an IT2 partner, rather than challenging a culturally dominant partner (remember negotiation is dominated by IT1 norms) had better formally accept the agenda (lip service). The IT2 party considers the agenda as non-binding because they need to maintain interconnection between issues, even at the risk of appearing chaotic to the IT1 partner. The tactic of sub-agreements, often unilaterally understood as binding by IT1 negotiators, can be resented as somewhat dangerous by the IT2 party. For them, such provisional agreements are non-binding until they have been validated within a *package deal*. Many negotiators do not want to be *locked-in* by the other side in what seems to be agreed, or in what has, supposedly, been formerly said. It may be that one party does not remember having said what the other party claims they said. A nasty debate may then take place on what the party with a selective memory supposedly said, implying a latent negative value judgement on their failure to recall (voluntary? involuntary?). This is why it is useful to make recaps in which each provisional agreement point is jointly discussed and stated, without however closing the discussion. Final agreement must remain open.

Some issues are more contentious than others. Generally speaking cooperative features are less contentious than distributive ones (e.g., price) or "punitive" clauses (e.g., delay penalties). Tactically, it is advisable to schedule negotiation issues according to their degree of contentiousness in order to avoid a blockade or undue (non-rationally justified) early breach of negotiation. The most contentious issues should not come at the beginning of negotiation, but later; however not too late. Problem-solving and exploration need to possibly jump from one issue which blocks the process to another which is easier to solve. Negotiators may connect issues (e.g., delivery date, possible delivery delays, and delay penalties). If both parties agree, contentious issues can be temporarily disconnected from noncontentious issues, which are easier to solve, thus creating a positive atmosphere. Any point must be open till the end. However, it is needed to finalize the agreement with commitment on both sides. A final tactical recommendation would be to systematically use positive frames rather than negative frames (see Chapter 6), and to avoid useless negative communication tactics such as threats, warnings, and punishment if they are not: 1) absolutely necessary, and 2) credible.

Instrumental communication (and persuasive) tactics

Instrumental communication (and persuasive) tactics involve the risk of being caught in communication misunderstandings. The first category is *positive (representative) communication tactics* based on the fair exchange of true information (Angelmar and Stern, 1978). *Self-disclosure* corresponds to a statement revealing information about one's own interests, positions, needs, etc. (e.g., "We have agreed on price x with you [the other party's] competitor" or "our cost price is x".) Self-disclosure is dangerous because of the risk of increasing information asymmetry to one's detriment. Self-disclosure is feasible only if there are rational expectations that it will be truly reciprocated self-disclosure. *Questions* are interrogative statements asking the other party to reveal information about themselves (e.g., "What are your prospects for next year? Have you reduced your backlog? Will your new plant be ready in time?"). Questions are positive because they are a proof of interest. However, they often contain an appeal to self-disclosure that may embarrass the questioned party who may legitimately answer elusively or not at all.

The second category comprises *communication tactics on the border of instrumental and representative communication.* Truthfulness may be there, however it cannot be verified. A *promise* is a declaration or assurance that one will do something or that a particular thing will happen (e.g., "We will deliver in time so that your production planning will go as planned"). The promise states an intention to provide the other party with a rewarding effect provided, naturally, that it is evaluated as both positive and truthful by the party to which it is addressed. The promise is close to the *reward*, that is, a statement describing pleasant consequences for the other party derived from something given in recognition of service, effort, or achievement (e.g.,

"We will give you free after sales service for one more year because you have agreed on the price"). Both promise and reward can be conditional on recip- rocation in the form of "if ... then" statements. The issue is whether or not promises and rewards are credible enough to generate reciprocal behaviour . *Commitment* is a statement engaging a party to work hard to do, support, or give something (e.g., "We will deliver top quality"), for example about thresholds for future offers or loyalty to the partner. Again, credibility and reliability are the main problematic issues: *lip service* commitments might erode credibility and undermine trust.

The third category of communication tactics is *instrumental communica- tion*; that is, manipulation of the other party by delivering information which is not false *per se*, however mostly aims to influence rather than inform. Two *instrumental communication* tactics (i.e., recommendation and positive nor- mative appeal) are positively framed. *Recommendations* predict a nice out- come to the other party if they follow a suggestion or proposal as to the best course of action, especially one put forward by an authoritative body (e.g., "Comply with EN56 European standard and you will have no problems"). There may be some reasons to believe in recommendation; however nobody knows for sure whether the predicted favourable outcomes will match the expectations since they are not under the instrumental communicator's con- trol. *Positive normative appeals* (also called normative leverage) indicate that the other party's behaviour has to conform to social norms (whose social norms in an ICBN setting?), for example by *appealing* to the other party's religious, professional, or moral standards as grounds for acting in a certain way (e.g., "If you go on following the agenda, we will be finished early").

A *Negative normative appeal*, which is equivalent to normative leverage when based on *negative* arguments, is a statement indicating that the other party's behaviour infringes social norms (e.g., "You should not arrive very late at our negotiation meetings as you have been doing up to now; this is not professional behaviour in business"). It is intended to change the other party's behaviour based on a "critical parent" approach in Eric Berne's Transactional analysis.[12] The danger is that the other party may find such latent reproach unfair especially because in ICBN both parties may not share the same "social norms". This is likely to generate negative emotions in the reprimanded party connected with a potential loss of face. In short, avoid negatively framed normative leverage in ICBN as much as possible.

A *Command* is a statement suggesting, or even requiring, that the other party behaves according to certain rules. The commanding party for instance gives an authoritative, peremptory order, a firm instruction to perform a spe- cific action (e.g., "[please] show your accounting books"). Commanding may be perceived as unduly authoritarian; feasible only when power asymmetry is largely in favour of the commanding party and interdependence small.

A *Threat* expresses an intention to inflict hostile action on someone in reprisal for something done or not done. It states a harmful intention to inflict on the other party an unpleasant or punishing deed (e.g., changing for another business partner, walking away). Serious threats have the potential to breach the relationship. A *Warning* is similar in nature, however lighter than a threat. Warnings consist in predicting that something **un**pleasant may occur to the other party because of non-compliance. A warning is intended to make the other party understand that there is a possible danger or problem. Its occurrence is however not supposed to be under the source's control. (e.g., "Please understand that we cannot offer this price beyond today. Tomorrow we may be obliged to ask for more"). The last type of these negatively framed communication tactics is *Punishment*, an unpleasant declaration that intends to show that a penalty will be incurred for doing something wrong. The infliction or imposition of a penalty is meant as retribution for an offence (e.g., "From now on we will discontinue our orders because of inacceptable delivery delays" [unsaid: "till you credibly commit to deliver in due time"]). Punishing statements are quite negative and somewhat arrogant. Punishment targets behavioural modification; however it is rarely and barely efficient as the target is likely to rebel against being considered a delinquent.

The fourth category of communication tactics, *Strategic misrepresentation*, consists in knowingly delivering "non-true" and manipulative information. A party may for example convey false information to the other side on the value they assign to a particular "good" in the negotiation. Cultures do not put the same value on communication attitudes such as frankness or speech openness: lying or dissimulating information may be perfectly acceptable in some cultures. Active, not passive, lying corresponds to strategic misrepresentation. Minor lies and lying by omission are the bread and butter of ICBN, well accepted in IT2 cultures. The IT1 concept of strategic misrepresentation (SM) is therefore subject to significant cultural variance. Two pragmatic issues must be addressed before using SM: 1) Is the strategic misrepresentation credible? 2) When will the strategic misrepresentation be unveiled? Beyond legitimate ethical concerns, it is advisable not to engage in SM if non-credible and likely to be quickly discovered.

Hardball tactics in ICBN

Tactics designed to extract concessions

Nibbling tactics, also called *Salami tactics*, consist in asking for additional advantages and/or rebates, at the end of the negotiation process, when after spending significant time and effort, the deal is near to a close. Nibbler negotiators raise additional demands on small issues (i.e., nibbles or "salami slices"). It might look mean and unpleasant to the nibbled negotiator who may ironically ask the nibbler what else he or she wants or express counter-demands which may be traded against the various nibbles. For Saner (2008, pp. 62–63), the salami tactic consists in cutting demands in small slices rather than trying to force acceptance demands at once:

Such small intermediate aims are achieved much more easily … the salami tactic is a sort of slow undermining of the other side. For example, we are negotiating a complicated deal with a computer salesman, and have already obtained the maximum rebate … And now at the last moment we demand one more item of software from the somewhat worn-down salesman. Rather than jeopardize the whole deal, he rather sheepishly adds it to the package – something he would have never done if we had negotiated the whole package from the very start.

Belittling

This tactic has not only to do with belittling the other party's alternatives, but also with the attempt at demeaning and depreciating their capacities, financial situation, their credibility, reputation, etc. The "belittler" is likely to adopt a patronizing style, a condescending attitude, through sneering and even disdainful communication. One should not be impressed by such arrogant behaviour, intended in fact at instilling doubt in one's own camp and at shaking one's resolve. The other party belittling one's side must be resisted by negative reciprocity (e.g., belittling their side to show that one's own camp is aware of their tactic, not naive, and unsusceptible to be manipulated), explicitly naming one's own BATNA, requiring respect and due consideration, etc.

Extracting last-minute concessions after agreement, but before signing the formal contract

This cynical tactic occurs especially when negotiating abroad and consists in last moment questioning of agreed upon terms, before closing and signing the deal. Sitting in a car back to the airport with the negotiation partners, the other party suddenly asks for a 5 or 10% rebate on a price which had been agreed upon and settled after a two-week negotiation. Either one accepts and makes a major concession yielding to what is a sort of blackmail (they know that the blackmailed negotiator does not want to fly back without a closed deal). Or the choice is for the blackmailed negotiator to say no and all the negotiation efforts are lost. Consequently, the advice is to say neither yes nor no. This may be somewhat frustrating because the blackmailed negotiator flies back home without a closed deal. Avoid showing anger and reprimanding the party which suddenly questions an already closed deal; however, signal unwillingness to yield under such undue time pressure. Renegotiation is in any case inevitable.

Mandated negotiator tactic: "I am not the boss!"

This is a frequent tactic for a mandated negotiator who does not have complete decision-making power, because his or her principal has given a compulsory negotiation mandate to instrumentalize his or her agency position to extract concessions. The mandate comprises instructions on key negotiation issues (e.g., reservation price, main aspects of the deal, BATNA, and so on) as well as leeway and manoeuvre margins on other issues. The counterpart of the mandated negotiator has no information on the content of the mandate, leaving the mandated negotiator free to take advantage of the situation, pretending that his or her hands are tied and/or that he or she has only limited discretion in negotiating.[13] The mandated negotiator may constantly refer to her or his principal, either by mentioning unverifiable instructions or by interrupting the negotiation to call her or his principal and later ask for further concessions. The principal then becomes an *invisible/implicit negotiator*, to the detriment of the full-fledged negotiator. Mandates need to be ascertained; the principal's positions should be checked, and/or the principal should be formally introduced into the negotiation process.

Take-it-or-leave-it offers

Such all-or-none offers are on the border of extortion. Unless there is compelling evidence that the party making a take-it-or-leave-it offer has some motives (strong power position, monopolistic market background, no dependence, etc.), it is better to bluntly ignore the take-it-or-leave-it offer and continue to explore other content options. Non-negotiable offers are not part of negotiation.

Manipulative, bluffing, and blurring tactics

Good guy/bad guy

Also called "Good Cop/Bad Cop", this tactic works only when negotiating in teams. Before the negotiation starts, and naturally without one's camp being aware of it, the other negotiation team has distributed roles between their team members. In this role distribution, an opponent is the "good guy": he or she displays openness and a listening ability, and behaves softly and reasonably as if he or she had a real concern for the other side's outcomes. Conversely, the "bad guy" is unilateral, communicates harshly and is demanding and tough, using threats and intimidation. However, it is relatively obvious that both the supposedly "good guy" and the apparently "bad guy" are working for the same camp. At some point, the bad guy may leave the negotiation table for the good guy to offer a seemingly soft solution, which in fact means for the other side yielding to their demands. To confront such a tactic, one's own camp may either decide to adopt the same tactic and also distribute roles of good guy/bad guy or openly reveal awareness of their plot. This tactic tends to substitute acting for negotiating, and may be detrimental to both Relationship-Building and to the joint exploration of mutually profitable solutions.

Bluffing

As a general concept, bluffing is an attempt to deceive someone into believing that one can or is going to do something. In negotiation, a bluff is an attempt to deceive the opponent by exaggerating and misrepresenting facts as to one's abilities or intentions, in order to make the other side's negotiators yield. For instance, bluffers try to make negotiators on the other team think that they are going to perform a particular action when in fact they have no intention to do so. Bluffing may involve deceitfully overstated financial capacity or supposed knowledge that the bluffer pretends to have (however, does not actually have). Associated terms for bluffing are many: deception, subterfuge, pretence, sham, fake, show, deceit, false show, idle boast, feint, delusion, hoax, fraud, masquerade, or charade. There is a hint of puffing and lying in what is more or less suspect to be a bluff. It may be worthwhile to use external sources to verify the bluffer's claims. Take-it-or-leave-it offers are frequent forms of bluffing as well as overly strong claims that some key aspects of the deal are non-negotiable. Such bluffing can be politely ignored. Outright scepticism may be signalled to the bluffing camp. An invitation to refocus on the deal content and to display more reasonable demands may be necessary.

Snow job

The metaphor in "Snow Job" is to disseminate a large quantity of information (i.e., "snow"), possibly based on difficult to understand, technical and expert knowledge, in the hope that the other party will have a hard time selecting which pieces of information are true and/or significant for the negotiation process. This entails the risk that the Snow Jobber will blur the whole exploration process. Information exchange becomes confused and problem-solving difficult. Despite being overwhelmed with expert language, the Snow Jobbed party should not hesitate to ask as many questions as needed in order to clearly understand, and challenge the Snow Jobber when answers are weak, confusing, and/or inconsistent.

Blurring issues

Chinese Stratagem 20 ("Muddle the water to catch the fish", i.e., create confusion and use this confusion to further your own goals) corresponds to this tactic. A negotiator may deliberately overestimate the importance of some issues, in the hope of trading them and obtaining concessions for really important issues. This biases problem-solving and the joint search for mutually profitable solutions. Furthermore it may backfire if the other party takes it seriously, yields on unimportant issues, and asks for reciprocal concessions on really important issues. When blurring issues are suspected, ask the other negotiator questions to investigate why they really want a particular outcome. Do not hesitate to expose the ploy and ask for priorities to be truthfully communicated.

Threats and warnings

As noted above, a threat in negotiation is a declaration by one party of their intention to inflict harm or damage on the threatened party (e.g., withdrawing from talks, looking for another partner, hurting their reputation, bringing them to court). Faced with such threats, the first recommendation is to ask the threatening party to reiterate and clarify their threats to oblige them to explicitly acknowledge what they are doing. A second step is to quickly evaluate the seriousness of their intentions and their capacity to put them in practice. A warning is slightly less severe than a threat: a party issues a statement predicting that an unpleasant consequence will occur to the warned party (e.g., this is illegal, you will not be able to implement this clause, to meet delivery dates). The credibility of warnings must be assessed before taking them seriously. Sometimes they may be purely instrumental and manipulative, and it is better to ignore warnings as if they had been unnoticed. If warnings are somewhat more credible, the best avenue is to discuss the likelihood of consequences.

Aggressive/commanding hardball tactics

Intimidation is based on a combination of threats, warnings, punishments, and negative normative appeal with effects anticipated as harmful and unpleasant. The potentially intimidated party risks yielding to avoid negative emotions (e.g., guilt and/or shame) and poor self-image. Intimidation can be either bluntly ignored or managed by the most emotionally stable negotiator in a negotiation team.

Trying to make a party wince

In this hardball tactic, there is no point in building a relationship. Making the other party wince reflects a deal-oriented tough strategy with a win-lose perspective, along with a focus on claiming rather than creating value. By continuously making extreme demands, by contending and eluding any concessive behaviour the hard bargainer hopes that the other party will finally flinch. Forget about building a relationship with the counterpart and adopt a (negative) reciprocal, mirror-game, negotiation style, and signal to the opponent a complete unwillingness to recoil. Reciprocate high demands by similarly high, unilateral counter-offers, fully centred on your interests and ignoring theirs. There is a small chance that a more cooperative stance will sooner or later emerge from this confrontation.

Aggressive emotional tactics

Such unashamed aggressive emotional tactics can be based on personal attacks, possibly even insulting statements, or – at least – feather ruffling ("to ruffle someone's feathers" is to purposely do or say something to cause confusion, agitation, irritation, or annoyance in that person). These personal attacks are intended to destabilize the other party, making them emotionally insecure and vulnerable in terms of negotiation rationality (e.g., yielding and conceding without reason). At least, this aggressive tactic must be calmly identified. A pause in the negotiation process may be called for if it does not stop. If unjustified hostile attitudes persist, it is important to clearly warn the aggressive party that they are damaging the long-term relationship and should therefore return to a well-mannered demeanour.

Countering hardball tactics

What should negotiators do when the other party behaves poorly, in an instrumental and manipulative manner, lie, cheat on key information, and the like (i.e., some of the hardball tactics described above)? Below are some "Countering tactics", which may be helpful to respond to an indelicate opponent. When it is obvious that the other party is lying (e.g., misrepresenting strategic information), should their ploy be angrily denounced with the risk of damaging the relationship and possibly losing a profitable deal? Better say nothing and go on in perfect cognizance of their tricky tactics, or deliver a slightly understated message indicating awareness that they are trying to fool you.

Courtesy tactic

Courtesy tactics consist in sending understated, however not too understated, indications as to your full awareness of the hardball tactics used by counterparts. By asking a barrage of questions they will be, little by little, obliged to concede, acknowledge, confess, that their statement was a misrepresentation of reality. Courtesy tactics entail being very polite, precise (low-context communication), very articulated and asking clear, unambiguous questions so that the other party cannot play on half-understanding of queries and must therefore answer clearly. This will lead the liar-deceiver to become more precise, reveal the fibs, and finally give up on them. Use a soft, diplomatic, unpretentious, uncommanding, and unaggressive style, being very (and slightly overly) polite to suggest ironic deference. Do not take revenge by mentioning that you have in any way won over the adversary. Pretend that you have seen nothing. This will have a face-saving advantage for them.[14]

Silence and sphinx tactic

The sphinx[15] tactic is based on not reciprocating communication when confronted with hardball tactics (which should not be confused with defecting in communication). Just do not say anything, look them directly in the eyes, stare at them, indirectly suggesting unwillingness to go further and wait for the "sphinxed" party to restart the communication. They will be destabilized. When doing this several times, they will certainly become aware that you do not want to be fooled further.

Concluding remarks

Tough and soft strategies are not really deliberate. Market background, interdependence, and power asymmetries often count more than the deliberate choice of a particular strategy. Most strategies are mixed and change/adapt over the negotiation process which is basically interactive, reciprocal, conditional, bilateral, and not unilateral. Most negotiation tactics, as I hope to have shown, must be employed with great prudence; if applied by the other party, they should be unveiled and countered.

Appendix: Checklists of basic characteristics of a negotiation

Table A8.1 Central features of a negotiation

Number of parties	Dyadic, triadic, four, or five parties and more – review possible coalitions and their stability
Number of players per party	One player vs. several players per party, monolithic versus non-monolithic party(ies)
Number and nature of negotiation issues	*Issues* to be examined and degree of dependence/connection between them
Negotiating for oneself vs. with a mandate	Mandate and mandatory vs. negotiating for oneself and/or with full power to make the deal
Time horizon	One-shot or repeated transactions/negotiations
Integrative/distributive *potential*	Actual common ground/perceived (subjective) common ground – degree of overlap between negotiation positions
Concern for one's own outcomes …	… as well as concern for the other party's outcomes (*Dual Concern Model with mirror effects on one's own side*)
Other party's concern for one's own outcomes	… as well as other party's concern for one's own outcomes (*Dual Concern Model with mirror effects on the other party*)

Table A8.2 Negotiation asymmetries

Information asymmetry	Logical: it's a game (cards are hidden)! However, information asymmetry should be assessed and properly managed
Dependence asymmetry	Interdependence is not necessarily symmetric (a party can be more dependent vis-à-vis the other party)
Power asymmetry	David against Goliath (example: a large order giver facing a weak subcontractor)
Asymmetry in number of participants per party	One against several (e.g., a single negotiator has to face several negotiators in the other camp)
Asymmetry in out-of-negotiation alternatives	One party may have more ATNAs and a stronger BATNA than the other party

Table A8.3 Differences between negotiating parties

Value differences	E.g., Frankness/honesty versus pragmatic centred on outcomes
Differences in interests	Assess interests, interest divergence, and interest convergence
Divergence in goals	Closing the deal or not? *Deal vs. Relationship?* Procrastinating to gain time?
Strategic *orientation*	Integrative vs. distributive, tough vs. soft, mixed strategies
Differences in time-related behaviour	Time culture (linear-economic vs. cyclical-holistic), attitudes to planning, deadlines, time pressure, etc.
Degree of need for personalized interaction	Do parties need to know each other? Do they need small talk and preliminaries?

Table A8.4 Formalizing the negotiation process and outcomes

Relevant external environment	Are actors in the macro-environment (i.e., public or regulatory bodies, trades unions, etc.) likely to intervene?
Links with other negotiations	Example in labour/social negotiation: links between company-level, industry-wide, and country-wide negotiations
Issue by issue vs. *package deal* termination	Intermediate (sub-)agreements (SA)? Are SAs conditional on final agreement? Wrongful termination of negotiation talks?
Agenda (in Latin: what needs to be done)	No agenda? More or less precise agenda? Unilaterally defined agenda? Negotiated agenda?
Negotiation schedule	Is a negotiation *schedule* tied to the agenda? Planning versus unplanned negotiation

Table A8.5 Organization variables

Place	The other party's site, one's own premises, or neutral ground
Time	Role of preliminaries /small talk, exploration phase, timing of concessions, etc.
Public, private, or secret negotiation?	Risks related to information leakage, which might jeopardize negotiation and/or be exploited by one party or the other
Third parties	Experts, interpreters, lawyers, mediator, conciliator, arbiter, journalists, participants-observers, ...
Communication mode (CM)	Face-to-face, by mail, by phone, by email, by teleconference, through third parties, or any combination of CMs over time

Notes

1 On ICBN strategies, see Saner (2003, 2008).
2 For example, sugary, sentimental, smooth, soppy, gushy, mushy, syrupy, or gooey.
3 Indirect reciprocity refers to general cooperative behaviour within a society. Indirect reciprocity can take two forms: (1) *Upstream reciprocity*: trustor A helps B, who indirectly reciprocates by helping C; (2) *Downstream reciprocity*: trustor A helps B, then C, observing A's trusting behaviour, helps A (Nowak and Sigmund, 2005).
4 For an IT1 defence and illustration of the normative superiority of interests-based over rights- or power-based strategies in negotiation, see Lytle et al. (1999).
5 See Fukuyama's (1994) chapter, "Face to face France".
6 About coalitions, see Faure and Rubin (1993), Bazerman et al. (2000), Raiffa et al. (2003), Shell (2006), Saner (2008, Chapters 10 and 11), Maude (2014, pp. 116–122), and Jeong (2016).
7 Both Free-Trade Area (FTA) and Customs Union have no custom duties between their member states; Customs Unions have common external tariffs vis-à-vis third countries, while FTA members keep independent external tariffs.
8 Members of a non-monolithic party (monolithic means "One-Stone like" in Greek) may differ on particular issues, while by and large sharing the same goals and interests. Conversely, members of a monolithic negotiation team are completely aligned in terms goals, interests, and expected outcomes.
9 Negotiation simulation prepared by J.-C. Usunier and A. Perrinjaquet, based on Bazerman and Neale (1992, chapter 14, pp. 128–132).
10 Differences are statistically significant at p<.01; minimal outcome is 120.
11 See Gunia et al. (2013); see also "When to Make the First Offer in Negotiations" From *Negotiation* by Adam D. Galinsky (2004); see also "Negotiation Opening Offer" by Dr D.P. Venter, www.negotiationtraining.com.au/articles/new-agreement/ about who should make the first offer in a negotiation, and how anchoring might affect the outcome.
12 Berne (1961).
13 See Mnookin, Peppet, and Tulumello (2004).
14 On the American diplomatic style, see https://history.state.gov/departmenthistory/short-history/style
15 In Greek tradition, a sphinx is a mythical creature with the head of a human, the haunches of a lion, and the wings of a bird. The sphinx devoured all travellers who could not answer the riddle it posed: "What is the creature that walks on four legs in the morning, two legs at noon and three in the evening?" The hero Oedipus gave the answer, "Man", causing the sphinx's death.

Part three

Agreements, ethics, and styles in ICBN

9 Negotiating different types of ICBN contracts

Sometimes, managers manage actions directly. They fight fires. They manage projects. They negotiate contracts.

(Henry Mintzberg)

Like Chapter 6, this chapter serves as a counterpoint to the ideal-types of Deal-Making (IT1) and Relationship-Building (IT2). It builds on the checklists presented in the preceding chapter to determine what should be treated in each major type of ICBN contract, on the basis of deal, relationship, or a combination of both. The basic characteristics of each type of contract are discussed in detail. Time issues presented in Chapter 4 are one of the guiding frameworks: one-shot (sales/procurement contracts) vs. repeated deals, time span of the agreement, strong future orientation of the arrangement (e.g., joint ventures), implementation issues beyond signing the contract (e.g., licensing/ franchising contracts), etc. Expectations of both parties as to the durability of the agreement as well as possible discrepancies between these expectations are examined in detail with illustrations. A number of legal issues related to particular agreements are discussed, such as the termination of contracts (e.g., licensing and franchising contracts), distribution of equity and man- agerial power (e.g., joint ventures, mergers and acquisitions), winner's curse (e.g., international corporate acquisitions), and non-disclosure agreements when key proprietary information is disclosed before finalizing the deal (e.g., know-how licences).

For each major type of ICBN contract (international and export sales, agent/distributor agreements, licensing/franchising contracts, international joint ventures, project and package deals, and mergers and acquisitions), the following analysis grid is used:

(A) type and purpose of contract, background market relationship, business context, one-shot or repeat negotiations, level of inter- dependence between the negotiating parties, deal complexity and nature of the relationship;

(B) main issues covered by this particular type of ICBN contract; and

(C) contract negotiation process (specifics for this type of contract) from pre-negotiation to face-to-face and finally post-implementation stages as well as possible forms of renegotiation.

A joint issue for all types of ICBN contracts is that they most often bring together a local and a foreign partner, frequently a multinational (global) company (MNC). While Local-Global and $Local_1$-$Local_2$ (companies from two different countries/cultures) partnering typically involve an intercultural negotiation encounter, Global-Global partnerships are likely to display ICBN characteristics only if the two (or more) MNCs involved still have a distinct country/culture of origin.

Typical ICBN contracts differ in terms of:

1) Time span, that is, not only over which period of time they are in effect, but also whether their duration is set and limited or not; whether short term contracts repeat over time, and whether planning trouble, delay, postponement, and rescheduling are likely to occur. In line with Chapter 4, special attention and care will be needed in ICBNs to avoid time-related conflicts and misunderstandings. This is illustrated with the termination of agency-dealership contracts as well as with the complex and uncertain completion of turnkey projects.

2) Partners, whether they share a common culture and a similar mindset, even broadly (like-minded, which is likely to be the case for instance between Western multinational companies), or conversely, when a global and local company with much cultural distance do not share culture, language, or relationship vs. deal basic assumptions.

3) Understanding what a signed contract involves in terms of rights and obligations; high-context cultures are fuzzier, more implicit, rely more on people and the relationship than low-context cultures which rely on precise, explicit contractual clauses and frown upon the perspective of renegotiation. Even if there are joint legal frameworks for contracts (e.g., sales contracts), interpretation of agreements is subject to differences in language and legal traditions. The part/type of deal and the part/type of relationship differ in each type of contractual arrangement. The six following types of ICBN contracts are examined:

- *International/export sales contracts* range from pure D to very R-oriented negotiations according to market background, standard vs. customized item being traded, etc. International sales contracts – export contracts are predominantly deal oriented, with one-shot discrete transactions, limited relationship development unless deals are repeated over time and both partners are willing to enter into a relationship.

- In *Agent-dealer-distributor contracts*, the Relationship is important and termination after successful collaboration needs to be managed with great care; sales deals with local customers are embedded within the contractual relationship with the local intermediary.

- In *License agreements*, the Deal is reflective of the extent of the licensor's trust in the capacities of the to-be-licensee. In the Post-agreement phase, the Relationship is important.
- *International joint ventures* negotiations are more Relationship than Deal-oriented; they are at first quite cooperative and future-oriented; building a good working relationship to manage the IJV seems logical; however, R may not resist the acid test of actual IJV implementation and development.
- *Turnkey-project* arrangements are very much deal oriented at the beginning (because of an auction process based on tenders and bidding, shortlisting, and final contractor selection). It is followed by the (sometimes painful) discovery during the implementation phase that extreme interdependence in a bilateral monopoly setting commands an R-orientation. Time management and the partner's ability to cooperate and coordinate their actions are essential.
- In *Mergers and acquisitions* (takeovers), information asymmetry between acquirers and acquired (merged) firms quite often causes a *Winner's Curse* scenario to emerge as in project sales. Two levels of negotiation are intermingled: a very calculative level, very deal-oriented [price per share for takeover or exchange ratio for shares of merging companies]; and a relational level, related to the post M&A implementation phase which requires joint action and a balance of power so that the acquirer does not "kill" the acquired company.

International sales contracts – export contracts

International sales – export contracts are often, not always, short-term, one-shot deals with little interdependence (if any), especially in a globalized market for standardized items, with a highly competitive market background and price as the main negotiation issue. There are three main cases: 1) *new-to-export* companies exporting based on passive *open distribution*; 2) international sales contracts for globally traded standardized B2B items (i.e., commodities); and 3) direct export sales of customized, often hi-tech, products and/or services, in B2B bilateral oligopolies.

Direct exports or exports intermediated from the country of origin are often used by newcomers to exporting activities (*new-to-export*) based at first on *open distribution*: a company receives orders from abroad without especially looking for them; it answers such inquiries, taking full risks in contracts, delivery, and payment. The problem of *new-to-export companies* (generally SMEs) is the lack of experience with international shipments, payment problems, and an underestimation of opportunistic behaviours in faraway markets. The second type, sales contracts for globally traded standardized items, is facilitated by online B2B purchase platforms (e.g.,

Alibaba, Europages) or online B2B marketplaces. Negotiation, which is often electronic, centres on price, quantity, shipping and insurance, and delivery date. This often comes with a strong power misbalance in favour of the buyer facilitated by the large number of competing sellers found on online B2B purchase platforms. Business originating from Internet platforms, especially in a B2B setting is pure Deal. The third case is based on direct exports; that is, the buyer and seller are acquainted and have a relationship based on product and/or service customization, which requires face-to-face negotiation. This is a worthy solution for niche industrial companies with very few clients worldwide (e.g., from 5 to 50), selling specialized products to foreign corporate customers in a B2B relationship.

ICBN sales contracts may be largely deal-oriented, especially in the case of a new, unknown partner, possibly in a politically unstable context, with high legal and cultural distance.[1] Strong deal orientation and an a priori one-shot deal, generally mean little interest and no willingness to bridge the cultural and/or linguistic gap. It could be repeat business, although embedded within successive one-shot deals with no particular relationship being developed.

Main issues

Generally export sales follow a deal-oriented pattern, legal and global, possibly a no trust, no relationship solution. This entails standard international sales contracts, which are key instruments to secure deal-related aspects. Such standard contracts are either imposed by the powerful party (i.e., their own standardized contract) and/or derived from an international standard contract. Potential recourse to litigation is based either on arbitration (ICC and others, see Chapter 7) or on the law and the courts of the powerful party. The deal conditions in terms of shipment, freight insurance, property, and risk transfer are based on ICC Incoterms standards. The payment is secured by a Letter of Credit through the intermediation of banks as third parties.

Contract negotiation process

For this type of export contract, especially in the case of globally traded standardized items, a lot of the negotiation now takes place online, through dedicated websites, email, Skype, with little or no face-to-face negotiation (except computer mediated conferencing). Relational expectations from the less powerful party may emerge over time after successful deals, especially if there are few alternative partners for the powerful party (e.g., a bilateral oligopoly market background). Repeat business and a non-standardized (i.e., customized) item require some face-to-face negotiation, travelling to meet the sales partner, investing in significant transaction costs, on technology, specifications, delivery schedule, shipping, etc. If in addition the representatives of both buyer and seller firm are the same over the years, asymmetric loyalty expectations may arise from an IT2 partner (being relational, HC, etc.). Loyalty expectations must, however, be kept under strict control, because they are not in the very nature of this type of business agreement.

Agent/distributor contracts

There are strong limitations to export sales and open international distribution for international business development and entry into foreign markets. In most cases, after some preliminary business deals, it is quickly necessary to have a local partner in the country of destination. This enables knowledge of and contact with the foreign market. Direct exports are not a real presence, unless in the case of niche industrial companies with very few clients worldwide described above.

Agent/distributor and dealer contracts correspond to exports intermediated by a middleman in the destination country, generally a foreign agent acting as an intermediary with local customers. Such agents most often represent multiple exporting companies. They are generally paid through commissions on sales. The degree of marketing delegation (on brand, promotion, advertising, etc.) from the exporter varies; it is often low. The exporting firm contracts with and invoices the final customer; the foreign agent is commissioned on the sale.

The foreign agent, being a small local partner, apparently has a weaker position compared with an international/global company in terms of size, professionalism, financial capacities, etc. However, the local partner brings key assets: a deep understanding of the local market, insider knowledge of the local culture, proficiency in the local language(s), familiarity with the institutional system, and a network of relationships with local companies. Who should adapt to whom in terms of language, culture, and negotiation style? Usually the local partner will adjust, speaking English and pretending to be the typical international business person. However, this adaptation could be partially misleading for those who are adapted to.

Agency contract may cover an exclusive, a non-exclusive, or a mix of exclusive and non-exclusive sales territories. If exclusive, the foreign agent will always receive fees for any sale on its contractual territory, even if the deal has been closed by the exporter without any agent's involvement. Conversely, in the case of a non-exclusive contract, the exporter may hire other non-exclusive agents for the same territory and/or directly sell to final customers, bypassing the agent(s). The main aspects of the agency contract abroad are:

1) The area(s) covered, depending on whether they are exclusive or non-exclusive sales territories, or a mix of both, according to particular sub-regions explicitly mentioned in the agency contract.
2) The product(s) and services covered.
3) The forms of commissioning (flat percentage fee, increasing or decreasing percentage according to sales figure, etc.).

4) The degree of marketing delegation (degree of leeway in terms of brands, trade documents, sales promotion efforts … if any).
5) Maintenance of a spare parts inventory (it is possible, however not always the case), as well as after sales service (rare for agents).
6) Contract duration: probation period, tacit or explicit renewal.
7) Clauses about possible cases of contract resolution; termination of the contract.
8) Legal precautions: clause designating the law governing the contract, arbitration clause, clause about provisions for possible litigation.
9) (Possibly) a clause concerning minimal sales to be reached by the agent for the contract to be maintained in force.

Dealerships are a stronger business relationship than agency contracts. A dealer represents a brand for a particular territory (generally on an exclusivity basis); it most often offers after-sales service and spare parts to local customers; and buys from its principal and resells to end customers. For example, Caterpillar (world leader in earthmoving equipment) has a worldwide network of dealers. Similarly local bottlers are Coca-Cola dealers; however, Coca-Cola has increasingly created local subsidiaries over the last 25 years.

Contract negotiation processes. There are two levels of contract negotiation: the first level is based on repeated deals (sales contracts with customers in the foreign market), the second level is non-repetitive (i.e., the intermediation contract with the foreign agent, which may cover several years before being terminated or renegotiated).

Interdependence issues have to be considered, taking into account that agents often represent many foreign exporters (FE). The FE is bound to the local agent (LA) for several years. Relationship development is needed and should sometimes (often) be proactive on the part of the FE. Global companies however sometimes change their internationalization strategies because they want to increase control over their foreign operations and consequently decide to replace foreign agents by sales subsidiaries (SS). This strategic move may lead to contract termination with the LA, despite the agent having done a good job over years and regardless of FE-LA relationship quality.

Agency or dealership agreements are indeed embedded in the relationship, especially if it is an exclusive contract. Implementation problems may arise on both sides. There may be no or very few deals, and the market is virtually closed to the FE if the agreement is exclusive. Alternatively, deals are closed with local customers without the agent being aware of it, because they were negotiated in the FE's home country. For instance when the FE, a multinational firm, deals directly with the headquarters of another MNC because of centralized purchasing systems, its local subsidiaries are subordinated to the headquarters' decision and have no reason to contact the LA, if even the subsidiary is aware of the LA's existence.

Figure 9.1 Three-party negotiations for agency/dealership agreements

Three-party sales negotiations follow the two-party negotiation of the agency-dealership contract. Like in any intermediation, sales deals therefore always involve foreign exporters, local agents, and local customers (see Figure 9.1). Choosing between a LA and a SS is a make or buy issue. A SS will replace the LA if direct contacts with the local market and with local customers as well as integrated distribution are required.

LA's opportunism is rather frequent. First, the LA may, willingly or unwillingly, close the market either by negligence and lack of involvement or for the benefit of a FE's competitor, the FE being unaware of the LA's covert opportunistic behaviour. The risk of a hidden market closure can be divided into two threats: Total market closure and partial market closure (for a particular product or for a particular sales territory). Second, the LA may unduly favour local customers and make a hidden quasi-coalition with some local customers against the FE (e.g., by reducing prices or granting special conditions), this being especially likely to arise in B2B markets. Third, the LA may discreetly represent the FE's competitors despite this being explicitly forbidden by the agency contract, assuming that exclusivity is bilateral.

Hence the key importance for the FE of a relationship with the LA, which paradoxically consists in both trust and capacity to control the LA's actions. This may give rise to expectations on the part of IT2 LAs that the FE will help even on personal, non-business related matters (e.g., taking care of a son or daughter sent abroad for a study period). These highly personal demands may appear to be curious to an IT1 FE who may not be used to rendering service as if he or she were almost a member of the extended family. FE negotiators may even find such requests for friendly assistance in non-business related matters shocking because this violates the IT1 norm of relatively strict separation between the personal sphere and business-related matters.

As noted above, agency agreements may no longer support the objectives of one party or context and circumstances may have evolved. In these cases, the agreement should be brought to an end. In case of termination, local courts often grant damage monies to former agents when agency contracts are terminated at the principal's (FE) initiative. Before starting the termination process it is therefore advisable to look at local practices and rules and to ask for expert advice. Problems in dissolving an agency agreement have to be resolved by negotiation, especially when the agent has no responsibility in the circumstances leading to contract termination. Creative and positive solutions have to be envisaged for the termination issue. The first piece of advice is to avoid litigation, especially with a local court which will certainly side with and support the agent; this is all the more likely when the local laws provide measures to financially repair agents and the local jurisprudence traditionally has been generous with evicted agents in damage monies (McCall, 2003). Consequently, it is recommended to come to an out-of-court settlement with the terminated agent or dealer. If the FE's market presence is the objective for the future, dodge any conflict that would result in a poor reputation for the FE in the local business environment. A positive solution is to associate the LA in the creation of the sales subsidiary which will take the form of a joint venture in exchange for their acceptance of the agency contract termination. Finally, it is generally better to negotiate a termination indemnity with the LA rather than going to local courts and receiving a higher penalty.

Licensing/franchising contracts

Type and purpose of contract, interdependence, and market relationship

Licensing/franchising contracts are deals that revolve around patented technology and know-how (i.e., non-patented technology) issues. Industrial property rights (IPR) are a central issue in such negotiations with the caveat that IPRs must be understood in the same way by both partners (for cultural differences on IPRs, see Li, 2004). Respecting IPRs and complying with industrial property rules may be a problematic issue as the IT2 paradigm does not attach the same formal and legal importance to IPRs as IT1 negotiators do. Very briefly stated it can be clipped into the following question. Are IPRs a private (IT1) or a public good (IT2)?[2]

Deal and Relationship are deeply intermingled in licensing agreements: the relationship is as important as the IPR-based deal itself, because such agreements involve long-term cooperation, with a win-win perspective and much integrative potential; however there are significant potential benefits for the party adopting an opportunistic stage. There is often a large gap in terms of knowledge and information between the potential partners that feed opportunistic behaviour on both sides. Control is key, especially for franchising, and being ready to litigate if needed in the case of trademark and patent infringement by the licensee or franchisee as well as non-respect of contractual rules. The major cultural-institutional-legal differences lie in the acceptance or not of the private appropriation of "proprietary" knowledge versus inventions and knowledge in general being viewed as a public good. It is worthwhile citing Benjamin Franklin, a strong partisan of the open and free use of knowledge.

… as we enjoy great advantages from the inventions of others, we should be glad of an opportunity to serve others by any invention of ours; and this we should do freely and generously. An ironmonger in London however, assuming a good deal of my pamphlet, and working it up into his own, and making some small changes in the machine, which rather hurt its operation, got a patent for it there, and made, as I was told, a little fortune by it. And this is not the only instance of patents taken out for my inventions by others, tho' not always with the same success, which I never contested, as having no desire of profiting by patents myself, and hating disputes. The use of these fireplaces in very many houses, both of this and the neighbouring colonies, has been, and is, a great saving of wood to the inhabitants.[3]

Licensing involves different forms of IPR: trademarks (brands, brand names)[4] and patents.[5] Incidentally, licensing may also cover intellectual property rights related to copyright. A licence is a right granted by the IPR owner (licensor) to manufacture and/or commercialize products or processes corresponding to a particular technology to a licensee. Licensing is most often associated with patents and trademarks, however not always; technology is also embedded in non-patented know-how: industrial designs, technical manuals, procedures, and/or pure know-how (i.e., somebody knows how to do it).

Licensing agreements: Clauses

As in the case of agency-dealership contracts, territorial clauses combined with exclusivity are the central parts of the license agreement. Rights to manufacture and/or commercialize combine with exclusivity/non-exclusivity. An exclusive licence precludes the patent owner from manufacturing and/or selling on the granted territories and no other licensee can be appointed. In a non-exclusive license, the licensee is generally not allowed to further license other companies. Manufacturing is generally limited to the territory of the licensor (i.e., the licensor gives up the right to manufacture in the licensee's country), while commercialization may be allowed for both exclusive territories (i.e., the licensor gives up the right to sell in these territories) and non-exclusive territories. In this case, licensor and licensee may be in competition for winning customers, which may evidently pose problems. Parties may foresee joint manufacturing operations, this having the advantage of increasing the licensor's control over quality, delivery dates, and reliability in delivering a product or service meeting the requirements of the licensed technology. However, the licensor must then significantly increase his or her financial and managerial involvement to the extent that both companies would create a joint venture which would be the licensee.

An additional issue is to decide which brand will be used for the products and/or services under licence. Licensors often prefer that their brand is not used by the licensee because there is uncertainty about their manufacturing and marketing abilities. The licensor's reputation could suffer from a licensee's poor image. The solution is generally to keep the licensee brand or corporate name and add in fine print "Manufactured under license from [the licensor corporate name]".

The license contract generally comprises a clause about reciprocal information as concerns new developments and a confidentiality clause by which the licensor is forbidden to spread information on the licensed technology to third parties (e.g., customers, competitors).

How is the licensor compensated: flat fee vs. commission? Generally, licensors prefer a large part of, if not all, their compensation in a flat fee because it protects them against the licensee failing to manufacture and/ or market according to the licence agreement. Conversely, licensees generally prefer a large part of, if not all, their compensation as a variable fee because it protects them against an outdated technology unsellable in their market area. Licence negotiation will often lead to balanced solutions where a flat fee is granted against know-how documents (plans, designs, technical manuals, procedures...) and a variable fee is established on sales as an incentive for the licensee to succeed in creating value out of the IPR they have acquired for a certain time period (to be negotiated as well as the probation period and tacit renewal).

Contract negotiation process

The strategic features of technology sales first and foremost imply answering the following question: Should the company license its proprietary technology or should it be kept for internal growth? Historical examples do not indicate a clear direction. Rank Xerox kept its photocopying technology for itself, but was later overwhelmed by competition when the technology fell into the public domain. Pilkington, a British glassmaker chose to license its float glass technology to its direct competitors (e.g., Corning Glass and Saint-Gobain), successfully using the huge licensing fees to move from its status as a local competitor to that of global player in the glass industry. Sony chose to keep its superior Betamax video recording technology, which never became the dominant standard in the market, except in the professional segment. Conversely, JVC chose to abundantly license its VHS technology which became the arch-dominant standard in the market, especially in the consumer electronics segment.

Negotiation preparation should take into account the place of licences and licensing as a foreign market entry mode in the international business strategy of the licensor. Licensing abroad may be either a full mode of entry into foreign markets, or mere technology sales (versus selling products). The search for and selection of potential licensees requires being more careful in the case of foreign market entry mode licences.

The strategic risk is that the licensee may become a competitor; an opposite risk is that the licensee may be incompetent, may not attain the desired objectives, and may close the market for which it has been granted exclusive rights. The prospective licensee may later become a competitor because their company enjoys growing sales and reputation. They may try to opportunistically get rid of their duties for diverse alleged reasons, for example, claiming to have developed a completely new technology or invoking some dispositions of the local legislation that allow licensees to repudiate licence agreements. Conversely, the success of the prospective licensee may be rather poor causing the licensor to lose market potential granted to the licensee, without gaining much in licensing fees. In both cases (too good, too bad), the information asymmetry should be bridged before and/or during the negotiation process by asking detailed and complete information from the prospective licensee and/or by performing audits, either financed by the licensee or by the licensor, or any negotiated scheme for sharing audit expenses. In any case, the licensor should try to hire their preferred auditing firm. If the prospective licensee refuses an audit, it is an indication that they are not self-confident about their own capacities to make the best out of the licence.

Sometimes licensing can lead to fake negotiation, for instance when negotiating a know-how licence in which the prospective licensee flakily negotiates in the hope of gathering technical information to copy and withdraw before closure for some sham reason. In the meantime, the prospective licensee can pretend to develop a forged and phony relationship which is abruptly terminated when the prospective licensee has gathered enough information to manufacture based on an imitative technology. In such cases the licensor may demand that the prospective licensee sign a non-disclosure agreement[6] before entering the licensing negotiation. A non-disclosure agreement strictly forbids the licensee to disclose information related to the to-be-licensed technology to third parties. It is often signed by the parties before entering into negotiation. The licensee may in fact take advantage of the negotiations (which it might not be willing to bring to an end) to gather information and learn about key details of the technology in order to later implement its own solutions without the licensor being compensated.

International joint ventures

Purpose and context of IJV agreements

In its most general definition, a joint venture is a cooperative agreement in which two or more businesses decide to pool resources for achieving a specific project or business activity (e.g., joint manufacturing, sales, R&D). A JV often is a separate company, with assets and equity contributed by its owners and founders. In an IJV, either two or more companies or a MNC and a local partner (most frequent acceptation of IJV) create a joint business entity for specific business activities. An IJV causes a priori a strong cooperative stance since it is an out-of-market, entrepreneurial alliance in which resources are shared and partners have to agree on how the IJV company will be managed. It is a joint project, long-term oriented, and very open in the early phase of negotiation. Since it is based on combined resources, an IJV seems at first more integrative than distributive: value creation appears to dominate over value claims in the early stages of IJV negotiation. Often partners already know each other (e.g., local partner is the former agent, a subcontractor, or a distributor). There may be complementarities in the contributions brought by each IJV partner (e.g., manufacturing vs. sales, knowledge of the local vs. experience with the global context; skills in technology and R&D vs. operations/management, and type of assets being brought to the JV by each partner). However, despite a pleasant atmosphere in the early phase of negotiating the joint project, relationships progressively deteriorate due to contextual differences, asymmetric contributions, power asymmetries, and the progressive discovery that interdependence is high after the IJV has been formed and starts its operations. IJVs need a readiness for continuous negotiation in the IT2 style.

Main issues

As a separate company, the objectives of the IJV cannot be reduced to those of the parent companies. However, problematic points at implementation must be carefully reviewed and discussed. The atmosphere during negotiation may suffer from the dependence and autonomy of the JV negotiators (oriented towards integrative value creation) vis-à-vis their parent companies (more oriented towards claiming value).

The main issues that will emerge are:

1) The goals for the JV vs. goals of both partners.
2) The compatibility of objectives and the relational background between future parent companies.
3) The joint assessment of critical (relevant) resources for the IJV.
4) The equity and asset contributions (e.g., cash, technology, facilities) as well as joint agreement on a balanced financial evaluation of partners' contributions.
5) Integration in the local context and relationships with public authorities and future local employees and management.
6) Key management positions in the IJV: how are positions assigned and IJV key staff recruited?
7) Clear assignment of responsibilities, management procedures, and reporting.
8) Scope and nature of the relationship especially in the case of significant cultural differences between partners.

9) The macro-environment where the IJV is going to operate has to be taken into account; the local rules concerning IJVs are particularly important if the country presents a rather hostile environment for both local employees and expatriate managers, with possible differences in legal traditions.
10) Communication and reporting rules and procedures that enable both partner "at home" and the "faraway partner" to have similar information on how the IJV works despite the distance.

There is no timeline for the IJV negotiation process: negotiation is continuous till termination, although less intense during the periods when the IJV is established in routine manufacturing and/or sales.

A complex and lengthy negotiation process

There are two steps in negotiating IJVs: a long negotiation at the start, followed by continuous negotiation when running the IJV together. The first step is to negotiate the IJV agreement, which can take several months and frequently more than one year with regular meetings and top executives from the parent companies joining only in the very final part. The pre-negotiation atmosphere may be rather positive and seemingly integrative, especially when doing pure information exchange in face-to-face negotiation. However, more distributive issues will emerge later such as the funding of the IJV, distribution of key positions, the evaluation of assets, and the way to compensate equity and asset contributions (e.g., royalties, dividends, and/or reinvestment of profits in the IJV).

The second step is permanent negotiation during the IJV's life. IJV contracts, even if well prepared, cannot foresee all implementation details, events, and minor conflicts arising throughout the duration of the IJV. Interdependence, which is often low at the start, becomes quite high when implementing the IJV, requiring a strong relational orientation in the IT2 perspective. Even with only two parties, deal complexity can be high, because the IJV is embedded in a complex series of side-agreements (e.g., a buy back agreement for IJV output, a licence agreement where the IJV is licensee and the licensor is a patent holding firm depending on the global parent company, a management contract, etc.). An IJV agreement may be integrated in a more complex scheme of arrangements designed to control the local partner in an unstable environment.

After the basic agreement is orally settled, negotiation will continue in writing the deal on paper; that is, drawing up an IJV contract as well as related contractual agreements. The presence of lawyers is necessary at this stage; they have to draft clauses related to the IJV and to possible litigation between its parent companies (e.g., arbitration, law governing the contract; see Chapter 7). An IJV is a sort of relational marriage. Like in any marriage, divorce is also possible. However unpleasant it may seem, the ways and means to organize a divorce negotiation should be envisaged from the start, for instance the IJV dissolution, or a possible transformation into a company entirely owned and managed by one of the initial partners.[7]

Project and package deals

Project and package deals are probably the most complex type of ICBN contract in terms of intercultural interaction, due to the great number of partners involved in large project and package deals with multiple negotiations taking place between culturally diverse contractors and subcontractors. In addition to the local country and cultural context in which a project will be completed (e.g., Brazil), many country-culture contexts are represented among the contractors when they join forces within a consortium (e.g., Japanese, American, and German engineering companies) as well as among a dense network of subcontractors from Asia, Europe, and South America.

The project business

The project business corresponds to important size and to (a priori) non-repetitive business deals. Examples of project sales abound: a transportation system (e.g., an underground train, a new airport, roads and motorways), a chemical plant, a brewery (or any food and beverage manufacturing unit), a power plant (nuclear coal-fired, solar, etc.). The list is endless as any type of industrial or service facility can be ordered from specialized engineering firms (e.g., Bechtel, Parsons, Fluor, Technip, Uhde), which act as the *contractor*(s). A *contractor* (sometimes a consortium of *contractor*s) is a company appointed to build a plant, a factory, or to complete the construction of any kind of unit project. The *owner* (in fact the future *owner*) is the buyer of the project and also occupies a seller's role for awarding this particular contract to competing *contractor*s.

   The global market size for specialized projects (e.g., an ammonia plant or a nuclear power plant) is as small in units as the project itself is large in dollar value; that is, sometimes more than USD 1 billion. Markets for large projects are discontinuous (e.g., the additional capacity brought by two large plants simultaneously opened may lead to global overcapacity, compromising any further deals for a significant period of time) and highly cyclical because they are based on derived demand (e.g., many projects are production capacity investments extremely sensitive to small changes in end-use markets). These markets as a whole are often referred to as *Turnkey* business, in as much as *contractor*s are supposed to deliver plants that work and that the *owner* can operate after thorough technical inspections and reliability checks. Another type of project contract, called *BOT* (build-operate-transfer) demands that the *contractor* not only construct but also operate the plant for a specified time (e.g., 3 years) jointly with the *owner*, then transferring the full management of the plant to the *owner*.[8]

Project sales are unitary projects, with a great degree of complexity in technical and managerial terms. Large financial amounts are involved, often related to public service (e.g., utilities, transportation), which require public-private partnerships, long-term project finance, and loans from public export banks and insurance companies (e.g., ECGD in the UK, Hermes and KfW in Germany, U.S. Eximbank, Japan Eximbank, COFACE in France). *Owners* are financed on the basis of long-term buyer credit schemes combined with an export credit insurance, which guarantees that the loans will be repaid even in the case of political risk or commercial risk (*owner* insolvency). The future *owner* is often a public sector organization or a public body.

Project and package deal negotiation process

Project and package deal negotiations are complex with multiple parties being involved, linked by chain contracts between the main *contractors* and a dense network of subcontractors. These negotiations start with a strong bargaining orientation, imposed by the bidding procedures of the WTO Agreement on Government Procurement (GPA), which any public sector buyer must follow.[9]

There are three different and successive negotiation processes (see Figure 9.2); success at each step being a condition for going on in a further round. The first step is an auction oriented negotiation process. The tender-bid-auction process is monopsonic in nature: There is only one buyer and multiple potential project *contractors*. The *owner* starts by issuing a publicly available tender document. Competing *contractors* prepare bids sent to the *owner* in response to the published tender offer. The *owner* then compares the bids as concerns price, performance, and technical credibility.

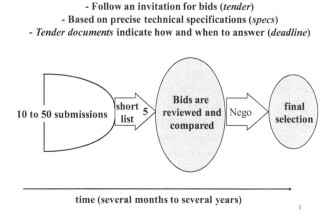

- **Submission Procedures (*bidding*)**
- **Follow an invitation for bids (*tender*)**
- **Based on precise technical specifications (*specs*)**
- ***Tender documents* indicate how and when to answer (*deadline*)**

10 to 50 submissions → short list → 5 → Bids are reviewed and compared → Nego → final selection

time (several months to several years)

Figure 9.2 Submission procedures for project sales

A "shortlist" of pre-selected *contractors* is published, especially when many heterogeneous bids have been received. "Shortlisted" *contractors* can compete for the final selection of a particular *contractor* who will be the privileged negotiation partner for the second step. The second negotiation step is a bilateral monopoly negotiation, which generally finishes with a signed deal. However, the possibility remains for each party to withdraw and exercise its BATNA (e.g., for the *owner* to restart negotiation with another shortlisted *contractor*). The third negotiation step arises out of implementation issues, especially planning, delays, and costs, and this takes place over the whole construction period and often later.

Before bidding, *contractors* undertake to prepare for the first step. They retrieve information on the project, even before tender documents are sent to potential bidders or officially published in newspapers and electronic platforms (e.g., European Union's TED, *Tenders Electronic Daily*). Some data collection and networking is needed to retrieve additional information and understand the project's political and economic context, map the decision-making process, and see who the key decision-makers are. Bidding and going through the whole negotiation process is costly (i.e., the costs of bidding and negotiation, sometimes with limited chances of being finally selected). Nobody pays for these costs, expect the potential *contractors*. To bid or not to bid, that is the question. The first choice after this initial phase is therefore a *go-no go* decision, that is, to submit a bid or not, given a realistic assessment of one's chances of success.

If the decision is to go and bid, the next task is to prepare a bid in response to the tender. Bid preparation may take several weeks; however there is time pressure for the *contractor* since a clear deadline is indicated in the tender documents as to when bid documents must be received by the future project *owner*. The *owner* will then compare offers and try to reduce the number of bids (if too large to be conveniently handled) to a shortlist of say four or five potential bidders, based on the seriousness and references of the potential *contractors* (previous achievements matter a lot). Rather than *shortlisting* the credible potential *contractors*, the *owner* may first prepare an official *bidding list*, thereby clearly indicating which *contractors* are invited to submit an offer. After a prospective supplier is selected, the *owner* may return to another shortlisted supplier if one-to-one negotiation ends in an impasse. The bidding phase is a curious mix of strong formalism and relational exploration (often unofficial, indirect, and underground). After shortlisting (if necessary) and the selection of the final bidder (*contractor*) the one-to-one negotiation will end-up with significantly different provisions from what may have been stipulated in the bidding documents.

There are several forms of bidding procedures according to the WTO. WTO procedures are precisely there to foster competition between potential *contractors*. Bidding procedures are different from one-to-one Deal-Making (allowed by GPA only in case of repeated orders, prototypes, etc.). Remember that the *owner* is in a monopsony situation: A future project *owner* is the only buyer for this particular project and simultaneously the *owner* is in a sort of monopolistic situation (i.e., the only "seller" of a task that several buyers/contractors are willing to make a bid for). Different selection procedures enable the future project *owner* to be more or less open to all firms and/or to restrict bids to technically competent and financially sound *contractors*. In a restricted tender procedure only prequalified bidders will be granted access to the competition and will be awarded the contract (i.e., shortlisted). Price and/or quality as choice criteria are combined with open/restricted tenders in various ways:

- Open tender and lowest bidder (i.e., lowest price bidder will be automatically selected).
- Open tender and best bidder (best price-quality ratio offers more leeway in selection).
- Restricted tender (with prequalification) and lowest bidder.
- Restricted tender (with prequalification) and best bidder.
- Closed tender procedure (only selected suppliers are invited to submit a bid) and competitive process.

The final negotiation with a single supplier (e.g., a bilateral monopoly) prompts a major change in the power relationships between *owners* and *contractors*. The first phase is based on an auction and therefore gives considerable power to the *owner* because of its monopsony situation. Furthermore, there are a handful of such projects worldwide for a one-year period in a cyclical business due to derived demand effects on new investments in production capacity. It is therefore difficult for a particular *contractor* to enter an alliance with other *contractors* (competitors) unless they make a consortium, after the shortlist phase, and share responsibility and risks with the agreement of the *owner*. The *owner* may indeed want previous competing *contractors* to join forces and share the deal. At a broader level (i.e., over some years and on a global market for a particular type of project) market sharing agreements may secretly develop for controlling prices and the attribution of deals.

The final negotiation is multi-issue, multi-partner (e.g., consortium for seller and/or buyer) with non-monolithic parties involved in complex face-to-face negotiation. Because multiple parties are involved, information exchange may at times be confused, especially when it comes to writing the contract(s) including delay penalties and litigation clauses. Post-agreement negotiation related to implementation issues, renegotiation, and delay penalties is very likely to happen.

Negotiation is expected to last beyond deal signature. This involves planning and scheduling issues (see Chapter 4 as well as examples on building contracts for the Olympic Games), unforeseen events, changes in *owner's* project specifications, a political change in *owner's* country, delays (e.g., at the time of writing, the Berlin Brandenburg Airport was delayed by 7 years[10]). Contentious issues emerge related to construction and delay penalties. The *owner* and the *contractor* may end up in a blockade situation with the ardent obligation to negotiate a way out of stalemate.

Issues in negotiating ICBN projects

A major issue in negotiating project deals is whether a particular sale is a single, isolated project with no repeat business or whether there is a long-term relationship with deals being regularly concluded over time. For instance, in the oil, chemicals, cement, and iron and steel industries, major players in these industries tend to develop privileged relationships with particular engineering companies and *contractors*. Another important issue is the contractor's experience with the country and/or region, its language(s), culture, and institutional/legal system. Because of the joint implementation process, time culture will strongly matter (see Chapter 4). Knowledge gaps and interpretation discrepancies between the *contractor* and *owner* will lead to continuous negotiation throughout the duration of the construction process. On both sides, communication skills will be in great need: the capacity to exchange information, to clarify misunderstandings, and to avoid conflict escalation by rationally going back to facts and joint interests are key competencies.

Corruption is a serious concern in such large deals, and bribery issues (see Chapter 10) may emerge as well as self-made administrative hurdles by poorly paid civil servants who want to extract some additional resources from supposedly rich contractors (e.g., asking for small bribes for customs clearance). The buyer-future *owner* "sells the deal" while the seller-*contractor* "buys the deal". A kind of blackmail can be exercised by an opportunistic *owner*'s team threatening the selected contractor that they will go back to another firm on the shortlist or evict them from the deal if they do not indulge in bribery. Being evicted would be a disaster for the potential contractor who has gone very far in negotiations and has invested millions of dollars in pre-contract transaction costs. During the construction phase, there is a need for small "lubrication payments" and other favours and advantages granted to various civil servants such as customs officers or public administration employees. Thus, in many contexts, the acceptance of some "greasing" mechanisms is inevitable to ease the implementation of the deal. The role of third parties in project implementation should not be underestimated. Some countries require that an agent (e.g., a "sponsor" in Saudi Arabia) and/or consultant be hired, officially or unofficially, to serve as a go-between facilitating the negotiation between *owner* and contractor.

The contract should be crystal-clear about the scope of obligations and the responsibilities of each party. If needed, technology transfer issues, licensing, and patents should be comprised in a covenant. Schedules and deadlines are also important negotiation issues; clear dispositions as to which party should be attributed responsibility for delays have to be drafted. Delay penalties are a high stake issue. If unlimited in time, they could reach stratospheric levels and compromise the project. It is therefore recommended to: 1) limit the delay penalties to a reasonable percentage per month (e.g., 0.2%); 2) stipulate a "grace period" of some months during which no delay penalties can be claimed; 3) set a limit in time for delay penalties, (e.g., 20 months after the agreed upon construction delivery date, after which no delay penalties can be claimed); and 4) designate who (*owner*, contractor, or others) is responsible for a construction delay. Indeed a great many firms, small and large, contribute to a project in the form of construction batches with sometimes several hundred subcontractors in the limelight. Multiple, related and linked, smaller negotiations take place due to what is often called a "project cascade", sometimes diluting and blurring responsibility. Coordination is key.

Like the next – and last – type of ICBN agreement examined (Mergers and Acquisitions), the issue of the *winner's curse* has to be openly confronted by potential *contractors*. A *contractor* who is awarded the contract for a project wins the deal in a descending auction by pricing under all its competitors. This is especially true when the tender is open and selection is at the lowest price. The *Winner's Curse*[11] is a well-known expression for the following paradox: the contractor who is awarded the contract (i.e., the winner) will surely incur a loss (i.e., the curse). The winner's final price will not cover their costs because of the harsh dynamics of competition between sellers in a monopsony situation. However, *owners* are more or less obliged to renegotiate the price when it clearly appears that costs will not be covered. Interdependence is so high when construction is advanced that *owners* can rarely stick to the Winner's Curse price.

Cross-border mergers and acquisitions

The deal versus relationship perspective perfectly applies to M&A ICBNs. Either the goal is mostly financial and determined by share price (i.e., a merely calculative deal orientation) or the aim is seen mostly as strategic, and therefore relational, with a view to integrate the acquired or merged business(es) into a larger and more efficient whole. Merged or acquired firms generally share the same industry culture, unless they are diversified conglomerates with multiple divisions. However, they may not share the same organizational and national cultures, making the concrete implementation of the alliance a challenge in terms of learning and adjusting to a new corporate culture.

Background aspects of M&A negotiations

M&As combine two sorts of business operations. The first form is takeovers which consist in the acquisition of a company (Target) by another company (Acquirer), with two quite different underlying relational patterns, hostile or friendly. In hostile takeovers, the acquired company is assumed to be ingested without its deliberate consent, in fact against its resolve. At first a hostile take-over seems both calculative and strategic; however it is not relational because it is based on a unilateral move of the acquirer, unwelcomed by the target. Later, the acquiring firm must "digest" the acquisition; that is, a corporate body that perceives itself as a vanquished entity willing to let the conqueror pay a high price in revenge for its defeat. Consequently, a purely relational negotiation is in order in the post-takeover phase if (and only if) the plan is to integrate the Target's strategic business units within the acquiring company. However, if the takeover is a pure deal operation, with the Acquirer seeking to sell out the Target's strategic business units (SBUs) at a significant profit, after replacing the management teams, downsizing, and reengineering the divisions to make them more attractive to potential acquirers, an apparent relational orientation from the Acquirer would be mere lip service.

Conversely, in friendly takeovers, there are talks before the operation between Target and Acquirer on a joint strategic perspective which combines deal and relationship aspects. The to-be-acquired company may obtain a number of guarantees from the potential Acquirer as to its employees, management, brands, etc. with the caveat that these demands must remain acceptable for the acquirer and have a positive impact on collaboration and efficiency in the post-acquisition phase. Relationship-Building is therefore a key ingredient of friendly takeovers. It is also an opportunity for joint learning, sensemaking (i.e., developing a shared framework between two previously separated entities), and sensegiving (i.e., influencing the way other actors, not involved in the alliance negotiation process, will under-stand their role at implementation stage).[12]

Mergers are assumed to contain a strong joint strategic perspective, espe-cially when they are "Mergers between equals" such as the recent merger between Lafarge and Holcim, respectively number one and number two in the cement industry worldwide.[13] Mergers between "unequals" occur when one company is obviously stronger, larger, and in better financial shape than the other. This supposed Merger may indeed hide an acquisition (generally a friendly takeover), making the difference between Mergers and Acquisitions not so clear in practice. The merger between Daimler and Chrysler was a merger between unequals that failed while the later alliance between Fiat and Chrysler proved successful.[14] Some acquisitions tend to be disguised in merger operations for pride reasons, including national pride. Real mergers take place between equals.

When a particular region of the world and a definite industry are sought after, potential targets for either a takeover or merger are not abundant. The standard corporate situation is not to be for sale on the global M&A market. There are rarely several potential targets available for acquisition but frequently there are at least two potential acquirers (sometimes more). The market for acquisition targets is often a monopsonist one, with a limited number of buyers who are very unlikely to collude to make it a contraried monopsony because they often compete head-to-head to acquire the target firm. Therefore the situation where there are more than two potential acquirers is more likely than the opposite situation. A duopsony market situation, in which two potential acquirers compete for the same and only target, is frequent in M&As. The reasons for a company being "on sale" or ready for an acquisition disguised in a supposed "merger" vary. Why are targets rare? They must be both attractive and ready for sale. Let us examine different scenarios for the situation of the target for acquisition and its likely motivation to go for sale on the M&A market. In the first possible scenario, the Target is in a poor financial situation and is losing market share to competitors. In the worst case scenario, the to-be-acquired company is possibly about to go bankrupt. However, due to information asymmetry, A may not be aware of this; in fact, the Target's shareholders want to withdraw before it is too late. In the second scenario, the Target may be commercially and financially strong; however the owner or majority shareholders want to sell for some reasons (e.g., CEO may be retiring with no heirs or nobody is willing to follow as next CEO). Another motivation to sell out a business would be limited long-term prospects for the Target as a local player in a national market when the industry is quickly globalizing. The third scenario holds that the Target is not on sale; however it is a public company, listed on the stock exchange, and (more or less) easy to acquire due to a largely dispersed/unconcentrated shareholder base. Scenarios 1 and 3 lead to relatively calculative and deal-oriented approaches, possibly in the form of a hostile takeover, especially for scenario 3. Scenario 2 calls for a relational and strategic rather than a calculative and deal-oriented approach.

Issues for M&A negotiations

The main issue when a friendly and relational approach is preferred is to choose the right partner, to outline the practical modalities, and to define joint objectives for the post-operation period. A proper and independent evaluation of the Target is imperative for the Acquirer. Therefore audits of the Target should be performed[15] with the view to reduce information asymmetry and evaluate the fit between Target and Acquirer's organizations and potential benefits either derived from business growth or resulting from cost savings due to joint operations. Information asymmetry is lower for listed than non-listed targets, due to the availability of information when listed and the lack of public information for privately owned targets. Cultural differences, both organizational and national, should be examined as well as their likely influence on post-merger integration, especially when the Target is involved in a hostile merger or acquisition environment. Unattractive targets (e.g., low-price, cheap but dangerous targets with structural losses) have to be avoided, especially when the Acquirer becomes a majority shareholder and has to pay for the losses which may at the end amount to several times the low acquisition price.

Legal and fiscal aspects should be thoroughly examined for the following:

1) The new entity should comply with antitrust legislation especially for M&As between large corporations with a hefty combined market share (i.e., European Union Directorate General IV and U.S. Federal Trade Commission Antitrust legislation). Antitrust issues for large M&As may oblige merging companies to divest and sell assets on a number of markets.

2) Taxation issues, especially if the merged entities have different tax systems.

3) How and where to incorporate the new entity, given the significant differences in company statutes evidenced by comparative company law.[16]

In choosing between a hostile versus an amicable M&A (acquisition), it has to be kept in mind that relationship problems are preprogramed by a hostile start. In case of a hostile takeover, Target's management must generally quit and the acquired company is provisionally destabilized. Cooperation and joint projects between Acquirer and Targets may be compromised. This is all the more likely to be the case for takeovers with prospects of re-engineering, downsizing, job cuts, and therefore with an antagonistic employee base. National interests in keeping the to-be-acquired company in local hands may emerge with the resentment of the local population and public authorities: in this case, public authorities generally do their best to avoid a foreign takeover of the local target, especially if it is a "national champion". All aspects of cultural differences apply and may well compromise a merger, especially when it is supposed to be between equals, even if it is not always true in practice. The same caveat on cultural conflict applies to an acquisition, especially when the acquired target shifts from a strong power position before acquisition to a dominated situation after being acquired.

M&A negotiation process

A lot of preparation and pre-negotiation are needed to develop shared knowledge and particularly knowledge of each other. Preliminaries are useful to create some socialization, even between former competitors which may also have been "colleagues" at times. Even when undertaking hostile mergers and acquisitions, a certain degree of dialogue may be desired by the acquirer in order to argue that the planned operation may not be as unfriendly as perceived and to try to change the deal's atmosphere. On average, however, negotiation takes a very different orientation whether it is a joint project (integrative by nature) or a one-sided operation (distributive by nature). It is also useful to decide which people in each company should be involved (e.g., major shareholders, board members, management, employee representatives, unions) because the consequences of an M&A operation are far-reaching.[17]

Logically, a value increase should emerge from the M&A operation. The negotiation process will include debates on creating value and claiming value, with some uncertainties on which partner has created value and how much he or she is allowed to claim. Like in any negotiation, there is a risk of the process ending with no agreement. Each party, acquirer and/or acquired, should be prepared to walk away if needed, especially early in the process when significant incompatibly surfaces. Alternatives to an M&A are often not sufficiently taken into account before entering the M&A negotiation. ATNAs and a BATNA should therefore be set for any M&A negotiation process; typical ATNAs may be: to invest resources in internal rather than external growth; to examine and explore other possible targets for an acquisition or merger; another M&A operation in a different SBU; investing in a greenfield operation in a foreign country instead of acquiring a local player. This last ATNA enables the investor to start with a fully controlled operation rather than taking over a local business with its own practices, national and corporate culture, which may not fit with the Acquirer. M&A negotiations should remain embedded in the complete set of ATNAs with the BATNA as best alternative.

Like in project sales, the *Winner's curse* (again) is quite likely. An acquirer who wins a deal (i.e., buys a Target for acquisition) in an ascending auction for a particular item will agree to a final price above the actual value of this item.[18] Information asymmetry is frequent in M&A negotiation; therefore the *Winner's curse* will be less significant with a target listed on a stock exchange than with a private company. When Honda and BMW competed for the acquisition of Rover, Honda asked for the target to be listed before making an offer, in contrast with BMW which accepted to buy a non-listed target and later had major difficulties with the acquisition.

Moral: It is always possible to make an offer to a Target for acquisition and win some money, but not on average. As an acquirer, a company has more chances of losing than gaining money. It is important to remember that targets for acquisition have full information on themselves while candidates for their acquisition have quite incomplete information. In takeovers and M&As, the acquired generally makes a better deal than the acquirer.[19] However, the real value creation comes in the post-acquisition phase when it becomes clear whether the strategic plans and the compatibility of corporate cultures enable value creation or not. That is why post-merger relationships between the joined entities are a key issue for M&As.

Notes

1 See Fainshmidt, White, and Cangioni (2014).
2 The TRIPS (Agreement on Trade-Related Aspects of Intellectual Property Rights) negotiated in the WTO has imposed minimal standards for protection of IPR worldwide (see www.wto.org/english/tratop_e/trips_e/intel2_e.htm). IPRs are still an important negotiation matter within the WTO with heated debates, especially for pharmaceutical patents and trademarks.
3 Benjamin Franklin, from chapter 10 of his Autobiography (which is available at the esteemed Project Gutenberg). Retrieved from http://slashdot.org/articles/01/03/18/1339201.shtml, accessed 21 August 2017.

4 The acceptability of a particular brand name for trademark registration must be proven (in terms of originality and anteriority) and covers only particular product or service categories. Brand names are different from shop signs, models, or designs: different legal responses exist according to country. Despite the existence of international conventions and an international organization (World Intellectual Property Organization, WIPO), trademark registration largely remains a matter to be treated at national level, except at EU level. Note that trademarks, as industrial property rights, are different from intellectual property rights (copyright for books, records, movie films, etc.).

5 *Patents* protect the inventor's rights (issues with originality, precedence, and applicability). Patents are still largely on a national basis, despite some international patent conventions (e.g., Paris Union of 1899, precedence right). Patent registration has the drawback of "informing" competitors. What is technically original is not necessarily patentable. There is much diversity in registration and patent prolongation procedures according to countries, despite the TRIPS agreement, international treaties (e.g., Patent Cooperation Treaty), and International Organizations such as the WIPO and the European Patent Office.

6 See Parker (2003).

7 See Urban (1996).

8 In the BOT or BOOT (build-own-operate-transfer) framework the *owner* hires the *contractor* to design and build the project, but also to operate the facility for a certain period of time. The facility is transferred to the *owner* at the end of the period.

9 See www.wto.org/english/tratop_e/gproc_e/gp_gpa_e.htm.

10 See Gavin Haines, "The farcical saga of Berlin's new airport – whatever happened to German efficiency?" *The Telegraph*, 1 June 2017, accessible at www.telegraph.co.uk/travel/news/the-crazy-saga-of-berlins-long-delayed-airport/

11 See Thaler (2012).

12 See Kumar and O'Nti (1998) and Kumar and Patriotta (2011), who illustrate by comparing unsuccessful and successful alliances (e.g., Nissan-Renault).

13 On the Lafarge-Holcim merger, see www.bloomberg.com/gadfly/articles/2016-07-13/lafargeholcim-50-billion-cement-merger-gives-no-cause-to-celebrate.

14 See Watkin (2007).

15 Audit costs may be paid by the Acquirer, by the Target, or shared between them. See De Beaufort and Lempereur in IBN (2003, pp. 301–307).

16 See De Beaufort and Lempereur (2003).

17 Cf. De Beaufort and Lempereur (2003).

18 Thus the introduction of the Vickrey auction (the winner is the highest bidder at the price of the second highest bidder), however with little success in practice.

19 A good illustration is the 2016 acquisition by the world leader in liquefied gas, Air Liquide, of the American company Airgas, at 40% more than the listed share value. By early 2018, Air Liquide's share had lost 15% of its 2016 value.

10 Ethical issues in ICBN

> The prudent man is always sincere, and feels horror at the very thought of exposing himself to the disgrace which attends upon the detection of falsehood. But though always sincere, he is not always frank and open; and though he never tells any thing but the truth, he does not always think himself bound, when not properly called upon, to tell the whole truth. As he is cautious in his actions, so he is reserved in his speech; and never rashly or unnecessarily obtrudes his opinion concerning either things or persons.
>
> (Adam Smith, *The Theory of Moral Sentiments*, 1790, p. 193)

"Mouth smiles, money smiles better", says a Ghanaian proverb. Money is always at the very centre of business negotiations, as price is discussed as well as "side price". This is all the more important when the whole process takes place across borders; that is, with a limited control of national regulatory authorities compared with the domestic scene. Traditionally, most laws, including tax and anti-corruption regulations, do not apply beyond national borders, although extra-territorial legislation has developed over the last 40 years. It is always tempting to win a deal by offering a bribe rather than by fair competition. Moreover, significant price and performance advantages over competitors sometimes do not suffice: some greasing money may be discreetly asked for by the buyers.

Bribery is considered by most business people as the key ethical issue in ICBN. More than one-third of a sample of U.S. executives ranked bribery as the top ethical concern out of ten possible ethical problems that may arise when negotiating international business.[1] Similarly, Australian and Canadian managers rank gifts, favours and entertainment, traditional small-scale bribery, and the confusing issue of whether gifts are intended as bribes or not in different cultures, as the three key ethical problems in international marketing out of a list of ten.[2]

However, there are other ethical concerns in ICBN which are related to *behaviour during the negotiation process*. Apart from buying the contract (through bribes), a party can:

- buy information in order to get strategic insight into the other party's basic interests, situation, and organization;
- buy the influence of members of the adversary negotiation team or of their principals;
- use instrumental communication to mislead the other party and gain advantage in the process, for instance by disclosing erroneous information on costs, investments, and dates;
- negotiate and sign clauses which, although legal in principle, will grossly disadvantage the other party in the future; in doing so, one party exploits the ignorance of the other;
- network with people and firms in the opposite negotiation group and do a number of reciprocal favours such as hiring their relatives or granting privileged access to positions that would normally be open to all applicants;
- negotiate, knowing in advance that they will not respect their commitments toward the other party or step out of the negotiation before an agreement is reached.

In the first section I examine the special case of negotiation ethics, especially in an intercultural context. Negotiation is not *per se* an ethical activity since instrumental communication, manipulative persuasion, and sometimes strategic misrepresentation are used to serve competitive goals. I provide a first explanation as to how and when moves by one party or the other can be viewed as unethical. The main ethical issue when negotiating internationally, that is, bribery, is analysed in the second section. The third section reviews a number of other ethical issues in ICBN. While they do not involve criminal activity as bribery does, they are important because the views of what is ethically acceptable may differ across negotiating parties. The fourth section presents ethical standpoints for ICBN and explains when particular ethical issues must be appreciated from a universalistic (IT1), culturally relativist (IT2), or morally pragmatic perspective (i.e., an attempt at combining IT1 and IT2 perspectives). The fifth section reviews recent advances in the fight against corruption at the global level that international negotiators should take into account. Finally, I propose some recommendations for action based on a compromise between the moral/legal and the pragmatic/competitive perspectives.

Ethicality in ICBN

Ethicality in ICBN is a special case of business ethics. There is little published literature on the topic of behaving fairly, ethically, and honestly in business negotiations. One reason may be that business negotiations are overwhelmingly confidential, that is, unobservable. Another reason is that negotiation activities are inherently competitive and there is a latent view that "everything is allowed". Taking advantage of a number of key asymmetries between both camps, related to information, power, or cognitive abilities, seems rather legitimate, especially if behaviour is unobservable and undetected. A lot of exploitative micro-moves in the negotiation process obey such a logic of being hidden and therefore remaining unnoticed (i.e., "leave nothing behind, even your footprints"): instrumental communication and/or strategic misrepresentation,[3] which aim at manipulating the other party, or non-reciprocation by one camp of voluntary information disclosure or a concession by the other side, etc. In general, exploitative micro-moves, although deceitful practices, are considered part of the negotiation game, in-between bluffing in a poker game and cheating in a game of cards. If a bluff or a small or strategic misrepresentation is later discovered by the exploited party, they tend not to complain because they fear being viewed as naive and being further exploited. However, when clearly on the cheating side, that is, for instance by concealing essential flaws and weaknesses in the items offered, there is legislation in most countries that protects the buyer from defects voluntarily hidden by the seller.

There are also more significant (macro) opportunistic moves such as concealing one's real intentions and negotiation goals, buying strategic information, secretly purchasing influence from third parties, and bypassing the mandatary negotiators on the other side of the table by settling the final agreement directly with their powerful principal from whom they receive a mandate with compulsory instructions. Opportunistic moves may take many other forms: covertly buying key information from an insider from the other party, who does not necessarily sit at the negotiation table; clandestinely enticing interpreters to work for your camp; or secretly inducing powerful third parties such as an arbiter to make their decision in your favour (a rare case). In the negotiation of know-how licences, the prospective licensee may enter into negotiation with the sole aim to gather proprietary information on the technology that the to-be licensor has not patented. The prospective licensee has the firm, but hidden, intention to step out of the negotiation process when enough data has been collected to replicate the know-how.[4]

However, the most significant category of unethical behaviour in business negotiations is buying influence on signing the deal, for instance, large-scale bribery in international contracts, especially by corrupting powerful public officials who are in a position to award the deal. The unethicality of bribing practices is directly revealed by their opacity: they should be invisible, therefore unseen and undetected. In practice, they rarely remain fully secret. Therefore, a number of intermediaries must be compensated (i.e., receive their own "brown paper packet") for closing their eyes on such corrupt behaviour, which is universally illegal.

In an intercultural context, ethical issues in negotiation become even more complex and trickier to deal with. This is first because some differences in communication style and culture, possibly language idiosyncrasies intermingled with ambiguous micro-moves, make it difficult to clearly assess whether these micro-moves are opportunistic or standard behaviour in a culture which is unfamiliar. For instance, indirect communication may be unduly equated with the use of instrumental and manipulative statements by another party which has a direct communication style. This party assumes that directness in information exchange signals frankness, honesty, and trustworthiness as a negotiation partner, and vice versa for indirectness. Similarly, in high-context (HC) communication cultures, there may be a large discordance between words and deeds, simply because it seems to HC negotiators self-evident that words and sentences should not be taken at face value (because these statements may, after being put in context, mean the contrary to what was explicitly said). Conversely, in LC cultures, negotiators are used to being more explicit, digital, precise, univocal, and to having much less discrepancy between words and deeds, although at times they may use vague speech. However, such broader discourse is "officially", explicitly meant to be – voluntarily – less explicit. LC negotiators will sometimes resent HC negotiators as being instrumental and manipulative, and sometimes think that HC people lie.

From these two examples, it is obvious that (inner) ethical judgements in ICBN micro-moves should be thoughtfully prepared, even more cautiously expressed, and phrased in such a way that they do not appear offensive to the HC partner. However, when it becomes clear that, beyond the artefacts of communication styles, micro-moves are repeatedly opportunistic, instrumental, and intentionally misrepresentative, a clear explanation is in order.

The second reason ICBN ethics are more complex than domestic/intracultural negotiations is the wide array of ethical behaviour worldwide, not so much in principle as in practice. In many local contexts, although it may be formally illegal and the author severely punished (if an individual is caught, which is rare), bribery is common practice. The realities and constraints of many countries (e.g., unpaid custom officers, poorly paid policemen) are conducive to self-serving practices for everyone in a position of power, small or large. Empirical research shows that general ethical beliefs as well as the relative importance of ethical issues vary according to country and culture, but not according to religion.[5] By and large, ethical principles are universal (i.e., cardinal virtues such as wisdom, courage, justice, temperance, humanity, and transcendence) and seem to apply globally,[6] whereas practices are local, and vary considerably. Beyond this broad simplification, the debate in intercultural ethics is between moral universalism and ethical relativism, a theme later developed in this chapter. A seemingly realistic position, especially in the business domain, is to "Do as the Romans in Rome": accept ethical relativism and endorse local corrupt practices, although with some reluctance. However, much anti-corruption legislation is extra-territorial in application; that is, it applies to most countries, beyond the particular context where the legislation was passed, provided that a national citizen and/or organization is involved. Even if tolerated in a local context where bribery has taken place, corrupters (individuals and/or organizations) may be prosecuted and their "sins" punished in their country of origin. There are many other arguments against simplistic ethical relativism:[7] 1) corruption is detrimental to local contexts in terms of both economic development and political stability; 2) even if, superficially, bribery seems accepted, a large part of the local population disapproves of it; there is much internal criticism of corrupt practices, especially where it is everyday practice; and 3) by adding one more bribe, a company feeds an already corrupt scene and increases the odds that fraudulent behaviour develops rather than dies out.

Bribery in ICBN

Forms of bribery

The practice is widespread and takes various forms:

- *Small and large gifts*: for instance, a multinational company offers a leading foreign politician a two week stay in a nice resort; the whole affair, including receptions, restaurants, and entertainment for the evenings, quickly reaches a cost of $50,000.
- *Percentages* based on the contract value itself. Here the form of illegal payment results in much larger sums being paid because of the size of the contract such as the sale of a turnkey plant.
- *Tips*: when civil servants are poorly paid, but hold authority and responsibility it may be "implicitly understood" that in exchange for carrying out poorly rewarded public duties, such officials may supplement their income. Thus obtaining information for the negotiation process or a tax form for a mandatory declaration may require some greasing payment, which can be assimilated to an implicit salary. In most cases, the authorities are well aware of the existence of such practices. In 2014, 232,000 Chinese civil servants and officials were punished for bribery charges, a 30% increase over 2013;[8] however, they accounted for only about 3% of the Chinese administrative system. Publicity surrounding these bribery affairs has augmented the fears of Chinese officials especially as some were invited to visit former colleagues in prison. But the "stick" was not sufficient for anti-corruption campaigns and, on such a large scale, it may have been excessively scary for poorly paid civil servants. A "carrot" was also needed. In early 2015, the Chinese authorities announced an average pay rise of 60% with the base salary of the lowest ranking civil servant being increased to Yuan 1,320 ($212), more than twice as much as they previously[9] earned, which was still not much.

In many countries, business activities are highly regulated and a host of different ministries are entitled to issue licences for various activities. Since inspectors from government bodies have the right to inspect companies at any time and for almost any reason, local managers spend much of their time on inspections. Inspectors have much leeway in their dealings with companies. As a consequence, bribing inspectors is a quick and efficient path for managers to obtain official approval. Such a situation is depicted by Werner as concerns the ex-Soviet republic of Kazakhstan, where "nothing is allowed but everything is possible [provided that you pay for it!]".[10]

Whether illegal payments are made and what sums are involved varies widely from one country and one industry to another. Bribes will be much more substantial in the construction industry or in Nigeria than in electronics or in Australia. Not everyone is corrupt. There is nothing worse than attempting to bribe someone who strongly disapproves of such immoral behaviour. Socially accepted bribing is akin to gift exchange in that it follows a culturally coded etiquette which indicates who is willing to accept a bribe, where and when it can safely be given, and what to say and do when presenting the bribe to the recipient. The direct method of passing cash is dangerous and ineffective. Accordingly, more indirect methods are often used:

- *Slush funds* are set up to make small payments by cheque, nominally as payment for services rendered. Systematically overstated expense reports are a commonly used means for funding slush funds: auditors may discover them when expense report copies are marked up from the actual expense, with markups averaging 1,000% of the real sum. A company can sell to a subsidiary without making any record of the transactions in their accounts and use this money to set up a slush fund that in turn feeds a secret bank account. This secret account is then used to pay "commissions" to intermediaries, civil servants, and influential people, clearly breaching the law.
- *Nominee and local consultancy companies*, to which phoney consulting contracts are awarded, may be used in different ways. For example, an adviser of the Transport Minister for country X who is well placed may be approached to influence the decision on an underground railway project in town Y. It will be suggested that he or she be made a part-time employee of the Luxembourg-based nominee company. Without having to move an inch, he or she will receive a salary each month which, for reasons of discretion and convenience, will be paid into an account in Switzerland. The adviser/consultant will take the money out of this bank account in Geneva, then discreetly spend it in an exclusive ski-resort. Money spent abroad is less visible than money brought back home.
- Two other solutions are frequently employed: the *over-invoicing* of certain transactions, expenditure, or receipts, and the *recording of fictitious transactions*. For example, a foreign company, obliged to pay a 10% commission to obtain the contract for the construction of a turnkey plant, artificially inflates the price of the contract, then records a commission for consultancy fees, without rendering any such service of this type. This allows the 10% commission to become a tax deductible

expenditure, and makes the payment apparently legitimate, whereas in fact it remains illegal.

The process of illegal payments

The process of secret payments involves the negotiators (briber/bribee), the way their relation is sealed, the authorities to whom they report, as well as the style of communication they use in this sensitive and precarious business. Both the donor and the recipient of the illegal payment take risks; bribery being punished in some countries by the death penalty. Donors, as individual negotiators, are poorly rewarded for the risks they take as they may be prosecuted while their organization wins a large contract. On the other side, the bribee's reward depends on the ultimate allocation of the money. If it goes into the bribee's own pocket, risk-taking can be viewed from the perspective of individual interest, opportunism, and moral standards. If the money goes to a political party, it is more difficult to assess the nature of individual responsibility because of the lack of direct and personal benefits.

Bribers and bribees are not isolated individuals. They work in negotiation teams and report to higher authorities. Whenever bribees personally request the bribe, they most often have to share it with other people. In turnkey contracts, both the contractor and the owner are complex organizations which comprise various companies, ministries, utilities, and agencies, all of which are involved in the decision-making process. A key issue is to keep the bribe secret when dividing it up within the owner's group which acquires the plant. Anyone who could potentially exert blackmail, such as a secretary who types a compromising letter or a minister who has to sign a letter related to the deal, must therefore be "paid off".

Messages exchanged during the bribery process will never be straightforward. First, communication between the potential parties serves to set the rules of the game, and to ensure that relationships will be "fair" (if fairness can ever exist in such affairs). Potential bribees may discreetly signal their willingness to be bribed by casually mentioning personal acquaintances and their influence and connections, as well as confidential information local acquaintances can find. This will be softly phrased, without once raising the subject of money. It may even be explicitly stated that money does not matter; demanding a bribe is largely implicit. Other potential bribees may complain about the poor salary earned as a customs officer, then hint at a missing document, and ultimately mention their effectiveness at granting customs clearance. This is an implicit call for compensation to the foreign business people who are seeking to obtain clearance of imported equipment.

Buying influence

Negotiators are sometimes led to buy "big influence", on the signature of large contracts, rather than "small influence" related to the day-to-day implementation of such contracts. It is not rare to see the ruler of a country (e.g., a president for life or a dictator) appear almost astonished to be criticized for having accumulated huge sums of money as a result of illegal payments while in power. Some dictators have transferred the equivalent of a large part of their country's foreign debt to foreign bank accounts. These rulers are instinctively convinced that the state is theirs and their family's property, and sincerely believe that power entitles them to use their position for personal enrichment. It may be more or less socially accepted if most people, on their own level, sell their personal power of influence. The practice is so ingrained that late President Mobutu of the Democratic Republic of Congo is reported to have said in a speech: "If you are going to steal, steal a small amount and do it intelligently, in a nice way. If you are going to steal so much that you become rich in a single night, you will be arrested".[11]

Local entrepreneurs in many developing countries cite bribery as the prominent obstacle to business life. Average citizens unfortunately get used to the behaviour of officials securing special privileges for themselves and their close friends and consider that politicians are primarily interested in taking advantage of their power position. Economic power is intermingled with political influence such as in the tradition known as *coronelismo* in Brazilian politics which corresponds to the case of wealthy landowners who can bribe, manipulate, and pressure the local electorate to vote for the candidates they choose. *Coronelismo* still flourishes in isolated and impoverished regions of the Brazilian countryside.

Bribery can almost be compared to a property right.[12] Legally accepted property rights (e.g., real estate property, shares, patents, etc.) permit companies and individuals to know a priori what they can reasonably expect in their dealings with other members of the community. These expectations manifest themselves in the laws, customs, and morals of a society. In the case of international bribery, the right – originally based on customary law, therefore unwritten and implicit – consists of deriving personal profit from a position of power over the signature of public deals. Property rights should be exclusive and transferable. An exclusive right occurs when one single individual receives all the profits, but also has to bear all the adverse consequences that may arise. These rights must be assignable and transferable since the individual must be able to proceed to effective arbitrage. He must be permanently in a position to exchange property rights on efficient markets on which these rights are quoted. Except for dictators who establish a quasi-ownership over their country, rights on the signature of deals are rarely exclusive. Moreover, in most cases, these rights are not transferable, or only in a very limited way, to an heir in dictatorship.

To maintain such "property rights" on the signature of deals, expenses have to be made: 1) to ensure respect of one's rights by others (bodyguards, secret agents, repression of enemies, elimination of economic and political opponents, etc.); and 2) to improve the efficiency of one's property rights, which may extend to paying for a sophisticated information network (i.e., spies). "Property rights" on the signature of large deals are temporary and partially exclusive; they should be considered only as subjective and implicit. Therefore business negotiators who are led to accept making illegal payments internationally face the risk of letting themselves be dragged along by the megalomaniac subjectivity of an authoritative ruler who, seeing the country as his personal property, sells the right to win business there. These rights are not transferable and no dictator rules for ever. Furthermore "property rights" on the signature of deals are never legally recognized; most countries officially prohibit the use of any position of authority for personal enrichment. Even when bribes are a widespread practice, it should be kept in mind that they are legally forbidden and punished if discovered.

Gifts and bribes

Often in ICBN, the seller's team in an export sale or the foreign partner in a joint venture may find it appropriate to offer gifts to their negotiation partners. It may make sense especially if they are hosted by their partners who spend time and effort accommodating them comfortably. Gifts are part of universal traditions of courtesy and obey local norms of reciprocity. It may be difficult to distinguish a bribe from a tip or a commission or consulting fee. The lack of a clear boundary between gifts and bribes is evidenced by local words. In Kazakhstan there are ten words for different types of gifts and ritual payments according to the context and the nature of the gift; for instance *kiit* and *minit* are gifts to in-laws, the first in the form of clothing, the second in livestock or money. However, the word for bribe, *para*, is used consistently to refer to illegal exchanges.

> ... a traffic policeman may extort a relatively small amount of money, the local equivalent of a few dollars, from an innocent driver. In a different context, a young man who needs a job might voluntarily pay a bribe of $500 to $1,500 to a military official, who in return will forge a document specifying that the young man is exempt from military service for health reasons ($500) or a document specifying that the young man has already completed his military service ($1,500).
>
> (Werner, 2000, p. 18)

What appears *at first sight* as a gift may be in fact close to bribery. For instance: are 12 bottles of Champagne – worth $600 – a gift or a bribe? Small gifts, say less than $50, are not considered bribes in most contexts, but they can also be perceived as somewhat ridiculous presents; that is, offensive to receivers as their small size possibly suggests a lack of true commitment and even contempt towards the receiver(s). Another area of difference is whether gifts are products or services. Gifts such as a sea cruise around the world or a paid ski holiday are generally more difficult to put into the "bribe" category. There is no direct money involved (it is paid for) or physical gift implied, although the receiver of this real bribe would have had to pay several thousand dollars for the trip.

To try to define the border between gifts and bribes it is necessary to list basic distinctive criteria:

1) *Size*: obviously the larger the gift, the more it tends to become a bribe; American legislation, for instance, allows gifts of small value as well as "lubrication payments".

2) *Intent*: a gift is not meant to be made in exchange for a favour whereas a bribe compensates for illegal action; *intentionality* is a basic element of the bribing process, either on the donor's or the receiver's side.

3) *Who is the recipient?* A bribe given to a head of state cannot be directly compared with that given to a customs officer for easing the customs process or obtaining a visa.

4) *Nature* of the "object" being given (tangible versus intangible) – as noted above, intangible gifts, offering trips, favours to relatives or near acquaintances, etc. are more difficult to consider as bribes, although they may be as much so as tangibles.

5) *Circumstances* in which the gift is given: if openly done, in official and public circumstances, it is less likely to be perceived as a bribe and more as a gift, than if the whole process is secret and hidden.

6) *Degree and nature of reciprocity*: Reciprocation for gifts often takes place instantly by the practice of cross-gifts; in the case of a bribe, there is no such reciprocation: money is given in exchange for key information, the awarding of contracts, etc.

7) *Existence of a legal definition of business gifts*, that is, the size and nature of legal business gifts to people who underwrite contracts.

8) *Local customs*: in some countries the traditional gift economy, based on the exchange of reciprocal presents and favours, is still very strong; for instance in Japan gift rituals remain central in social life.

9) *"Poisonous gifts"*: In order to exert pressure, the briber may send a gift to somebody who has not asked to be bribed and feels embarrassed with the "gift". The receiver may send it back without complaining, because he or she would be suspected of having asked for it.

Personal connections, networking, buying, and disclosing information

Information is a key issue in business negotiations. There is a grey area between what is ethical and what is not as concerns information exchange as shown by the following questions/dilemmas (Volkema, 1999, p. 59):

> Is it appropriate to seek information from friends and associates during a negotiation? Is it ethical to offer gifts or pay friends and associates

for this information? Is it appropriate to hide your bottom line during a negotiation? Is it ethical to distort your bottom line? To lie about it? Is it right to talk to an opponent's supervisor or subordinate? To try to recruit subordinates of your opponent with the understanding that they will bring important information with them?

Often, the cultivation of social networks appears as a prerequisite to obtaining key information.[13] However, there is some ambiguity involved in trying to develop personal connections, because some informants in the buyer's team may be used against their own camp, and favours obtained through networking may unduly discriminate against competing sellers.

Using agents for networking and influencing purposes

In international tenders, for instance, the organizational links within the owner consortium are often not clearly defined. A state-owned utility may acquire a turnkey factory under the supervision of different ministries and banks; various consultants may also intervene. The areas of responsibility are vaguely defined. As influences can be diverse and relational networks complex, an agent who is an insider in the client organization may offer a chance to escape the labyrinth by identifying the relevant officials and assessing the extent of their influence, and may ultimately influence them. The agent may therefore: 1) supply the seller with confidential information on the client organization; 2) supply the seller with information on competitors; 3) spread misleading information to discredit a competitor, or to avoid imminent signature of the contract with this competitor; 4) identify potential bribe recipients among influential people; and 5) share out the illegal payment among bribees.

The agency relationship involves delegating decision-making from the principal to the agent. Agent-principal relationships may give rise to opportunistic behaviour. Each individual may seek to extract personal profit from any flaws in the agency contract. Flaws will be large in the case of corruption, since "bribery contracts" are never written down. It is not unheard of for bribes to be given to intermediaries without the contract being ultimately won. Because of the risks incurred when hiring an agent, agency costs relate to controlling the agent. Possible retaliation measures against the agent and/or a bonus on the signature of the deal may dissuade the agent from behaving opportunistically. "Commissions" must be paid at the last possible moment, once the signature of the deal is imminent and the selection of the final contracting party is effectively decided and cannot be changed. Games akin to hide and seek will often be played between the contractor and the agent in this final stage. As a result it may be worth considering an extension of the agency relationship. Providing for the continuation of the relationship after the deal is signed will ensure that the agent controls his or her behaviour in the hope of future gains.

290 Agreements, ethics, and styles in ICBN

Ethical aspects of disclosing information to the other party

There are various ways to manipulate the other party by: 1) strategic mis-representation, for instance, when a seller's team discloses alleged technical problems of a well-placed competitor; 2) hiding key information (e.g., a new technology is about to make the patent for a licensing agreement obsolete); 3) falsifying information; that is, willingly altering figures, data, and information in order to influence the other party's decision-making process; or 4) putting pressure by raising false arguments (e.g., "our future CEO will refuse such deals: sign now or it will be too late!").

There are, for instance, significant differences between Brazil and the United States in terms of strategic misrepresentation: Americans perceive themselves less likely to misrepresent information and to bluff (feign threats, lead on opponents) than Brazilians. Moreover, Americans tend to consider this kind of behaviour as less appropriate than Brazilians. There are also significant differences between American, Canadian, Australian, and Dutch people as concerns a number of controversial practices when negotiating sales (false promises used to close sales, cheating on the bidding process, spying on competition), the Dutch and Canadians being on average more tolerant of strategic misrepresentation than Americans and Australians.[14]

Taken at first glance, all these tactics seem to be unethical from a universalist point of view. However, they are used in ICBN, at least on the fringe, because the true reality is never so clear-cut. When the (future) buyer states that one of your competitors is ready to offer the same performance for a price 10% lower, it is quite difficult to check whether it is a pure lie, a simple bluff, or a slightly transformed truth. Different cultures do not value honesty and sincerity to the same degree, especially when it relates to information exchange. Americans value the exchange of representative information as a key attitude for building trust between the parties. For other cultures, playing with words and information is acceptable even between long-term business partners, especially because high-context communication (IT2) partners assume that messages will be interpreted and not taken literally.

Negotiators who asks for information disclosure and receive confidential information from the other party must in some way reciprocate. There are ethical issues involved in asking questions and giving answers in ICBN. Would it be fair for a party to ask for the disclosure of proprietary information by the other party? Should the other party consequently feel obliged to answer, given that the disclosed information may be exploited if negotiation talks break? The answer to both questions is obviously, no. However, one should be aware that there is always less ethical pressure involved in asking questions than in answering them. Negotiators whose cultures value openmindedness, sincerity, and frankness can be unfairly exploited by partners who mostly ask questions. Herb Cohen (1980, p. 103) remarks:

Some of us assume that the more intimidating or flawless we appear to others, the more they will tell us. Actually, the opposite is true. The more confused and defenseless you seem, the more readily they will help you with information and advice... With this approach you will find it easy to listen more than talk. You should prefer asking questions to giving answers. In fact you ask questions even when you think you know the answers, because, by doing so, you test the credibility of the other side.

Networking

Networking may involve the use of insider contacts at the detriment of competitors. To network with people and firms it is often necessary to exchange a number of reciprocal favours such as hiring relatives, granting privileged access to positions that would normally be open to all applicants, etc. What is acceptable or not when networking and socializing is differently perceived in ICBN. Nepotism, for instance, which is considered evil by IT1 negotiators, may be normal and even necessary for IT2 negotiators because of strong ingroup orientation. Ingroup bonds involve loyalty relationships which can be based on kinship or patronage. The concrete virtue manifested in loyalty is maintaining allegiance, even when faced with conflicts with other members of the ingroup or when experiencing unfair treatment from the most powerful members. Ingroup versus outgroup orientations have a deep influence on actual systems of ethics and morality. Strong ingroup orientation (IT2) increases loyalty among insiders and legitimizes nepotism, patronage, and clientelism while simultaneously lessening moral obligations towards outsiders. It might, for instance, be considered perfectly virtuous for the ingroup to lie to or steal from the outgroup to whom no loyalty is owed. The Mafia as an ingroup-oriented secret society favours strict loyalty.[15]

Conversely, outgroup orientation (IT1) values universal rules, applied to everybody: human rights ethics are a typical feature of outgroup orientation. Impersonal rules applied by independent judges to anyone is typical of high outgroup orientation. Objectivity and reciprocity are preferred over subjective relationships and loyalty; or, stated differently, loyalty is not toward people but to the impersonal rules and values that govern the society as a whole. While the mix of friendship and business in negotiation is fairly universal, attitudes towards networking and social relationships in ICBN differ significantly between ingroupist and outgroupist ethics.

The IT1 outgroupist approach to business networks emphasizes that relationships between companies, built out of the history of the companies' dealings with each other, matter as much as mere elements of the deal itself; that is, hard data on product specifications, price, and terms of contract. In business networks, personal contacts matter because they serve to reduce the uncertainty linked to complex deals by face-to-face exchange of information on technical, organizational, and commercial matters. "Mutual trust, respect and personal friendship between participants allows confidential information to be exchanged".[16] Personal contacts also enable interacting partners in the network to assess each other's competence, to negotiate implementation issues and beyond-the-letter-of-the-contract issues in complex negotiations. In case of critical problems, they offer a framework for quick information exchange and decisions about corrective measures. Personal contacts also play a social role. However, market rationality and the doing orientation keep the lead in the IT1 view of networking. People are there to "close the deal", not to enjoy the charms of social life or to indulge in patronage. Relationships should be "good but distant".

> ... companies are not likely to encourage interaction which is only socially based. There is an expectation that other elements of inter-action (such as information exchange, product sales or purchases and adaptations) would also result. There is evidence from the research that buyers are more inclined to maintain "good but distant" relationships than salesmen. Yet some suppliers see the dangers of too close an involvement of their salesmen with customers, in that they may lose their objectivity and take actions in the interests of the social relationships, rather than in the wider interests of their company.
>
> (Ford, 1990, p. 83)

The very notion of *guanxi* can to a large extent be considered as the Chinese and more broadly East Asian form of networking based on the continuous maintenance of relationships with the appropriate organizations and individuals within these organizations. Chinese *guanxi* corresponds to *Kankei* in Japan and *Kwankye* in Korea, that is, after-hours socialization which become important forums for meeting and convincing key decision-makers in a socially more comfortable atmosphere.[17] *Guanxi* mixes social behaviour and business practices in a complex set of disinterested and interested personal interactions. It is not necessarily directed at short-term results and consists of an investment in relationships which may or may not be called upon in the future. The practice of *guanxi* translates into large sales forces for maintaining contacts and large account receivables (in a way similar to the liberal credit policy in Japanese *Keiretsu*). Firms engaged in a connected set of companies, called *guanxihu*, do their best to avoid embarrassing a business partner experiencing temporary financial problems. *Guanxi* has been shown to be strongly favourable to the performance of international joint ventures in China as well as for foreign-invested enterprises in China and Chinese domestic firms.[18]

The Chinese concept of *guanxi* shares some common traits with the Western concept of networking, especially the continuity of business relationships and a framework for understanding the relationships between firms engaged in cooperative rather than competitive behaviour. There are, however, some significant differences which Luo and Chen (1997, pp. 3–4) explain as follows:

... *guanxi* primarily relates to personal, not to corporate, relations, and exchanges that take place amongst members of the *guanxi* network are not solely commercial, but also social, involving the exchange of *renqing* (social or humanized obligation) and the giving of *mianzi* (face in the society), or social status. This feature often leads *guanxi* to be named "social capital". In contrast, networking in Western marketing and management literature is the term primarily associated with commercially based corporate-to-corporate relations. Because of this difference, many Western business people are often in danger of overemphasizing the gift-giving and wining-and-dining components of a *guanxi* relationship, thereby coming dangerously close to crass bribery or to be perceived as "meat and wine friends" which is a Chinese metaphor for mistrust.

From an ethical perspective, the question is not only "Does *guanxi* work?", it is also whether *guanxi* is always ethical. To some extent, *guanxi* is a word which is synonymous in Chinese with corruption. There is debate, even within China, whether *guanxi* is moral or an unfortunate, though necessary, evil for those willing to do business in China.[19] Dunfee and Warren highlight the problematic aspects of *guanxi*: it benefits a few at the expense of many, it may result in the violation of important fiduciary duties, and may violate universal ethical norms. Furthermore, it may not be supported by those involved:

A community of bureaucrats may support *guanxi* because it operates to their personal advantage. In contrast, a community of managers expected to deal with the bureaucrats may not support *guanxi* because they must compete in broader markets and managers need to make staffing and business decisions on the basis of merit.

(Dunfee and Warren, 2001, p. 201)

Commitment ethics

Commitment is a serious concern for ICBN ethics, dealing not so much with the process itself but with negotiation outcomes, after the contract has been implemented. A relativist approach of what "commitment" means is needed. The English word "commitment" cannot be appropriately translated in many languages because it loses much of its strength as a self-obligation; that is, as an IT1 ethical attitude of *doing* what one has promised to *do*. This further relates to the discrepancy between words and deeds: do parties say what they will do and will they do what they say they will do? The degree of linkage between words, promises, and real commitment towards the other party may differ in ICBN. Negotiating partners should discuss early what commitment means for them in a number of key areas, before implementation and the fulfilment of obligations. Domains of commitment must be discussed to assess parties' reliability. Additional mechanisms such as delay penalties, conflict arbitrage, and renegotiation clauses may be necessary to redress poor commitment ethics. Time commitments related to deadlines, delay, delivery dates, project planning, etc. should not a priori be considered as self-enforceable. They must be agreed upon during the negotiation process and not discovered too late; since attitudes toward time differ, delivery dates, construction time, and the treatment of possible delays must be considered with a view of how parties can be *jointly* committed.

Commitment ethics may widely differ as concerns the respect of contract clauses: the renegotiation of clauses may seem standard practice to one party (IT2) and an outright violation of obligations to the other (IT1). The degree of commitment to the letter of the contract may differ between the parties. If a party tries to escape responsibility by evoking exceptional circumstances, unless this comes under a *Force Majeure* or a *Hardship* clause, it may lead to severe conflict.

Ethical standpoints: Universalism, cultural relativism, and moral pragmatism

When faced with ethical issues in ICBN, there are two extreme positions: relativism and universalism. Relativism is based on the view that moral perceptions and ethical judgements as well as rules are basically local and do not apply elsewhere; universalism, on the other hand, favours the view that most rules cross borders and apply everywhere because they are based on universal moral principles.[20] Many normative approaches to ethics in intercultural negotiations reflect the IT1 cultures and values, with a strong emphasis on deontological ethics that attempt to develop universal standards for resolving ethics conflict faced by individuals and organizations. The empirical literature suggests that there are significant differences across cultures in the tolerance towards controversial practices in sales negotiations and in business-related ethical beliefs.[21] Before describing ethics standpoints, it is necessary to assess the degree of relativity of ethical attitudes.

Cultural relativity of ethical attitudes

Figure 10.1 presents a framework for assessing the cultural relativity of ethical conceptions.[22] Any activity may be considered both from the legal and regulatory point of view (*legality*) and in terms of its degree of acceptability as a social practice (*legitimacy*). Unlike legality, that is, the quality of being lawful, legitimacy is the quality of what is just and equitable, conforming to established standards of usage and behaviour but not necessarily completely legal. Views of what is a *legitimate* activity help to settle debates by reference to personal evaluations of the requirements of natural justice rather than by strict reliance on the letter of the law. The notion of legitimacy is therefore much more indistinct because it is based on a mix of individual and

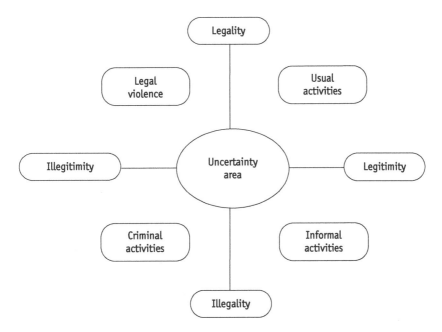

Figure 10.1 A framework for assessing the cultural relativity of ethical attitudes
Source: Usunier and Verna (1994, p. 31)

social assessments. Natural law, with its moral underpinnings, is much more suffused with conceptions of legitimacy than positive law, which is founded on legal formalism and on the different sources of law.

In Figure 10.1, there are four types of activities: "*normal activities*" which are both legal and legitimate; "*informal activities*", at the margin of legality but often legitimate: underground economy, moonlighting, or informal economy in developing countries; "*criminal activities*" which are intentionally carried out in breach of the law, and are totally devoid of legitimacy; and "*legal violence*" in which an activity is legal but not legitimate (e.g., forcing the population to accept a hazardous factory, the export of toxic waste).

In the case of bribery, it is clear that socio-economic explanations are not excuses for unacceptable practices. However, there must be some strong economic and social reasons for bribery, although unlawful, to continue to flourish. Three implicit economic explanations for illegal payments correspond to the most common bribery scenarios in ICBN. Far from being mutually exclusive, these forms of payment, which "ease" negotiation processes and facilitate favourable outcomes, are combined in traditional societies where most people, on their own level, sell their personal power of influence.

The first case (*implicit salary*) is that of small-scale, everyday corruption of poorly paid civil servants who supplement their income by taking advantage of their power. Passing through customs or obtaining a tax form for a mandatory fiscal statement may require the "greasing of palms". Small bribes may be viewed as an implicit salary; that is, as fringe benefits for civil servants or managers who may go months without receiving their salary. This semi-official situation is tolerated as long as bribes do not exceed a "fair" level. If a police officer, a customs officer, or a tax inspector is poorly paid but holds authority and responsibility, it may be "implicitly understood" that in exchange for carrying out poorly rewarded public duties, he or she may supplement his or her income. This can be assimilated to an implicit salary, in so far as the public authorities are aware of such practices and consider this implicit salary as justified by the low level of the official salary. Depending on the context, small-scale payments may be perceived as an informal or a criminal activity. In some developing countries, it is still standard social practice to pay civil servants for obtaining some permission, while it is considered criminal in many countries.

The second economic explanation is that illegal payments would be related to an *implicit property right* when the person who has the final say on a contract feels entitled to waive this right in return for money. This situation where a dictator in its wider sense, namely someone at the very top with all-inclusive decision power, sells his or her right to award deals, is a form of legal violence.

The third form of illegal payment may be viewed as an *implicit agency contract* between a principal who seeks to win the deal in a negotiation process and an agent who penetrates relational networks, supplies information, and exerts influence. Depending on the country, it may be considered either a normal or informal activity, socially accepted but at the fringes of legality.

Universal ethics: The example of the FCPA (Foreign Corrupt Practices Act)

Ethical universalism is based on the view that core ethical principles are universally applicable, whenever and to whomever, independently of country, culture, territory, and group membership. The U.S. Foreign Corrupt Practices Act of 1977, revised in 1988, is an example of such a universalist approach to ethics *and* rules. It applies extraterritorially, that is, American anti-bribery legislation applies to American companies whenever the illegal action takes place outside U.S. territory and with foreign companies and individuals. It has been strictly implemented over time. For instance, in February 2015, Goodyear paid USD 16 million to settle charges against its subsidiaries in Angola and Kenya, which had paid USD 3.2 million in bribes to local officials.[23] This legislation typifies the universalist orientation of U.S. and Northern European cultures.[24]

The FCPA makes it illegal for companies to influence foreign officials by personal payments or transfers of money to political groups. This law obliges firms to introduce internal accounting controls. The FCPA's definition of what constitutes bribery is very wide. It does, however, exclude small payments known as "backhanders" and tips paid to minor civil servants to speed up customs clearance and any administrative formalities.

After the introduction of this legislation, over 40 articles appeared in the management literature in the United States criticizing the FCPA on the basis that it was detrimental for American companies abroad. Some critics claimed that the FCPA placed American companies at a competitive disadvantage compared with European and Japanese competitors. In some countries such as Sweden, France, Switzerland, and Germany, although illegal payments paid to nationals were illegal and not tax deductible, those paid to foreign officials were.[25] In response to the FCPA the majority of American multinationals substantially reduced or eliminated these practices. In a few cases, they abandoned their export business. More generally, they turned their former agents into separate companies, independent of themselves, so they could buy and sell in their own right. Sometimes they even abandoned their long-standing competency as a prime contractor and acted as subcontractors for German, Japanese, and Korean companies. A further frequent criticism of the FCPA is that it has destabilized political regimes that are friendly to the United States. It is alleged that the leaders of these countries have sometimes been forced into making compromising revelations.

Studying affairs of corruption in the Middle East for ten years, Gillespie (1987) carried out an analysis of about 60 cases of corruption involving foreign companies. She concluded that arguments against the FCPA were not strictly met by the facts. Some regimes remained stable despite major scandals (e.g., Turkey, Egypt, Saudi Arabia); others fell (e.g., Marcos of the Philippines) for more deep-rooted reasons. Furthermore, Gillespie's study of the changes in the export market share of the United States (in comparison with its major international competitors) showed that U.S. foreign trade with the Middle East had not been adversely affected by the FCPA. However, Foster outlines the limitations of the universalist view in the following terms:

> We need to recognize that this process of developing "universal standards", of searching for and relying on objectifiable fact is *not* universal, that it is, in part, a uniquely Western process and that many other cultures neither subscribe to this world view of ethics nor have histories and traditions supportive of it. In fact, it is precisely because of the profoundly opposite world view held by traditional Asian cultures in this regard that Americans find themselves in the mystifying position of having Chinese associates "change" contract terms on them right after they have signed the deal.
>
> (Foster, 1995, p. 212)

Cultural relativism

The ethical position of cultural relativism considers that what is right or wrong, good or bad, depends on one's culture. This is based on the view that rules are applicable locally in the ingroup territory. Thus "When in Rome, do as Romans do". Empirical contributions tend to support ethical relativism. There are, for instance, differences between people from Hong Kong, Singapore, Hawaii, and Canada, as concerns the belief that money works wonders, the belief in social responsibility, the belief in *guanxi* (i.e., networking), and Machiavellianism. Ethical norms are also situation-contingent: when confronted with giving a bribe, managers tend to not support corruption if they are the CEO of the bribing company; however, they are more lenient if their job is threatened by refusing the bribe and therefore losing the business.

Ethicality is relative to the degree of economic development: the less developed, the more corrupt (on average and with exceptions naturally). It is also relative to Hofstede's cultural dimensions: collectivism, high power distance, and high uncertainty avoidance positively correlate with corruption level.[26] If moral reasoning, although based on some universal principles, is relative to local conditions, especially as concerns negotiation behaviour, it is important to make some minimal but necessary adjustment when negotiating business internationally. Host country conditions have to be taken into account as well, as shown by the following statement from a top manager:

> You cannot say to a country manager, "Don't do this, don't do that, now here are your goals for country X where all of your competitors do this and that. I don't want to hear any excuses if these objectives are not met". Under those circumstances, either rules will have to be broken or ambitious goals will not be achieved. The way to avoid this kind of impossible situation is to build a consensus among practitioners for enforceable rules. ... The example of the FCPA is a case in point. Although it would be more satisfying to punish the person who demands the bribe than the company that pays it, obtaining legal prohibitions in the major industrial countries and targeting the companies that bribe rather than the local citizens who demand payment is likely to have greater impact.
>
> (Reported in Berenbeim, 1997, p. 26)

Moral pragmatism

When addressing cross-cultural ethical conflicts, three critical questions should be asked:[27] 1) Is this situation high in moral significance? 2) Do I have a high level of influence over the outcome of the situation? 3) Is there a high level of urgency to resolve the situation? Between pure ethical universalism and complete relativism, lies a third possible view which is a pragmatic and respectful view of how ethical behaviour can be developed in ICBN. It involves the development of ethical concerns and attitudes related to the situation, given the legality and the legitimacy of a definite action, both of which can differ in the home and the host country. Let us call it "moral pragmatism"; it is based on the Confucian view of *Shu* emphasizing the importance of reciprocity in establishing human relationships and the cultivation of "like-heartedness". Moral pragmatism is concerned with the welfare of the global collectivity, directing human relationships to the betterment of the common good. It is not a strictly pragmatic perspective which would involve a somewhat cynical analysis of the effectiveness of these practices in the winning of contracts. This approach avoids the risks of the simplistic attitudes whereby illegal payments are either completely condemned or alternatively unequivocally accepted on the basis of being merely "realistic".

Useful guidelines for those confronted with ethical issues are provided by the definition of a "moral personality" proposed by John Rawls in his *Theory of Justice*.[28] A moral personality is characterized by the capacity to conceive good and the capacity to develop a sense of justice. The first capacity is realized through a rational project for one's life. The second capacity implies a continuing desire to act in a way that one believes is just. Thus for Rawls, moral personalities have chosen their own goals; and they prefer those conditions which enable them to fully express their nature of rational, free, and equal beings. The unity of the person is then manifested by the coherence of one's own project. This unity is based on a higher order aspiration to follow the principles of rational choice in a way which is suitable with a person's sense of justice. It means that if people are asked to perform an action which violates their sense of right and wrong, it is better not to do it, even if it means not behaving as a Roman in Rome. Rawls's definition of a moral personality remains a rather Western IT1 one, in that rationality, individualism, and the sense of equality with others are strongly emphasized.

In many other cultural contexts, especially Asian countries, where moral personalities actually exist, these traits would not be emphasized in such a definition. Moral pragmatism is better in any circumstance where things are intentionally hidden, suggesting that even local people are not certain about the legitimacy of what they do. Moral pragmatism complements cultural relativism. For instance, one party may exploit the other party by taking argument of its alleged "difference" in order to gain advantage after the contract has been signed. Although some flexibility with the letter of the contract is obviously needed (because contracts are never fully "complete": there are always loopholes and minor inconsistencies even in the best drafted contracts), a party which does not stick to its obligations must in some way be forced to honour them. A way of finding adequate corrective measures is to discreetly take local advice about what happens locally when a company, an individual, or an agent does not fulfil a certain part of its commitments: how is the issue raised and addressed, how is the conflict managed and what are the preferred solutions? Who are possible intermediaries for problem-solving?

Individual ethics, corporate interests, and social welfare

The first consideration is pragmatic: business people who make illegal payments take (real) personal risks for (potential) organizational benefits;

they do it either because of corporate loyalty or personal interest (e.g., sales commissions or promotions). Doing this, they 1) involve their company in the risk of being implicated in a scandal; and 2) risk themselves being implicated, indicted, imprisoned, and ultimately sentenced to imprisonment. In the case of turnkey sales, the favourite domain for large bribes, it is important to clarify the mandate for negotiation which is given to the project negotiators by the engineering company or consortium of contractors.

The payment of a bribe directly involves the individual responsibility of donors while their companies risk being drawn indirectly into the scandal. The risk of indictment and prosecution is an individual matter. The loss of a business based on bribery is an organizational issue. However, there is reason to believe that a company will not support an indicted employee, even when the instruction to bribe was implicitly backed by the company. They may prefer to plead guilty and accept fines, leaving their indicted employee with his or her personal responsibility in front of foreign courts. A pragmatic view for an individual requires reference to a personal norm, not to a corporate one.

Bribery is highly detrimental to social welfare in the recipient country. The big loser in the bribe system is the recipient country, because it pays in the end for bribes which are inevitably included in the full contract price. Bribery has adverse consequences; for example factories or equipment are either left idle or surplus to market needs because contracts have not been signed for sound economic reasons. Bribery significantly reduces commitment to quality and delivery dates when bribes are a central issue in the negotiation process. Local managers may be discouraged because their technical expertise is poorly considered. As a consequence, they will spend most of their time trying to attain those political positions where illegal payments enable significant personal enrichment. Bribes may ultimately be powerful motivators for under-performance. For example, technical advisers participating in the buyer's negotiating team may be bribed by being fictitiously employed by a fake consultancy company. Their objective interest is that their "consultancy fees" should be paid abroad for as long as possible; therefore the contract should be negotiated slowly and construction should extend over a long period of time. Keeping to deadlines would stop their bribes.

Evolution in the fight against bribery in international contracts

Since the U.S. adopted the FCPA in 1997, they have been constantly fighting at the international level for such legislation to be adopted by the major industrialized countries. They have used different international organizations as forums for promoting global anti-bribery legislation, including the 8th International Conference Against Corruption which issued the Lima Declaration against Corruption, a blueprint for action. The major achievement is the OECD Convention on Combating Bribery of Foreign

Public Officials in International Business Transactions, which is an extension of the principles contained in the FCPA among the OECD countries.

The OECD Convention on Combating Bribery of Foreign Public Officials

The convention was adopted in November 1997. As of May 2017, it was ratified by 43 signatory countries.[29] The text makes it compulsory for countries to criminalize bribery of foreign public officials. It does not specifically cover political parties; however, business-related bribes to foreign public officials made through political parties and party officials are covered. The negotiators agreed to apply "effective, proportionate and dissuasive criminal penalties". The convention requires that countries be able to seize the bribe or property of similar value or that they apply monetary sanctions of comparable effect.

The convention is not self-enforcing: countries have to modify their existing laws and enact new ones to comply with the provisions of the convention which outlaws:[30] 1) kickbacks to obtain or retain government business; 2) tax deductibility of bribes as business expenses; 3) off-the books accounting practices; 4) loose public procurement procedures which facilitate bribes and collusion; and 5) bribing through intermediaries, consultants, and agents.

Most signatory countries have now ratified the OECD convention and modified their national legislation to make it locally enforceable. Over the last 15 years, Asia-Pacific countries and Latin America have followed the initiative against corruption. In Tokyo, in November 2001, the Third Annual Conference of the ADB/OECD adopted an Anti-Corruption Initiative for Asia-Pacific, whereby 17 Asian and Pacific governments endorsed a regional action plan to fight corruption. In 2018, 31 countries in the Asia-Pacific region have endorsed the Action Plan and committed to its goals.[31] Similarly, in 2017, the Inter-American Convention against Corruption (adopted in 1996) has been ratified by 33 countries.

Other efforts at combating bribery

The International Chamber of Commerce has also played an active role by drafting a self-regulation code for companies. The ICC "Rules of Conduct to Combat Extortion and Bribery" deal with ethical issues in ICBN such as payments to sales agents and other intermediaries, business entertainment and gifts, and political contributions. Contrary to the OECD convention, it covers bribery within the private sector as well as toward public officials.

At the corporate level, it appears that the formulation of global corporate ethics codes involves 95% of CEOs and 78% of company boards of directors.[32] Bribery is a topic covered by a vast majority (92%) of the ethics code. Many ethics codes provide concrete operationalizations of what is a bribe and how to deal with it. Some, not all, target compliance by providing managers involved in foreign operations with precise procedures and guidelines. In relative terms, corruption tends to deter investors from negotiating foreign direct investment in countries with high levels of corruption.[33]

There are basically two sides in bribery: that of donors, which are principally concerned by the conventions and codes previously described, and that of the recipient countries which are less directly concerned. Corruption in international deals will not cease by the simple virtue of donors becoming suddenly honest and drying up the supply of bribes. In most potential recipient countries no strong anti-bribery codes exist or they are not actually enforced.

The level of corruption of particular countries can be measured, based on composite indicators for the perception of corruption. They are published on a yearly basis by Transparency International (www.transparency.org), an NGO which is considered as the most influential global anti-corruption organization. Data is based on mean scores of seven to nine surveys per country, rarely fewer. The highest scores correspond to the lowest levels of corruption, for example, in 2016, Denmark and New Zealand ranked first with a score of 90, Finland was third at 89, followed by Sweden (88), and Switzerland (86). Germany ranks tenth (81) while the U.S. ranks 18th (81) and France ranks 23rd (69). Countries plagued by endemic corruption have low scores (around 40). Among the most corrupt countries in 2016 (according to Transparency International), all with scores below 20, are Venezuela, Yemen, Eritrea, Uzbekistan, Afghanistan, Sudan, North Korea, South Sudan, and Somalia with the last rank (176) and the lowest score (10).[34]

A number of countries where corruption is endemic show increased severity against offenders. China for instance (scoring 40 on the Transparency corruption scale in 2016, with rank 79, an improvement over previous years) is combating bribery, going as far as the execution of senior officials, like the Vice Governor of Southern Jiangxi province who was convicted of having accumulated about 850,000 dollars in bribes.[35] The move to combat corruption started in early 2000. In 2002, a top banker was sentenced to 15 years imprisonment on bribery charges. He had been found to have taken about 500,000 dollars' worth of bribes when he was chairman of the group which controls one of China's largest banks.[36]

Money laundering

International negotiators, especially when they are in a position of seller or "favour-seekers", should not forget that if bribes remain unnoticed at contract winning stage, they are often discovered later when bribees try to launder dirty money. Money laundering is a natural complement to bribery: if money has unavowable sources, it is often made legitimate by the way of complex bank circuits with offshore banks designed to hide the dubious origin of the funds. Money can be converted in readily movable assets such as diamonds. Grey cash amounts can also be laundered by crediting fake cash entries (restaurant meals, hotel bills) later recovered by invoicing fees to the accomplice hotel or restaurant. A popular avenue for money laundering is to combine it with legitimate business activities. Bauer gives the following example:

> Other layering techniques involve buying big-ticket items – securities, cars, planes, travel tickets – that are often registered in a friend's name to further distance the criminal from the funds. Casinos are sometimes used because they readily take cash. Once converted into chips, the funds appear to be winnings, redeemable by a check drawn on the casino's bank.
>
> (Bauer, 2001, p. 20)

Money laundering has been combated with success over the last 25 years by the Financial Action Task Force (FATF, founded in 1989). In 2018, FATF is a 37-member intergovernmental organization which works under the auspices of the OECD.[37] FATF standards are implemented by commercial banks in signatory countries which must declare to the public authorities any fund transfer of significant amount that appears to have suspicious origin.[38] Moreover, the FATF issues a list of non-cooperative countries and territories which are then under pressure to conform to their standards.

Concluding remarks: Recommendations for action

When the scale of an ethical issue is large and/or when it involves corrupt behaviour which is legally prohibited in any country, a universalist stance to ethical issues should be adopted. Conversely when confronted with minor ethical problems involving unsaid divergence in interpretation of what is ethical behaviour and what is not, it is better to adopt a culturally relative attitude toward ethics in negotiation. Moral pragmatism is to be adopted when a party asks for benefits which are at the fringe of legality but rather legitimate in a social perspective. Recommendations for action are the following:

1) As a negotiator on the seller's side, do not propose grease money: it is contrary to universal principles and has adverse consequences for the bribee's country; moreover, it is not a normal, that is, both legal and legitimate, way of winning business deals.
2) If asked for a bribe by the other party, you have to decide with your company whether this should be included in the negotiation process or not; as an individual negotiator, always keep in mind that: (a) this is illegal; (b) profits go to the bribing organization and not to the individual briber who takes the most risks. Remember that ethical issues in ICBN are both organizational and personal: companies never go to jail whereas negotiators may.

3) Do not try to win over competitors by offering larger bribes to greedy buyers. This just feeds the "inflation" of bribes.
4) Lubrication payments can be made, provided that the payment does not unduly border on a bribe.
5) Cultural relativism can be adopted in non-bribe ethical issues such as making personal connections, networking, buying information, and hiring agents and intermediaries for smoothing the negotiation process.
6) Do not confuse ethical issues with mere communication misunderstandings and/or a biased view of your partners' honesty.

The final word may be given to Adam Smith, cited in the epigraph of this chapter, when he describes key aspects of what he calls the "character of virtue".

Notes

1   According to Mayo et al. (1991).
2   Chan and Armstrong (1999).
3   Knowingly delivering "non-true" and manipulative information: one party may for example convey false information on the value they assign to a particular "good" in the negotiation.
4   See Parker (2003).
5   See Loe et al. (2000, 2013, p. 193).
6   See Koehn (2013); Melé and Sánchez-Runde (2013).
7   See Demuijnck (2015).
8   *The Economist* (2015).
9   *MarketWatch*, "China's millions of government workers to get huge 60% pay raise", 22 January 2015. www.marketwatch.com/story/chinas-millions-of-government-workers-to-get-huge-60-pay-raise-2015-01-21, retrieved 3 February 2016.
10   Werner (2000, p. 18).
11   Péan (1988, p. 139).
12   On the notion of property rights, see the founding article by Demsetz (1967).
13   On international negotiations and social networks, see Money (1998).
14   Donoho et al. (1999).
15   See Gambetta (1988) and Bigoni et al. (2016).
16   Ford (1990), p. 81.
17   Yeung and Tung (1996).
18   Luo (1995), Luo (1997), Luo and Chen (1997).
19   Tsang (1998).
20   Melé and Sánchez-Runde (2013), Sánchez-Runde et al. (2013), Morales-Sanchez and Cabello-Medina (2013).
21   See Donoho et al. (1999), Merrilees and Miller (1999), Volkema (1999), Ang (2000), Hui and Au (2001), Rawwas (2001), Melé and Sánchez-Runde (2013), Demuijnck (2015).
22   Usunier and Verna (1994).
23   Horn (2015).

24 Demuijnck (2015).
25 Bribes are no longer tax-deductible in the countries mentioned.
26 Becker and Fritzsche (1987), Husted et al. (1996), Husted (1999), Ang (2000), Hui and Au (2001), Rawwas (2001), Robertson et al. (2002), Loe et al. (2013), Seleim and Bontis (2009).
27 Buller et al. (1997).
28 Rawls (1971) and Follesdal (2015).
29 Countries having ratified the OECD convention are the 35 OECD member countries and 8 non-member countries: Argentina, Brazil, Bulgaria, Colombia, Costa Rica, Lithuania, Russian Federation, and South Africa. Regular updates of steps taken to implement the Convention country-by-country can be found at www. oecd.org
30 Hamra (2000). See German (2002) for a detailed account of how the OECD Convention on bribery translates into national legislation, in the Canadian case.
31 Afghanistan; Australia; Bangladesh; Bhutan; Cambodia; People's Republic of China; Cook Islands; Fiji Islands; Hong Kong, China; India; Indonesia; Japan; Kazakhstan; Korea; Kyrgyz Republic; Macao, China; Malaysia; Mongolia; Nepal; Pakistan; Palau; Papua New Guinea; the Philippines; Samoa; Singapore; the Solomon Islands; Sri Lanka; Thailand; Timor-Leste; Vanuatu; and Vietnam.
32 Berenbeim (1999).
33 Habib and Zurawicki (2002).
34 Transparency International (2017).
35 ABCnews (2002).
36 Xinhua News Agency (2002); Chen (2015).
37 Morris-Cotterill (2001), see www.oecd.org/cleangovbiz/toolkit/moneylaundering.htm and www.fatf-gafi.org/ retrieved 28 January 2016.
38 Myers (2001), Roberge (2011).

11 Some elements of the national style of business negotiation

Kill with a borrowed knife.
> (Chinese Stratagem 3, Play the competitors against each other)

Hide a knife in a smile.

> (Chinese Stratagem 10, Manipulate friendship and hospitality)

Among the national styles of business negotiation, the American (U.S.) style is most often the explicit or implicit baseline for comparison. Most empirical articles use a comparison between at least two country-cultures (CCs) and American negotiators are contrasted in various ways (i.e., negotiation simulations, self-report questionnaires, interviews, observations) with negotiators from mainly the 12 CCs that are examined in this chapter. This is coherent with the predominantly U.S. origin of knowledge described in Chapter 1. In ICBN, images of the other negotiating party are based on a collection of traits. They sometimes border on stereotypes, are occasionally misleading, and are often highly meaningful. They amount to a basic portrait of how a party's national culture influences their negotiation behaviour, process, and outcomes. The set of 12 miniature portraits of negotiation style in this chapter are based on a combination of *emic* traits that are particular to each cultural/national context, *etic* ICBN literature (comparative studies across CCs, rarely with large sets of CCs, more frequently across two, three, or four CCs), and ICBN studies that examine intercultural interaction in ICBN and that sometimes compare how negotiators behave intraculturally versus interculturally, offering key insights into the issue of cultural adaptation to different partners.

Ideally, this exercise in mutual reflection should be done for each bilateral ICBN relationship, for example, defining the Brazilian negotiation style in terms of how it is perceived by the Americans, the French, the Japanese, etc. There is no doubt that negotiations between Chinese and Indians do not resemble those between American negotiators and Chinese or Indians. It follows that a matrix design would be necessary if we were to accurately describe not only how particular negotiating styles are perceived by other CCs but also how culturally different negotiators adjust to each other.

Unfortunately, such a design would be too complex. We cannot deny the pivotal role of American negotiation knowledge, culture, and English language (exactly as in Google Translate, where translation always goes through English) in defining archetypes of negotiation styles. For the purposes of clarity (in fact, necessary simplification), ICBN styles are more or less based on an average of what is seen through Western eyes.

This chapter describes some elements of national and regional styles of business negotiation. At the risk of adopting what could be termed a Western stereotyping classification, this chapter describes salient traits of the following "styles" in ICBN (listed in alphabetical order): American (US-IT1), Black African (IT2), Brazilian (IT2), British (IT1), Chinese (IT2), French (IT1), German (IT1), Indian (IT2), Japanese (IT2), Mexican (IT2), Middle Eastern (IT2), and Russian (IT2) negotiation styles.

American style

The United States is very high on individualism (score at 91) and displays low Power Distance (40) in a relatively egalitarian society. It is also relatively low in Uncertainty Avoidance (46), consistent with a high risk-taking ability and the emphasis on entrepreneurship and the valuation of the *self-made man*. The American negotiation style – individualistic and action-oriented – reflects major aspects of the U.S. national character: emphasis on doing, on ability and skills, competence, professionalism, decision-making, and explicit communication.[1] As a consequence, American negotiators usually exhibit the following talents: they are rather well prepared, serious about business matters and interests, pragmatic and accurate in writing contract clauses. U.S. managers have fairly well-defined autonomy and room for manoeuvre as mandated negotiators. However, clear limits are also set, and they have to report to their principals. In the negotiation process, Americans often consider that decisions have to be made on the spot by the individual who has the most expertise or responsibility in a given area. The motto "Separate people from problems" is in fact the climax of the IT1 paradigm. When reflexively elaborating on their own negotiation style, Americans are extremely self-critical. Acuff (2008), for instance, grades American negotiators on the classical scale used in U.S. education as very good on personal integrity (A), having rather high aspirations (B+), not too bad on preparing for ICBN (B-); however unacceptably poor (D) on communication and cultural skills (listening abilities, cultural IQ, patience, adapting to the negotiation process in the partner's CC), and on ability (or willingness) to build solid relationships (D). An excessive competitiveness in negotiation and a lack of integrative/*win-win* orientation are also graded D, while Americans completely fail on language skills (F).

Nevertheless, professionalism is a quality that is very widely recognized in American negotiators. In business negotiation, it means careful selection of the negotiators and above-average methodical preparation. They are also noted for being rather *win-win* oriented despite being competitive. In their failure to take sufficient account of the culture of other parties, the Americans, like the French, tend to be an "ethnocentric-missionary" people. They are quite convinced (as are the French) that their system is "The best way", and that the other side would do well to adopt their system of values and behaviour.

A great deal of attention is (pragmatically) paid to precise issues to be debated, to facts and evidence, to an attitude oriented towards matter-of-fact discussions and to a tight negotiation time schedule. This renders Americans susceptible to becoming irritated by negotiating parties who are more interested in general principles or even pure logical reasoning (i.e., the ideologist mindset). This may also lead them to interpret the non-linear style of their negotiating counterparts as delaying tactics. They will resent package deal, global negotiation as a way of reconsidering what has already been decided and as a failure to respect a preset agenda.

A strong positive emphasis is placed on frankness and sincerity; Americans show willingness to make the first move by disclosing information in the hope (sometimes unfulfilled) that their opponent will do likewise. They are sometimes ready to adopt the "John Wayne Style", by pushing frankness to the bounds of arrogance. This can be resented by negotiators from cultures where self-assertion must be contained within strict limits.

A genuine naivety, ingenuousness and a "retarded adolescent" style (noted by the anthropologist Margaret Mead²) can sometimes lead Americans to choose positions that are very tough because they are – genuinely – disappointed. This occurs mainly when, having demonstrated their quite genuine sincerity, they then feel that they have been badly treated, since their open-mindedness has been taken advantage of. However, sincerity and frankness are by no means universal cultural values, contrary to what a good number of Americans may believe.

The American sense of equality between buyer and seller means that they "let the best man win". This can surprise people who deal with Americans, since Americans value personal assertiveness and so can appear tough, as there is little sympathy for anyone who loses. In the U.S. business mentality, no consolation prizes should be awarded to "losers".

The Americans are reputed for being informal in everyday life. In fact, compared with other peoples, they are formal in different areas. When it comes to negotiating the details of agreements, Americans can become quite formal and anxious about the preciseness and explicitness of written contracts which are therefore drawn up with care. These contracts, the law between the parties, are also the basis for attitudes which are readily oriented towards recourse to litigation and legal battles with the assistance of lawyers.

Americans, although generally future oriented (*the future is bigger and better*), tend to be focused on the short and medium term when it comes to negotiation and business. For example, at the end of the Vietnam War, the Vietnamese were at a time advantage in the US–Vietnamese peace talks in Paris, because they had rented a villa with a two-and-a-half year lease, whereas the Americans rented hotel rooms on a week-to-week basis. The U.S. time pressure in business may be easily explained by the system of quarterly reporting to shareholders and the Stock Exchange. U.S. companies depend heavily on the financial markets; labour mobility is high. Accordingly, people must get quick results and show a faster return than their foreign counterparts. This "short-termism" may disadvantage Americans in ICBN.

Black African style

The way Black Africans love to just talk amazes those used to more purposeful speech. Africans simply do not have the same relationship to the universe as Europeans and Americans do. Differences relate to basic concepts such as time and space. Poetry has a powerful meaning for Africans. The African is a very verbal person: Africans are almost all polyglots; language is an instrument for enjoying the pleasure of speaking. As a result, negotiations can sometimes seem to be rather ill directed, not just because Africans enjoy debating, but also simply because they enjoy speaking. In the Black African "palaver" style of communication, speech is abundant, very high-context, quite indirect, sometimes circular, and slow in coming down to focused issues (see Figure 5.2 in Chapter 5). African negotiators seem not always to be aware of their own communication style's influence on foreign negotiation partners.[3]

Although money matters, like everywhere in the world, there is never a pure economic individual motivation. Money does not have the same value as in Europe. Westerners are accustomed to an age-old tradition of exchange based on money which has acquired a strong symbolic value as reward for work, as a means of saving, as a measure of personal success, and as the fair price of things.

> ... [in Africa] attitudes towards money follow different rules. Money is only a means of obtaining enough for survival and projection of self-image, whereas its other attributes fade into the background ... this money is taken without remorse, and in good humour ["baksheesh"], and usually benefits not just the person who receives it but also the whole family. The African system of distribution functions in such a way that money goes to the one who needs it: the employee whose salary does not allow him to live decently, the high-ranking civil servant who supports a large family in the village for example.
>
> (Gruère and Morel, 1991, pp. 122–123; my translation)

Power is quite unequally distributed in most African countries (power distance score 70), in Black African collectivistic societies (low individualism score at 23) with rather low democratic standards and endemic corruption. Black-African countries range from 10 to 45 on the 2016 TI corruption index.[4] The reality of ethnic belongingness and ingroups should never be ignored. During the process of business negotiations, the influence of the extended family and ethnic background will inevitably make its presence felt, whether through people participating or benefiting from the negotiations.

The concept of time is simply not the same. This has a direct influence on the progress of business negotiations. As noted by Weiss and Stripp (1985, p. 39) in the case of Nigeria,

> Time is simply considered flexible. Lateness to meetings (even of several hours) is common. In the same vein, the foreigner who hurries through a negotiation – even after a very late start – will often be suspected of cheating.

In the *being-* and *ingroup*-oriented Black African societies, much emphasis is put on relationships. Black Africa is a mosaic, involving various characteristics of diversity: ethnic, religious (Christianity, Islam, animism), and linguistic. There too, as in the Middle East, a map of the "human landscape" must be prepared in advance. Universalist IT1 negotiators do not consider their Black African counterparts first as members of a particular ethnic group, a clan, and an extended family, rather they tend to consider them predominantly as individuals.[5]

Darley and Blankson (2008, p. 380) outline conditions for developing relationships in Africa:

> To take into account the collectivistic, slight feminine and high power distance nature of the African culture, arrangements and conditions that conform with good character, allow for fulfillment of social obligations, respect elders, and value social relevance and welfare of others, should facilitate collaborative partnerships. There should also be extensive communication, increased interaction, and ongoing consultation.

Brazilian style

Brazil is a federal state, independent from Portugal for quite some time (1822). The country is to a large extent a melting pot; it is unified by the generalized use of the Portuguese language despite some other communities having arrived over a century ago (Japanese in Sao Paulo, Germans and Italians in the southern states). Brazilian culture is, like most Latin cultures, relatively high Power Distance (69) and collectivistic (i.e., the individualism score is relatively low at 38). Brazil shares high social and income inequality with its surrounding Spanish-speaking neighbours. The country has a recent democracy and a tradition of authoritarian right-wing regimes supported by large landowners (*fazendeiros*). However, it is hugely different from other countries in Latin America because of its language and history.

As negotiators, Brazilians are reported to be rather integrative and win-win oriented as well as having a tendency to equal distribution between buyer and seller, irrespective of role.[6] Decision-making style is rather top-down and high Power Distance at 69. The hierarchical nature of Brazilian organizations is reflected in decisions being centralized at top levels, with intellectual rather than pragmatic, implementation-oriented planning, and a somewhat conflictual atmosphere due to inadequate responsibility and authority distribution across management levels. However despite relatively high Power Distance, Brazilian negotiators mix egalitarian with hierarchical behaviour.[7] Brazilians are more concerned with the other party's outcomes. They are also more ingroup oriented than Americans, and tend to be more accommodative in conflicts with ingroup members than with outgroup negotiators.[8]

Brazil is both relationship and contract/deal-oriented. Although Brazilian negotiators report themselves as being rather contract-oriented (in Salacuse, 1999), long-term relationships are also important for Brazilian companies. Brazilian negotiators may be unwilling to impersonally talk business if rapport and personal acquaintance have not been established. Similarly, Amado and Vinagre Brasil (1991, p. 58) describe the strong personal and relational attitudes in the Brazilian culture.

> Brazilian people are obsessed with relationships and with personal bonds… [in] this distinction between the individual (*o individuo*) and the person (*a pessoa*) … the *individual* is the impersonal subject of universal laws, while the *person* is the subject of social relationships, with their emotions and uniqueness. The tendency of Brazilians is therefore to reduce the power of the anonymous individual (or laws) to live and solve processes at a personal level.[9]

Despite being noted as rather conflict avoidant, Brazil is a very litigious country, in fact number two for the number of lawyers per capita after the U.S.[10] Brazilian negotiators are reportedly high in risk-taking, despite a high level of Uncertainty Avoidance (76). Time-orientation is notably polychronic and time-relaxed in line with low time sensitivity self-reported at 0 in Salacuse (1998).[11] The communication style of Brazilian negotiators is rather high-context; they are somewhat fuzzy communicators, moderately indirect in communication, discursive and often engaging in non-task focused digressions. They are very talkative, with virtually no silence periods; implicitly, silence is probably understood by Brazilian negotiators as a latent sign of possible disagreement. Brazilians do not fear conversational overlap, and what may be perceived by negotiators of other cultures as aggressive communication tactics. Brazilian negotiators frequently command the other party, using "no", assembled in typically Brazilian "no, no, no". However, this should not be misinterpreted as a sign of systematic opposition and negativity. Brazilians are reputed for being nice, mild, friendly, and good-natured.

Brazilians share the Americans' rank-ordering of what is most important for negotiators: 1) Preparation and planning skill, 2) Thinking under pressure, 3) Judgement and intelligence, 4) Verbal expressiveness, 5) Product knowledge, and 6) Perceive and exploit power.[12] Brett et al. (1998) report empirical evidence of both low- and high-power norms in Brazil.

> The Brazilian participants endorsed norms for distributive tactics in negotiation, suggesting that Brazilian negotiators will use power strategies in negotiation. However, they also were more egalitarian than hierarchical and viewed both information and alternatives (BATNA) as power in negotiation, suggesting that Brazilian negotiators will not use power strategies in negotiation.

To sum up, Brazilian negotiators are collaborative rather than competitive, as much *win-win* as *win-lose* oriented, concerned with relationships, and value preparation on an equal footing with improvisation.[13]

British style

The UK displays a moderately high individualism score (67) and low Power Distance (35), despite being a rather socially stratified country, with a strong emphasis on social class and educational background (e.g., public schools and Oxbridge graduates). British society, with a traditionally strong and liberal institutional system, is medium-high on the Uncertainty Avoidance scale (65), with very low prevalence of corrupt behaviour (TI 81).

Like the French, the British have been strongly affected by their tradition of diplomatic negotiation and their country's position as head of a far-flung empire, the *Commonwealth of Nations*. The British style is characterized by a "soft-sell" approach which is essential for negotiating. British coolness is not an empty phrase. An air of confidence, restraint, and calm is essential for any negotiators in the position of seller. They must never be seen to be pushy in negotiation.

The British cultivate a sense of being quite different from their American cousins. They are more inclined to value tradition and have the reputation of being less motivated by money than the Americans. The welfare state still exists to a large extent in the UK, and British people are still more inclined to make the most of their free time. This situation may at times slow down the decision-making process.

On the basis of simulated negotiations, it has been shown that the negotiator's role (purchaser or vendor) has a strong influence on negotiation outcomes in the United Kingdom, British buyers obtaining significantly superior profits compared with British sellers.[14] This is consistent with the British reputation of having a "soft-sell" type of approach, where the vendor must take care not to annoy the purchaser by being too pushy, turning up too often, making too many proposals, or by adopting an attitude that is too action oriented.

Although seemingly closest to the Americans, the British are not necessarily those who resemble them the most in the field of business practice.

Language-related issues (the style in which they write clauses, for instance) are treated differently by the British and the Americans. Whereas U.S. people easily accept a somewhat simplified "international English" that will be used for drafting agreements, the British, like the French, take pride in language, and are sensitive to style for its own sake. The British communication style is rather contextual, often understated, slightly indirect, so that foreign negotiators sometimes need to interpret the British position. British negotiators see themselves as rather non-emotional, looking for specific and detailed, low context agreements, and relatively win-win, integrative oriented.[15]

Chinese style

China is the oldest civilization in the world with its ideographic writing system. Pictograms are more concrete than letters. They constantly refer to images of the real world which promote holistic and concrete thinking. Westerners have a more abstract and analytical thinking style because they need to chain letters to sounds, sounds to words, and words to concepts. The *Wu Xing* example in Chapter 6 is typical of how the five elements can be concretely used as a symbolic/holistic register to balance their attitudes during the negotiation process.

The Chinese social organization is hierarchical and based on Confucian rules of interpersonal behaviour, a mix of loyalty and reciprocity norms guiding both vertical (i.e., superior-subordinate) and horizontal (i.e., between peers) interactions. The most well-known principle, although found in the Bible, is "*Do not do unto others what you would not want others to do unto you*". While respect for social hierarchy (*Shehui Dengji*) has top priority, a strong insistence on interpersonal harmony (*Renji Hexie*, see p. 194 in Chapter 6) is valued as a counterbalance.

China, with its deep influence of obedience-encouraging Confucianism, is a highly collectivistic (i.e., a very low individualism score at 20) as well as a very high Power Distance (80) society in a relatively centralized and somewhat authoritarian country. Paradoxically, the Chinese are relatively low in Uncertainty Avoidance (30), which is in line with the entrepreneurial and risk-taking attitudes of Chinese people. Persistence and obstinacy are also noted characteristics of hard working Chinese. In a collectivistic, rather ingroup conscious, and Confucian society, strong family ties, networking, and nepotism are daily realities. Reciprocity-based *guanxi* (see Chapter 10) is the relational network based on the long-term bilateral exchange of favours. *Guanxi* is mostly related to Confucian teaching on the art of managing horizontal interactions and relationships between peers (persons and/ or organizations) while keeping an eye on possible vertical/hierarchical aspects of the relationship. The *guanxi* Chinese networking system needs to be taken into account, as the development and maintenance of appropriate connections is key to business and may help in negotiating beyond the negotiation table itself.[16] Most of the *guanxi* relationships are based on a combination of blood (immediate and extended families), educational ties, and geography; that is, common membership in the same clan or village. Ingroup orientation is strong and people from outgroupist cultures must regard the Chinese networking activities without prejudice. China is a naturally collusive society, and it is no surprise that it scores relatively high on endemic corruption (TI at 40).

Pye also notes the role played by differences of attitude relating to the concept of "friendship". Thus it seems that whereas the Americans view friendship in terms of a feeling which rests on a natural mutual exchange, in other words mainly on an economic principle of reciprocity, the Chinese view friendship in social terms of loyalty. The idea is that of a long-lasting obligation:

> What the Chinese neglect in terms of reciprocity they more than match in loyalty. They not only keep their commitments, but they also assume that any positive relationship can be permanent. A good example of this is the number of Chinese who have tried to establish pre-1949 ties with U.S. companies and individuals – as though nothing had happened in the intervening days.
>
> (Pye, 1986, p. 79)

Chinese negotiator communication style is rather indirect communication, due not only to a shame-avoidant culture, but also to the language and to the ideographic writing system. Chinese communication is not only about exchanging information and persuading. Chinese people are concerned with *face* (*Mianzi*), a sort of social mask which protects a person against being publicly exposed to *shame*. Face can be hurt (by highlighting misbehaviour), injured (by statements that appear insulting), or even withdrawn (by outright revelation of wrongdoing). All of these result in a *loss of face*. Face can be lost, but also given, borrowed, lent, saved, etc. IT1 guilt-regulated behaviour is often opposed to shame regulated behaviour (typical of IT2 societies). Expressing guilt is Western style and outgroupist (IT1); it is understood as a way to obtain mercy and pardon from others. It is accepted that those who are courageous enough to sincerely confess mistakes will deserve pardon. Such forgiveness for sinners confessing their sins is not easily granted in non-Western societies. For IT2 negotiators, it is probably more adequate for correcting errors without expressing a low-profile, subdued sense of shame, rather than outright and explicit acknowledgement of responsibility for mistakes.[17] The face of Chinese negotiators should therefore be carefully preserved, and overly direct communication with them should absolutely be avoided.

The Chinese style of business negotiations has been the most widely studied, *per se* (often with *emic* Chinese cultural concepts relevant to ICBN), in comparison with the American style, other East-Asian countries/cultures, and within larger comparison sets.[18] One of the main experts on business negotiation with the Chinese, Lucian W. Pye (1982, 1986) lists the following factors, which combine to demonstrate that the Chinese are tactical, skilful, and fairly tough negotiators:

> As hosts, the Chinese take advantage of their control over the pace of negotiations. First they set the agenda, then they suggest that the Americans start the discussions...their proposals become the starting point from which all compromise follows.
>
> (Pye, 1986, p. 77)

The Chinese deliberately adopt a fairly passive attitude, taking care not to show enthusiasm, concealing any feeling of impatience, playing their game impassively so as to force their opponents to be the first to show their hand. They do not shy away from appearing very manipulative (see Chapter 8), with a view to disconcerting the other side and in the ultimate hope of obtaining further concessions. They will attribute an exaggerated import-ance to minor details, which in reality are of no consequence to them, or return to discussion of points where full agreement seemed to have previ-ously been reached. The Chinese are quite sensitive to the relational aspects of negotiations, which are prioritized. They try to maintain long-term, har-monious personal relationships whereas deal-oriented American negotiators would value objective information exchange and competitiveness.[19] Graham and Lam (2003, p. 82) note:

> All too often, Americans see Chinese negotiators as inefficient, indirect, and even dishonest, while the Chinese see American negotiators as aggressive, impersonal, and excitable.

The bureaucratic orientation of the People's Republic of China is still to be noted despite WTO accession and the major role of China in global trade. Socialism has imposed strong government control on industry, which has however been relaxing over the last 25 years. As a consequence, Chinese negotiators tend not to be capable of individual decision-making. Before an agreement is reached, official approval must most often be sought by Chinese negotiators from their principals.

Chinese business people tend to overrate the advantage offered by their large population in terms of market opportunities, even though per capita purchasing power has been considerably increasing over the last 25 years. A persuasion tactic used by Chinese negotiators is to mention the foreign negotiators' competitors and suggest that they could do business with another company (*Jiao Ta Liangshi Chuan*, "threatening to do business else-where").[20] The foreign partners should recall that they also have alternatives since Chinese negotiators may sometimes underestimate the opportunities offered to their foreign partners by other markets.

Chinese negotiators think of themselves as being win-win oriented (82), despite the fact that most of the studies mentioned in note 18 consider them as rather win-lose with an underlying fixed pie assumption. Sun-Tzu's Chinese stratagems are supposed to be useful for Chinese negotiators. However they feature war and battle, give advice for winning over the enemy by cunning and manipulative tactics. Chinese stratagems clearly emphasize a *win-lose* (or, even worse, *lose-lose*) situation with a defeated loser and a winner who has overpowered the vanquished by losing less.

Chinese decision-making process is rather top-down and Chinese negotiators self-reportedly prefer a strong leader to consensus in the team.[21] Like the Japanese, the Chinese are less economic-time minded and more long-term oriented than Westerners. As noted by Pye (1986, p. 78) "The Chinese use time shrewdly. If they sense that business people are in a hurry to leave China, they may slow down negotiations and turn the deadline to their advantage". The noted patience of Chinese negotiators[22] is used by them for developing time-based manipulation tactics, by slowing down the process, and by making additional demands when their IT1, economic time-minded, partners are under strict pressure to respect deadlines.[23]

French style

The French are said to be somewhat difficult to negotiate with. As noted earlier, the French tend to be Cartesian ideologists and find it sometimes difficult to accept convincing facts and evidence, if they feel that facts contradict intellectual logic. As emphasized by Burt (1984, p. 6): "Although they [the French] may consider themselves to be experts at negotiating, at times they tend to be amateurish and inadequately prepared". Because of their tendency to lock up the other side in perfect Cartesian reasoning, French negotiators risk being themselves imprisoned in their logic. A self-inflated collective self is the result of both the love of winning arguments and a bloated sense of French history (*la Grande Nation*).[24] The French communication style subtly combines high and low context communication and can be at times direct. French society paradoxically combines egalitarian and hierarchical orientations. French negotiators self-report to be win-win players and rather contract-oriented and they have been shown in fact to be rather integrative in negotiation.[25]

The French are conflict prone. They do not mind confrontation and sometimes even enjoy it. The French negotiating style is competitive and inherently confrontational. They also tend to use emotional and theatrical ways of behaving in negotiation. In France (as in the United Kingdom) social class remains an important feature of society. Consciousness of social status is very strong in France, as is Power Distance. French negotiators are sensitive to the organizational status of their foreign counterparts, and require equivalence.

France is still one of the most centralized nations in the world, with a very long tradition of Paris-based decision-making (inaugurated by Hugh Capet, in 987). High-ranking *élite* civil servants (*énarques* and *polytechniciens*) have a substantial say in business deals which involve large companies and their subsidiaries. At times, some French negotiators may be resented as arrogant and disdainful: in a very high-power-distance society, which is at the same time individualistic, power display may be exacerbated, to the detriment of politeness and courtesy. The paradox of a high individualism score (63) combined with high Power Distance (68) in a centralized and somewhat bureaucratic country, relatively high in Uncertainty Avoidance (59), explains some of the French interaction style in negotiation. French negotiators self-report to be very concerned with writing general agreements (70), with a win-win orientation (80), low on risk taking (90), and with a top-down decision-making system (60) consistent with French centralization and high Power Distance.

German style

One of the striking aspects of Germany is its relatively high level of Uncertainty Avoidance (score of 65 on Hofstede's index of Uncertainty Avoidance). A key German term is *sicher* (sure, safe). The Germans do not like *unsicherheit*, a sense of insecurity which makes them feel uneasy in business, as well as in their whole life. When faced with partners who generate such uncertainty, Germans will quickly develop *Mißtrauen* (mistrust). They need to be *versichert*, that is, reassured. This cannot be done through superficial and wordy arguments, but only with hard facts, sound arguments, tests, and so on. Reliability is key for relationship development.

The German love of formality is one thing that stands out clearly. For example, the title of *Doktor*, even *Professor Doktor*, is a recognized sign of ability (*Kompetenz*) and will be employed as part of a personal identity. Formality and the presence of constraining rules (which are generally respected) in the decision-making process on the German side are characteristics of the German system, which seeks to avoid uncertainty.[26] As a consequence, German managers prefer handling conflicts based on the application of impersonal regulations (i.e., rights-based strategies), while American managers support a more informal and pragmatic integration of interests between the parties. Explicit contracting is related to the German low-context style with the view that long term trusting relationships are only possible if parties reliably stick to general principles.[27]

These rules are often the end result of a reasonably solid consensus. The respect for accepted rules is more internalized by the Germans than forced upon them. Germany is rather low Power Distance (35) and German organizations are well known for their capacity to build consensus between their members, especially between employers and employees (*Mitbestimmung*).

Decisions in a German company are taken at a fairly slow pace. The machine is "well oiled", but it is also rather cumbersome. Procedures are important and a fairly substantial number of signatures will be required for any final agreement. This is because the Germans have a strong legal system and emphasize rights when negotiating, insisting on intellectual property, coming back to contract clauses and to the famous *AGB* (*Allgemeine Geschäftsbedingungen*), the general business clauses imposed by the seller on any buyer. The German contract orientation comes with a significant dominance of the seller's role in intracultural negotiations between Germans.[28]

Great pride is taken in the technical quality of products manufactured in Germany; thus a reaction of disbelief is instinctively provoked when Germans are faced with non-German products, which fail to conform to German DIN standards. As a result, readiness to participate in detailed discussions with German technical experts is essential when negotiating with Germans.

German earnestness is no myth. The Germans are people who keep their word, and who will respect the agreement made, whether it takes a written or an oral form. They loathe anything that approaches flippancy, in particular negotiation for negotiation's sake, or the failure to keep appointments and to meet deadlines. Germans, when they negotiate with the Italians or the French, often resent their Latin counterparts' unreliability in keeping to their commitments.

Germans prefer explicit and direct communication. They display a clearly monochronic temporal style as well as low emotionalism.[29] In negotiations, German negotiators expect that he schedule and agenda will be respected. During negotiations, the role of emotions and friendship is fairly limited; Germans keep their distance. They feel that overly personal relationships could interfere with the desired outcomes resulting from their work.

There is ambivalence in the way Germans are perceived by others: they are both admired and disliked. As stated by Barzini (1983, p. 94), this "has its roots not only in their less amiable traits – arrogance, tactlessness and obtuseness – but also in their great virtues, their excellence in almost all fields". Germans should be considered as individuals more than any nationality in the world, with a high individualism score (65).[30]

Indian style

India is a subcontinent with much regional and linguistic diversity. It is the largest democracy in the world and a federal state. Sanskrit, the ancient language of India is the matrix of Indo-European languages; that is, most Western languages including English, French, German, and Italian. Although India has been deeply influenced by British colonization (and marginally by Portuguese, Dutch, and French colonizers), its culture(s) has also massively influenced other countries both in the West and in the East, in terms of philosophy, religion, and science, just to name a few areas. As more than 80% of the Indian population are Hindus, Hinduism is the dominant religion and extends its influence on secular life. Some aspects of the Hindu culture are occasionally misunderstood by foreigners such as the caste system, which still exists despite being legally forbidden. Indian ambiguity is reflected in cultural dimensions scores: India is high Power Distance (77), however as much individualistic (48) as collectivistic, and is characterized by rather low Uncertainty Avoidance (40).

Kumar (2004) notes that Indian negotiators paradoxically combine two types of behaviour patterns, one based on Hindu culture, the other based on Western influence. While the primary, Hindu, mode of behaviour is in line with scores on cultural dimensions values (collectivistic to a moderate extent and high Power Distance), the secondary mode is based on a more individualistic and pragmatic stance. Despite being considered a collectivistic culture (the Indian individualism/collectivism (IC) score at 48 is slightly above the global average score of 43), Indian high-context negotiators may simultaneously use features of collectivistic and individualistic behaviours, depending on the negotiation context. India's Uncertainty Avoidance at 40 is well below the world average at 65, however it is relatively inconsistent with India's rather strong rules and procedures orientation, a reputation for administrative red tape, and a significant level of corruption (TI score at 40).

Kumar (2004, p. 53) sees two key Indian characteristics, *brahmanical idealism* and *anarchical individualism* as explaining the dynamics of Indian negotiating behaviour.

> Brahmanical idealism represents an introverted form of thinking. Cooperative behavior and teamwork among Indians are extremely difficult. ... A major implication of Brahmanical idealism is that aspiration levels (expectations) of Indian negotiators are likely to be very high. On the positive side, high aspiration levels are essential for attaining integrative solutions. On the negative side, high aspiration levels slow down the process of reaching an agreement...

The high aspirations of Indian negotiators bear as a consequence that they may not be satisfied with outcomes that do not meet their expectations. They are especially concerned with minimizing negative outcomes. Indian negotiators consider their decision-making process as top-down and their risk-taking ability as quite high.[31] However, in everyday negotiation practice, Indian bureaucracy, its red tape, some nepotism, and a rather hierarchical society combined with individual pride, require empathetic understanding from their foreign counterparts.

A second key cultural characteristic of Indian negotiators noted by Kumar (2004, p. 51) is what he calls *anarchical individualism*, an Indian creolization pattern of their secondary individualistic mode of behaviour.

> Anarchical individualism may also detract from the negotiating team's ability to concentrate on the task at hand – much of their time and effort might go in either critiquing other team members or responding to criticisms levelled against them. This may distract them from truly trying to concentrate on developing an integrative solution to the

problem at hand. Finally, internal disunity within the Indian negotiating team may convey an impression to the other party that they are
not really serious about negotiations. Anarchical individualism renders
intra-group cooperation highly problematical. Anarchical individualism
may impart a high degree of unpredictability in the negotiation process.
... More broadly, both Brahmanical idealism and anarchical individualism work to slow down the speed of the negotiation.

Several authors note that negotiating with Indians requires patience at each
level of the negotiation process, during information exchange as well as for
finalizing an agreement, and recommend making no concessions until the
very end.[32] Foreign negotiators should neither lose their nerve nor try to
speed up a process to close a deal, which may appear to Indian negotiators
as clearly suboptimal. Kumar notes (2004, p. 53):

> An extensive preoccupation with detail and what many may perceive
> to be an overcritical attitude are also reflective of the same idealistic
> mindset. You cannot directly challenge that mindset.

Japanese style

Numerous books and articles are devoted to the Japanese style of negotiation
and more generally to the Japanese mentality and style of management.[33]
The Japanese are well prepared, especially when it comes to familiarising
themselves with their negotiation partners' culture. Japanese seem at first a
rather ethnocentric people but, paradoxically, are also very conscious of this
ethnocentrism (e.g., the crucial distinction between *Nihon-Jin,* a Japanese
person versus *Gaï-Jin,* a foreign person as virtually two different types of
human beings). They are also well prepared in terms of defining their basic
interests and are willing to defend them quite vigorously. The Japanese culture is moderately high Power Distance (54), collectivistic with a relatively
low individualism score (46), and record high on Uncertainty Avoidance
(92). Japanese negotiators are likely to use negotiation strategies based on
power differentials to extract more for themselves from the joint outcomes;
however this also leads to higher joint gains. Although they make use of
distributive, information-based persuasion tactics to increase the power differential in their favour, Japanese negotiators are known for being *win-win*
oriented. The purchaser's role is dominant. Vendors must be fully aware of
this fact and adapt their behaviour accordingly.[34]

Although at heart Japanese people are very sensitive and emotional, they
seek to conceal their true emotions as far as possible. Japanese communication style is high-context and indirect. Like all Asians they must not be
made to "lose face": their foreign counterparts should avoid a communication style that would be resented by Japanese negotiators as being overly
direct.

Within a group of Japanese negotiators it is difficult to determine who really performs what function and who holds what power; it is always unwise to rely solely on "who says what" as a clear indication of "who holds power". Consensus building is important in Japan (i.e., *ringi-sho*), to the extent that a final answer to a negotiated agreement may be waited upon for several weeks or months by the foreign partner, simply because the sophisticated and lengthy consultation process investigating implementation details is under way within the Japanese organization.

High context Japanese negotiators display quite a high level of tolerance of ambiguity despite their high level of Uncertainty Avoidance. Whereas Americans may perceive ambiguity to be a sign of weakness, or a lack of masculinity and assertiveness, for the Japanese there is no conflict between masculinity and ambiguity.[35]

Japanese people are also long-term oriented, both past and future oriented with an ability to merge the past and future into an extended present (see *Makimono* time in Chapter 4). Lifetime employment is the rule in large companies. These companies are often backed by large banks which, as shareholders, do not strive for a quick return. They are more concerned with the soundness of the long-term business strategy of companies. This partly explains why Japanese negotiators do not feel as strongly pressured by timelines as do their Western counterparts.

Like most Asians, the Japanese tend to prefer an agreement based on trust over a detailed written contract. Even though this agreement may be loosely worded, in their view it is a better expression of the mutual trust that has developed between the parties. Japanese negotiators do not like the perspective of litigation based on the formal confrontation of claims in a court; there are only 7 lawyers per 100,000 inhabitants in Japan against 281 in the United States.[36]

The empathy of Japanese people may be very high: the interpersonal sensitivity of Japanese people and their sincere interest in foreign cultures and people makes them friendly hosts at business lunches or dinners. As noted earlier, Japanese businessmen spend time and money entertaining their negotiating partners to establish a rapport built on trust. However, Japanese negotiators remain strongly aware of what their basic interests are, and they are reputed to be tough negotiators. Graham recounts in the following terms a meeting in Tokyo between the president of a large Japanese industrial distributor and the marketing vice-president of an American machinery manufacturer, looking for a long-term agreement. After the traditional exchange of business cards, they spoke through an interpreter, despite the fact that the Japanese president understood and in fact spoke English.

> The Japanese president controlled the interaction completely, asking questions of all of us Americans through the interpreter ... After this initial round of questions for all the Americans, the Japanese president focused on developing a conversation with the American vice-president

... The Japanese president would ask a question in Japanese. The interpreter then translated the question for the American vice president. While the interpreter spoke, the American's attention (gaze direction) was given to the interpreter. However, the Japanese president's gaze direction was at the American. Therefore, the Japanese president could carefully and unobtrusively observe the American's facial expressions and nonverbal responses. Additionally, when the American spoke, the Japanese president had twice the response time. Because he understood English, he could formulate his responses during the translation process.

(Graham, 2003, p. 27)

Mexican style

Mexico is a high-power-distance country (81), ranking among the highest worldwide; as a consequence, decision-making is fairly centralized and "Mexicans logically prefer to deal abroad at the higher levels of government and business and on a personal and private basis".[37] Personal leverage – *palanca* – is important and influence is key to negotiation power. Mexican negotiators tend to be well positioned in their society, exhibiting their status and stamina.

As in many Latin American collectivistic societies (i.e., a low 36 individualism score for Mexico), family and political ties are extremely important in Mexico for determining individual influence. Strong ingroup orientation is expressed in bonds of loyalty and solidarity among the top people in both business and government. The dominant political party, PRI, is also a structure allowing patronage and networking in Mexican society, where relationships are a key issue. Although corruption has been combated by public authorities in recent years, bribery is still common in Mexico (TI score at 30). *Ubicacion*, that is, where one is plugged into the system, is important for determining a negotiator's status. Hernández Requejo and Graham (2008) mention 11 key elements of the Mexican culture that can explain the high relational orientation of Mexican negotiators: *La Familia* (i.e., family as a combination of the extended family and close friends); *Amigos* (i.e., a Mexican preference for doing business with people they know); *Confianza* (i.e., confidence extending to reliance and trust); *Riesgo* (i.e., a risk-taking attitude moderated by a rather fatalistic acceptance of possible negative outcomes); *La Ley* (i.e., a complex legal system, not always scrupulously respected); *Convencer* (i.e., persuasion; *convencer* which means *to convince*, is based on subjective rather than data-based arguments); *Puntualidad* (a relaxed attitude to time); *Buenos Modales/Etiqueta* (i.e., good manners and etiquette are related to conflict avoidance, indirect communication and polite confrontation); *Patriarquismo/Machismo* (i.e., Power Distance combines with the authority of the patriarch); *Formalidad/Lucirse* (i.e., Formality and show-off: professional appearance combined with class-consciousness are ostentatiously demonstrated); *El Acuerdo/El contrato* (i.e., an assumed acceptance of the incompleteness of contracts and a consequent preference for relational dispute resolution and the avoidance of litigation).[38]

Body language is important to most Latin Americans: it conveys emotions, especially when a negotiator is trying to persuade the other party. To their American neighbours in particular, Mexicans appear at times overly dramatic, emotional, and sentimental (Salacuse, 1999). Conversely, Mexican negotiators often resent their foreign partners for being reserved, inexpressive, and cold.

Truthful communication is not always to be expected from Mexicans and frankness should not be taken for granted. Paz (1962) explains that: "The Mexican tells lies because he delights in fantasy, or because he is desperate, or because he wants to rise above the sordid facts of his life". The use of instrumental communication strategies by high-context communication Mexican negotiators allows them to increase their profits, by manipulating their negotiation partner.

In a comparative study across 17 countries,[39] Mexicans appeared as competitive negotiators (this being evidenced by a fairly low level of joint profits) and the Mexican buyers were those who obtained the lion's share of the profits (almost 57% of the joint outcome), the highest position for buyers out of the 17 countries. Mexicans have been shown to be more win-win oriented when they negotiate interculturally than intraculturally, especially if the foreign negotiators themselves have an integrative orientation. The Mexicans positively react to their partner's problem-solving orientation by becoming themselves more problem-solving oriented and finally more satisfied with the negotiation outcomes.[40]

The Mexicans have a relaxed concept of time, expressing a polychronic pattern whereby schedules are not given precedence over relations with people. The *mañana* philosophy of time is based on a strong present orientation, which is detrimental to the accuracy of long-term planning and to real commitment vis-à-vis dates and deadlines. The etymology of the word for business in Spanish (*negocio*) is based on a negation of "*ocio*" (leisure, good time). Extreme activity, workaholism, and high time consciousness are not strong values in Spanish-speaking Mexico.

Mexicans have a problematic identity problem with their big neighbour, the U.S., and there is high sensitivity "to their perceived dependent relationship with the U.S. and their long memory of patronizing and demeaning actions taken by the U.S. as a government, by American companies and by Americans as individuals".[41] It is worth noting that a large part of the Mexican territory was conquered by the United States in a short war in 1845–1846 which led to the annexing of California, New Mexico, and Texas. It is therefore understandable that the relationship between Americans and Mexicans is not an easy one (understatement) and that a large Hispanic population still lives in formerly Mexican states of the U.S.

Middle Eastern style (Arab-Muslim countries)

If a "Middle Eastern style" truly exists, the following caveat should be borne in mind. The countries considered here are exclusively Arab-Muslim countries. Iran is Shiite Muslim, but not Arab; Turkey which is Ottoman and Muslim is not Arab; however it has dominated the Arab world for centuries. Yet it would be a mistake to ignore the enormous diversity of the Middle East. Christian minorities (Lebanese Maronites, Egyptian Copts, Iraqi Nestorians, Armenians, members of the Orthodox churches, etc.) are present almost everywhere and are influential in some countries. It is therefore essential to be fully aware of the fact that a world that is somewhat hastily classified as Arab-Islamic is also composed of Arabs who are not Muslims and Muslims who are not Arabs. It is noteworthy that Middle Eastern civilizations were largely the founders of European civilizations. They have left many traces behind, and as far as art and culture are concerned, their influences were dominant for many centuries during the Middle Ages. The pride of the persons with whom foreign negotiators are dealing must be –genuinely – respected.

On average, Middle Eastern Arabic (MEA) countries are high Power Distance (77), Collectivistic (38), and rather high Uncertainty Avoidance (68).[42] Due to their collectivist orientation, Arab negotiators place emphasis on building trust and relationships before they start negotiating business. Cultural sensitivity should extend much beyond looking at the list of "dos and don'ts" in a particular area of the world. Cultural insensitivity can lead first to hostility and finally to aborted negotiation. Negotiations can fail because the negotiator is unwilling/unable to pay the respect considered appropriate by the other party; alternatively, without leading to an impasse, cultural hostility on the MEA side blurs and slows down the negotiation process leading to suboptimal outcomes and low satisfaction on both sides. Personal and group reputation are important matters; thus a key issue is preserving and saving face, the concept of honour being of utmost importance in the Middle East. To Westerners, losing face may be embarrassing, but to Arabs, losing face is the decisive disgrace. Therefore their negotiation counterparts should be aware that they have to grant face to MEA negotiators; reciprocal respect for each other's honour and dignity is essential for MEA negotiators. Negotiating with high-context, polychronic Arab Middle Eastern negotiators requires significant patience because of their polychronic time pattern which gives precedence to interaction with people over task related concerns.[43]

Knowledge of the subgroup to which the negotiator belongs (e.g., ethnic, religious, national, and cultural) is essential; relationships between the negotiators in the MEA team must be carefully explored and understood, to find out who is who and what relationship each negotiator has with the others in an MEA group of negotiators.

The role of intermediaries ("sponsors" in Saudi Arabia) is important. As a result of European colonization over the last two centuries, the majority of "Middle Eastern" business people speak French or English and understand

European civilization; whereas the reverse is rarely true. Intermediaries must be employed for a simple reason: Europeans and Americans systematically underestimate the cultural divide. Local interpreters can be a problem because, although fluent in Arabic, they may belong to a different national, religious, or ethnic group and be resented by the negotiators of the country where negotiation takes place.[44]

One must expect a great deal of emotion, theatricality, and demonstrativeness, interspersed with true pragmatism. The mixture is often bewildering. Friendship is sought, relationships are personalized, and the idea of a cold "business-like" relationship is difficult to envisage. Once a true friend has been made (which is far from straightforward), the sense of loyalty can be very strong.

Arab Middle Eastern executives are more inclined to use an avoidance style than are Americans. In terms of the dual concern model, MEA negotiators use more integrative-problem-solving as well as an avoidant style in handling conflict, whereas American negotiators use more obliging, contending-dominating, and compromising avenues for conflict resolution.[45] During the negotiation process, MEA negotiators tend to have a fixed pie assumption that leads them to believe that it is not really feasible to maximize joint outcomes while trying to maximize one's share of the pie. In the case of Qatari negotiators, Tinsley et al. (2011, p. 505) write:

> Qataris even view maximizing own gain as antithetical to maximizing joint gains, and see yielding as necessarily correlated. Similarly, Qataris view defending honor as incompatible to the goals of Relationship-Building and Giving Face. That is, they seem to believe defending one's honor can be so important that it sacrifices abilities to give face to and build a relationship with the other party.

On another note, it should be remarked that Islamic values permeate daily life. For example, if the negotiations lead to consideration of a loan and interest rate, although this problem is not insurmountable, a great deal of caution is essential. The question of *riba*, which is usually translated as "interest", never fails to pose problems for Koranic law and the different legislative assemblies entrusted with its interpretation. These assemblies have been more or less strict in their interpretation of *riba*, which is mentioned several times in the Koran, as being forbidden. Thus specific financial operations, excluding the imposition of a method of repayment for loans which is fixed in advance, have been settled in accordance with Islamic law and on the basis of ancient practices. Rather than loans, they are joint operations where the banker brings the financing and clients their facilities and business talents. *Mudhâraba* corresponds to project financing with no recourse for the banker or investor if the business is discontinued; *musharaka* is similar except that the client brings part of the financing; *murabaha* is a sort of leasing agreement. Due to the relative complexity of the financial system, the weakness of economic governance in some MEA countries, and pervasive ingroup collusion, some of those countries exhibit relatively high TI levels of corruption; however there is much variance from 28 (Lebanon) to 43 for Bahrain, 46 for Saudi Arabia, and 61 for Qatar.

Russian style

Over 70 years of communism has left some deep impressions on Russian society. The results include a lack of understanding of basic economic concepts such as free-market price, company valuation, or the balance sheet. Unfamiliarity with free-market mechanisms is progressively being remedied by management education.[46] High Power Distance (77) and Collectivism (39) are characteristic not only of the ex-USSR but also of its successor, the Russian Federation. Strict obedience to authority and the fear of negative consequences of wrongdoing, combined with an extreme Uncertainty Avoidance level (95) translated into low levels of individual initiative and strong risk aversion of mandated Soviet negotiators. As noted by Beliaev et al. (1985, p. 105):

> Each negotiator is well trained in the party discipline; obedient, with a well-developed sense of hierarchy; hard-working and trained for stress, but with narrow horizons; loyal to the state and fearful of mistakes because of the risk of falling to the level of the average Soviet citizen; cautious, tough, and inflexible because of the strictness of their instructions; and willing to subordinate personal life to the demand of the position.

The Soviet style, still a part of the Russian style even after the disintegration of communism, has been described as fairly tough and unilateral. Negotiators tend to make extreme initial demands, to view adversaries' concessions as weakness, to make only minimal concessions, and to ignore deadlines. On the other hand, the Soviet-style Russians were good payers, and did respect contracts which were drafted in a very detailed way. This changed after the introduction of a highly opportunistic version of the free-market economy, with sometimes a lack a respect for the letter of contracts, and no efficient legal system and courts for the foreign party to defend its rights. There is much support for the view that the fundamentals of Russian negotiators are like those of the Soviet era: conflict and struggle-prone, unconcessive, lacking initiative, secretive, and obstructing, and tending to play a zero-sum game. Paradoxically, however, Russian negotiators are looking for good relationships with their negotiation partners.[47]

There is in fact a consensus of opinion describing Russian negotiators as "competitive" and "uncompromising", likely to be distributive and fixed-pie oriented, and ready to exert power strategies in negotiation.[48] This suggests that such contending and competitive behaviour is considered locally as standard practice. The ethical system of Russians widely differs from that of Americans. According to Lefebvre:

Something that an American considers normative positive behavior (for example, negotiating and reaching a compromise with an enemy, and even any deal with another individual), a Soviet man perceives as showing Philistine cowardice, weakness, as something unworthy (the word "deal" itself has a strong negative connotation in contemporary Russian).

(Lefebvre, 1983, quoted in Graham, Evenko, and Rajan, 1992, p. 396)

Communist centralized planning, based on detailed five-year plans, did not endow Soviet citizens with a sense of economic time. Given the complexity of coordination between government bodies, the Soviet citizen gave up trying to meet exact schedules. In Russia today, this logically results in a highly present and short-term-oriented society.

Russia is still undergoing fundamental transition. The bureaucratic controls have progressively been relaxed, giving birth to a new society with deep contrasts. New entrepreneurs appear very different from former Soviets, and are almost Western in style, insofar as they are full of initiative and show great flexibility. These gains, however, are largely undermined by the prevailing lack of reliability, opportunistic behaviour, and the confusion between business and wild capitalism. Incidents involving payment defaults and failure to enforce negotiated contracts are frequent. Many new Russian entrepreneurs do not feel bound by business norms and contracts because either they ignore them or they view them as foreign and therefore inapplicable in their context. The 2016 Transparency International score of 29 is clear evidence of high endemic corruption.

Notes

1 In Salacuse (1998, 1999), American negotiators report to be high in risk taking, using a direct communication style, and they are the highest in self-reported informality.
2 Margaret Mead (1948).
3 Nigerian negotiators (Nigeria serving as a proxy for Black Africa) self-report being highly formal in negotiation interactions, a direct communication style, rather win-lose oriented with 47 in Salacuse (1998, 1999).
4 The 2016 TI (Transparency International) corruption perceptions index is the classic measure for corruption level. It is high for "clean", non-corrupt countries such as Denmark and New Zealand (90) and low for countries with high and endemic corruption (lowest scores are South Sudan at 11 and Somalia at 10). See www.transparency.org.
5 The advantage of the universalistic/individualistic view is to increase inter-group tolerance and reduce hostility between conflicting ethnic groups. The disadvantage is increased individual isolation, since individuals are less supported in their personal life by ingroup members.
6 Graham (2003, p. 45), examining differences in competitiveness and equity, finds Brazilian negotiators to be relatively high in terms of joint profits in

Kelley's game, with almost equal distribution between buyer and seller (no role effect). However, Brazilian negotiators self-report to be rather win-lose at 44 in Salacuse's (1998) study.

7 Brett et al. (1998) report empirical evidence of both low- and high-power norms in Brazil.

8 Pearson and Stephan (1998).

9 Amado and Vinagre Brasil's accurate socio-historical description is an excellent account of the Brazilian national character (1991, pp. 51–59).

10 One lawyer per 326 inhabitants in Brazil vs. 300 in the U.S.; source: "The Most Litigious Countries in the World", *Clements Worldwide*, available at: www.clements.com/resources/articles/The-Most-Litigious-Countries-in-the-World, accessed 26 February 2018.

11 See Levine (1988), Graham (2003), Salacuse (1998, 1999). Time sensitivity is self-reported at 0 in Salacuse (1998, 1999); Brazilian negotiators self-report being rather contract-oriented (67), high in risk-taking (90), and low on time sensitivity (0) in Salacuse (1998, 1999). Communication style is indirect (20 self-reported, the highest score in Salacuse's study). Self-reported emotionalism is high (89).

12 Adler (2002).

13 Sobral, Carvalhal, and Almeida (2008).

14 Campbell et al. (1988); Graham (1993).

15 Salacuse (1998, 1999).

16 Luo (1995), Luo and Chen (1997), Tung (1996).

17 See Ha (1995), Tangney (1995). Face saving is strongly related to indirect communication. There is a risk of involuntarily making the other lose face by being overly direct. In Salacuse (1998, 1999), Chinese negotiators self-reporting about their negotiation style, rank second out of 12 CCs for indirect communication.

18 See for instance for the *emic* approaches of the Chinese business negotiation style (Pye, 1982, 1986; Shenkar and Ronen, 1993; Fang, 1999; Ghauri and Fang, 2003; Fang, 2006, Fang and Faure, 2011; Karsaklian, 2016; Hernández Requejo and Graham, 2008), in comparison/interaction with Americans (Graham and Lin, 1987; Eiteman, 1990; Adler et al., 1992; Graham and Lam, 2003; Lee et al., 2006; Liu et al., 2012), with other East-Asian countries/cultures (Tung, 1996; Movius et al. (2006), and within larger comparison sets (Graham, 1993; Graham et al. (1994), Salacuse, 1998, 1999; Morris et al. 1998).

19 Lee et al. (2006).

20 Hernández-Requejo and Graham (2008, pp. 227–228).

21 In Salacuse (1998, 1999), Chinese negotiators report a win-win orientation (82), a rather indirect communication style (18, rank), a rather top-down decision-making (54) and preferring strong leadership to team consensus (91).

22 Ghauri and Fang (2003, p. 430).

23 On the negotiation process with the Chinese, especially post-negotiation, see Ghauri and Fang (2003).

24 Cogan (2003).

25 See Graham (1993), Brett et al. (1998), Salacuse (1998, 1999), and Adair et al. (2004).

26 Hofstede (2001).

27 Tinsley (1998).

28 Campbell et al. (1988), Graham (2003).

29 German negotiators report to have a direct communication style (9) and low emotionalism (36) in Salacuse (1998, 1999).

30 Considering German negotiators as pure individuals is the best way to avoid negative biases when negotiating with them. After all, they are not personally responsible for every event of German history.

31 Salacuse (1998, 1999).

32 Kumar (2004), Hernández Requejo and Graham (2008).

33 The Japanese style of business negotiation has been described in books such as De Mente (1987), Hodgson et al. (2008), in chapters in a book or articles (Van Zandt, 1970; Oh, 1984; Tung, 1984; Hayashi, 1988; Graham, 1993; Drew et al., 1999; Graham and Sano, 2003), compared with the U.S. (Graham, 1981; Tung, 1996; Goldman, 1994; Brett and Okumura, 1998; Adair et al., 2001; Adair et al., 2004), or compared with other countries (Graham et al., 1988; Salacuse, 1998, 1999; Tinsley, 1998; Pornpitakpan, 1999; Brannen and Salk, 2000; Adair et al., 2004; Movius et al., 2006).

34 See in particular Adair et al. (2004), Graham (1981, 2003), Graham and Hernández-Requejo (2008), Graham et al. (2014); in Salacuse (1998, 1999), all Japanese negotiators (100%) self-report to be win-win oriented.

35 See Hawrysh and Zaichkowsky (1990); in Salacuse (1998, 1999), Japanese negotiators are the highest on communication indirectness.

36 See www.tentmaker.org/Quotes/lawyers-per-capita.html accessed 21 February 2018.

37 Fisher (1980, p. 28).

38 See Chapter 11 on the Mexican negotiation style in Hernández Requejo and Graham (2008).

39 Graham (1993).

40 See the empirical studies of Halvor and Rognes (1995) in the case of Norwegian versus Mexicans, and Mintu-Wimsatt and Graham (2004) on Canadian Anglophone and Mexican exporters.

41 Fisher (1980, p. 40); see also Carlos Fuentes (2012), *The Crystal Frontier*, London: Bloomsbury.

42 Based on average scores in Hofstede (2001, p. 500) between Saudi Arabia, Egypt, United Arab Emirates, Iraq, Kuwait, Lebanon, and Libya.

43 See Feghali (1997), Wunderle (2007), Khakhar and Rammal (2013).

44 Wunderle (2007, p. 36) comments on the issue concerning U.S. troops in Iraq as follows:

[because of] their disproportionate influence and their personal biases, interpreters can favor some groups at the expense of others. Animosity toward interpreters can also impair the U.S. mission. For example, U.S. forces that used Kuwaiti interpreters were received coldly by Iraqis because of the animosity between Iraqis and Kuwaitis. Similarly, an interpreter's tribal and sectarian affiliations might interfere with U.S. objectives and operations.

45 Elsayed-EkJiouly and Buda (1996).

46 Holden (2002).

47 Kimura (1996), Kremenyuk (1996), Roemer et al. (1999).

48 Rajan and Graham (1991), Graham et al. (1992), Graham (2003), Adair et al. (2004).

Recommendations for effective intercultural business negotiations

1/ Preparing

Rule 1: Be prepared to prepare; however do not over-prepare
Rule 2: Be prepared for the other side's unpreparedness
Rule 3: Map the human landscape and prepare for respectful behaviour
Rule 4: Assess intercultural obstacles (and opportunities) as early as possible
Rule 5: Key information must be collected prior to the negotiation
Rule 6: Prepare for the type of deal which will be negotiated
Rule 7: Empathy is not enough; examine the key elements of both the relationship and the deal and prepare for understanding their interface during the negotiation process

2/ Communicating and dealing with people

Rule 8: Take time for adequate preliminaries (especially if first-time encounter with long run partnership potential)
Rule 9: Give face to the other side and to your team partners; protect also your own face
Rule 10: Be ready for different communication styles
Rule 11: Constantly check the accuracy of communication
Rule 12: Do not over-interpret, especially when faced with ambiguous micro-moves
Rule 13: Let your intuition guide you in the interpretation of non-verbal communication
Rule 14: Have interpreters work on your side
Rule 15: Use interpreters as cultural consultants only if so decided
Rule 16: When interacting in English, use simple and clear words as well as short sentences
Rule 17: Never release key information in the hope of reciprocity

3/ Developing strategic behaviour in intercultural business negotiations

Rule 18: Define what your basic interests are
Rule 19: Identify the expectations of the other party and the common ground for negotiation
Rule 20: Be ready to breach negotiation, however avoid mentioning walk-away options
Rule 21: Be equipped for tough strategies from the other side
Rule 22: Do not overinvest in benevolent integrative moves if the other party is not likely to reciprocate

4/ Managing issues, power, and conflict

Rule 23: Control location … or take your time when not "at home"
Rule 24: Change negotiation style when needed
Rule 25: Be prepared to resist some rough and manipulative tactics; bring them to light
Rule 26: Control your concessions
Rule 27: Be flexible with the negotiation agenda

5/ Managing time in the negotiation process

Rule 28: Allow yourself plenty of time
Rule 29: Never tell the other side when you are leaving
Rule 30: Plan modestly
Rule 31: Be ready for temporal clash

6/ Fostering trust and developing relationships

Rule 32: Use go-betweens to help build a trustful relationship
Rule 33: Check that third-parties are neutral and do not play against you
Rule 34: Introduce lawyers as late as possible in the negotiation process
Rule 35: Be prepared to negotiate beyond negotiation
Rule 36: Litigation should be avoided because it does major damage to the relationship
Rule 37: Try to develop long-term relationships rather than close short-term deals

References

ABCnews (2002). Acting tough as part of anti-corruption stand, China executes official, ABCnews. November 11, 2002.

Acuff, F. L. (2008). *How to negotiate anything with anyone anywhere around the world*. AMACOM Div American Management Association.

Adachi, Y. (1998). The effect of semantic difference on cross-cultural business negotiations: A Japanese and American case study. *Journal of Language for International Business*, 9, n. 1, 43–52.

Adair, W. L., Okumura, T., and Brett, J.M. (2001). Negotiation behavior when cultures collide: The United States and Japan. *Journal of Applied Psychology*, 86(3), 371–85.

Adair, W. L., Brett, J. M., Lempereur, A., Okumura, T., Shikhirev, P., Tinsley, C., and Lytle, A. (2004). Culture and negotiation strategy. *Negotiation Journal*, 20(1), 87–111.

Adair, W.L. and Brett, J.M (2005). The negotiation dance: Time, culture, and behavioral sequences in negotiation. *Organization Science*, 16(1), 33–51.

Adler, N. J. (1986). *International Dimensions of Organizational Behavior*. Boston: PWS-Kent.

Adler, N. J. (2002). *International dimensions of organizational behaviour*, 4th edn. Cincinnati: South-Western.

Adler, N. J., and Graham, J. L. (1989). Cross-cultural comparison: The international comparison fallacy? *Journal of International Business Studies*, 20(3), 515–537.

Adler, N. J., Brahm, R. and Graham, J. L. (1992). Strategy implementation: A comparison of face-to-face negotiations in the People's Republic of China and the United States. *Strategic Management Journal*, 13(6), 449–466.

Alchian, A. A. and Demsetz, H. (1972). Production, information costs, and economic organization. *American Economic Review*, 62 (December), 777–795.

Amado, G., and Vinagre Brasil, H. (1991). Organizational behavior and cultural context: The Brazilian Jeitinho. *International Studies of Management and Organization*, 21(3), 38–61.

Ancona, D. G., Okhuysen, G. A. and Perlow, L. A. (2001). Taking time to integrate temporal research, *Academy of Management Review*, 26(4), 512–529.

Ang, S. H. (2000). The power of money: A cross-cultural analysis of business-related beliefs, *Journal of World Business*, 35(1), 43–60.

Angelmar, R. and Stern, L. W. (1978). Development of a content analysis scheme for analysis of bargaining communication in marketing, *Journal of Marketing Research*, 15, February, 93–102.

Association for Overseas Technical Scholarship (1975). *Nihongo no Kiso [Foundations of Japanese]*, Tokyo: AOTS-Chosakai.

Axelrod, R. (1984). *The Evolution of Cooperation*, New York: Basic Books.

Baber, W.W. and Fletcher-Chen, C. C-Y. (2015). *Practical Business Negotiation*, Abingdon: Routledge.

Barkai, J. (2008). Cultural dimension interests, the dance of negotiation, and weather forecasting: A perspective on cross-cultural negotiation and dispute resolution. *Pepperdine Dispute Resolution Law Journal* 8, 3.

Barry, B., Smithey Fulmer, I, and Van Kleef, G. A. (2004). I laughed, i cried, i settled: The role of emotion in negotiation. In M. J. Gelfand and J. M. Brett (Eds.), *The handbook of negotiation and culture* (pp. 71–94). Stanford: Stanford University Press.

Barzini, L. (1983). *The Europeans*. London: Penguin Books.

Bauer, P. (2001). Understanding the wash cycle, *Economic Perspectives*, 6(2), 11–14.

Bazerman, M. H. and Neale, M. A. (1992). *Negotiating Rationally*, New York: The Free Press.

Bazerman, M. H., Curhan, J. R., Moore, D. A. and Valley, K. L. (2000). Negotiation, *Annual Review of Psychology*, 51, 279–314.

Bazerman, M. H. (2002). *Judgment in Managerial Decision Making*, 5th edition, New York: John Wiley.

Beaufort, V. De and Lempereur, A. (2003). Negotiation mergers and acquisitions in the European Union. In P.N. Ghauri and J.-C. Usunier (Eds.), *International Business Negotiations* (pp. 291–323). Oxford: Pergamon/Elsevier.

Becker, H. and Fritzsche, D. H. (1987). A comparison of the ethical behavior of American, French and German managers, *Columbia Journal of World Business*, 22(4), 87–95.

Behfar, K., Friedman, R. and Brett, J.M. (2004). The team negotiation challenge: Defining and managing the internal challenges of negotiating teams, 1–33, Working Paper available at http://ssrn.com/abstract=1298512

Beliaev, E., Mullen, T. and Punnett, B. J. (1985). Understanding the cultural environment: U.S.-U.S.S.R. trade negotiations. *California Management Review*, 27(2), 100–12.

Benabou, C. (1999). Polychronicity and temporal dimensions of work in learning organizations, *Journal of Managerial Psychology*, 14(3/4), 257–268.

Bentham, J. (1996). *The collected works of Jeremy Bentham: An introduction to the principles of morals and legislation*. First published 1789. Oxford: Clarendon Press.

Berenbeim, R. E. (1997). Can multinational business agree on how to act ethically? *Business and Society Review*, 98, 24–28.

Berenbeim, R. E. (1999). Global corporate ethics practice: A developing consensus, *The Conference Board*, Research Report 1243-99-RR.

Berg J., Dickhaut J. and Mccabe K. (1995). Trust, reciprocity and social history, *Games and Economic Behavior*, 10, 22–142.

Berne, E. (1961). *Transactional analysis in Psychotherapy*. New York: Grove Press.

Bigoni, M., Bortolotti, S., Casari, M., Gambetta, D. and Pancotto, F. (2016). Regional disparities in Italy may have to do with trust and cooperation. *LSE Business Review*. Sept. 13.

Bista, D. B. (1990). *Fatalism and Development*, Calcutta: Orient Longman.

Bluedorn, A. C. (1998). An interview with anthropologist Edward T. Hall. *Journal of Management Inquiry*, 7(2), 109–115.

Bluedorn, A. C., Kalliah, T. J., Strube, M. J. and Martin, G. D. (1999). Polychronicity and the inventory of polychronic values (IPV): the development of an instrument to measure a fundamental dimension of organizational culture, *Journal of Managerial Psychology*, 13(3/4), 205–230.

Bourgeois, F. and Martinez-Tournalia, F. (2015). *Conducting negotiations in France. The sudden breaking off of negotiations ("La rupture abusive des pourparlers")*, EVERSHEDS LLP. Accessed June 8, 2018, from www.eversheds-sutherland.com/documents/global/france/Conducting_negotiations_in_France_note.PDF

Brannen, M. Y. and Salk, J. E. (2000). Partnering across borders: Negotiating organizational culture in a German-Japanese joint venture, *Human Relations*, 53(4), 451–487.

Brett, J. M. and Okumura, T. (1998). Inter- and intra-cultural negotiations: US and Japanese negotiators. *Academic of Management Journal*, 41(5), 495–510.

Brett, J. M., Adair W. L., Lempereur A., Okumura T., Shikhirev P, Tinsley C. H., and Lytle A. (1998). Culture and joint gains in negotiation. *Negotiation Journal*, 14(1), 61–86.

Brett, J. M., Shapiro, D. L. and Lytle, A. E. (1998). Breaking the bonds of reciprocity in negotiations. *Academy of Management Journal*, 41(4), 410–424.

Brett, J. M. (2000). Culture and negotiation, *International Journal of Psychology*, 35(2), 97–104.

Brett, J. M., Friedman, R. and Behfar, K. (2009). How to manage your negotiating team, *Harvard Business Review*, 85(9), 105–109.

Brooks, R. R. (2015). Observability & verifiability: informing the information fiduciary. Working Paper, University of Chicago. www.law.uchicago.edu/files/file/brooks_observability_verifiability.pdf

Brülhart, M., and Usunier, J. C. (2004). Verified trust: reciprocity, altruism and noise in trust games. Available at papers.ssrn.com

Brülhart, M. and Usunier, J.-C. (2012). Does the trust game measure trust? *Economics Letters*, 115, 20–23.

Buchan, N. R., Croson, R. T. A. and Dawes, R. M. (2002). Swift neighbors and persistent strangers: A cross-cultural investigation of trust and reciprocity in social exchange. *American Journal of Sociology*, 108(1), 168–206.

Buchan, Nancy R.; Johnson, Eric J. and Croson, Rachel T.A. (2006). "Let's get personal: An international examination of the influence of communication, culture and social distance on other regarding preferences". *Journal of Economic Behavior and Organization*, 60: 373–398.

Buller, P. F., Kohls, J. J. and Anderson, K. S. (1997). A model for addressing cross-cultural ethical conflicts. *Business & Society*, 36(2), 169–193.

Bülow, A. M. and Kumar, R. (2011). Culture and negotiation. *International Negotiation* 16(3), 349–359.

Burt, D. N. (1984). The nuances of negotiating overseas. *Journal of Purchasing and Materials Management* (Winter), 2–8.

Campbell, N. C. G., Graham, J. L., Jolibert, A. and Meissner, H. G. (1988). Marketing negotiations in France, Germany, the United Kingdom and United States, *Journal of Marketing*, 52(April), 49–62.

Caputo, A. (2013). A literature review of cognitive biases in negotiation processes, *International Journal of Conflict Management*, 24(4), 374–398.

Carnevale, P. J., Cha, Y. S., Wan, C. and Fraidin, S. (2004). Adaptive third parties in the cultural milieu. In Michele J. Gelfand and J. M: Brett (Eds.), *The handbook of negotiation and culture* (pp. 280–294). Stanford: Stanford University Press.

Carroll, J.B. (1956). *Language, Thought and Reality: Selected Writings of Benjamin Lee Whorf*. Cambridge, MA: MIT Press.

Caves, R. E. (2000). *Creative Industries: Contracts Between Art and Commerce*. Cambridge, MA: Harvard University Press.

Cellich, C. and Jain, S.C. (2004). *Global Business Negotiations: A Practical Guide*, Mason, OH: South Western.

Chapman, M. and Jamal, A. (1997). Acculturation: Cross cultural consumer perceptions and the symbolism of domestic space. *Advances in Consumer Research*, 24, 138–143.

Chan, T. S. and Armstrong, R. W. (1999). Comparative ethical report card: A study of Australian and Canadian Manager's perception of international marketing ethics problems, *Journal of Business Ethics*, 18, 3–15.

Charles, M. (2005). Language matters in business communication. *Journal of Business Communication*, 44, 260–282.

Chen, C. C., Chen, X.-P. and Meindl, J. R. (1998). How can cooperation be fostered? The cultural effects of individualism-collectivism. *Academy of Management Review*, 23 (2), 285–304.

Chen, D. (2015). China's Anti-Corruption Campaign Enters Phase Two, The Diplomat, 2 July 2015, retrieved 28 February 2016 from http://thediplomat.com/2015/07/chinas-anti-corruption-campaign-enters-phase-two/

Chinese Culture Connection (1987). Chinese values and the search for culture-free dimensions of culture. *Journal of Cross-Cultural Psychology*, 18(2), 143–164.

Cogan, C. (2003). *French negotiating behavior: Dealing with la grande nation*. US Institute of Peace Press.

Cohen, H. (1980). *You Can Negotiate Anything*, New York: Bantam Books.

Cohen, R. (1993). An advocate's view. In G. O. Faure, and J. Z. Rubin, (Eds.), *Culture and negotiation: the resolution of water disputes* (pp. 22–37). Thousand Oaks, CA: Sage.

Cohen, R. (2007). *Negotiating across cultures: International communication in an interdependent world*. Washington: US institute of Peace Press.

Colson, A., Druckman, D. and Donohue, W. (2013). *International Negotiation: Foundations, Models, and Philosophies – Christophe Dupont*. Dordrecht: Republic of Letters Publishing.

Conte, J. M., Rizzuto, T. E., and Steiner, D. D. (1999). A construct-oriented analysis of individual-level polychronicity. *Journal of Managerial Psychology*, 14(3/4), 269–287.

Darley, W. K. and Blankson, C. (2008). African culture and business markets: implications for marketing practices, *Journal of Business & Industrial Marketing*, 23(6), 374–383.

David, R. (1987). *Le Droit du commerce international, réflexions d'un comparatiste sur le droit international privé*, Economica: Paris.

De Mente, B. (1987). *How to do Business with the Japanese*, N.T.C. Publishing: Chicago, IL.

De Moor, A. and Weigand, H. (2004). Business negotiation support: Theory and practice. *International Negotiation,* 9(1), 31–57.

Demsetz, H. (1967). Toward a theory of property rights. *American Economic Review*, 57(May), 347–359.

Demuijnck, G. (2015). Universal values and virtues in management versus cross-cultural moral relativism: An educational strategy to clear the ground for business ethics. *Journal of Business Ethics* 128(4): 817–835.

D'Iribarne, P. (2003). *The logic of honor: National traditions and corporate management*. New York: Welcome Rain Publishers, 256.

Donoho, C. L., Polonsky, M. J., Swenson, M. J., and Herche, J. (1999). A cross-cultural investigation of the universality of the personal selling ethics scale, *Journal of Euromarketing*, 8(1/2), 101–16.

Drew, M., Herbig, P., Howard, C. and Borstorff, P. (1999). At the table: observations on Japanese negotiation style. *American Business Review*, 17(1), 65–71.

Druckman, D., Benton, A.A., Ali, F. and Bagur, J.S. (1976). Culture differences in bargaining behavior. *Journal of Conflict Resolution*, 20, 413–449.

Dunfee, T. W. and Warren, D. E. (2001). Is guanxi ethical? A normative analysis of doing business in China, *Journal of Business Ethics*, 32, 191–204.

Dupont, C. (1994). La Négotiation: Conduite, Théorie, Applications, 4th edition, Paris: Dalloz.

Dupont, C. and Audebert-Lasrochas, P. (2013). The Congress of Vienna Negotiations. In Colson, A., Druckman, D. and Donohue, W., *International Negotiation: Foundations, Models, and Philosophies* (pp. 101–148). Dordrecht: Republic of Letters Publishing.

Earley, P. C., and Mosakowski, E. (2004). Cultural intelligence. *Harvard Business Review*, 82(10), 139–146.

The Economist (2015). Who wants to be a mandarin? Public service is less fun if you can't take bribes. *The Economist*, June 6, 2015.

Eiteman, D. K. (1990). American executives' perceptions of negotiating joint ventures with the People's Republic of China: Lessons learned, *Columbia Journal of World Business* (Winter), 59–67.

Elberse, A. (2007). The power of stars: Do star actors drive the success of movies? *Journal of Marketing*, 71(4), 102–120.

Elfenbein, H. A., Curhan, J. R., Eisenkraft, N., Shirako, A., and Baccaro, L. (2008). Are some negotiators better than others? Individual differences in bargaining outcomes. *Journal of Research in Personality*, 42(6), 1463–1475.

Elsayed-EkJiouly, S. M., and Buda, R. (1996). Organizational conflict: A comparative analysis of conflict styles across cultures. *International Journal of Conflict Management*, 7(1), 71–81.

English, T. (2010). *Tug of War: The Tension Concept and the Art of International Negotiation*, Common Ground Publishing.

Ess, C. and Sudweeks, F. (2006). Culture and computer-mediated communication: Toward new understandings. *Journal of Computer-Mediated Communication*, 11, 179–191.

Evans, F. B. (1963). Selling as a dyadic relationship: A new approach. *American Behavioral Scientist*, 6, May, 76–79.

Fainshmidt, S., White, G. O. and Cangioni, C. (2014). Legal distance, cognitive distance, and conflict resolution in international business intellectual property disputes. *Journal of International Management*, 20(2), 188–200.

Fang, T. (1999). *Chinese business negotiating style*. London: Sage.

Fang, T. (2006). Negotiation: the Chinese style. *Journal of Business & Industrial Marketing*, 21(1), 50–60.

Fang, T., and Faure, G.-O. (2011). Chinese communication characteristics: A Yin Yang perspective. *International Journal of Intercultural Relations*, 35(3), 320–333.

Faure, G.-O. and Sjöstedt, G. (1993). Culture and negotiation: An introduction, in G. O. Faure & J. Z. Rubin (Eds), *Culture and Negotiation* (pp. 1–13). Newbury Park, CA: Sage Publications.

Faure, G.-O. and Rubin, J. Z., editors (1993). *Culture and Negotiation*. Newbury Park, CA: Sage Publications.

Feghali, E. (1997). Arab cultural communication patterns. *International Journal of Intercultural Relations*, 21(3), 345–378.

Fehr, E. and Gächter, S. (2000). Fairness and retaliation: The economics of reciprocity. *Journal of Economic Perspectives*, 14, 159–181.

Fenn, P, Lowe, D. J. and Speck, C. (1997). Conflict and dispute in construction. *Construction Management and Economics*, 15(6), 513–518.

Ferraro, G. P. (1990). *The Cultural Dimension of International Business*, Englewood Cliffs, NJ: Prentice-Hall.

Fershtman, C. and Gneezy, U. (2001). Discrimination in a segmented society. *Quarterly Journal of Economics*, 116, 351–377.

Fisher, G. (1980). *International Negotiation: A cross-cultural perspective*. Yarmouth, ME: Intercultural Press.

Fisher, G. (1988). *Mindsets*, Yarmouth, ME: Intercultural Press.

Fisher, R., Ury, W. L. and Patton, B. (2011). *Getting to yes: Negotiating agreement without giving in*. New York: Penguin.

Follesdal, A. (2015). John Rawls' Theory of Justice as Fairness. In *Philosophy of Justice* (pp. 311–328). Dordrecht: Springer.

Ford, D., editor (1990). *Understanding Business Markets*, London: Academic Press.

Foster, D. A. (1995). *Bargaining Across Borders*, New York: McGraw-Hill.

Foster, G.M. (1965). Peasant society and the image of limited good. *American Anthropologist*, 67, 293–315.

Fuentes, C. (2012). *The Crystal Frontier*, London: Bloomsbury.

Fukuyama F. (1994). *Trust: The social virtues and the creation of prosperity*, New York: Free Press.

Gächter, S. and Herrmann, B. (2009). Reciprocity, culture and human cooperation: previous insights and a new cross-cultural experiment. *Philosophical Transactions of the Royal Society of London B: Biological Sciences*, 364(1518), 791–806.

Galinsky, A. D. (2004). *When to make the first offer in negotiations*. Harvard Business School Working Knowledge – 9/2004. http://hbswk.hbs.edu/archive/4302.html, accessed March 2018.

Galinsky, A. D., Leonardelli, G. J., Okhuysen, G. A., and Mussweiler, T. (2005). Regulatory focus at the bargaining table: Promoting distributive and integrative success. *Personality and Social Psychology Bulletin*, 31(8), 1087–1098.

Galtung, J. (1981). Structure, culture and intellectual style: An essay comparing Saxonic, Teutonic, Gallic and Nipponic approaches, *Social Science Information*, 20(6), 817–856.

Gambetta D. (1988). Mafia: The price of distrust. in D. Gambetta (ed.), *Trust: Making and Breaking Cooperative Relationships*, Oxford: Blackwell, 159–175.

Geertz, C. (1983). Local Knowledge. New York: Basic Books.

Gelfand, M.J. and Brett, J.M., editors (2004). *The Handbook of Negotiation and Culture*. Palo Alto: Stanford University Press.

Gelfand, M.J., Lun, J., Lyons, S. and Shteynberg, G. (2011). Descriptive norms as carriers of culture in negotiation. *International Negotiation*, 16(3), 361–381.

Gelfand, M. J., Brett, J. M., Gunia, B. C., Imai, L., Huang, T.-J., and Hsu, B.-F. (2013). Toward a culture-by-context perspective on negotiation: Negotiating teams in the United States and Taiwan. *Journal of Applied Psychology*, 98(3), 504–513.

George, J. M., Jones, G. R. and Gonzalez, J. A. (1998). The role of affect in cross-cultural negotiations. *Journal of International Business Studies*, 29(4), 749–772.

German, P. M. (2002). To bribe or not to bribe – A less than ethical dilemma, resolved? *Journal of Financial Crime*, 9(3), 249–258.

Ghauri, P., and Fang, T. (2001). Negotiating with the Chinese: A socio-cultural analysis. *Journal of World Business*, 36(3), 303–325.

Ghauri, P. N. and Fang, T. (2003). Negotiating with the Chinese: A process view in P.N. Ghauri and J.-C. Usunier (Eds.), *International Business Negotiations* (pp. 411–433). Oxford: Pergamon/Elsevier.

Ghauri, P. N. and Usunier, J.-C. (2003). *International Business Negotiations*. Oxford: Pergamon/Elsevier.

Gillespie, K. (1987). Middle East response to the US Foreign Corrupt Practices Act, *California Management Review*, 29(4), 9–30.

Glenn, E. (1981). *Man and Mankind: conflict and communication between cultures*, Horwood, NJ: Ablex.

Goldman, A. (1994). The centrality of 'Ningensei' to Japanese negotiating and interpersonal relationships: Implications for U.S.-Japanese communication. *International Journal of Intercultural Relations*, 18(1), 29–54.

Goldsmith, D. J. (2001). A normative approach to the study of uncertainty and communication. *Journal of Communication*, 51(3), 514–533.

Goleman, D. (2006). *Emotional intelligence*. New York: Bantam books.

Goodenough, W. H. (1971). *Culture, Language and Society*, Modular Publications, 7, Reading, MA: Addison-Wesley.

Graham, J. L. (1981). A hidden cause of America's trade deficit with Japan, *Columbia Journal of World Business*, Fall, 5–15.

Graham, R. J. (1981). The role of perception of time in consumer research. *Journal of Consumer Research*, 7, March, 335–342.

Graham, J. L. and Herberger, R. A. Jr (1983). Negotiators abroad: Don't shoot from the hip. *Harvard Business Review*, 61(4), 160–168.

Graham, J. L. (1985). Cross-cultural marketing negotiations: A laboratory experiment. *Marketing Science*, 4(2), 130–146.

Graham, J.L. and Meissner, H.G. (1986). *Content analysis of business negotiations in five countries*. Working Paper. Los Angeles: University of Southern California.

Graham, J. L. and Lin, C.-Y. (1987). A comparison of marketing negotiations in the Republic of China (Taiwan) and the United States, in *Advances in International Marketing*, 2, 23–46, Greenwich, CT: JAI Press.

Graham, J. L., Kim, D. K., Lin, C.-Y. and Robinson, M. (1988). Buyer-seller negotiations around the Pacific Rim: Differences in fundamental exchange processes. *Journal of Consumer Research*, 15(1), 48–54.

Graham, J. L. and Sano, Y. (1989). *Smart bargaining: Doing business with the Japanese*, 2nd edn, Cambridge, MA: Ballinger.

Graham, J. L., Evenko, L. I. and Rajan, M. N. (1992). An empirical comparison of Soviet and American business negotiations. *Journal of International Business Studies*, 23(3), 387–418.

Graham, J. L. (1993). Business negotiations: Generalizations about Latin America and East Asia are dangerous, *UCINSIGHT*, University of California Irvine GSM, Summer, 6–23.

Graham, J. L. (1993). The Japanese negotiation style: Characteristics of a distinct approach. *Negotiation Journal*, 9(2), 123–140.

Graham, J. L. (1993). Business negotiations: Generalisations about Latin America and East Asia are dangerous. *UCI Irvine/Research*, 6–23.

Graham, J. L., Mintu, A. T. and Rodgers, W. (1994). Explorations of negotiation behaviors in ten foreign cultures using a model developed in the United States. *Management Science*, 40, 1 (January), 72–95.

Graham, J. L. (2003). Vis-à-vis: International business negotiations. In P.N. Ghauri and J.-C. Usunier (Eds.), *International Business Negotiations*, 2nd edn (pp. 23–50). Oxford: Pergamon/Elsevier.

Graham, J. L., and Lam, N. M. (2003). The Chinese negotiation. *Harvard Business Review*, 81(10), 82–91.

Graham, J. L. and Sano, Y. (2003). Business negotiations between Japanese and Americans in P.N. Ghauri and J.-C. Usunier (Eds.), *International Business Negotiations*, 2nd edn (pp. 393–410). Oxford: Pergamon/Elsevier.

Graham, J. L., Lawrence, L. and Hernández Requejo, W. (2014). *Inventive Negotiation: Getting Beyond Yes*. London: Macmillan.

Grayson, K., Johnson, D. and Chen, D.-F. R. (2008). Is firm trust essential in a trusted environment? How trust in the business context influences customers. *Journal of Marketing Research,* 45 (April), 241–256.

Greif A. (1994). Cultural beliefs and the organization of society: A historical and theoretical reflection on collectivist and individualist societies. *Journal of Political Economy*, 102(5), 912–950.

Gruère, J.-P. and Morel. P. (1991). *Cadres Français et Communications Interculturelles*. Paris: Eyrolles.

Gudykunst, W. B. and Ting-Toomey, S. (1988). Culture and affective communication. *American Behavioral Scientist*, 31, 384–400.

Gudykunst, W.B., Matsumoto, Y., Ting-Toomey, S., Nishida, T., Kim, K., and Heyman, S. (1996). The influence of cultural individualism-collectivism, self construals, and individual values on communication styles across cultures. *Human Communication Research*, 22(4), 510–543.

Gunia, B. C., Swaab, R. I., Sivanathan, N., and Galinsky, A. D. (2013). The remarkable robustness of the first-offer effect: Across culture, power, and issues. *Personality and Social Psychology Bulletin*, 39(12), 1547–1558.

Gunia, B. C, Brett, J. M., and Gelfand, M. J. (2016). The science of culture and negotiation, *Current Opinion in Psychology*, April, 8, 78–83.

Guttman, J. M. (2000). On the evolutionary stability of preferences for reciprocity. *European Journal of Political Economy*, 16(1), 31–50.

Ha, F. I. (1995). Shame in Asian and Western cultures. *American Behavioral Scientist*, 38(8), August, 1114–1131.

Habib, M. and Zurawicki, L. (2002). Corruption and foreign direct investment, *Journal of International Business Studies*, 33(2), 291–307.

Hall, E. T. (1959). *The Silent Language*, Garden-City, NY: Doubleday.

Hall, E. T. (1960). The silent language in overseas business. *Harvard Business Review,* 38(3), 87–96.

Hall, E. T. (1976). *Beyond Culture*, Garden City, NY: Anchor Press/Doubleday.

Hall, E. T. (1983). *The Dance of Life*, Garden City, NY: Anchor Press/Doubleday.

Halvor, N. J. and Rognes, J. (1995). Culture, behavior, and negotiation outcomes: A comparative and cross-cultural study of Mexican and Norwegian negotiators. *International Journal of Conflict Management*, 6(1), 5–29.

Hamra, W. (2000). Bribery in international business transactions and the OECD convention: Benefits and limitations. *Business Economics*, October, 33–46.

Harnett, D. L. and Cummings, L. L. (1980). *Bargaining Behavior: An International Study*. Houston: Dame Publications.

Harris, P. R. and Moran, R. T. (1987). *Managing Cultural Differences*. Houston: Gulf Publishing.

Harris, P. R. Moran, R. T. and Moran, S. (2004). *Managing Cultural Differences: Global Leadership Strategies for the 21st Century*. Oxford: Butterworth-Heinemann.

Haugland, S. (1998). The cultural dimension of international buyer-seller relationships. *Journal of Business-to-Business Marketing*, 4(4), 3–33.

Haworth, D. A., and Savage, G. T. (1989). A channel-ratio model of intercultural communication: The trains won't sell, fix them please. *Journal of Business Communication*, 26, 231–254.

Hawrysh, B. M. and Zaichkowsky, J. L. (1990). Cultural approaches to negotiations: Understanding the Japanese, *International Marketing Review*, 7(2), 28–42.

Hayashi, S. (1988). *Culture and Management in Japan*, Tokyo: University of Tokyo Press.

Henrich, J., Boyd, R., Bowles, S., Camerer, C., Fehr, E., Gintis, H., McElreath, R., Alvard, M., Barr, A., Ensminger, J. and Henrich, N. S. (2005). Economic man in cross-cultural perspective: Behavioral experiments in 15 small-scale societies. *Behavioral and Brain Sciences*, 28, 795–815.

Hernández Requejo, W. and Graham, J. L. (2008). *Global negotiation: The new rules*. London: Macmillan.

Hirschman, A. O. (1970). *Exit, Voice, and Loyalty: Responses to Decline in Firms, Organizations, and States*, Cambridge, MA: Harvard University Press.

Hodgson, G. M. (2004). Opportunism is not the only reason why firms exist: why an explanatory emphasis on opportunism may mislead management strategy. *Industrial and Corporate Change*, 13(2), 401–418.

Hodgson, J. D., Sano, Y and Graham, J. L. (2008). *Doing business with the new Japan: succeeding in America's richest international market*. Rowman & Littlefield.

Hofstede, G. (1989). Cultural predictors of national negotiation style. In Frances Mautner-Markhof (ed.), *Processes of International Negotiations*, Boulder, CO: Westview Press, 193–201.

Hofstede, G. (1991). *Cultures and Organizations: Software of the mind*, Maidenhead: McGraw-Hill.

Hofstede, G. (2001). *Culture's Consequences*, 2nd edn, Thousand Oaks: Sage Publications.

Hofstede, G. and Usunier, J.C. (2003). Hofstede's dimension of culture and their influence on international business negotiations. In P.N. Ghauri and J.-C. Usunier (Eds). *International Business Negotiations*, 2nd edn (pp. 137–154), Oxford: Pergamon/Elsevier.

Holden, N. J. (2002). *Cross-cultural management: A knowledge management perspective*. Harlow, UK: Pearson.

Hoon-Halbauer, S. K. (1999). Managing relationships within Sino-Foreign joint ventures. *Journal of World Business*, 34(4), 344–371.

Horn, G. (2015). M and A due diligence failures: FCPA and Goodyear. *The National Law Review (Barnes & Thornburg LLP)*. Retrieved March 2, 2015 from www.natlawreview.com/article/m-and-due-diligence-failures-fcpa-and-goodyear.

Hui, M. K., and Au, K. (2001). Justice perceptions of complaint handling: A cross-cultural comparison between PRC and Canadian customers, *Journal of Business Research*, 52, 161–173.

Husted, B., Dozier, J. McMahon, J. and Katten, M. (1996). The impact of cross-national carriers of business ethics on attitudes about questionable practices and form of moral reasoning, *Journal of International Business Studies*, 27(2), 391–411.

Husted, B. (1999). Wealth, culture, and corruption, *Journal of International Business Studies*, 30, 2, 339–360.

Inglehart, R. (Ed.). (2004). *Human beliefs and values: A cross-cultural sourcebook based on the 1999–2002 values surveys*. Buenos Aires: Siglo XXI.

Jeong, H.-W. (2016). *International Negotiation: Process and Strategies*, Cambridge: Cambridge University Press.

Jones, R. and Lim, K. (2012). Singapore Airlines A380 turns back after engine problem. *Reuters-Asia*, March 27, 2012. www.reuters.com/article/uk-singaporeair-a380/singapore-airlines-a380-turns-back-after-engine-problem-idUSLNE82Q01V20120327, accessed July 5, 2018.

Kahneman, D., Knetsch, J. L. and Thaler, R. (1987). Fairness as a constraint on profit seeking: Entitlements in the market, *American Economic Review*, 76, 728–41.

Kalé, S. H. (2003). How national culture, organizational culture and personality impact Buyer-seller interactions in P.N. Ghauri and J.-C. Usunier (Eds.), *International Business Negotiations* (pp. 75–93). Oxford: Pergamon/Elsevier.

Kaplan, R. B. (1966). Cultural thought patterns in inter-cultural education. *Language Learning*, 16, 1–20.

Karsaklian, E. (2016). The invisible negotiator in the land of paradox management. *Journal of US-China Public Administration* 13(5), 333–347.

Karsaklian, E. (2017). *Sustainable Negotiation: What Physics Can Teach Us About International Negotiation*, Bingley: Emerald Publishing.

Kaufman, C. D., Lane, P.M. and Lindquist, J. D. (1991). Exploring more than 24 hours a day: A preliminary investigation of polychronic time use, *Journal of Consumer Research*, 18(3), 392–401.

Kaufman-Scarborough, C. and Lindquist, J. D. (1999). Time management and polychronicity. Comparisons, contrasts and insights from the workplace, *Journal of Managerial Psychology*, 14(3/4), 288–312.

Kelley, H. H. (1966). A classroom study of the dilemmas in interpersonal negotiations, in K. Archibald (ed.), *Strategic Interaction and Conflict*, Institute of International Studies, University of California, Berkeley, CA.

Kern, M. C., Lee, S., Aytug, Z. G., and Brett, J. M. (2012). Bridging social distance in inter-cultural negotiations: "you" and the bi-cultural negotiator. *International Journal of Conflict Management*, 23(2), 173–191.

Kersten, G. E. and Noronha, S. J. (1999). Negotiation via the World Wide Web: A cross-cultural study of decision making. *Group Decisions and Negotiations*, 8, 251–279.

Kersten, G. E., Köszegi, S. and Vetschera, R. (2002). Effect of culture in anonymous negotiations: An experiment in four countries. *35th Annual IEEE Conference on System Science*, 1, 7–10.

Khakhar, P. and Rammal, H. G. (2013). Culture and business networks: International business negotiations with Arab managers. *International Business Review*, 22(3), 578–590.

Khuri, F. (1968). The etiquette of bargaining in the Middle-East. *American Anthropologist*, 70, 693–706.

Kim, D., Pan, Y. and Park, H. S. (1998). High- versus low-context culture: A comparison of Chinese, Korean, and American cultures. *Psychology & Marketing*, 15(6), 507–521.

Kimura, H. (1996). The Russian way of negotiating. *International Negotiation*, 1(3), 365–389.

Kirkbride, P. S., Tang, S. F. Y. and Westwood, R. I. (1991). Chinese conflict preferences and negotiating behavior – Cultural and psychological influences. *Organization Studies*, 12(3), 365–386.

Kluckhohn, F. R. and Strodtbeck, F. L. (1961). *Variations in Value Orientations*, Westport, CT: Greenwood Press.

Knittel, B. and Stefanini, A. (1993). Indian Joint-Venture: Les Leçons de l'Expérience. *Annales des Mines - Gérer et Comprendre*, March, 17–23.

Koehn, D. (2013). East meets West: Toward a universal ethic of virtue for global business. *Journal of Business Ethics*, 116, 703–715.

Kolb, D. M., and Williams, J. (2004). Everyday negotiation. In Carrie Menkel-Meadow and Michael Wheeler (Eds.), *What's Fair: Ethics for Negotiators* (pp. 264–269). San Francisco: Jossey Bass.

Kolb, D. M., and McGinn, K. L. (2008). Beyond gender and negotiation to gendered negotiations. Harvard Business School Working Paper 09-64.

Kolb, D. M. (2009). Too bad for the women or does it have to be? Gender and negotiation research over the past twenty-five years. *Negotiation Journal*, 25(4), 515–531.

Kopelman, S., and Olekalns, M. (1999). Process in cross-cultural negotiations. *Negotiation Journal*, 15(4), 373–380.

Kozan, M. K. and Ergin, C. (1999). The influence of intra-cultural value differences on conflict management practices. *The International Journal of Conflict Resolution*, 10(3), 249–267.

Kranton, R. E. (1996). Reciprocal exchange: A self-sustaining system. *American Economic Review*, 86(4), 830–851.

Kremenyuk V. A. (1993). A pluralistic view point. In G. O. Faure and J. Z. Rubin (Eds.), *Culture and negotiation: the resolution of water disputes* (pp. 47–54). Thousand Oaks, CA: Sage.

Kremenyuk, V. A. (1996). Negotiations in the Former Soviet Union: New structure, new dimensions. *International Negotiation*, 1(3), 351–364.

Kumar, R. (1997). The role of affect in negotiations: An integrative overview. *Journal of Applied Behavioral Science*, 33(1), 84–100.

Kumar, R. and Nti, K. O. (1998). Differential learning and interaction in alliance dynamics: A process and outcome discrepancy model, *Organization Science*, 9(3), 356–367.

Kumar, R. (1999). Communicative conflict in intercultural negotiations: The case of American and Japanese business negotiations. *International Negotiation*, 4(1), 63–78.

Kumar, R. (2004). Culture and emotions in intercultural negotiations: An overview. In M. J. Gelfand and J. M. Brett (Eds), *The handbook of negotiation and culture* (pp. 95–113). Stanford: Stanford University Press.

Kumar, R. (2004). Brahmanical idealism, anarchical individualism, and the dynamics of Indian negotiating behavior. *International Journal of Cross Cultural Management*, 4(1), 39–58.

Kumar, R. and Patriotta, G. (2011). Culture and international alliance negotiations: A sensemaking perspective. *International Negotiation*, 16(3), 511–533.

Lang, W. (1993). A professional's view. In G. O. Faure and J. Z. Rubin (Eds.), *Culture and Negotiation*, (pp. 38–46). Newbury Park, CA: Sage Publications.

Langosch, M., and McCarthy, K. J. (2017). Culture in mergers and acquisitions. In T.K. Das (ed.) *Culture and Behavioral Strategy* (pp. 125–154). Charlotte, NC: Information Age Publishing.

Lax, D. and Sebenius, J. K. (1992). The Manager as Negotiator: The Negotiator's Dilemma: Creating and Claiming Value. In S. Goldberg, F. Sander & N. Rogers (Eds), *Dispute Resolution* (2nd ed., pp. 49–62). Boston: Little Brown and Co.

Lee, K.-H., Yang, G. and Graham, J. L. (2006). Tension and trust in international business negotiations: American executives negotiating with Chinese executives. *Journal of International Business Studies*, 37, 5, 623–641.

Lee, S., Adair, W. L., and Seo, S. J. (2013). Cultural perspective taking in cross-cultural negotiation. *Group Decision and Negotiation*, 22(3), 389–405.

Lefebvre, V. D. (1983). Ethical features of the normative hero in Soviet children's literature of the 1960s-70s, *Studies of Cognitive Sciences*, 20, Irvine, CA: School of Social Sciences..

Leung, K. (1997). Negotiation and reward allocations across cultures. In P.C. Earley and M Erez (Eds), *New Perspectives on International Industrial/Organizational Psychology* (pp. 640–675). San Francisco: Jossey-Bass.

Levine, R. V. (1988). The pace of life across cultures. in Joseph E. McGrath (ed.), *The Social Psychology of Time*, Newbury Park, CA: Sage Publications, 39–60.

Li, S. (2004). Why is property right protection lacking in China? An institutional explanation. *California Management Review*, 46(3), 100–115.

Li, J. and Labig, C. E. Jr (2001). Negotiating with China: Exploratory study of relationship-building, *Journal of Managerial Issues*, 13(3), 345–359.

Linton, R. (1945). *The Cultural Background of Personality*, New York: D. Appleton-Century.

Liu, L. A., Friedman, R., Barry, B. Gelfand, M. J. and Zhang, Z.-X. (2012). The dynamics of consensus building in intracultural and intercultural negotiations. *Administrative Science Quarterly*, 57, 269–303.

Loe, T. W., Ferrell, L. and Mansfield, P. (2013). A review of empirical studies assessing ethical decision making in business. *Journal of Business Ethics*, 116, 279–301 (citation classics from the JBE), originally published in *Journal of Business Ethics* (2000), 25(3), 185–204.

Lorenz, E.H. (1988). Neither friends nor strangers: Informal networks of subcontracting. In Diego Gambetta (ed.), *Trust: Making and Breaking Cooperative Relationships* (pp. 194–210), Oxford: Blackwell.

Louhiala-Salminen, L., Charles, M., and Kankaanranta, A. (2005). English as a lingua franca in Nordic corporate mergers: Two case companies. *English for Specific Purposes*, 24, 401–421.

Luft, J. and Ingham, H. (1961). The johari window. *Human Relations Training News*, 5(1), 6–7.

Luna, D., Peracchio, L. A. and de Juan, M. D. (2002). Cross-cultural and cognitive aspects of web site navigation. *Journal of the Academy of Marketing Science*, 30 (4), 397–410.

Luo, Y. (1995). Business strategy, market structure, and performance of IJV. *Management International Review*, 35(3), 249–64.

Luo, Y. (1997). Guanxi and performance of foreign-invested enterprises in China. *Management International Review*, 37(1), 51–70.

Luo, Y. and Chen, M. (1997). Does guanxi influence firm performance? *Asia Pacific Journal of Management*, 14, 1–16.

Lytle, A. L., Brett, J. M., and Shapiro, D. L. (1999). The strategic use of interests, rights, and power to resolve disputes. *Negotiation Journal*, 15(1), 31–52.

McKeon, R. (ed.) (2001). *The basic works of Aristotle*. New York: The Modern Library.

MacLeod, M. (2000). Language barriers. *Supply Management*, 5 (14), 37–38.

Maddux, W.W., Kim, P. H., Okumura, T. and Brett, J.M. (2011). Cultural differences in the function and meaning of apologies. *International Negotiation*, 16(3), 405–425.

Madhok, A. (1995). Revisiting multinational firms' tolerance for joint ventures: A trust-based approach. *Journal of International Business Studies*, 26(1), 117–137.

Mainemelis, C. (2001). When the muse takes it all: A model for the experience of timelessness in organization. *Academy of Management Review*, 26(4), 512–529.

Marks, M. L., and Mirvis, P. H. (2011). A framework for the human resources role in managing culture in mergers and acquisitions. *Human Resource Management*, 50(6), 859–877.

Markus, H. R. and Kitayama, S. (1991). Culture and the self: Implications for cognition, emotion and motivation. *Psychological Review*, 98(2), 224–253.

Matsumoto, M. (1988). *The unspoken way: Haragei – silence in Japanese business and society*, New York: Kodansha International.

Maude, B. (2014). *International Business Negotiation: Principles and Practice*, Palgrave Macmillan.

Mayo, M. A., Marks, L. J. and Ryans, J. K. Jr (1991). Perceptions of ethical problems in international marketing. *International Marketing Review*, 8(3), 61–75.

McCall, J.B. (2003). Negotiating sales, export transactions and agency agreements. In P.N. Ghauri and J.-C. Usunier (Eds), *International Business Negotiations* (pp. 223–241). Oxford: Pergamon/Elsevier.

Mead, M. (1948). *Male and Female*, New York: William Morrow.

Mehrabian, A. (1971). *Silent messages*. Belmont, CA: Wadsworth.

Melé, D. and Sánchez-Runde, C. (2013). Cultural diversity and universal ethics in a global world. *Journal of Business Ethics*, 116(4), 681–687.

Menkel-Meadow, C. (2001). Negotiating with lawyers, men, and things: The contextual approach still matters. *Negotiation Journal*, 17(3), 257–293.

Merrilees, B. and Miller, D. (1999). Direct selling in the West and East: The relative roles of product and relationship (Guanxi) drivers, *Journal of Business Research*, 45, 267–273.

Mesquita, B. (2001). Emotions in collectivist and individualist contexts. *Journal of Personality and Social Psychology*, 80(1), 68.

Mintu-Wimsatt, A. and Graham, J. L. (2004). Testing a negotiation model on Canadian Anglophone and Mexican exporters. *Journal of the Academy of Marketing Science*, 32(3), 345–356.

Mishima, Y. (1954). *Shiosai* (French translation), Paris: Gallimard (original Japanese edition, 1954).

Mnookin, R. H., Peppet, S. R., and Tulumello, A. S. (2004). *Beyond Winning*. Cambridge, MA: Harvard University Press.

Money, R. B. (1998). International multilateral negotiations and social networks. *Journal of International Business Studies*, 29(4), 711–727.

Morales-Sanchez, R. and Cabello-Medina, C. (2013). The role of four universal moral competencies in ethical decision-making. *Journal of Business Ethics*, 116, 717–734.

Morand, D. A. (1996). Politeness as a universal variable in cross-cultural managerial communication. *International Journal of Organizational Analysis*, 4 (1), 52–74.

Morris, M. W., Williams, K. Y., Leung, K., Larrick, R., Mendoza, M. T., Bhatnagar, D., Li, J., Kondo, M. Luo, J.-L. and Hu, J. C. (1998). Conflict management style: Accounting for cross-national differences. *Journal of International Business Studies*, 29(4), 729–747.

Morris, M. W., Leung, K., and Iyengar, S. S. (2004). Person perception in the heat of conflict: Negative trait attributions affect procedural preferences and account for situational and cultural differences. *Asian Journal of Social Psychology*, 7(2), 127–147.

Morris, M. W., and Gelfand, M. J. (2004). Cultural differences and cognitive dynamics: Expanding the cognitive perspective on negotiation. In Michele J. Gelfand and J. M. Brett (Eds.), *The handbook of negotiation and culture* (pp. 45–70). Stanford: Stanford University Press.

Morris-Cotterill, N. (2001). Money laundering, *Foreign Policy*, May/June, 16–22.

Morschbach, H. (1982). Aspects of non-verbal communication in Japan. In L. Samovar and R. E. Porter (Eds.), *Intercultural Communication: A Reader*, 3rd edn. Belmont, CA: Wadsworth.

Mosterd, I. and Rutte, C. G. (2000). Effects of time pressure and accountability to constituents on negotiation, *International Journal of Conflict Management*, 11(3), 227–247.

Movius, H., Matsuura, M., Yan, J. and Kim, D.Y. (2006). Tailoring the mutual gains approach for negotiations with partners in Japan, China, and Korea. *Negotiation Journal*, 22(4), 389–435.

Myers, J. (2001). International standards and cooperation in the fight against money laundering, *Economic Perspectives*, 6(2), 9–10.

Myler, L. (2016). There's a B2B marketplace for that (or there soon will be), *Forbes*, Oct 11, 2016.

Naipaul, V. S. (1981). *Among the Believers: An Islamic Journey*. London: André Deutsch.

Neale, M. A., and Bazerman, M. H. (1992). Negotiating rationally: The power and impact of the negotiator's frame. *The Executive*, 6(3), 42–51.

Nowak, M. A., and Sigmund, K. (2005). Evolution of indirect reciprocity. *Nature*, 437, 1291–1298.

Oh, T.K. (1984). Selling to the Japanese, *Nation's Business*, October, 37–38.

Ollivier, A. and de Maricourt, R. (1990). *Pratique du marketing en Afrique*, Paris: Edicef/Aupelf.

Ott, U. F. (2011). The influence of cultural activity types on buyer-seller negotiations: A game theoretical framework for intercultural negotiations. *International Negotiation*, 16(3), 427–450.

Palmer, D. K. and Schoorman, F. D. (1999). Unpackaging the multiple aspects of time in polychronicity, *Journal of Managerial Psychology*, 14(3/4), 323–344.

Parker, V. (2003). Negotiating licensing agreements. In P.N. Ghauri and J.-C. Usunier (Eds.), *International Business Negotiations* (pp. 243–273). Oxford: Pergamon/Elsevier.

Parlamis, J. D., and Geiger, I. (2015). Mind the medium: A qualitative analysis of email negotiation. *Group Decision and Negotiation*, 24(2), 359–381.

Paz, O. (1962). *The Labyrinth of Solitude*, New York: Grove.

Péan, P. (1988). *L'Argent Noir*, Paris: Librairie Arthème Fayard.

Pearson, V. M. S. and Stephan, W. G. (1998). Preferences for styles of negotiation: A comparison of Brazil and the US. *International Journal of Intercultural Relations*, 22(1), 67–83.

Perrinjaquet, A., Furrer, O., Usunier, J. C., Cestre, G., and Valette-Florence, P. (2007). A test of the quasi-circumplex structure of human values. *Journal of Research in Personality*, 41(4), 820–840.

Pike, K. (1966). *Language in Relation To a Unified Theory of the Structure of Human Behavior*, The Hague: Mouton.

Pinkley, R. L., and Northcraft, G. B. (1994). Conflict frames of reference: Implications for dispute processes and outcomes. *Academy of Management Journal*, 37(1), 193–205.

PON (2012). Management report on BATNA basics: Boost your power at the bargaining table. Program on Negotiation (PON) at Harvard Law School. Available from www.pon.harvard.edu

Pornpitakpan, C. (1999). The effect of cultural adaptation on business relationships: Americans selling to Japanese and Thais, *Journal of International Business Studies*, 30(2), 317–338.

Potter, R. E., and Balthazard, P. A. (2000). Supporting integrative negotiation via computer mediated communication technologies: An empirical example with geographically dispersed Chinese and American negotiators. *Journal of International Consumer Marketing*, 12(4), 7–32.

Prime, N. and Bluedorn, A.C. (1996). Culture, time and business negotiation: An empirical study in France and the United States, Proceedings of the ISIDA Conference on Time, Palermo, 59–78.

Pruitt, D. G., and Lewis, S. A. (1975). Development of integrative solutions in bilateral negotiations. *Journal of Personality and Social Psychology*, 31(4), 621–633.

Pruitt, D. G. (1981). *Bargaining Behavior*, New York: Academic Press.

Pruitt, D. G. (1983). Strategic choice in negotiation. *American Behavioral Scientist*, 27(2), 167–194.

Pruitt, D. G. and Rubin, J. Z. (1986). *Social Conflict: Escalation, Stalemate and Settlement*. New York: McGraw-Hill.

Putnam, L. L and Roloff, M. E. (1992). Communication perspectives on negotiation. In L.L Putnam and M.E. Roloff (Eds.), *Communication and Negotiation* (pp. 1–14). Thousand Oaks, CA: Sage.

Pye, L. (1982). *Chinese Commercial Negotiating Style*, Cambridge, MA: Oelgeschlager, Gunn and Hain.

Pye, L. (1986). The China trade: making the deal, *Harvard Business Review*, 46(4), 74–84.

Raiffa, H., Richardson, J. and Metcalfe, D. (2003). *Negotiation Analysis: The Art and Science of Collaborative Decision Making*, Cambridge: Belknap Press.

Rajan, M. N. and Graham, J. L. (1991). Nobody's grandfather was a merchant: Understanding the Soviet commercial negotiation process and style. *California Management Review*, 33(3), 40–57.

Ramirez-Marin, J. Y. and Brett, J.M. (2011). Relational construal in negotiation: Propositions and examples from Latin and Anglo cultures. *International Negotiation*, 16(3), 383–404.

Rao, A. and Schmidt, S. M. (1998). A behavioral perspective on negotiating international alliances. *Journal of International Business Studies*, 29(4), 665–694.

Rawls, J. (1971). *A Theory of Justice*, Cambridge, MA: Belknap Press of Harvard University.

Rawwas, M. Y. A. (2001). Culture, personality, and morality: A typology of international consumers' ethical beliefs, *International Marketing Review*, 18(2), 188–209.

Ribbink, D. and Grimm, C. M. (2014). The impact of cultural differences on buyer–supplier negotiations: An experimental study. *Journal of Operations Management*, 32(3), 114–126.

Roberge, I. (2011). Financial action task force. *Handbook of Transnational Governance: Institutions and Innovations*, 45–49.

Robertson, C. J., Crittenden, W. F., Brady, M. K. and Hoffman, J. J. (2002). Situational ethics across borders: A multicultural examination, *Journal of Business Ethics*, 38, 327–338.

Roemer, C., Garb, P. A., Neu, J., and Graham, J. L. (1999). A comparison of American and Russian patterns of behavior in buyer-seller negotiations using observational measures. *International Negotiation*, 4(1), 37–61.

Rogers, E. M., Hart, W. B., and Miike, Y. (2002). Edward T. Hall and the history of intercultural communication: The United States and Japan. *Keio Communication Review*, 24, 3–26.

Rosenbloom, B., and Larsen, T. (2003). Communication in international business-to-business marketing channels: Does culture matter? *Industrial Marketing Management*, 32, 309–315.

Rubin, P. A. and Carter, J.R. (1990). Joint optimality in buyer-seller negotiations, *Journal of Purchasing and Materials Management*, 26(2), 20–26.

Rudd, J. E. and' Lawson, D. R. (2007). *Communicating in Global Business Negotiations: A Geocentric Approach*, Thousand Oaks: Sage Publications.

Sako, M. (1992). *Prices, Quality and Trust: Inter-firm Relations in Britain and Japan*, Cambridge: Cambridge University Press.

Salacuse, J. W. (1993). Implications for practitioners. In G. O. Faure and J. Z. Rubin (Eds.), *Culture and Negotiation* (pp. 199–208). Newbury Park, CA: Sage Publications.

Salacuse, J. W. (1998). Ten ways that culture affects negotiating style: Some survey results. *Negotiation Journal*, 14(3), 221–240.

Salacuse, J. W. (1999). Intercultural negotiation in international business. *Group Decision and Negotiation*, 8(3), 217–236.

Salacuse, J. W. (2004). Negotiating: The top ten ways that culture can affect your negotiation. *IVEY Business Journal*, 69(1), 1–6.

Samiee, S. (1998). The Internet and international marketing: Is there a fit? *Journal of Interactive Marketing*, 12, 5–21.

Sánchez-Runde, C. J., Nardon, L. and Steers, R. M. (2013). The cultural roots of ethical conflicts in global business. *Journal of Business Ethics*, 116, 689–701.

Saner, R. and Yiu, L. (1993). Conflict handling styles in Switzerland, *Die Unternehmung*, 2, 181–193.

Saner, R. (2003). Strategies and tactics in international business negotiations in P.N. Ghauri and J.-C. Usunier (Eds.), *International Business Negotiations* (pp. 51–73). Oxford: Pergamon/Elsevier.

Saner, R. (2008). *The Expert Negotiator*, 3rd edn, Leyden: Brill.

Sapir, E. (1929). The status of linguistics as a science. *Language*, 5, 207–214.

Sawyer, J. and Guetzkow, H. (1965). Bargaining and negotiation in international relations in H. Kelman, (ed.), *International Behavior*, New York: Holt, Rinehart and Winston.

Scanzoni, J. (1979). Social exchange and behavioral interdependence, in R.L. Burgess and T.L. Huston (Eds.), *Social Exchange in Developing Relationships* (pp. 61–98). New York: Academic Press.

Schuster, C. P. and Copeland, M. J. (1999). Global business exchanges: Similarities and differences around the world, *Journal of International Marketing*, 7(2), 63–80.

Schwartz, S. H. (2009). Culture matters: National value, cultures, sources and consequences. In C.-Y. Chiu, Y. Y. Hong, S. Shavitt and R. S. Wyer Jr (Eds), *Problems and Solutions in Cross-cultural Theory, Research and Application* (127–150). New York: Psychology Press.

Schweitzer, M. E., and Kerr, J. L. (2000). Bargaining under the influence: The role of alcohol in negotiations. *The Academy of Management Executive*, 14(2), 47–57.

Sebenius, J. K. (1992). Challenging conventional explanations of international cooperation: negotiation analysis and the case of epistemic communities, *International Organization*, 46(1), 323–365.

Sebenius, J. K. (2001). Six habits of merely effective negotiators, *Harvard Business Review*, 79(4), 87–97.

Sebenius, J. K. (2002). Caveats for cross-border negotiators. *Negotiation Journal*, April, 121–133.

Sebenius, J. K. (2002). The hidden challenge of cross-border negotiations, *Harvard Business Review*, 80(3), 76–85.

Segall, M. H., Dasen, P. R., Berry, J. W. and Poortinga, Y. H. (1999). *Human Behavior in Global Perspective*, Needham Heights, MA: Allyn and Bacon.

Seleim, A., and Bontis, N. (2009). The relationship between culture and corruption: A cross-national study. *Journal of Intellectual Capital*, 10(1), 165–184.

Semnani-Azad, Z. and Adair, W. L. (2011). The display of dominant nonverbal cues in negotiation: The role of culture and gender. *International Negotiation*, 16(3), 451–479.

Shell, G. R. (2006). *Bargaining for advantage: Negotiation strategies for reasonable people*. New York: Penguin.

Shenkar, O., and Ronen, S. (1993). The cultural context of negotiations: The implications of Chinese interpersonal norms. In L. Kelley and O. Shenkar (Eds), *International Business in China* (pp. 191–207). London and New York: Routledge.

Simintiras, A. C., and Thomas, A. H. (1998). Cross-cultural sales negotiations: A literature review and research propositions, *International Marketing Review*, 15(1), 10–28.

Slocombe, T. E. (1999). Applying the theory of reasoned action to an individual's polychronicity, *Journal of Managerial Psychology*, 13(3/4), 313–322.

Smith, A. (1790). *The Theory of Moral Sentiments*, 6th edn. Sao Paulo: MεταLibri.

Smith, P. B., Dugan, S., Peterson, M. F. and Leung, K. (1998). Individualism: collectivism and the handling of disagreement: A 23 country study. *International Journal of Intercultural Relations*, 22(3), 351–367.

Sobral, F., Carvalhal, E. and Almeida, F. (2008). The influence of culture on negotiation styles of Brazilian executives. *Management Research: Journal of the Iberoamerican Academy of Management*, 6(2), 107–119.

Sorokin, P. and Merton, R. (1937). Social time: A methodological and functional analysis. *American Journal of Sociology*, 42, 615–629.

Stahl, G. K., and Voigt, A. (2008). Do cultural differences matter in mergers and acquisitions? A tentative model and examination. *Organization Science*, 19(1), 160–176.

Sugimoto, N. (1998). Norms of apology depicted in U.S. American and Japanese literature on manners and etiquette. *International Journal of Intercultural Relations*, 22(3), 251–76.

Sussman, L. and Johnson, D. M. (1993). The interpreted executive: Theory, models, and implications. *Journal of Business Communication*, 30, 415–434.

Tangney, J. P. (1995). Recent advances in the empirical study of shame and guilt. *American Behavioral Scientist*, 38(8), 1132–1145.

Thaler, R. (2012). *The winner's curse: Paradoxes and anomalies of economic life*. New York: Simon and Schuster.

Thomas, K. W. (1992). Conflict and conflict management: Reflections and update. *Journal of Organizational Behavior*, 13(3), 265–274.

Thompson, L., Neale, M. A., and Sinaceur, M. (2004). The evolution of cognition and biases in negotiation research: An examination of cognition, social perception, motivation, and emotion. In Michele J. Gelfand and J. M. Brett (Eds.), *The handbook of negotiation and culture* (pp. 7–44). Stanford: Stanford University Press.

Tinsley, C. H. and Brett, J. M. (1997). Managing workplace conflict: A comparison of conflict frames and outcomes in the U.S. and Hong Kong, paper presented at the Annual Meeting of the Academy of Management, Boston.

Tinsley, C. H. and Pillutla, M. M. (1998). Negotiating in the United States and Hong Kong. *Journal of International Business Studies*, 29(4), 711–727.

Tinsley, C. H. (1998). Models of conflict resolution in Japanese, German, and American cultures. *Journal of Applied Psychology*, 83, 316–323.

Tinsley, C. H., Curhan, J. and Kwak, R. S. (1999). Adopting a dual lens approach for overcoming the dilemma of difference in international business negotiations, *International Negotiations*, 4, 1–18.

Tinsley, C. H. (2004). Culture and conflict: Enlarging our dispute resolution framework. In Michele J. Gelfand and J. M. Brett (Eds), *The handbook of negotiation and culture* (pp. 193–210). Stanford: Stanford University Press.

Tinsley, C. H., Turan, N., Aslani, S. and Weingart, L. R. (2011). The Interplay between culturally- and situationally-based mental models of intercultural dispute resolution: West meets Middle East. *International Negotiation*, 16(3), 481–510.

Transparency International (2017). Transparency International Corruption Perceptions Index 2016, retrieved March 12, 2018 from www.transparency.org/news/feature/corruption_perceptions_index_2016.

Traoré Sérié, R. (1986). La promotion du Livre en Côte d'Ivoire, Communication au Colloque Marketing Pour le Développement, Abidjan, December.

Triandis, H. G. (1983). Dimensions of cultural variation as parameters of organizational theories. *International Studies of Management and Organization*, 12(4), 139–169.

Triandis, H. C. (1995). *Individualism and Collectivism*. Boulder, CO: Westview.

Trompenaars, F. (1993). *Riding the waves of culture*, London: Nicholas Brealey.

Trompenaars, F., and Hampden-Turner, C. (2011). *Riding the waves of culture: Understanding diversity in global business*. London: Nicholas Brealey Publishing.

Tsang, W.K. (1998). Can guanxi be a source of sustained competitive advantage for doing business in China, *The Academy of Management Executive*, 12(2), 64–73.

Tse, D. K., Francis, J. and Walls, J. (1994). Cultural differences in conducting intra- and inter-cultural negotiations: A Sino-Canadian perspective. *Journal of International Business Studies*, 25(3), 537–555.

Tung, R. L. (1984). How to negotiate with the Japanese, *California Management Review*, XXVI(4), 62–77.

Tung, R. L. (1996). Negotiating with East Asians in P.N. Ghauri and J.-C. Usunier (Eds.), *International Business Negotiations* (pp. 369–381). Oxford: Pergamon/Elsevier.

Ueda, K. (1974). Sixteen ways to avoid saying no in Japan, in J.C. Condon and M. Saito (Eds.), *Intercultural Encounters in Japan* (pp. 185–192). Tokyo: Simul Press.

Ulijn, J. M., O'Hair, D., Weggeman, M., Ledlow, G., and Hall, H. T. (2000). Innovation, corporate strategy, and cultural context: What is the mission for international business communication? *Journal of Business Communication*, 37, 293–316.

Ulijn, J. M., Lincke, A. and Karakaya, Y. (2001). Non-face-to-face international business negotiation: How is national culture reflected in this medium? *IEEE Transactions on Professional Communication*, 44(2), 126–137.

Urban, S. (1996). Negotiating international joint ventures. In P.N. Ghauri and J.-C. Usunier (Eds.), *International Business Negotiations* (pp. 231–251). Oxford: Pergamon/Elsevier.

United States Institute of Peace (2002). *U.S. Negotiating Behavior*, Special Report 94, October, www.usip.org.

Usunier, J.-C. (1991). Business time perceptions and national cultures: A comparative survey, *Management International Review*, 31(3), 197–217.

Usunier, J.-C. and Valette-Florence, P. (1994). Perceptual time patterns (time styles): A psychometric scale. *Time and Society*, 3(2), 219–241.

Usunier, J.-C. and Verna, G. (1994). Ethique des Affaires et Relativité Culturelle, *Revue Française de Gestion,* 99(3), 23–40.

Usunier, J.-C. and Valette-Florence, P. (2007). The time-styles scale: A review of developments and replications over 15 years. *Time and Society*, 16(2/3), 349–382.

Usunier, J.-C. and Roulin, N. (2010). The influence of high- and low-context communication styles on the design, content, and language of business-to-business web sites. *Journal of Business Communication*, 47(2), 189–227.

Usunier, J.-C. (2011). Language as a resource to assess cross-cultural equivalence in quantitative management research. *Journal of World Business*, 46(3), 314–319.

Usunier, J.-C. and Lee, J. (2013). *Marketing Across Cultures,* 6th edn, Harlow: Pearson.

Usunier, J.-C., Van Herk, H. and Lee, J. (2017). *International and Cross-Cultural Business Research*, London: Sage Publications.

Van Zandt, H.R. (1970). How to negotiate with the Japanese, *Harvard Business Review*, November–December, 45–56.

Volkema, R. J. (1999). Ethicality in negotiations: An analysis of perceptual similarities and differences between Brazil and the United states, *Journal of Business Research*, 45, 59–67.

Von Glinow, M. A., Shapiro, D. L., and Brett, J. M. (2004). Can we talk, and should we? Managing emotional conflict in multicultural teams. *Academy of Management Review*, 29(4), 578–592.

Von Stackelberg, H. (2010). *Market structure and equilibrium*. Berlin: Springer Science & Business Media. Originally published in German in 1934 as *Marktform und Gleichgewicht*.

Wade-Benzoni, K. A., Okumura, T., Brett, J. M., Moore, D. A., Tenbrunsel, A. E. and Bazerman, M. H. (2002). Cognition and behavior in asymmetric social dilemmas: A comparison of two cultures, *Journal of Applied Psychology*, 87(1), 87–95.

Waller, M. J., Giambatista, R. C., and Zellmer-Bruhn, M. E. (1999). The effect of individual time urgency on group polychronicity. *Journal of Managerial Psychology*, 13(3/4), 313–322.

Walton, R. E., and McKersie, R. B. (1965). *A behavioral theory of labor negotiations: An analysis of a social interaction system*. Ithaca, NY: Cornell University Press.

Watkins, M. (2007). Why DaimlerChrysler never got into gear. *Harvard Business Review* [Online]. Available at: https://hbr.org/2007/05/why-the-daimlerchrysler-merger.

Weiss, S. E. (1994a). Negotiating with "Romans": Part 1. *Sloan Management Review*, 35(2), 51.

Weiss, S. E. (1994b). Negotiating with "Romans": Part 2. *Sloan Management Review*, 35(3), 85.

Weiss, J. N. (2015). From Aristotle to Sadat: A short strategic persuasion framework for negotiators. *Negotiation Journal*, 31(3), 211–222.

Weiss, S. E., and Stripp, W. (1985). *Negotiating with foreign businesspersons: An introduction for Americans with propositions for six cultures*. Working Paper 85-6, New York: Graduate School of Business, New York University.

Weitz, B. (1979). A critical review of personal selling research: The need for contingency approaches, in G. Albaum and G.A. Churchill, Jr (Eds.), *Critical Issues in Sales Management: State of the art and future needs* (pp. 76–126). Eugene University of Oregon.

Werner, C. (2000). Gifts, bribes, and development in Post-Soviet Kazakhstan. *Human Organization*, 59(1), 11–22.

Wheeler, M. (2013). *The Art of Negotiation: How to Improvise Agreement in a Chaotic World*. New York: Simon & Schuster.

Williamson, O. E. (1975). *Markets and Hierarchies: Analysis and Anti-trust Implications: A Study in the Economics of Internal Organization*. Free Press: New York.

Willinger, M., Keser, C., Lohmann, C., and Usunier, J. C. (2003). A comparison of trust and reciprocity between France and Germany: experimental investigation based on the investment game. *Journal of Economic Psychology*, 24(4), 447–466.

Wong, R. Y. and Hong, Y. (2005). Dynamic influences of culture on cooperation in the prisoner's dilemma. *Psychological Science*, 16(6), 429–434.

Woodward, N. H. (1999). Do you speak internet? *HR Magazine*, 44(4), 12–16.

Wunderle, W. (2007). How to negotiate in the Middle-East, *Military Review*, March-April, 33–37.

Xinhua News Agency (2002). Top banker sentenced on bribery charges, October 11, 2002.

Yeung, I. Y. M. and Tung, R. L. (1996). Achieving business success in Confucian societies, *Organizational Dynamics*, 24(Autumn), 54–65.

Zartman, I. W. (1993). A skeptic's view. In G. O. Faure and J. Z. Rubin (Eds.), *Culture and Negotiation*, (pp. 17–21). Newbury Park, CA: Sage Publications.

Author index

Subject index